Ireland and the Federal Solution:
The Debate over the United Kingdom Constitution,
1870–1921

For almost fifty years the issues of Irish self-government and the increasing complexity of government business were the primary stimulants to constitutional debate in the United Kingdom. Politicians and publicists devoted considerable energy and attention to devolution, federalism, and "home rule all round" as possible means of resolving the urgent political, administrative, and constitutional problems confronting the United Kingdom.

John Kendle analyses the many issues involved in the debate over decentralization. Concern about the relationship between the United Kingdom and the self-governing colonies/dominions stimulated much of the debate, but the "Irish question" was its focal point and many of the federal and devolutionary schemes proposed were designed to accommodate the demand for Irish home rule while preserving the union. Scots and Welsh demands are also examined and placed in context. Imperial federation was continuously and exhaustively discussed and promoted from the late 1860s through World War I and Kendle argues that it is not always possible to separate the arguments for closer imperial union from the proposals for internal change.

In *Ireland and the Federal Solution*, Kendle shows that federalism was never central to British thinking and was rarely articulated in detail; its advocates never came to terms with the issue of financial relations within the United Kingdom and underestimated the opposition of the Irish, both Nationalist and Unionist, to federalist plans. Ironically, the Irish question remained both the most powerful impetus to federalist thought and the source of the strongest resistance to it. It gave rise to a vibrant and important debate which still merits our attention today.

John Kendle is a member of the Department of History at St John's College in the University of Manitoba.

Ireland and the Federal Solution

The Debate over the United Kingdom Constitution, 1870–1921

JOHN KENDLE

McGill-Queen's University Press
Kingston and Montreal

© McGill-Queen's University Press 1989
ISBN 0-7735-0676-4

Legal deposit first quarter 1989
Bibliothèque nationale du Québec

Printed in Canada on acid-free paper

This book has been published with the help of a gran
from the Social Science Federation of Canada, using
funds provided by the Social Sciences and Humanities
Research Council of Canada.

Canadian Cataloguing in Publication Data

Kendle, John, 1937–
Ireland and the federal solution: the debate over the United
Kingdom constitution, 1870–1921

Includes bibliographical references and index.
ISBN 0-7735-0676-4

1. Great Britain – Constitutional history. 2. Home rule
(Ireland). 3. Home rule (Scotland). 4. Home rule (Wales). 5.
Great Britain – Politics and government – 1837–1901. 6. Great
Britain – Politics and government – 1901–1936. I. Title.

DA959.K46   1989   941.08   c88-090277-9

Contents

To the memory of
Leslie Upton

Preface

From the 1870s to 1921 considerable energy and attention were devoted by politicians and publicists to home rule all round, devolution, and federalism as possible means of resolving the urgent political, administrative, and constitutional issues confronting the United Kingdom. The increasing complexity of government business, the gathering forces of nationalism in Ireland, Scotland, and Wales, and a concern to maintain and strengthen the role in imperial affairs of the parliament at Westminister combined to keep the possibility of decentralizing power at the forefront of political and public debate for much of the period.

Central to all such discussion was the "Irish question" and many of the federal and devolutionary schemes that surfaced were designed to accommodate the demand for Irish home rule while preserving the Union. Ireland and the problems associated with granting it some form of self-government therefore bulk large in this volume but it is not a book exclusively about Irish home rule. It is a study of the motives and attitudes of all participants in the debate over constitutional change and an examination of the various schemes and proposals that emerged. Scottish and Welsh demands are examined and placed in context. Similarly, much of the debate over internal constitutional change took place at a time when many people were concerned about the relationship between the United Kingdom and the self-governing colonies. Imperial federation was continuously and exhaustively discussed and promoted from the late 1860s through World War I. It is not always possible to separate the arguments for closer imperial union from the proposals for internal change. This overlap of interests, organizations, and participants is an important dimension of the book. Finally, an effort has been made to sort out what the participants in the debate believed they meant when they spoke and wrote of "federalism," "devolution," "home rule all round," and "federal devolution."

I am grateful to the staff of the following institutions: the British Library; the Public Record Office; the House of Lords Record Office; the Institute of

Historical Research; the Institute of Commonwealth Studies; the Royal Commonwealth Society; the University of London Library; the Bodleian Library; Rhodes House Library; the University of Birmingham Library; Durham University Archives; the Wiltshire Record Office; Cambridge University Library; St John's College, Cambridge; Trinity College, Dublin; the National Library of Ireland; the National Library of Wales; the National Library of Scotland; the Scottish Record Office; the New York Public Library; the University of Minnesota Library; the Humanities Research Center, University of Texas, Austin; the National Library of Canada; the Public Archives of Canada; University of Toronto Archives; Queen's University Archives; the Manitoba Provincial Library; the University of Manitoba Library; and St John's College Library, University of Manitoba.

This project has been generously supported by the Social Sciences and Humanities Research Council of Canada which by awarding me two research grants and a Leave Fellowship enabled me to secure the necessary time for research and writing. The first draft of this book was written during 1985-6 when I was the Commonwealth Fellow at St John's College, Cambridge. My thanks to the Master and Fellows of the College for providing me with a quiet and congenial setting in which to work. I am particularly grateful to Ben Farmer, Peter Clarke, Nicholas Mansergh, and Henry Pelling for their many kindnesses. I am indebted to Leslie Head and Paula Halson of Cambridge, England, and to Carol Adam of Winnipeg for so rapidly and efficiently typing my drafts, and to Charles Beer for his excellent editorial advice. A special thanks to Judy for her support.

I was introduced to the field of imperial and commonwealth history by Leslie Upton. He encouraged me in my pursuit of a scholarly career, provided penetrating and constructive criticism of my early work, and was instrumental in helping me obtain a university position. I valued his friendship and I dedicate this book to his memory.

Ireland and the Federal Solution

Introduction

Gladstone introduced his first home rule bill on 8 April 1886. Although the bill was defeated two months later on 8 June, Gladstone's initiative opened a major constitutional discussion within the United Kingdom over how the government of the islands could be made both more efficient and less remote from the bulk of the inhabitants. From 1886 until 1921 there was constant debate over the best way either to devolve or delegate or distribute power. Should the unitary form of government be preserved as it was? Or should the sovereignty of the Westminster parliament be maintained while certain powers and authority were devolved upon subordinate regional or national legislatures? Or should the unitary system be scrapped and a federal constitution adopted with a division of sovereignty between central and provincial parliaments? Much of the discussion revolved around Ireland and the need to meet its demand for some form of self-government. While Wales and Scotland often echoed Irish demands neither country mounted a political or nationalist campaign to compare with Ireland's. If they had done so the British government might have been compelled to move more systematically than it did. On the other hand, many advocates of constitutional change were not nationalists of any stripe, but rather men more interested in relieving the congestion in parliament. For almost forty years the issues of Irish self-government and congestion in parliament were the primary stimulants of constitutional debate in the United Kingdom. Only with the passage of the Government of Ireland Act in 1920 did concerted discussion cease; not to revive until the 1960s.

When Gladstone introduced his bill the British public was not well informed about other possible systems of government. Devolution and federalism had never been matters of public debate in the United Kingdom; and home rule had not been adequately defined. Few men in public life, whether politicians or journalists, had a concrete knowledge of alternative modes of government. Their limited grasp of the significant differences between devolution and federalism led many of them to misuse terms with the result that, in the 1880s, at the very beginning of concentrated discussion, "devolution," "federalism," "home rule," "federal home rule," "home rule all round," and "federal devolution" were used indiscriminately to describe proposed changes to the British constitution. This interchanging of terms persisted throughout the period and inevitably led to confusion and misunderstanding. Ironically, the protagonists of change were often the worst offenders. What, therefore, did the politicians and publicists of those years mean when they spoke and wrote about "federalism," and what historical precedents and analogies did they draw upon?

The notion of federalism has existed since ancient times but most of the ancient and medieval systems had been confederal rather than federal in nature and, with the exception of the Swiss, had proven too weak to withstand imperial foes. Modern federalism dates from the formulation of the United States constitution in the 1780s. Its success had owed much to the development by the Americans of a system which, while protecting the rights of the individual states, vested more power and authority in the central government than had been the case in the looser leagues and alliances which had passed as federations in previous eras. Essentially, American federalism was a system in which legislative powers were divided between two levels of government, central (federal) and regional (state); the division always being subject to amendment and judicial review. The novelty and success of this system of coordinate federalism attracted widespread attention throughout the nineteenth century, and was adopted in varying forms by Canada (1867), Germany (1871), and Australia (1900). It was also the model used to adapt the Swiss system (1848 and 1874) and was closely examined and discussed in South Africa before 1910.

The concept was therefore not unknown in the United Kingdom and by the time serious consideration was given to changes in the British constitution there were a number of works to turn to for information and analysis. First and foremost, of course, was *The Federalist*, the eighty-five essays written by Alexander Hamilton, John Jay, and James Madison in 1787–8 in support of the adoption of the United States constitution. Although there was no specifically British edition until 1911, it was read and discussed throughout the nineteenth century, particularly by imperial statesmen, Colonial Office officials, and advocates of imperial federation. It was often referred to during the Canadian, Australian, and South African constitutional debates. One of the earliest and most sustained commentaries on the American system was Alexis de Tocqueville's *Democracy in America* published in two volumes in 1835 and 1840. English translations were available within a few months and circulated extensively in political circles. John Austin had discussed the problem of the location of sovereignty in a federal system in his *Province of Jurisprudence Determined* (1832), a work which was highly influential in the period 1870-1930, while James Bryce's analysis of the *American Commonwealth* (1888) long attracted both British and colonial statesmen. E.A. Freeman's first and only volume of his *History of Federal Government from the Foundation of the Achaian League to the disruption of the United States* (1863) raised many key points about the nature of federalism, but probably even more successful in making some knowledge of federal theory and problems fairly common among British politicians, lawyers, and publicists during the late nineteenth and early twentieth centuries was A.V. Dicey's *Law of the Constitution* (1885) in which a section had been devoted to "Parliamentary Sovereignty and Federalism." And finally, J.S. Mill had included a chapter on "Federal Representative Governments" in *Considerations on Representative Government* (1860), one of the most widely read political works of the nineteenth century. Thus while federalism may not have been a subject of much public discussion, the better-informed politicians, writers, legal experts, and publicists had some familiarity with its intricacies and knew it was more than devolution and certainly more complicated than a simple division of legislative powers.

In addition to the United States constitution and various legal, philosophic, and constitutional works, the British politician or publicist could turn to Britain's own relationship with its self-governing colonies for evidence of "home rule," "devolution," and "federalism." In fact, it was often suggested that the empire itself was quasi-federal in nature, and a model to be emulated. The nature of Britain's relationship with its colonies of settlement had perplexed and bedevilled its statesmen since the late eighteenth century but by the 1850s a devolutionary system had been adopted in British North America, Australia, and New Zealand. The Westminster parliament remained sovereign but certain powers had been devolved to the colonies. Within those defined spheres they had become self-governing. This form of home rule was especially attractive to Gladstone, both in mid-century and in the 1880s when he turned to a consideration of home rule for Ireland.

A federal solution to particular colonial problems was first suggested in the 1840s and 1850s when the British government was anxious to devise stable systems of government in New Zealand and Australia within which self-governing powers could be properly wielded and administered. Earl Grey, the secretary for war and the colonies (1846–52), vigorously promoted federalism in both areas. While his federal scheme proved unworkable in New Zealand and unappealing to the bulk of Australians, the discussion his suggestions engendered meant that considerable familiarity with the federal concept – particularly the American system – existed in some political and civil service circles by the 1860s.[1]

In that decade a stronger and more sustained federal movement within British North America, backed by many British officials, culminated in the passage of the British North America Act in 1867. The colonies of Nova Scotia, New Brunswick, and Canada (divided as of 1 July 1867 into the provinces of

Ontario and Quebec) united in a federation known as the Dominion of Canada. By the mid-1870s three other provinces, Prince Edward Island, British Columbia, and Manitoba (formerly the Red River Settlement), had joined the dominion, thus strengthening its existence and underlining the potential of federal structures. Canada now had the first federal government in the British empire. Understandably, the British North America Act became a much studied document in constitutional circles throughout the empire. One of Gladstone's first requests preparatory to drafting his first home rule bill was for a copy of the BNA Act.[2]

The British North America Act had been modelled after the United States constitution but it differed from that document in fundamental ways. First, the BNA Act preserved the British system of parliamentary (and hence responsible) government within a federal framework. It was a unique achievement and established a precedent for future federations within the commonwealth. Second, the Canadians wanted a stronger central government than the Americans and therefore opted to leave residual powers to the dominion government rather than to the provinces. Certainly that is what they and most observers of the time believed had been done. In drafting section 92 of the BNA Act the Canadians had clearly defined the powers of the provinces and thus had presumably left the residuum to the dominion. But in section 91, which outlines the authority of the central government, the Canadians had also chosen to list twenty-nine specific dominion powers. Throughout the late nineteenth century the courts more often than not interpreted sections 91 and 92 in favour of the provinces. This subtle and gradually shifting change in the basis of Canadian federalism often escaped contemporary commentators in the United Kingdom. To their mind what was particularly attractive about the Canadian example was the marriage of federalism at the local level with self-government in the imperial setting. It seemed to suggest that a larger union and local interests could be preserved both within an individual state and within the larger imperial framework. Many others beside Gladstone found it essential to consider the Canadian version of federalism before drafting their schemes for reform of the United Kingdom's constitutional practices.

Apart from initiatives in specific colonial areas there had also been a revival of interest in federalism among those interested in broader imperial problems. Particularly attracted were those concerned with giving the white settlement colonies some say in imperial decision-making and with preserving the unity of an increasingly wide-flung empire. Federalism had been much debated in the 1770s and 1780s as a possible means of keeping the American colonies within the imperial fold and was resurrected again in the 1820s as the reform and free trade movements gathered strength. At that time, and for about another thirty years, federalism principally meant the addition of colonial representatives to the Westminster parliament, or, as it was so often called, to the imperial parliament. This was not, of course, pure federalism, nor were the extra parliamentary schemes such as advisory councils and imperial boards suggested by many empire federalists of the 1850s and 1860s, but the supraparliamentary schemes that appeared in increasing profusion from the 1860s were definitely federal in nature. Imperial federation was discussed continuously by British and colonial publicists and politicians until the 1920s. It was seen by many as a means of preserving the strength and unity of the empire in a world of increasing challenge and friction. Many of the advocates of closer union of the empire were deeply involved in the debate over "federalism" for the United Kingdom. Not surprisingly, they often turned to the American example and various colonial analogies for information and insight.[3]

CHAPTER ONE

Early Schemes and Ideas, 1840–1885

Given the resurgence of interest in the federal idea in the colonial and imperial settings in the 1840s, it is not surprising that a few Irish and English politicians speculated about its possibilities as a solution to the problems inherent in the Anglo-Irish relationship. The United Kingdom of Great Britain and Ireland had been established by the Act of Union of 1800. It had ended the separate existence of the Kingdom of Ireland which had lasted since 1534, and had abolished the separate Irish parliament, a body that dated back to the thirteenth century. Although the Irish parliament had been subjected to the sovereignty of Westminster for much of its existence – even Grattan's parliament of 1782–1800 had been severely circumscribed – it had had a symbolic significance, and by the late eighteenth century Irishmen expected it to develop much as the legislatures in the Americas had done. The American and French revolutions and the Rebellion of 1798 in Ireland aroused grave fears in London and put an end to such hopes. The British were only too aware of the strategic significance of Ireland. It seemed unwise to permit the emergence of a self-governing colony or perhaps an independent state on Britain's doorstep. Pitt opted for the union of Ireland with Great Britain. On 1 January 1801 the British and Irish parliaments were united, and Ireland was thenceforth represented in the House of Commons by 100 MPs (later increased to 105). Until 1921 Irishmen would attempt to either modify or secure the repeal of the Act of Union.

The initial demands for repeal reached a peak in the autumn of 1843. Daniel O'Connell was at the height of his powers and the Repeal Association, widely supported both inside and outside Ireland, appeared to pose a considerable threat to the British government. In this atmosphere, compromise solutions were sought and "federalism" was seriously considered for the first time. Its leading exponent was Sharmon Crawford, an Ulster landlord, best known for his advocacy of land reform and tenant-rights. For years Crawford had wavered between a fervent anti-repeal stance and some appreciation of

O'Connell's position. He had always been aware that the union was not a success insofar as Ireland was concerned but he was equally convinced that the establishment of two separate parliaments with equal powers would endanger the connection between Great Britain and Ireland and weaken their resources. He preferred a scheme which would retain the union with Great Britain in major matters affecting Ireland while ensuring that an Irish parliament would be able to control Irish domestic affairs. By 1840 Crawford had broken with O'Connell's repeal policy and favoured retention of the union, but on "federal" lines.[1]

In a letter to O'Connell of 1 August 1843 Crawford advocated local parliaments for not only Ireland but also England and Scotland. He reasoned that "The principle of self-government by representation should be carried out through every institution of the State; and local taxation, whether in a parish or a town, should be imposed and managed, and the bye-laws affecting the locality enacted, by a body representing the locality which that taxation or those laws affect, and the whole kept under control and regulation, by the central power of imperial representation."[2]

Enthusiasm for federalism increased throughout 1844 and O'Connell was drawn inexorably to it. Anxious to have the federalists in his camp, he published a manifesto on 12 October 1844 announcing his interest in a federal scheme.[3] His initiative shocked his younger supporters, particularly those in the *Nation* group, and infuriated Crawford who found O'Connell's tactics disingenuous. O'Connell had not, of course, outlined a particular scheme but he had effectively challenged the federalists to do so.

Crawford took up the challenge in four letters to the *Northern Whig* in mid-November.[4] He drew upon the experiences of such colonial governments as Canada, Nova Scotia, and New Brunswick to argue that "local representation was the principle underlying British rule."[5] He was particularly attracted by the Canada Act of 1840 and thought that Ireland would be satisfied with similar legislative powers. The Irish legislature was to have the power to pass laws and impose taxation in Ireland subject to certain limitations. For example, any bill passed by the Irish parliament which made any provision with regard to religion or religious worship or grants or payments for the purpose of religion was to be subject to the veto of the imperial parliament. Similarly, customs and excise duties throughout the United Kingdom were to remain the exclusive responsibility of the imperial parliament. Ireland was also to pay a fixed sum each year into the imperial exchequer as its contribution to various imperial expenses. In return, Ireland would continue to have representation in the imperial parliament.

Crawford's scheme was more devolutionary than federal in nature. There was no clear-cut division of sovereignty; the imperial parliament retained veto powers in crucial areas; and no imperial parliament was established separate from the parliament for England, Scotland, and Wales. Crawford's scheme attempted to deal with many of the key issues that were to be at the centre of all later discussions: control of customs and excise, the protection of religious minorities, and Irish representation in the imperial parliament. In trying to marry colonial and federal precedents he anticipated the predisposition of later constitutional architects. But since his scheme was not adopted by any political group, Crawford, unlike Butt or Gladstone or Asquith, did not have to grapple with the inconsistencies and difficulties inherent in his proposal.

O'Connell's own flirtation with federalism quickly ended. He recognized that it was of no interest to repealers and that his particular view of federalism – no Irish representatives at Westminster and complete British control of imperial foreign policy – was anathema to Crawford and his supporters. For the Young Irelanders federalism was but the shadow of repeal. In fact, they recognized that Crawford's scheme was not truly federal but essentially devolutionary. In their eyes, either form of government would only continue "Ireland's moral and intellectual subjection to England." Neither would give Ireland the independence that their nationalism demanded.[6] The reaction of the leading politicians in London was predictably conservative. Repeal or the establishment of a half-way house such as devolution or federalism appalled most of them. Lord John Russell was clearly alarmed and urged the duke of Leinster, the leader of the Whigs in Ireland, to write to his friends urging them not to give support "to what is called Federal Union. The union is a fundamental part of our political system. It cannot be compromised or cut into fragments to make repeal more easy to swallow." He was personally determined to "stand by the Legislative Union."[7] Sir James Graham also warned Peel that federalism was the device around which "the two extremes in Ireland" would converge as a stepping-stone to the larger goal of repeal.[8]

Among the criticisms that surfaced during late 1844 some of the most pointed were in the *Morning Herald*. On 4 October an unsigned editorial raised two major issues. The first, the difficulty in discriminating under a federal system between national and imperial questions, reflected either a lack of knowledge of federalism or the difficulties imbedded in combining constitutional revisions at the national level (the United Kingdom) with the retention of imperial unity. The *Herald*'s confusion had only been compounded by Crawford's ill-devised scheme. The second issue was of even more concern: what was "to prevent an Irish dependent Parliament from doing tomorrow what an Irish dependent Parliament did in 1782 – declaring itself independent?" Such an eventuality was at the centre of unionist anxiety until the early 1900s.[9]

Again on 26 October the *Morning Herald* writer, possibly Isaac Butt, the future home ruler, commented deprecatingly on federalism: "To be a province, *which Ireland now is not*, may be bad enough; but to be a province with a provincial assembly, *which Ireland would be in the federative plan*, would be infinitely worse."[10] Five days later the *Herald* reminded its readers that many who contemplated federalism considered it "the shelter under which cowards hid their treason."[11] On 1 November the same writer reemphasized how subversive of the British constitution federalism would be – the division of the Union into federal states was "utterly irreconcilable with every principle, utterly at variance with every form and practice of our constitution." Moreover, if the choice were one between federalism and separation the writer believed most loyalists in England and Ireland would choose separation. Interestingly, the writer pointed to the difficulties that might beset the monarch if faced with conflicting advice from different responsible assemblies: "Out upon absurdity! This is, indeed, to degrade the English nation – this is, indeed, to shake the British throne. Compared with this mass of confusion, repeal assumes the form of constitutional order – ay, SEPARATION ITSELF is loyalty."[12] In this atmosphere "federalism" had little chance of being accepted, and after 1844 it quickly faded from the forefront of public discussion.[13]

Over the quarter-century between O'Connell's flirtation with "federalism" and the reaffirmation of the idea by Isaac Butt in 1870 there was little attention given in Ireland or Great Britain to devolution or federalism. The famine, the Young Irelanders, the Irish Republican Brotherhood, and the problems of religion and land dominated the scene. Such efforts as there were at change were violent rather than constitutional. Nevertheless, the idea or concept of federalism was not lost sight of completely. The creation of the Dominion of Canada in 1867 and the adoption in the BNA Act of a federal constitution, as well as the victory of federal forces in the American Civil War, served to remind those concerned about congestion in parliament and the rights of Ireland vis-à-vis England that a constitutional relationship other than union did exist and could be explored.

The most interesting development of the 1870s was Isaac Butt's advocacy of self-government, or "home government," for Ireland in conjunction with a federal union between Great Britain and Ireland. Butt's federal ideas never gained wide support, certainly not among committed nationalists, while the imperial dimensions of his scheme made it unpalatable to most Irishmen and uncongenial to Englishmen for whom the idea of a loose association through the crown was too tenuous to accept. Nevertheless, Butt's initiative was important. Not only did his venture coincide with a resurgence of interest in imperial federation but he also stimulated the first debate on federalism as a solution to the problems of the United Kingdom.

Butt's ideas had shifted considerably since he had criticized federalism in the *Morning Herald*. Although still a unionist, he now recognized the force of many of Crawford's arguments and his proposals bore a certain resemblance to those of the 1840s. Butt's Home Government Association met for the first time on 1 September 1870 in Dublin. In November an address was circulated outlining the aims of the new body. Adherents were asked to support not only a demand for "the restoration to Ireland of that right of domestic legislation, without which Ireland can never enjoy real prosperity or peace" but also "a Federal Union between the three portions of the United Kingdom as may still combine them into one great Imperial State."[14] Butt clearly wanted more than a simple repeal of the Union and a return to the mythical independence of Grattan's Parliament of 1782. He wanted what he referred to as "federalism." Butt outlined his ideas in a pamphlet entitled *Home Government for Ireland, Irish Federalism: Its Meaning, Its Objects, and Its Hopes*, which was published in August 1870 and went through four editions during the next four years. In his first preface, Butt emphasized that he was suggesting an outline for discussion and not a complete system. He always resisted specific details on the ground that arguing about minutiae would distract attention from the principles.[15] The essence of his argument rested on the failure of the Union and the need to provide self-government for Ireland while maintaining the unity of the United Kingdom and the empire. But he was also very conscious of the increasing congestion in the Westminster parliament and in the third edition of his pamphlet he argued that a federal constitution would also go a long way toward resolving that difficulty.[16]

Butt made it clear that he wanted to suggest a way by which it would be possible "to realize ... independence without breaking up the unity of the empire, interfering with the monarchy, or endangering the rights or liberties of any class of Irishmen."[17] He reasoned that "a Federal Union between the countries as would give an Irish Parliament control over all the domestic affairs of Ireland, while an Imperial Parliament still preserved the unity and integrity of the United Kingdom as a great power among the nations of the world" would provide a peaceful solution to the problem of nationality, self-government, and the unity of classes.[18] He "was sure that it would meet with the approval of many persons in both countries who would not support a measure which would simply repeal the Act of Union, without making some provision to secure a united action of the two countries in all matters that can concern them as one Imperial state." He was equally persuaded that "under a Federal arrangement Ireland could enjoy all of self-government and distinct nationality which would be necessary for the full development of her national life." As for the idea that federation would constitute a lowering of the national flag, Butt believed that "in a Federal Union, Ireland would take a higher place, and would exercise a greater influence than she did do, or ever could do, under the Constitution of 1782. I propose that Constitution perfected by a Federal Union with England. This ought to have been done in 1800. Instead of this the Irish Constitution was destroyed."[19]

Butt was familiar with the federal system of the United States and with the federal experiments in Germany, Switzerland, and, most recently, Canada.

He seemed much taken with the British North America Act and suggested that in Canada a model existed for a change in the relationship of Ireland to Great Britain.[20] In essence his proposal was as follows: "England, Scotland and Ireland, united as they are under one sovereign, should have a common executive and a common national council for all purposes necessary to constitute them, to other nations, as one state, while each of them should have its own domestic administration and its own domestic Parliament for its own internal affairs."[21]

Butt proposed to leave the constitution and powers of the imperial parliament unchanged. It would continue to be composed of English, Scottish, and Irish representatives and would have full control over all legislation affecting the crown of the United Kingdom and the administration of the royal power. It would remain "the great Council of the Empire" with power to legislate for India and the colonies, to determine foreign and defence policies, to tax for imperial purposes, and to advise the sovereign on matters of war and peace. Butt made it clear that Ireland and, presumably, the other constituent parts of a new federal structure, would be obliged to contribute to the interest on the national debt, the civil list of the crown, the expenses of the army and navy, and the maintenance of foreign ambassadors and colonial establishments. He did not mention whether the imperial parliament or the Irish parliament would control customs and excise.[22]

As for the Irish parliament, Butt proposed an Irish House of Commons of between 250 and 300 members chosen in an election separate from that of representatives for the imperial parliament. He also recommended the restoration of an Irish House of Lords of unspecified size in order to attract the Irish aristocracy to his proposals. Butt was emphatic that the Irish parliament would have "supreme control" in Ireland "except in those matters which the Federal Constitution might specifically reserve to the Imperial Assembly." Apart from taxation for imperial purposes, Ireland would have "complete control" over the revenue and resources of Ireland: "Every matter relating to the internal administration of the country – our railways, our post office, our public works, our courts of justice, our corporations, our systems of education, our manufacturers, and our commerce, would all be left under the management of our domestic Parliament." Butt reasoned that under such a constitution Ireland would enjoy, for the first time, "a government carried on by ministers responsible to the Irish parliament, and answerable to that Parliament for each and every of their acts." He reassured his readers that "Those ministers would stand in the same relation to the Parliament as the ministers in Canada or in the great Australian Colony stand to the colonial Parliament." Butt's use of the phrases "supreme control" and "complete control" when referring to the powers of the Irish parliament suggests that he had a divided sovereignty in mind and that his scheme was truly federal in nature rather than simply devolutionary. However, his failure to mention customs and excise specifically and his insistence that Ireland would control all matters relating to commerce suggest that he had not systematically thought through the implications of his "federal" proposal.[23]

Both his federal intentions and his vagueness on key issues were underlined when he turned to the working of his scheme. He envisaged the imperial parliament meeting to discuss its business in a session lasting no more than two months a year. Ireland would continue to send 105 representatives to vote on all questions of imperial concern and, of course, would be joined in the deliberations of the imperial parliament by the representatives of England and Scotland.[24] So far the scheme seemed clear enough; however, Butt then suggested that

In England the English members and the English peers would assemble in a separate Parliament for the transaction of all purely English affairs. Whether they would still form one parliament with the Scotch members is a question with which Ireland would have nothing to do. If Scotland, like Ireland, wished for a separate Parliament, an arrangement might easily be made by which the sittings of the English and the Imperial Parliament might be held at intervals so timed as to summon the Scotch and Irish representatives to take part in the discussions of Imperial affairs ... Very possibly a system might be framed under which, consistently with the Constitution, the English parliament might be summoned for English purposes in an English session, and in an Imperial session for Imperial purposes, at which latter the Irish and Scotch representatives would be present.

This was cumbersome and confusing and could have had little appeal to any serious constitutionalist. Butt clearly wanted Ireland and, if they wished, England and Scotland to have separate legislatures. And he realized that within a federal system Ireland should not have a say in English and Scottish domestic affairs. Nevertheless, to suggest that the full federal structure could be achieved on a piecemeal basis at the provincial or state level while the hesitant region still participated at the central or imperial level revealed confusion. As far as he was concerned, "These are details which have more to do with the facilities for the transaction of English business than with the principles of our Federal Union."[25]

Despite these vagaries in his scheme Butt had raised one of the basic difficulties that would confront all home rulers – "the question of the retention or non-retention of the Irish representatives in a British as opposed to an 'Imperial' parliament."[26] It was a problem that was to bedevil all future discussion over home rule and which was to destroy Gladstone's schemes in particular. To pure federalists, of course, the logic was irrefutable – the only way to ensure the integrity of the United Kingdom, and the empire, and protect the nationalities in Ireland, Scotland, and Wales was a federal system for the United Kingdom. Butt's ideas addressed various devolutionary issues but because they went so far beyond the immediate needs of Anglo-Irish compromise they failed to attract sufficient adherents among repealers and even among the conservative landlord class.

Butt's federalist scheme was treated with suspicion by repealers because it did not ensure an independent Irish parliament. On the other side, conservative Irishmen and Englishmen also feared federalism. To them it seemed a step toward separation and thus to the disintegration of the empire. The colonial analogy was not persuasive because the colonies were far away and posed no strategic threat if they became independent, whereas the thought of an independent or quasi-independent Ireland was alarming. Butt believed Ireland could achieve full nationhood within the empire. He respected the empire and wanted Ireland to remain a part of it but even he acknowledged that "No one could guarantee an eternal Union of two countries ... the hour of separation might come."[27] As his own experiences were to underline, many Irishmen, even in the 1870s, were already emotionally attracted to separation. [28]

One of the most interesting aspects of the debate over Butt's federal ideas was the degree to which the Anglo-Irish problem was viewed in the wider imperial context. The subject of the transfer or demission of power had been extensively discussed in imperial circles since the 1830s and it was only natural that the Anglo-Irish issue would be viewed from other than a purely Anglo-Irish perspective. Most British statesmen, of course, responded negatively, treating home rule as a threat to imperial unity. For example, Salisbury argued that the triumph of Irish nationalism on the doorstep of the imperial centre would lead inevitably to the disintegration of the far-flung empire. [29] That attitude pervaded discussions over devolution and federalism right down to 1921. Butt's ideas, of course, ran counter to that assumption. He believed that the unity of the empire depended on the continuing unity of England and Ireland, and that federalism was the means to ensure both. His viewpoint also echoed throughout the debates of the next fifty years.

Discussion of Butt's ideas took place primarily in the newspapers and learned journals and at ill-attended public meetings. It was not until 30 June 1874 that he raised the issue in the House of Commons. On that date Butt moved "That this House resolve itself into a Committee of the Whole House, to consider the present parliamentary relations between Great Britain and Ireland."[30] In introducing his motion, Butt drew heavily upon his pamphlet. He wanted to see an Irish parliament established which would be solely responsible for Irish affairs. The imperial parliament would continue to have exclusive control over imperial matters. The best system to accommodate those separate interests and needs would be a federal union between Ireland and Great Britain. Only under such a federal arrangement would Ireland obtain self-government and the United Kingdom remain intact. He did not mention Scottish, Welsh, or English interests nor did he go into much detail about the federal scheme itself. He simply said that the division of Irish from imperial affairs might not be as difficult as many assumed, and he cited both the American and Canadian constitutions as successful examples of the division of powers. He also made a point of referring to the increasing difficulty of discussing business in the House. Clearly the Commons was overburdened with work when important legislation had to be rushed through with minimal debate. He suggested that the adoption of a federal system would benefit the conduct of the everyday business of parliament.

The majority of the MPs who spoke on 30 June and 2 July were opposed to the federal idea. Overall the debate covered most of the criticisms that were frequently to surface about the implementation and operation of federalism. Many speakers thought home rule or federalism would be inconsistent with the safety of the empire. To permit a weakening of the union would lead to a weakening of both the United Kingdom and the empire. Others pointed out that all previous federal systems had been adopted by states wishing a closer union. Under Butt's scheme it would not be possible to set up a federation unless the kingdoms were first separated. It seemed ludicrous to many that the first step towards federation would be the dissolution of the Union. To them it seemed obvious that if it was permitted it would lead to separation. The problems associated with reorganizing the British constitution, determining the division between imperial and Irish or Scottish or Welsh or English affairs, and redividing the administrative offices of state were all raised by Butt's critics. Only one speaker, John George MacCarthy, the MP for Mallow, spoke in favour of the federal idea. He pointed out that federation was neither a fanciful nor a "new-fangled system" but "one of the oldest and best settled in the world's history." It had worked well in the Achaian League of early times and in the United Netherlands of the Middle Ages.

It existed for seven centuries in Switzerland. Under it the United States of America have grown ... This system has thriven in Sweden and Norway since 1814. Austria and Hungary have recently adopted it. The new Imperial German Constitution had adopted it ... Self-government has been reconciled with Imperial unity under the British Crown in the Channel Islands and the Isle of Man. The Imperial Parliament has adopted this as a fixed principle in dealing with all its colonies of European race ... The Federal system is that towards which civilized society is naturally tending all over the world ... Federalism is a principle more akin to national, free, and beneficial legislation than this forced centralization ... the Federal proposal is in accord with common sense ... One very obvious practical advantage is that it would relieve the plethora of business in the House ... Another ... would be ... the domestic affairs of Ireland would be transacted by men who know all about them, who would have time to attend to them ... It is only by exercising some degree of self-government that a country gains political experience, tolerance, and self-control.

MacCarthy then proceeded to outline a possible division of powers and ended by recommending the establishment of a Supreme Court in conjunction with a federal system.[31]

This, of course, was anathema to Butt's critics, and both in the 1874 debate and in another, briefer, and even more desultory debate of 1876, he had little chance of gaining adherents. If anything, the 1876 debate underlined even more emphatically the inchoate thinking of the federalists, the depth of grievance of the Irish nationalists, the entrenched resistance of English and Irish unionists, the lack of appeal that home rule all round yet had for the Scots and Welsh, and the limited awareness and understanding of federalism in the House and in the wider community.[32] Overall both debates suggested most of the main criticisms that were to surface during the next fifty years in all discussions of devolution and federalism, and revealed the deep-rooted fears and assumptions of those opposed to any change in either the relationship between Ireland and Great Britain or the British constitution generally.

The parliamentary debates of the mid-1870s attracted relatively little comment and only one article of any substance appeared, but since it was by Edward A. Freeman, an acknowledged expert on federalism, it is of interest. Freeman had published the first volume of his *History of Federal Government from the Foundation of the Achaian League to the Disruption of the United States* in 1863. In that book Freeman had argued that the division of sovereignty between the central and local states was "essential to the absolute perfection of the federal idea." For example, a "true and perfect Federal Commonwealth" would be "any collection of states in which it is equally unlawful for the Central Power to interfere with the purely internal legislation of the several members, and for the several members to enter into any diplomatic relations with other powers." Under a true federation sovereignty was divided and coordinate, "the Government of the Federation and the Government of the State ... each equally claiming allegiance within its own range." Freeman argued that federalism was essentially a compromise, "something intermediate between two extremes." For him a federal government was most likely to be formed when the question arose "whether several small states shall remain perfectly independent, or shall be consolidated into a single great state." That is, a federation would be the result of integrative not disintegrative forces. Clearly, for Freeman, federation was a form of government that was the creation of circumstances. It could not be transferred easily to places where circumstances had not prepared the ground for it. In 1863 Freeman had been quite emphatic about the unsuitability of federalism to the United Kingdom. "No one could wish to cut up our United Kingdom into a federation, to invest English Counties with the rights of American States, or even to restore Scotland and Ireland to the quasi-Federal position which they held before their respective Unions. A Federal Union, to be of any value, must arise by the establishment of a closer tie between elements which were before distinct, not by the division of members which have been hitherto more closely united." Freeman also raised the problem of a federal monarchy. Was it possible? At the least it would be a delicate and difficult political machine to work. He concluded that a federal state would also be a republican state.[33]

Freeman made many of the same points in his article "Federalism and Home Rule" published in the *Fortnightly Review* about a month after the 1874 debate.[34] He was quick to admit that neither dependence nor quasi-independence nor incorporation had resolved Anglo-Irish difficulties, and he recognized that "home rule" was increasingly the cry. But what was "home rule?" It appeared to mean an imperial parliament for the settlement of imperial business, i.e., business in which England, Scotland, and Ireland were all interested, and a special Irish parliament for purely Irish affairs. Freeman asked what was to happen to those matters specially English or specially Scottish or those which concerned the whole of Great Britain but not Ireland? Would there also be separate parliaments for England and Scotland? If not, Irish members would be able to vote on English and Scottish business while English and Scottish members would not be able to vote on Irish business. This would not be fair. Perhaps it would, as Butt hinted, be necessary for it to be ordained by law that on purely English and Scottish measures, Irish members should have no votes. It would be hard to define what was English, Scottish, and Irish business. Even with an Irish parliament the Irish members would still be inferior at Westminster, only sometimes having votes while the others would always have votes. This would not prove satisfactory to anyone, particularly the Irish.

As for the federal system, it was "suited for some times and places, and not suited for others." Freeman restated the point that a federal system was the right one if it was a step toward closer union but the wrong one if a step back to a looser relationship: "In the case of every successful Federation, the Federal system has appeared as a principle of union." Moreover, were not three required to make a federation rather than two? Freeman concluded: "To my mind then the scheme of the Home Rule seems unpracticable, and the analogies, past and present, by which they try to support it seems to me to wholly off the question. I am indeed inclined to think that total separation would be a less evil than such a scheme of Federation, or whatever it is to be called, as is now proposed." Freeman agreed that the Irish had legitimate grievances that would not be resolved by insult or coercion, but in his opinion Butt's "federal" proposal would not settle them.

There was much in this article that had already been raised in the 1840s but, given the prestige of the author and the natural conservatism of most anti-home rulers and anti-federalists, it was much cited over the years. It was, of course, true that no interest in federalism or even in devolutionary "home rule all round" existed in Scotland and Wales, let alone England, in the 1870s.

Without a common impulse federalism or devolution throughout the United Kingdom would be difficult to achieve. The lack of impulse reflected the degree to which many in Britain, certainly most Englishmen, were wedded to the concept of undivided sovereignty and therefore to both a unitary system of government and a united empire. Although Butt had no success in convincing most Irishmen or Englishmen of the merits of Irish self-government, or of federalism, his was an important stance. He laid the base on which Parnell was to more successfully make the case for home rule and he initiated the first major debate on "federalism" for the United Kingdom.

While federalism as a solution to United Kingdom problems faded in the late 1870s, there continued to be some debate and discussion over what was meant by home rule. As it became clear by the early 1880s that Parnell and his supporters were a new and formidable group in British political life which would have to be either countered or accommodated, there was increasing speculation about constitutional change. Once again federalism was considered.

Many of the commentators were concerned about the congestion of business in parliament which had been exacerbated by the "obstruction" tactics of Parnell and his party. In their estimation, Westminster's capacity to function and the respect in which it was held were being seriously diminished. MPs were overworked and often lacked experience about particular regions. Although the writers were agreed that changes needed to be made, they differed over methods. The difficulty in demarcating between national and imperial subjects was widely acknowledged, since so many issues and interests appeared to overlap, but Frederick Heygate's solution, the merger of the Irish vice-royalty with the crown and the holding of levees in Dublin, seemed hardly adequate.[35] One writer, Sir George Campbell, the MP for Kirkcaldy, realized that simply improving local county government would not relieve an overburdened and congested parliament nor meet demands for "self-rule in the provinces." So, after examining the American, Canadian, and Austro-Hungarian systems, he advocated a decentralization of local affairs to provincial assemblies and the establishment of a separate central parliament to handle imperial business. He thought the provinces might be Wales and Scotland, Northern England, Southern England, London and its surroundings, possibly East Anglia, and a special mining province in the north. Campbell was not sure how to deal with Ireland because it had many of "the race difficulties in the way of self-governing institutions" with which the British were familiar in the colonial empire. As he put it, "Ireland is in a condition ... analogous to one of the South African colonies, in which only British authority prevents collision between a colonist minority and a native majority." Nevertheless, Campbell wanted a system that combined "national union and greatness, with a considerable amount of self-rule in the provinces." He admitted the crudity of his scheme but noted, quite rightly, that the whole subject had not as yet been treated very seriously in the British Isles. Campbell's ideas were rough-and-ready but his observations on congestion and on the tensions within Ireland were perceptive.[36]

Justin McCarthy, the MP for Longford, shared Heygate's and Campbell's concerns about congestion but he went further in his criticisms and in his proposed solution. "What," he asked, "can be said for a system which insists that the Imperial Parliament shall neglect the business which it alone can do, in order to undertake business which it never can do effectively, and which it never ought to have undertaken?" He pointed particularly to the numerous private bills on highly local matters that preoccupied so much parliamentary time. He thought the only reasonable solution was to leave to England, Scotland, and Ireland (again no mention of Wales) the work each understood and really cared about, while letting the imperial parliament meet for the settlement of strictly imperial business that concerned all three kingdoms.[37]

Despite his sympathy for federation McCarthy was muddled on key issues. For example, while he professed a liking for American and Canadian systems he was prepared not only to deal with Ireland in advance of England and Scotland but to contemplate the presence of colonial representatives in the imperial parliament as a step toward imperial federation. The first would have meant approaching federalism for the United Kingdom in an awkward, piecemeal manner, and the second would have allowed colonial representatives a voice in English, Scottish, and Irish affairs. Unlike many later theorists, McCarthy did not contemplate a third parliamentary tier devoted strictly to imperial affairs and divorced from the concerns of the nation-state.

The vagaries and obvious inconsistencies in McCarthy's scheme left him, and more generally the federalist position, open to the criticism of the inveterate foes of the concept. Edward Wilson savaged McCarthy's reasoning and the predilection of many writers on "home rule" and "federalism" to argue by analogy. Pointing to successful federal institutions in the United States, Canada, and Germany was of limited value unless one recognized that "the conditions under which federal principles would have to be applied to the United Kingdom differ from those prevailing in the Austrian and German Empire, in Canada and the United States." Wilson accused the federalists of refusing to discuss details and failing to admit that outside the home rule party there were no adherents of federalism in the United Kingdom. Wilson thought home rule would lead to separation or even civil war, and that a federal constitution would mean a written constitution and a revolution in the British constitutional and political system. He admitted that parliamentary congestion existed but he saw the solution in the transfer of local affairs to nonlegislative bodies. Wilson also made the point that the adoption and development of federal institutions had always been in the direction of consolidation, not disintegration. This, of course, was Freeman's argument.[38]

Goldwin Smith, the former Regius professor of history at Oxford, fresh from a protracted correspondence with J.X. Merriman, the South African politician, about the merits and failings of Canadian federalism, derided McCarthy's arguments, pointing out that the "federal system requires, for its successful application, a number of states tolerably equal in magnitude, free at least from dangerous predominance; nor is a federation likely to prosper unless it is originally founded in good will and a strong sense of mutual need, such as arises when a group of small communities is threatened by a powerful enemy." In any United Kingdom federation England would greatly predominate. These were valid points, but Smith's real reasons for opposition lay deeper and were far less rational: "The Celts of Ireland are as yet unfit for parliamentary government ... Left to themselves, without what they call English misrule, they would almost certainly be ... the willing slaves of some hereditary despot, the representative of their old coshering chiefs, with a priesthood as absolute and as obscurantist as the Druids ... What they really need is not an increased measure of that for which they are but half-prepared, but the occasional admixture of more paternal government."[39]

The most interesting comments in the early eighties were made by Albert Venn Dicey, Vinerian professor of law at Oxford and a fellow of All Souls. Dicey was to be the most vehement and persistent critic of Irish home rule and of federalism for the United Kingdom. He published a number of books and articles directly attacking and criticizing both Gladstonian and Asquithian ventures. His ideological commitment to Unionism affected his analysis of the British constitution but his standing was such that his views on federalism had a pervasive influence throughout the debate over constitutional change in the United Kingdom. Once stated, Dicey's essential arguments did not shift over the next forty years.

Dicey's first major statement on home rule, "Home Rule from an English Point of View," appeared in the *Contemporary Review* in July 1882.[40] He frankly admitted his aim was to establish the truth of the proposition "that any system of 'Home Rule' or of 'Federalism,' is at least as much opposed to the interests of Great Britain as would be the national independence of Ireland." He did not find it absurd for Irishmen to desire home rule or independence but he did believe it was incumbent on those who did not share that ambition to examine the proposals and, if necessary, point out the "fallacies of federation."

Dicey was familiar with the ideas of Isaac Butt and with the constitutions of the United States and Canada. He assumed that the federalists wanted to adopt a constitution modelled on that of the United States. If so, it would not affect Ireland alone. The whole of the United Kingdom would be involved. There would need to be a written constitution which would have to define the respective powers of the central and state governments and provide for an arbiter, perhaps a superior court, to decide disputes between the central and state authorities. Dicey pointed out what many tended to overlook "that a Federal constitution implies an elaborate distribution and definition of political powers; that it is from its very nature a sort of compromise." He admitted that under a federal system the break with the past would be lessened; a federal union might in the eyes of foreign powers simply be the United Kingdom in another form; and Ireland might still contribute to the imperial exchequer so the loss would be minimized.

Nevertheless, such a "constitutional revolution" would mean the dislocation of all British constitutional arrangements; the power of Great Britain would be diminished; and the chance of further disagreement with Ireland would be enhanced. The first was of special concern to Dicey. For him the latent power of the British constitution, "the true source of its life and growth," was the "absolute omnipotence, the sovereignty of Parliament," i.e., of the King, Lords, and Commons combined. The sovereignty of parliament was nothing but "unlimited power." Federation would mean divided sovereignty and the loss of the omnipotence of parliament. "Home Rulers," he argued, "whether they know it or not, are prepared to touch the mainspring of the British constitution." Also the court or tribunal, the final arbiter, would have the power to determine whether or not a law was constitutional. Parliament would therefore be doubly weakened. Ironically, the monarch, as Butt had surmised, might well become stronger under a federal arrangement because the monarchy alone would represent national unity in its fullest sense. He concluded that "federalism would dislocate every English constitutional arrangement."

As to British power, he wondered how the army was to be divided? No matter how it were done it seemed obvious to Dicey that "The central Government would again, merely from that division of powers which forms part of Federalism, be as feeble against foreign aggression as against local resistance." Moreover, he believed federalism was as likely to cause divisions between England and Ireland as remove them. For a government to work with anything like success there had to exist among the citizens a spirit of genuine loyalty to the union which must predominate over loyalty to the state, but in a federation national allegiance and local allegiance would divide and perplex the feelings of even loyal citizens. Dicey was convinced Irish citizens would always be more loyal to Ireland than to the British federation.

The essence of Dicey's argument in 1882, and for the next forty years, was summed up as follows:

[Federalism] revolutionizes the whole constitution of the United Kingdom; by undermining the parliamentary sovereignty, it deprives English institutions of their elasticity, their strength, and their life; it weakens the Executive at home, and lessens the power of the country to resist foreign attack. The revolution which works these changes holds out no hope of conciliation with Ireland. An attempt, in short, to impose on England and Scotland a constitution which they do not want, and which is quite unsuited to the historical traditions and to the genius of Great Britain, offers to Ireland a constitution which Ireland is certain to dislike, which had none of the real or imaginary charms of independence, and ensures none of the solid benefits to be hoped for from a genuine union with England.

Dicey also distrusted self-government for Ireland for other reasons, as he made clear to James Bryce in November 1882.[41] Much like Goldwin Smith, he doubted if there existed an Irish political capacity for self-government. The necessary neighbourliness, "the good influence of landowners etc.," essential to the success of local government was wanting in Ireland. But he admitted he had little faith in local self-government in any setting. To him good administration was "in many cases better than local self-government." In early January 1885 he wrote once more to Bryce about the dangers of a separate parliament for Ireland: "The alternative for good or bad is ultimately between Union & separation (complete independence) ... If I were an Irishman I have little doubt I shd be an out & out Nationalist & therefore anger or indignation at fair Nationalism is out of place in my mind ... As at present advised I am inclined to say, one's maxim shd be no Federalism – no discussion no martial-law. Substitute for the time strict enforcement of ordinary law & strict protection for legal rights. If this policy is found at last absolutely unworkable then, tho' with the greatest regret I shd advocate separation."[42]

Later in 1885 Dicey published his lectures on *The Law of the Constitution*. The book became immensely popular and remained a standard text until well into the twentieth century. His arguments about the sovereignty of parliament and the rule of law were accepted unquestionably for many years. In particular, the lecture on "Parliamentary Sovereignty and Federalism" reiterated his belief in the necessity of preserving the Union and in the inherent weaknesses of federalism. Anyone who had read his article in the *Contemporary Review* of July 1882 would not have been surprised by his conclusions.

In his lecture, Dicey compared the British parliamentary system with the federal system of government, especially that of the United States. To him the federal government in the United States represented the most advanced form of federalism, the Swiss and Canadian examples being merely copied from the United States. The major distinction between the British and American systems of government was that in the United Kingdom supreme authority was vested in parliament (defined as the King, Lords, and Commons) while in the United States limited executive, legislative, and judicial authority was distributed among bodies "co-ordinate with and independent of the other."[43] Dicey argued that a federal state required for its formation two conditions: first, a body of countries, colonies, or provinces "so closely connected by locality, by history, by race, or the like, as to be capable of bearing in the eyes of their inhabitants, an impress of common nationality"; and, second, the citizens of the proposed component parts must possess not only a desire for national unity but "the determination to maintain the independence of each man's separate State." The aim of federalism was to give effect, as far as possible, to both sentiments. In Dicey's words, "a federal state is a political contrivance intended to reconcile national unity and power with the maintenance of 'state rights'." This was done by preparing a written constitution "under which the ordinary powers of sovereignty" were elaborately divided between "the common or national government and the separate states." Whatever concerned the nation as a whole was placed under the common government and all matters not of common interest remained in the hands of the several states. Therefore the essential characteristics of federalism were the supremacy of the constitution; the distribution of powers; and the authority of the courts to act as interpreters of the Constitution. The essential distinction between a federal and a unitary system was the "tendency of federalism to limit on every side the action of government and to split up the strength of the state among coordinate and independent authorities." There was nothing parallel in the British constitution, said Dicey, where the "one fundamental dogma of English constitutional law is the absolute legislative sovereignty or despotism of the King in Parliament." Dicey concluded that a federal system would always be weaker than a unitary state of equal resources because no one authority would have enough overriding power. Moreover, federalism meant "legalism – the predominance of the judiciary in the constitution – the prevalence of a spirit of legality among the people." Federalism would substitute litigation for legislation.[44]

Dicey obviously favoured a unitary form of government and his analysis of federalism reflected that predisposition. He tended to exaggerate both the rigidity of a federal system and its potential fragility in the face of internal pressures and external foes. Over the years, his arguments and assumptions were to crop up again and again in the speeches and articles of others and his constructs were to determine the nature of the Unionist response. He could not have known, of course, that Gladstone had begun to contemplate some form of home rule for Ireland and that his book would soon be much thumbed by all involved in the debate over constitutional change in the United Kingdom.

During the early 1880s there was only one serious attempt by a government politician to find a solution to the Irish demand for greater control of its own affairs. It was made by Joseph Chamberlain, president of the board of trade. He began modestly in late 1884 with suggestions little different from a reform of local government but by the end of 1885 he was increasingly attracted by a federal solution modelled on the constitution of the United States.

When Chamberlain embarked on negotiations over Irish governmental reform, he did so knowing that the recent enlargement of the franchise would considerably increase the power of the Irish nationalist MPs led by Parnell. Those MPs would vehemently oppose a renewal of the Prevention of Crime

Act which was due to expire in 1885. A protracted dispute over the issue would weaken the Liberal government in the run-up to the next election scheduled to be held in 1886. It seemed obvious to Chamberlain that it would be in the interests of the Irish and of Liberal electoral fortunes to pursue any opportunity of decreasing the tension. This does not mean that Chamberlain was not genuinely committed to some reform of the constitutional relationship between Ireland and Great Britain. He had, after all, pursued the idea as early as 1879. It was simply that Chamberlain believed he could marry his commitment to reform with his interest in Liberal party success, while always ensuring that the integrity of the United Kingdom and the empire was preserved.

In November 1884, during widespread discussion in Liberal and Irish political circles about the proposed renewal of the Crime Act, Captain William Henry O'Shea, the Nationalist MP for County Clare and an established intermediary between Parnell and Chamberlain, delivered to Chamberlain "a short note" purporting to contain Parnell's views on both the Crime Act and Irish local government. Chamberlain immediately drafted his own scheme. The two proposals were similar. Both men wanted to establish a system of representative local government in Ireland and to create a national body with more extensive authority on all-Irish matters. The key difference was that Parnell did not want such reforms to interfere with the achievement of an Irish parliament while Chamberlain saw them as satisfying Irish needs. Thus Parnell's "Irish board" was to have only administrative functions, whereas Chamberlain's "central board" had administrative and minimal legislative authority.[45]

Chamberlain outlined his ideas in a letter dated 17 December 1884 to Henry Duignan, a Walsall solicitor, and a longtime supporter:

I can never consent to regard Ireland as a separate people with the inherent rights of an absolutely independent community. I should not do this in the case of Scotland, or of Wales, or, to take still more extreme instances of Sussex, or of London. In every case the rights of the county or district must be subordinated to the rights of the whole community of which it forms only a portion. Ireland by its geographical position, and by its history is a part of the United Kingdom, and it cannot divest itself of the obligations or be denied the advantages which this condition involves.

Accordingly, if nationalism means separation, I for one am prepared to resist it. I see in it the probability, almost the certainty, of dangerous complications and an antagonism which would be injurious to the interests of the larger country and fatal to the prosperity of the smaller. Sooner than yield on this point I would govern Ireland by force to the end of the chapter.

Chamberlain was, of course, never to yield on that point. Nevertheless, "if nationalism [meant] home rule" he had no objection in principle. He simply wished to know what home rule meant. For example, he objected to the home rule proposed by Isaac Butt because not only would it not work but, in his estimation, it "would infallibly lead to a demand for entire separation." On the other hand, he believed Ireland had "a right to a local government more complete, more popular, more thoroughly representative, and more far-reaching than anything that has hitherto been suggested." He believed there were "questions, not local in any narrow sense, but which require local and exceptional treatment in Ireland and which cannot be dealt with to the satisfaction of the Irish people by an imperial parliament."

Chief among them are the education question and the land question, and I would not hesitate to transfer their consideration and solution to an Irish board altogether independent of English government influence.

Such a board might also deal with railways and other communications and would, of course, be invested with powers of taxation in Ireland for these strictly Irish purposes ... If [these proposals] were carried out the Irish people would have entire independence as regards all local work and local expenditure ... while the imperial parliament would continue to regulate for the common good the national policy of the three kingdoms.[46]

This proposal, while not a restitution of a full Irish parliament, was clearly a step up from simply a reform of local government. It even hinted at legislative devolution and at a demarcation of local and national domains. Nevertheless, Parnell did not find it attractive. On 5 January 1885 he had reminded O'Shea that "in talking to our friend you must give him clearly to understand that we do *not* propose this local self-government plan as a substitute for the restitution of our Irish parliament but solely as an improvement of the present system of local government in Ireland. The claim for restitution of parliament would still remain."[47] He particularly disliked Chamberlain's scheme because it proposed legislative functions as well as administrative. It conceded too much rather than too little. To accept such a scheme would imperil the demand for a full Irish parliament: "The two questions of the reform of local government and the restitution of an Irish parliament must ... be left absolutely separate ... The central local government body which I propose will not have legislative functions, only administrative. I could not put it forward as a substitute for a parliament."

As far as Parnell was concerned, Chamberlain's scheme suggested the establishment of a central board "with more extensive powers than I have claimed, as a substitute for an Irish parliament." The central board would "be empowered to legislate regarding the settlement and solution of the land question and should have full control over this matter. This is a power I have not claimed as it would cross the borderline between legislative and administrative functions which I have endeavoured to follow in all important particulars."[48] On 21 January 1885 Parnell underlined his position in dramatic fashion during a speech in Cork, when he declared "no man has the right to fix the boundary of the march of a nation. No man has a right to say, 'Thus far shalt thou go and no further' ... we have never attempted to fix the *ne plus ultra* to the progress of Ireland's nationhood and we never shall."[49]

Although Chamberlain must have been aware of Parnell's objections, he decided to push ahead with his scheme. On 25 April he circulated to his cabinet colleagues a memorandum entitled "Local government in Ireland."[50] It was a far more detailed proposal than his earlier one but reflected his thinking since late January. Perhaps because he had heard of Parnell's concerns, Chamberlain reduced the central board's legislative powers and dropped the land question from the board's jurisdiction. Nevertheless, the board's powers over education, public works, and communication were retained as were its legislative responsibilities in those areas. Once again Chamberlain made it clear that he opposed separation "or even a separate parliament under the same sovereign" but wished to meet "in the fullest possible way the legitimate aspirations of the Irish people towards entire independence in the management of their local affairs." He would therefore "give the widest possible interpretation to the term local government; and would include in it not merely local and municipal affairs but also questions which may be described as national although they do not concern imperial interests."

The majority of Chamberlain's colleagues disliked the proposal. Lord Spencer, the Irish viceroy, and Henry Campbell-Bannerman, the chief secretary, were especially concerned, but their views were widely shared and, in fact, were to be echoed in later years over ever more ambitious schemes. Spencer outlined his concerns to Chamberlain on 26 April.

The proposal removes from the hands of the executive government all administrative work, with the exception of that connected with law, justice, prisons and police. It takes from government all patronage connected with the department which it absorbs.

Without further discussion I am hardly prepared to agree to this which is a fundamental change in our principle of a government.

Are you prepared to give up these duties of government in Scotland and England, duties now performed by various offices like the home office and the local government board?

I see further a grave danger in constituting a representative body which may assume to itself the right of speaking for the Irish nation ... It will be impossible to prevent this central body from taking up general questions and passing resolutions upon them. These may and often will be in direct opposition to decisions of the imperial parliament, and of the executive government in Dublin, and will create serious difficulties.

The influence and pressure from such a representative body will be difficult to resist ...

Although the central board will be confined to administration it will be difficult to resist its functions becoming legislative hereafter.[51]

Chamberlain's central board scheme was considered by the cabinet on 9 May 1885, and while supported by Gladstone and all the commoners except Hartington was opposed by all the peers except Lord Granville. The scheme was therefore rejected. Dismayed and disgruntled, Chamberlain resigned on 20 May 1885 over Gladstone's decision to introduce an Irish land-purchase bill unaccompanied by the reform of local government, but his resignation was neither accepted nor withdrawn. Three weeks later Gladstone's ministry fell, having been defeated on 9 June over Hugh Childers's budget.

In the weeks following his setback in cabinet Chamberlain continued to wrestle with the problem of constitutional reform. In June he publicly proclaimed the necessity of giving "the widest possible self-government to Ireland ... consistent with the maintenance of the integrity of the empire" and, on one occasion, even suggested that Scotland might be similarly treated.[52] In July an article based on Chamberlain's cabinet memorandum appeared in the *Fortnightly Review* and carried the analysis further.[53] In this article general remarks were made about the need for local government reform throughout the United Kingdom, and the congestion of business in parliament was condemned. It seemed clear to the writer that "no mere extension of local government upon the ordinary and restricted lines will relieve the parliamentary congestion which has long since become a national calamity." It affected imperial and local matters and had to be remedied. The central government interfered altogether too much with local government in Scotland and Ireland. The interference in the latter was that of an "alien authority." It provided the additional factor of "the prejudice of race and nationality." The continuance of such a system would be "unjust to Ireland, useless to England and dangerous to both."

The problem of the government of the empire was "How can the work of legislation and administration in the United Kingdom be so adjusted as to secure the integrity of that kingdom, while giving to each of its component parts the best means of providing for its own public wants and developing its own resources?" The answer was division and subdivision of labour. "The imperial Parliament cannot satisfactorily attend to its legitimate work as the great legislative body of the empire without delegating to some other authorities the task of dealing with all matters which possess a local character." But local matters could be matters concerning a single county and those which while concerning several counties did not concern one of the four countries – England, Scotland, Ireland, and Wales – comprising the United Kingdom. These matters might be called domestic rather than local. Therefore to make the legislative and administrative machinery of government for the United Kingdom workable it would be necessary to establish both boards at the county level (County Boards) and councils at the level of each of the four countries (National Councils). In order to relieve the imperial parliament from undue pressure of work "the business of private bill legislation for these countries should be transferred to Edinburgh and to Dublin."

The establishment of a National Council, elected by the Irish people and endowed with national authority, would enable the Imperial Parliament to delegate to a body of sufficient weight, capacity, and power, duties which Parliament now endeavours to perform, but the performance of which necessitates the neglect of other and more important matters upon which the attention of the great legislative assembly of the Empire should be concentrated. By the creation of County Boards and National Councils we should secure in the United Kingdom a rational division of the duties and labours of government. The imperial Parliament, the National Councils, and the County Boards would together form ... a hierarchy of legislative and administrative authority, all based upon the only true principle of government – free election by the governed. For all parts of the United Kingdom the establishment of such a system of government would be advantageous.

The writer believed adoption of the idea would bestow "an immense national boom upon Ireland." It would strengthen the empire because it would remove a reproach. Moreover, "We live in an epoch when our relations with our dependencies and our whole scheme of Imperial administration is undergoing close scrutiny. Upon what terms is the mother country to be associated with its colonies? How far are the latter to be represented in the Government of the former? In what proportions are the burdens of the empire to be divided between the two?" At such a time a solution to the relationship of England and Ireland must be found for "an alienated Ireland means a weakened England, and even a weakened Empire."

This was an intriguing proposal. The focus was still Ireland but the implications of the analysis had been extended to England, Scotland, and Wales, while the context had been considerably broadened to include the imperial implications. Chamberlain might not have written the article but he did endorse it. It was an indication of how his thoughts were shifting. The proposal still emphasized delegation and thus did not suggest the weakening of parliamentary sovereignty. It certainly was not federalism and nowhere did the writer use that term, but it was not unlike many of the schemes for home rule all round that were to surface in the late eighties and in the 1890s.

At no time during his rumination did Chamberlain depart from his opposition to a separate parliament for Ireland. Although he realized by the late summer of 1885 that Parnell would have nothing to do with a "central board" or a "national council," Chamberlain, in turn, would have nothing to do with Parnell's single chamber for Ireland. Chamberlain was always interested in strengthening the imperial parliament and hence the empire. Although he had not yet mentioned a "federal" solution, it was clear by the autumn that he was familiar with federal systems. In referring to Parnell's plan he noted: "The powers he claims for his separate Parliament are altogether beyond anything which exists in the case of the State Legislatures of the American Union, which has hitherto been the type and model of the Irish demands; and if this claim were conceded, we might as well for ever abandon all hope

of maintaining a United Kingdom. We should establish within less than thirty
miles of our shores a new foreign country, animated from the outset with un-
friendly intentions towards ourselves." Such a policy would be ruinous to
Ireland and dangerous to England. Chamberlain went on: "It is said by
[Parnell] that justice requires we should concede to Irishmen the absolute
right of self-government. I would reply that it is a right which must be considered in relation to the security and welfare of the other countries in juxtaposition to which Ireland is placed ... as neighbours neither one nor the
other has any right so to rule his own household as to be a source of annoyance
or danger to the other. Subject to that limitation, I, for my part, would concede the greatest possible measure of local government to the Irish people,
as I would concede it also to the English and the Scotch."[54]

Chamberlain's musings, and those of most of his contemporaries, were
given a dramatic wrench in mid-December, when Herbert Gladstone unwit-
tingly revealed to an astonished public that his father was contemplating home
rule for Ireland. Since the recent election had left the Irish Nationalists
holding the key to parliamentary success, the Liberal leader's intention had
to be taken seriously. Speculation was immediately rife. What form would
"home rule" take? Would the Irish continue to sit at Westminster? If so, there
would be many problems. Not only would the Irish inevitably have a say in
Scots, Welsh, and English affairs but so would the latter in matters imping-
ing on Irish interests. Moreover, would an imperial ministry enjoying the
confidence of the House in domestic matters automatically be obliged to
resign if defeated on a foreign question with Irish help? Tim Healy, the Nationalist MP, found that one "a poser" and concluded that "the federal idea
cannot work unless you have a local and an imperial Parliament."[55]

Healy's comment revealed how little he knew about federalism, but
Chamberlain was not so uninformed. Reluctantly, he began to give the idea
serious thought, and by 26 December he had come grudgingly to the conclusion that the only way of giving "bona fide Home Rule" would be the adoption of the American Constitution:

1. Separate legislation for England, Scotland, Wales, and possibly Ulster. The three
   other Irish Provinces might combine.
2. Imperial Legislation at Westminster for foreign and Colonial affairs, Army, Navy,
   Post Office and Customs.
3. A Supreme Court to arbitrate on respective limits of authority. Of course the House
   of Lords would go. I do not suppose the five legislations could stand a Second
   Chamber a piece. Each would have its own Ministry responsible to itself. There
   is a scheme for you. It is the only one which is compatible with any sort of Imperial
   unity, and once established it might work without friction ... I am not going to
   swallow separation with my eyes shut.[56]

It was obvious that Chamberlain had turned to "federalism" as the one possible means of resolving the constitutional problem while keeping the United Kingdom, and thus the empire, intact. It was to be a primary motivation for unionists until 1921. It is not fully clear what Chamberlain meant by "federalism," although it would seem that, for a time at least, he did seriously consider a true division of sovereignty. His anxiety and his confusion were revealed in further letters to Labouchere at the turn of the year. On 27 December he scrawled: "I wish someone would start the idea of a Federal Constitution like the United States. I do not believe people are prepared for this solution yet, but it is the only possible form of Home Rule. It is that or nothing. In my opinion Mr. Gladstone cannot carry his or any other scheme just now." A week later he wrote, almost despairingly, "The difficulties of any plan are almost insurmountable, but the worst of all plans would be one which kept the Irishmen at Westminster while they had their own Parliament in Dublin."[57] Only time and political opportunity would reveal what Gladstone had in mind.

CHAPTER TWO

Gladstonian Home Rule

Gladstone had long been involved in Irish affairs and his ministries of 1868–74 and 1880–5 initiated major pieces of legislation that dealt with the issues of the church and the land. He had not, however, publicly stated his interest in any scheme of home rule or devolution during those years. Many later observers pointed out that in a speech at Aberdeen in 1871 Gladstone had declared that if Ireland were given home rule, Scotland and Wales would also be entitled to it. Those observers took comfort from such a comment and interpreted it as supportive of home rule all round, failing to note that he had immediately gone on to say: "Can any sensible man, can any rational man, suppose that at this time of day, in this condition of the world, we are going to disintegrate the great capital institutions of this country for the purpose of making ourselves ridiculous in the sight of all mankind?"[1] Clearly Gladstone did not favour home rule in the early 1870s. He equated its adoption with the fragmentation of the United Kingdom and the potential disintegration of the empire. Over the next fifteen years he mellowed somewhat toward the acceptance of some form of devolution but always adhered to the principle that the unity of the United Kingdom and the empire would have to be maintained.

Gladstone did, however, favour local self-government, i.e., local government, and over the next decade he was drawn to more extensive schemes.[2] On 26 November 1879, in his second Midlothian speech, Gladstone spoke of the congestion of parliament and the need to relieve it by devolving some responsibility to subordinate authorities.[3] In mid-November 1880 he submitted to cabinet a suggestion for the devolution to parliamentary committees of responsibilities for portions of the United Kingdom. It would have expanded the function of the committees from specific topics to specific areas. Gladstone believed his scheme would "neutralise and reduce" obstruction. He did not have separate authorities in mind but "sub-formations out of the body of the House itself." He hoped the scheme would "supply the means of partially meeting and satisfying ... the call for what is styled (in bonam partem) 'Local Government,' and (in malem) 'Home Rule.'" The committees would have had neither financial nor executive powers and would have been obliged to report directly to parliament.[4] This suggestion, modelled on the ideas of Sir Erskine May, was in keeping with Gladstone's stated interest in an extension of local government and with his awareness of the problems of congestion in parliament. Modest though the proposal was, it did not appeal to the cabinet and was rejected.

A year later, when asked what his position was vis-à-vis Parnell, he wrote, "I am rather advanced as to Home or local rule, not wishing to stipulate excepting for the supremacy of Parliament, and for not excluding Scotland in principle from anything offered or done for Ireland."[5] For Gladstone home rule had "for one of its senses Local Government, an excellent thing to which I should affix no limits except the supremacy of the Imperial Parliament, and the right of all parts of the country to claim whatever might be accorded to Ireland." He told Granville that "This is only a repetition of what I have often said before, and I have nothing to add or enlarge. But I have the fear that when the occasion for action comes, which will not be in my time, many Liberals may perhaps hang back, and may cause further trouble."[6]

In February 1882 Gladstone spoke only mildly against a motion for the repeal of the Act of Union with Ireland. When the queen complained, he asserted that government must not be imposed upon those who did not wish it. He reminded her that Canadian self-government had once been regarded "as a thing fatal to the unity of the Empire."[7] Nevertheless, he had no intention of extending to Ireland the kind of home rule that existed in Canada. This was underlined two months later when, in response to a new land purchase proposal, Gladstone submitted a "Provincial Councils" scheme for the consideration of his cabinet colleagues. It was an expansion of his earlier local government ideas but was still emphatically devolutionary. There were to be four provincial councils which would take over the powers of the Land Commission and the duties of the commissioners of national education. The primary functions of the councils would have been the purchase of estates for resale and the provision of advances to tenants to enable them to purchase their holdings. Although Gladstone had carefully avoided recommending anything approaching a national body, his scheme was too advanced for the majority of his colleagues and was given little serious attention before he was diverted by the negotiations leading to the Kilmainham Treaty and then by the Phoenix Park murders.[8] At the end of 1882 Gladstone was still quite emphatic: "Irish Home rule. Not the least chance of any question as to any sort of assembly (for Ireland) in Dublin. That question if any where is not in the nearer future."[9]

By the early 1880s the Liberal party had publicly stated many times that it was prepared to extend local government to Ireland, and Gladstone himself had taken the initiative on at least two occasions in devising some form of devolutionary structure. He was therefore annoyed and alarmed when Lord Hartington, the secretary for war, asserted in January 1883 that it would be "madness ... to volunteer to give Ireland more extended self-government unless we receive from the representatives of the Irish people some assurance that this boon would not be misused."[10] Such a statement made it seem as if the Liberals were backing away from their previous commitment. It threatened to weaken the Liberals' position in Ireland and endanger the changed and more encouraging relationship with Parnell. Hartington's remarks occasioned a lengthy letter to Granville in which Gladstone was revealingly frank about his thinking on constitutional change. In reference to local government for Ireland, he pointed out:

There has also come prominently into view a new and powerful set of motives which, in my deliberate judgement, require us, for the sake of the United Kingdom even *more* than for the sake of Ireland, to push forward this question.

Under the present highly centralised system of Government, every demand, which can be started on behalf of a poor and ill-organised country, comes directly on the British Government and Treasury; if refused it becomes at once a head of grievance, if granted not only a new drain but a certain source of political complication and embarrassment, the peasant proprietary – the winter's distress – the state of the labourers – the loans to farmers – the promotion of public works – the encouragement of fisheries – the promotion of emigration – each and every one of these questions has a sting, and the sting can only be taken out of it by our treating it in correspondence with a popular and responsible *Irish* body – competent to act for its own portion of the country.

Every consideration, which prompted our pledges, prompts the recognition of them, & their extention rather than curtailment.

The Irish Government have in preparation a Local Government Bill.

Such a bill may even be an economy of time. By no other means that I can see shall we be able to ward off most critical and questionable discussions on questions of the class I have mentioned.

The argument that we cannot yet trust Irishmen with popular local institutions is [a] mischievous argument ...

By acting on principles diametrically opposite, we have broken down to 35 or 40 what would have been a party, in this Parliament, of 65 Home Rulers, and have thus averted (or at the very least postponed) the perilous crisis, which no man has as yet looked in the face: the crisis which will arise when a large & united majority of Irish Members demand some fundamental changes in the legislative relations of the two countries.[11]

Nothing could be more explicit. Local government was designed as a balm to injured feelings and a sop to aspirations. It was the damper of revolution. There was no deep-rooted commitment to self-government here; rather the reverse. It was designed to hold home rule at bay and to accommodate the less committed among the Irish MPs.

Gladstone was initially drawn to Chamberlain's central board scheme for the same pragmatic reasons. He had an extended conversation with Spencer about it on 29 April 1885 but found that only he, Sir Charles Dilke, and Chamberlain favoured it.[12] Gladstone summarized his thoughts in a memorandum dated 6 May. He indicated that his opinions were strongly "in favour of some plan for a Central Board of Local Govt in Ireland on something of an elective basis." He was under no obligation to act with Chamberlain, but "independently of all questions of party, of support, & of success, I looked upon the extension of a strong measure of Local Govt like this to Ireland, now that the question is effectually raised by the Crimes' Act, as invaluable itself, & as the only hopeful means of saving Crown & State from an ignominious surrender in the next parliament after a mischievous & painful struggle."[13] Despite its tactical attractions, Chamberlain's scheme was defeated in cabinet on 9 May 1885.

Far from being cowed by the opposition in his cabinet to any form of constitutional change, Gladstone continued to reflect upon the problem. He quickly realized that even if Chamberlain's scheme had been acceptable to his colleagues it would not have satisfied the Irish Nationalist desire for a far more extensive version of self-government. He continued to ponder on the means by which some form of home rule could be granted while preserving the integrity of the United Kingdom and the empire, and in doing so he gradually moved away from purely local and provincial schemes toward acceptance of a national body for Ireland. By August he had been sent information on the Austro-Hungarian union and in October he had obtained copies of the Canada Act of 1840 and the British North America Act of 1867. He found the latter particularly interesting.

Until the defeat of his government on 9 June and during the early months in opposition, Gladstone hesitated to commit himself or the Liberals publicly on the question of home rule, despite Parnell's declared intent to attain it and the Conservatives' obvious interest in the issue. Gladstone hoped the Irish Nationalists and the Conservatives would work something out and that home rule would be introduced by the Conservatives. This would presumably have enabled Gladstone to keep his party together.[14] While there was extensive discussion within the Liberal party throughout late 1885, Gladstone kept his ideas to himself. Nevertheless, it was generally understood that provided the unity of the empire and the sovereignty of parliament were preserved Gladstone was not averse to devolving enlarged powers upon portions of the United Kingdom in order to improve the management of affairs and meet local aspirations. To him this was the only possible way to avoid a serious crisis and was in keeping with his thinking on constitutional reform since at least the late 1870s. [15]

There was no public hint of Gladstone's advanced degree of commitment to home rule until mid-December 1885, when his son without parental approval indicated that his father was seriously considering a home rule scheme. This revelation severely limited Gladstone's bargaining and tactical positions and virtually obliged him to make his interest public. When his party resumed office in February 1886, its main preoccupation until its demise in July was a home rule bill.

The election of late 1885 had given neither Salisbury's government nor the Liberals a clear-cut victory. The Liberals did have a majority of eighty-six over the government but since the Parnellites had won exactly eight-six seats they held the balance of power. Although Salisbury stayed in office, Gladstone realized that the Conservatives had no incentive to continue their relationship with Parnell, certainly not now that Gladstone's own adoption of home rule had become public. By the end of the year he recognized that he and his party would soon be dependent upon the Parnellites and obliged to introduce a home rule bill. And so it proved. The Salisbury government was defeated on 27 January 1886 and Gladstone's third ministry was sworn in on 3 February. Gladstone was immediately preoccupied with the preparation of home rule and land purchase bills. [16]

In considering what form his proposal might take, Gladstone was not without advice from newspapers, journals, and publicists. During 1885 there had been a number of speculative articles about constitutional change in the United Kingdom. Lord Castletown had argued in the *Fortnightly Review* that only local government reforms were palatable because they would avoid the transfer of too much power and would preserve the integrity of the empire. He believed both federalism and home rule would lead to either civil war or the disintegration of the United Kingdom. A federation of the United Kingdom would suggest "a partnership of national groups" as in the United States but in fact would provide Ireland with an opportunity to break the link. Once a system was acknowledged "which gives a distinct or quasi-independent Parliament to Ireland, with taxing powers, legislative powers, etc., ... sooner or later the day will come when that Parliament will refuse to obey the Imperial Parliament." Both C. Raleigh Chichester in the *Dublin Review* and Edward William O'Brien writing in the *Nineteenth Century* agreed. They favoured county boards and the maintenance of the integrity of the empire. O'Brien particularly distrusted national councils, which in his estimation would be parliaments in all but name and would threaten imperial unity.

Two other writers thought federalism might provide a solution. Using the Canadian analogy, J. Leslie Field argued in the *Nineteenth Century* that a federal system might work in Ireland itself if six states were created: two for Ulster in order to separate as much as possible Catholic from Protestant; one for Dublin; and one for each of Leinster, Munster, and Connaught. Under such a scheme imperial, foreign, colonial, and customs matters would still remain the responsibility of Westminster but all else would be devolved, including police. G.B. Lancaster Woodburne, writing in the *National Review*, went a step further and advocated imperial federation as a solution to the Irish problem. He believed home rule could be safely granted within the framework of imperial federation. He reasoned: "If we were to give a separate legislature to Ireland, as we do to many of our Colonies, and let Irish representatives sit in an Imperial assembly, the danger would be dead, for, by giving the Irish Home Rule, the great cause of irritation between England and Ireland would be removed, and at the same time the Irish would contented, having secured for themselves the management of their own affairs, to remain part and parcel of that Empire in whose imperial business they had a voice." He also felt Scotland should have a separate Parliament.

The *Spectator* railed against these various schemes. At the very end of 1885 it argued "that a Federal system conceded for the sake of Ireland would very soon indeed spread to Scotland and Wales ... So that Scotland and Wales, which have never asked for Federalism, would be positively encouraged to ask for it at once; while England, which has not the smallest wish for a local Assembly distinct from Parliament, would be almost forced by the mere law of symmetry to accept what she has never even thought of wishing for." This would mean the break up of the old historic constitution. "If," the *Spectator* continued, "we once admit that because the Irish Members show a large majority for Home-rule they ought to have Home-rule, it will be simply impossible to refuse it to a large majority of Scotch Members or a large majority of Welsh Members. Indeed, we do not see any reason why it should stop there. England north of the Trent is more distinct from England south of the Trent than England north of the Trent is from the Scotch Lowlands. London is more distinct from the rural districts of Southern England than the rural districts of Southern England are from the Midland Counties. The contagion of disintegration will spread rapidly." In so far as the *Spectator* was concerned, this break-up of the United Kingdom would proceed from "pure weakness, from want of tenacity."[17]

Herbert Gladstone's revelation that his father was seriously considering home rule for Ireland elicited a quick response in the newspapers and magazines. The comments were both perceptive and revealing. The *Times* examined federalism in a major article on 26 December 1885 entitled "What Home Rule Means." It pointed out that the division of legislative functions between an imperial and local legislatures was exceedingly difficult. It would mean "a series of far-reaching and hitherto unconsidered changes in the English Constitution." There would be a written constitution and the conse-

quent loss of flexibility of an unwritten one. There would need to be a
Supreme Court as in the United States but with it would vanish "the historic
independence and the boasted omnipotence of the Imperial Parliament." Protection of minorities and religious interests would be necessary but difficult.
This article made a number of valid points but it reflected the hostility of the
Times to any substantive change as well as its unwillingness to see loss of
privileges for the landed and propertied classes. Above all the *Times* feared
the disintegration of the empire.[18]

Two writers pointed out the problems involved in determining whether or
not Irish MPs should remain at Westminster. If they did they would interfere
with Scottish, Welsh, and English affairs, but if they did not there would arise
the problem of taxation without representation.[19] Ulster was also recognized
as a problem and this led one commentator to argue the necessity of protecting
minorities by beginning not with a separate parliament for Ireland but with
smaller measures of "local self-government for counties."[20] Sir James Stephens
equated home rule with Irish independence. He wondered what "effectual
precaution can possibly be taken against the efforts of an Irish Parliament
to effect a separation between Ireland and Great Britain?" Unlike Canada,
Australia, South Africa, and New Zealand, Ireland was tied too closely to
Great Britain by geography, law, capital, and administration to be granted
independence. He also believed the object of the Irish nationalists was to
confiscate the property of the landlords and if the land question were resolved
there would probably be few demands for independence. These arguments
were to recur repeatedly over the next thirty-five years as the unionists and
federalists grappled with the question of Irish home rule.[21]

One colonial observer did not think much of Irish independence or federation. J.X. Merriman explained to G.J. Goschen, the veteran Liberal politician, in February 1886:

> In some degree Colonialists are fond of connecting [the Colonial question and the
> Irish difficulty] and advocates of Federation try to believe that the same measure of
> Home Rule which loosens the one tie can be made in some way to knit the dependencies
> more closely. I confess it seems to me to be almost impossible to believe that Ireland
> can safely be placed in the position of a British colony or that England could tolerate
> the loyalty tempered by threats of dissolution of the connecting tie, that passes current
> in communities who live on the other side of the world. If the experiment is ever tried
> I hope that two or three states will be created, in view of a balance of power, rather
> than one homogeneous Ireland where the minority will be crushed out of existence.[22]

In February 1886 important analyses of Gladstone's options were published
by James Bryce in the *Nineteenth Century*, Joseph Chamberlain in the *Fortnightly
Review*, and E.A. Freeman in the *Contemporary Review*. Bryce correctly pointed
out that up to December 1885 home rule had been little discussed in Great

Britain, but on reviewing the policies placed before the country in the past few weeks he found they were of three kinds: first, "the Hold-on policy," keeping government as at present; second, "the policy of small concessions" which would involve giving county government, creating various local boards, "perhaps provincial boards, perhaps central boards for special purposes," following the precedents of English local government; and third, "the policy of Home Rule" which would mean letting Ireland have "a local legislature, with powers sufficient to throw on the Irish people the responsibility for making and administering their own law and its administration." Bryce thought the first would be difficult if not impossible, while the second did "not touch the capital difficulty of governing Ireland." It would not appease the Nationalists nor would it remove any of the troubles of Irish local administration. For Bryce it was "a Half-way house policy. It carries us half way to Home Rule, gives none of the advantages which are claimed for Home Rule, loses such advantages as the Hold-on policy retains, and leaves the English Parliament in a position where there is really no stopping. It sets us on an inclined plane, whence the descent to Home Rule is all but certain." For the Ulster Unionists such concessions would be seen as the beginning of the end. On the other hand, home rule was a loose term. Whether it meant a federal system or body in Dublin with wide or narrow powers was unclear. Bryce doubted that the Irish really desired absolute separation, but if there was to be constitutional change he did not want the Irish to be given an armed force beyond what was needed for civil order for he believed it would lead to separation. Bryce was adamant that nothing should destroy the sovereignty of parliament; landowners had to be protected; and "No scheme of Home Rule or local self-government is admissible which does not recognise and provide for the case of the Ulster Protestants."[23]

In his canvas of various home rule proposals, Chamberlain admitted that his National Councils scheme would now be rejected by the Irish Nationalists, while the establishment of a relationship between Ireland and Great Britain similar to the one between Great Britain and a self-governing colony such as Canada would be difficult because Canada was virtually independent. An independent Ireland would not be consistent with Gladstone's ideas. As for an Irish parliament within a United Kingdom, Chamberlain doubted its feasibility given the problems that would arise over finance and the representation of Ireland in the imperial parliament. That left the last option, an American form of federal government with Ireland having possibly two legislatures – one for Ulster – and Scotland, Wales, and England each having one. It would mean an overall imperial parliament charged with the control of foreign and colonial affairs, military and naval expenditure, customs, and the post office. The House of Lords would probably be abolished. Chamberlain argued that such a scheme involved "the absolute destruction of the historical constitution of the United Kingdom, the creation of a *tabula rasa*, and the establishment thereupon of the United States constitution in all its details." Chamberlain thought it might work, but "it is hardly conceivable that the people of Great Britain as a whole are prepared for such a violent and complete revolution." Chamberlain, of course, still preferred the maintenance of parliamentary sovereignty and in this article he did not forcefully espouse the federal solution in the way one might have expected given his comments of December 1885. By this stage he doubted if any scheme of home rule that satisfied Parnell would be acceptable to the British parliament.[24]

E.A. Freeman also surveyed the home rule question in February 1886. His analysis of the various schemes that had been proposed was in line with his earlier writings. He believed most Irishmen meant by home rule "a modified independence for Ireland, such a measure of independence as shall not wholly sever the political connection between Great Britain and Ireland, but which shall still make Ireland for many purposes a separate state." Federalism would certainly be one method of achieving that end, but since there was no real pressure as yet for the break-up of the larger island into smaller home rule entities, Freeman doubted it would work. He was convinced there needed to be more than two members to effect a successful federation. Moreover, in his opinion, if one member held an "Imperial" position while the other was simply local the relation was not federal or even quasi-federal. He believed that "what is federal cannot be Imperial, and ... what is Imperial cannot be federal." This, of course, is not strictly so, but the argument had considerable influence at the time. He was more to the point when discussing Irish representation at Westminster and the status of Ulster. The problem of members voting on some issues and not on others posed great difficulties of definition. As he put it, "To make a written constitution, and to make two classes of members of the House of Commons with different rights, are very serious changes in English Law and practice." And what of Ulster? He believed "The Protestant corner has as good a right to Home Rule as the rest of the island," but he shrewdly pointed out "what is Home Rule for the rest of the island will not be Home Rule for the Protestant corner." Here, thought Freeman, was "a pretty question for constitution makers." Perhaps home rule could be given to Protestant Ulster on different grounds or terms from that given to the rest of Ireland or Ireland as a whole could have home rule as against Great Britain and Protestant Ulster home rule as against Ireland.[25]

By the time these articles appeared Gladstone had already given his home rule bill considerable thought and had gathered around him a variety of materials to draw upon. Nevertheless, he probably paused to reflect because many of the comments cut to the heart of the dilemma facing him: how to preserve unity while permitting diversity. As he sat down to draft, therefore, he must have been grateful for G. Shaw Lefevre's timely survey of the various constitutions adopted in Norway-Sweden, Austria-Hungary, Canada, and the United States, and his reminder about the problems associated with finance, representation at Westminster, and the division of powers in a federal system. He also undoubtedly agreed with another writer, Frank Hill, that the main object in granting home rule to Ireland was to strengthen the union between Great Britain and Ireland. Whatever the solution adopted, "the redistribution of functions between a central legislature and local chambers is a necessity of efficient Parliamentary government in a great and varied State such as the United Kingdom."[26]

With all this in mind, in addition to the spate of letters from colleagues and a reading of Burke and of Dicey's *Law of the Constitution*, particularly the chapter on semi-sovereign assemblies, to stir his thoughts, Gladstone began in the early months of 1886 to formulate his scheme.[27] Gladstone had always believed that in order to strengthen the empire the central government's power should be reduced to a minimum. He had been a strong supporter of the extension of responsible government to the colonies. In fact, he was to argue in 1886 that the colonies had shown that responsible government did work and that a model, tested and proven in the colonial world, existed for the resolution of Irish demands for greater control over domestic affairs. He believed the Irish should have an executive responsible to the legislature, i.e., full cabinet government as granted to the Canadian, Australian, and New Zealand colonies earlier in the century. Gladstone argued that the smaller the degree of interference with local affairs the greater the possibilities for the continued unity of the empire. Gladstone was a pragmatist who was convinced that the extension of responsible government to Ireland would strengthen rather than weaken the empire. He was equally determined to relieve the over-burdened Westminster parliament and thus strengthen it for its imperial tasks.

In looking for precedents he turned to both foreign and colonial experiences. In August 1885 Granville sent him "a full account of the Austro Hungarian Union,"[28] but he was particularly interested in Canadian developments, and on 9 October he asked the Liberal chief whip, Richard Grosvenor, to send him "a copy of the Canada Union & Government Act *1840* and Canada Government (Dominion) Act *1867*." In doing so, he admitted that "I have been working on Ireland." The Canada Act of 1840 and the British North America Act of 1867 were in Gladstone's hands the next day and were avidly studied.[29] His thoughts were further stimulated by the receipt, on 30 October, of Parnell's "Proposed Constitution for Ireland."[30] Parnell suggested an elective chamber responsible for Irish affairs but with no power to interfere in imperial matters. The chamber was to have 300 members of whom 206 were to be elected, with Protestant representation proportionate to population. Ninety-four members were to be appointed but that arrangement would cease after the first full session. The Irish chamber was to have the authority to raise revenues by both direct taxation and custom duties. It was also to have the power to maintain a police force. Ireland would pay £1 million to the imperial exchequer in return for the right of the crown to levy taxes for imperial purposes. The representation of Ireland in the imperial parliament might be retained or given up. If it were given up, the speaker might decide what imperial questions the Irish could take part in. Although Parnell's proposal did not address all the difficulties as fully as Gladstone would have wished, it was in line with his own thinking.

Gladstone was also influenced by a memorandum written for Carnarvon in October 1885 by Sir Robert Hamilton, the under-secretary at Dublin Castle.[31] Hamilton was particularly interesting on the political and economic condition of Ireland. He pointed out the degree of ignorance about Ireland that prevailed among English and Scottish MPs. He asked rhetorically: "Is it conceivable that if the great majority of the Scotch Members were unanimous in advocating some measure for Scotland, it would not be seriously considered by both parties, with the view of granting it if Imperial interests would allow? ... surely the time has arrived for taking into consultation the Representatives of the Irish people in settling how they are to be governed." He went on to argue that the concession to Ireland of the right to raise its own revenues would no more "conflict with the integrity of the Empire than the exercise of it does in the case of our great self-governing Colonies. It no doubt would be inconvenient to have different tariffs in Ireland and Great Britain, but there are no Imperial interests involved in the matter ... as England will always be the great market for Irish produce, the Irish are not likely to take any step which would destroy the market. In this relation, England can do without Ireland, but Ireland cannot do without England." Hamilton's pragmatism and his colonial references must have appealed to Gladstone.

Basically Hamilton saw no problem in granting legislative independence. Under his scheme "Ireland would have no power granted to her by her Constitution to raise local forces." Great Britain would control the troops in Ireland and the Irish militia. They would have to depend on the basic good will and sense of the Irish to protect property, but Great Britain could retain "for the present" the control of the constabulary and by having special provisions in the constitution to protect special classes and interests. It was clear to Hamilton that "No mere creation of County Boards will be acceptable to the people now."

He did not consider the exclusion of the Irish from Westminster would be a problem because he did not think Ireland was much interested in foreign and imperial affairs. Anyway, he believed imperial federation would occur eventually and that Ireland would take its place in such an arrangement. It did not seem practical to let Irish representative into Westminster for only imperial affairs. It could only be done with "an entire remodelling of the

Imperial Parliament ... and the establishment of local Councils in England and Scotland to deal with purely local affairs." At the moment, Great Britain was not prepared to pay that price and the division of imperial and domestic questions would be difficult. Hamilton argued that if Ireland was not given a parliament the British would face more parliamentary problems and an increased cry for separation. For him, "the sole danger to guard against is the disintegration of the Empire." The extension of self-government to Ireland would help avoid that.

Gladstone must have found Hamilton's memorandum a most helpful document when he read it in February, shortly before he settled down to two months' intensive work on his land, financial, and constitutional schemes. It confirmed his own point of view and helped him focus on the key issues of finance, exclusion or retention, and protection of the minority.

In working out his proposals, Gladstone worked virtually alone. The only member of his cabinet who was as convinced of the need for home rule as himself was John Morley, the chief secretary for Ireland. Morley provided sound and sympathetic support but no original ideas. Nevertheless, he was a firm advocate of the exclusion of Irish representatives from the imperial parliament and on that issue he may have been influential, although it should be added that most of those cabinet members sympathetic to Gladstone's proposal were equally adamant on that point. Gladstone had no strong feelings on the matter. For him it was not an issue of principle but a matter of practicality. That being so, it made some sense to remove the Irish representatives. This was not, at least initially, a problem because Gladstone had also been willing to give the Irish control over customs and excise. It was only when he was obliged to bow to the howls from the British manufacturers and retain customs and excise within the powers of the imperial parliament that the exclusion of the Irish representatives presented real difficulties for him.

In addition to the advice and general support of Morley, Gladstone also received encouragement and backing from Spencer. In fact, it is clear that if Spencer had not been prepared to go along, Gladstone would probably not have been able to go as far as he did in 1886. Gladstone would not have moved, could not have moved, without Spencer, but Spencer, like Morley, did not supply ideas or suggestions. Those were primarily Gladstone's. Gladstone did, of course, seek and receive civil service support. Throughout the weeks of preparation of the home rule and land purchase bills, from early February to early April, Gladstone received considerable statistical material from Edward Hamilton and R.E. Welby at the Treasury which was of enormous help to him in preparing his financial scheme.

Gladstone began his drafting with a far more open mind than the bulk of his colleagues. He was prepared to grant fuller powers to the Irish than his associates could dream of tolerating. He was wedded to the belief that only by loosening the bonds of empire – only by granting full self-government on the colonial model to Ireland – would the Anglo-Irish problem be resolved and the empire strengthened. Gladstone did not share the beliefs of those around him that the only way to strengthen the empire was to maintain a strong central government in the United Kingdom and firm imperial control over Ireland. He still tended to view the imperial relationship from an earlier, more assured perspective rather than from one conditioned by the imperial crises of recent years. The problems in South Africa and Egypt in the early eighties had underlined Britain's vulnerability. They had made most British politicians more defensive, more inclined to look for ways to preserve the strength and integrity of the empire. It was not accidental that the Imperial Federation League had been founded in 1884 or that pressure was mounting to initiate a conference between Britain and her major colonies to discuss common problems of defence and trade. In this age of increased *realpolitik* the suggestion that home rule be granted to Ireland was anathema to many. They believed it would weaken Britain's defences and undermine her strategic security. Moreover, it would lead to the disintegration of the empire. It would encourage other colonies to further loosen the ties. At a time when Britain was more aware than ever of her gathering military, naval, and economic vulnerability, the grant of home rule to Ireland seemed absurd to most Englishmen, if not to most Scots, Welsh, and Irish. Such a fundamental change in the relationship could not be contemplated.

In early February Gladstone began to draft. For the first month or so he was preoccupied with land and financial questions, and it was not until mid-March, after his third draft of the land purchase bill had been completed, that he turned his attention for the first time to his legislative proposal.[32] He had spread about him the Canada Act of 1840, the British North America Act of 1867, various foreign examples of dual and federal governments, and a memorandum prepared on 2 March by Sir Henry Thring, the Treasury draftsman, which contained excerpts from the Constitution of the United States outlining the powers of Congress, restrictions on the states, the powers of the president, and amendments to the Constitution; sections 91 and 92 of the BNA Act; "Prerogatives of the Crown as extracted from Blackstone's Commentaries"; and "Prerogatives of the Crown preserved in a Colonial Bill."[33]

It is clear from the evidence in the Gladstone Papers that the most important influence on him in preparing the home rule bill was Canada's internal and external constitutional relationships. Gladstone was much attracted by the way the grant of responsible government had led to the strengthening rather than the weakening of the tie between the United Kingdom and her senior white settlement colony. Similarly, he found it interesting that the division of powers between the federal and provincial governments in Canada appeared to have successfully preserved both unity and diversity. He prepared a bill incorporating both dimensions of the Canadian example with the intention of granting Ireland as much autonomy as possible while preserving the unity of the United Kingdom and the empire. Gladstone's own copy of the British North America Act was heavily underlined and marked up in the margins, particularly section 91 dealing with the legislative authority of the Canadian parliament. He often lifted whole phrases, even clauses, in the preparation of his first draft.

Nevertheless, as Dunne has pointed out, Gladstone was preparing an Irish bill and he had to be conscious of the pressure around him; both in his cabinet and in the House. For example, the "powers granted to the Irish body bore no comparison with those enjoyed by the Dominion Parliament, particularly in the control of taxation, trade and commerce, the military and defence. On the other hand, the Irish body was to have a wider range of powers than the Canadian provincial parliaments had, and unlike them was to have all residuary powers, potentially very important."[34] Despite leaving the residuary power with the Irish parliament, Gladstone severely restricted its operations. Using section 91 of the BNA Act as his guide, Gladstone determined that the Irish legislature should have no power relating to the crown, peace or war, the army, navy, militia, volunteers, the defence of the realm, treaties and other relations with foreign powers, dignities or titles of honour, prize or booty of war, offences against the law of nations, treason, alienage or naturalization, trade, navigation, or quarantine, the postal and telegraph service, beacons, lighthouses or sea marks, the coinage, the value of foreign money, legal tender, weights and measures, copyright or patent rights. In addition, he placed certain restrictions on the powers of the Irish legislature. It was not to make any law respecting the establishment or endowment of religion or prohibiting its free exercise. It was not to impose any disability or confer any privilege because of religious belief nor to hinder the establishment or maintenance of a denominational school, institution, or charity nor to hinder the right of a child to attend a publicly funded school without attending the religious institution at the school. At the last moment he was persuaded by Hugh Childers to leave the power to determine customs and excise duties at Westminster. Gladstone would have been happy to allow the Irish that right, but Childers had advised him on 18 March that "I feel confident that English and Scottish public opinion will never tolerate any plan which gives to an Irish Legislature power to impose Customs duties; so as to make Ireland a 'Foreign country' and trade with Ireland 'Foreign Trade.'"[35]

The bill reflected the restrictions within which Gladstone worked and the safeguards and compromises that he knew to be necessary. When he sat down to frame his bill, he had drawn up nine "Principles of Construction" and throughout the process he was guided by them. They read as follows:

1   Strict and thorough severance of Imperial from local affairs
2   Reservation of the first
3   transference of the second
4   on the principle of trust which is adverse to Exceptions
5   one great exception of necessity – finance

6   and one of policy – Protection
7   Safeguards for the minority
8   Safeguards for property (Land)
9   Safeguard for vested interest[36]

He had not been unaware, as some of his later critics said he had been, of the need to address the issue of taxation and representation. Early in the drafting process he had scribbled a note to himself in the form of a query: "Taxation or Representation. A. Shall we retain powers of taxation. B. Shall Irish members continue to sit? These subjects are inseparable." In the end he decided that exclusion was the only sensible answer because a division of imperial from local subjects was to his mind impossible and would lead to endless difficulties in parliament. Also Great Britain would not tolerate 103 Irish members at Westminster, while Ireland would fight against a reduced number such as forty which would be more in line with her population. He was also convinced that Ireland could not man two parliaments.[37] Similarly, Gladstone did consider the possibility "whether any particular portion of Ireland might be excepted and might continue as now." He found it difficult to see how an effective land purchase scheme "could be made applicable to any such excepted position" and he did not pursue the matter. Presumably this was an oblique reference to Ulster, although in general Gladstone seemed unaware of the potential difficulties with that region. His concern for the minority was a concern for the Protestants and the propertied – the two were usually synonymous – throughout Ireland, not just in a single area.[38]

Gladstone's first draft was printed for the cabinet on 20 March and discussed on 26 March. G.O. Trevelyan, the secretary for Scotland, and Chamberlain resigned immediately, the latter claiming that there were "great dangers to the security of the Empire" in Gladstone's proposal.[39] A second draft was prepared by 31 March and revised by the cabinet on 1 April. It was at that meeting that Gladstone agreed to drop the word "Parliament" and to substitute the more cumbersome "Irish legislative body," but it is clear that Gladstone did mean the "legislative body" to be a parliament and the Parnellites accepted it as such. Although the document was more or less set in its final form by 1 April, revisions continued until 8 April when Gladstone introduced his bill in the House. That Gladstone did wish the Irish legislative body to have full parliamentary powers was clear from his insistence on the grant of responsible government to Ireland on the colonial model.[40] Similarly, his expectation that Great Britain would not use the royal veto in "ordinary cases" suggested that he hoped the Irish legislature would be more independent in practice than the numerous exceptions and restrictions constraining it suggested.[41]

Any effort to change the relationship between Great Britain and Ireland or to tinker with the British constitution was bound to arouse fear and controversy. The ones that provided Gladstone with the most difficulty – Irish representation in the Westminster parliament; Irish contributions to the imperial exchequer; and the protection of minorities – he confronted and attempted to resolve. As has been seen, Gladstone's concept of imperial unity did not necessitate retention of the Irish members. Admittedly, he would have found it difficult to form a cabinet in February if he had insisted on inclusion, but he saw no need to push the point. Exclusion would presumably have been acceptable to the Irish if they had been given control of customs and excise and the management of their own defence requirements, but the former was intolerable to key British business interests and the latter would have meant the virtual independence of Ireland, or at the least, a status within the empire equivalent to Canada's. That was unthinkable.

Gladstone's adherence to total exclusion, coupled with the retention of customs and excise at Westminster and a continuing Irish contribution to the imperial exchequer, immediately led to cries of "taxation without representation." Although it was an issue obviously exploited for political advantage, it was a fundamental and exceedingly grave problem which Gladstone did not adequately address. All he would do by way of compromise was to give the Irish a right to attend the Westminster parliament whenever there was a question of altering the tax for Ireland or changing the original statute.[42] This suggestion was never fully explored but it is doubtful if it would have been acceptable. Gladstone had run smack into the problems posed by attempting to provide a degree of self-government to one portion of a state while retaining the overall unity of the state. He had been attracted to the Canadian imperial and domestic constitutional precedents but he had never considered the full adoption of the Canadian domestic system for the United Kingdom. Despite the discussions about federalism that surrounded him in late 1885 and early 1886, he was never attracted to it as a solution to the problems of either the United Kingdom or the empire. Gladstone, like his critics, was cautious and conservative. He recognized the need to grant some degree of self-government to Ireland but he too believed in the integrity of the United Kingdom and its constitution. For him as for others the sovereignty of parliament was indivisible and he could not fully contemplate a federal system. The most he could offer was a cumbersome linking of a unitary state and quasi-federal features.

Finance was a difficult problem to resolve. After the Act of Union in 1801 the Irish exchequer remained separate from Britain's until 1817 when the two were amalgamated. From then until 1919 the exchequer was one and no separate accounts were kept for English, Irish, Scottish, or Welsh trade, investment or taxes. All revenues were paid directly into the imperial exchequer and all decisions about customs and excise, taxes, rates, and licensing were made by the central parliament or local councils.

Gladstone's decision to introduce home rule for Ireland necessarily raised the question of how revenues were to be divided and who was to control customs and excise and how much latitude in the raising of taxes was to be devolved to an Irish parliament. Gladstone's original proposal to hand control of customs and excise to the Irish had been a logical extension of his wish to remove all the Irish MPs from Westminster. As we have seen, his subsequent decision to retain such control had left his proposal open to the charge of no taxation without representation, a charge highly damaging to his devolutionary plans. This difficulty had resulted from attempting to weld a colonial model and a federal model. Under the colonial model the colony ceases to have representation in the imperial parliament and the imperial parliament no longer has the right to tax the colony. Gladstone, however, had wanted to reserve to the imperial parliament certain powers such as defence, resulting from Ireland's geographical proximity to Great Britain. This meant that Ireland should continue to pay something toward defence. Gladstone therefore made Ireland's contribution to the imperial exchequer the first charge on her revenues under the 1886 bill. That decision, coupled with the removal of Irish MPs from the imperial parliament, led to the claim of no taxation without representation.

Gladstone also had difficulty in determining what would be Ireland's fair share of the imperial burden and he devoted much of February and early March to the question. The lack of reliable statistics made it an almost impossible task. Edward Hamilton had provided him with a breakdown of Irish revenue and expenditure on 15 January and this was followed on 17 February by Welby's and Hamilton's first paper on Irish finance.[43] Over the next six weeks Hamilton and Welby either jointly or separately prepared a further nine papers on Irish finance for the prime minister and Gladstone submitted at least two papers to the Treasury officials for comment. In essence, Gladstone began by arguing that one-twelfth should be Ireland's contribution to the imperial exchequer, even though Hamilton had advised him in his initial analysis that one-twentieth would be a more accurate, and certainly fair, assessment.[44] Faced with Gladstone's contention, Welby and Hamilton responded in more detail underlining that "Mr. Gladstone when he takes 1/12 as the basis of the Irish contribution, practically increases the contribution which Ireland at present makes to the Imperial Exchequer." They wondered "whether 1/15 or 1/16 would not more accurately represent a fair adjustment between the two countries."[45] While not entirely convinced, Gladstone did finally accept one-fifteenth. Parnell, of course, did not accept that figure. Like Hamilton and Welby he believed a proportion of one to twenty nearer the true, and fairer, position.[46]

Gladstone's difficulties with finance did not end with determining the amount the Irish should contribute to the imperial exchequer. It was necessary for him to decide how that money should be raised and what fiscal powers would be extended to the Irish parliament. In the end he decided that the Irish parliament would receive all the revenue collected in Ireland through either direct or indirect taxation and from it pay the one-fifteenth imperial levy. Indirect taxation, i.e., customs and excise, would remain under imperial control, leaving Ireland with only the power to impose direct taxes. There was, of course, a difference of opinion over whether or not the levy should be a first charge or a residual sum. The Irish understandably wanted it to be residual so that Irish needs could be taken care of first. This was not appealing to many in Britain, who pointed out that the Irish contribution would quickly dwindle to nothing since the Irish government would use its revenues for the development of Irish resources or the care of Irish needs rather than transfer them to the imperial exchequer. To the British this seemed to imply that the Irish wanted the benefits of self-government without assuming any of the wider responsibilities. Gladstone finally made the levy a first charge on Irish revenues.

Another problem arose over the exclusion of the Irish from any further involvement in the setting of customs and excise duties. Since three-quarters of Irish revenue was derived from customs and excise, the proposal seemed especially anomalous. To resolve this particular problem, Gladstone proposed that Irish members be allowed to return to Westminster, at the discretion of the imperial parliament, when changes in the measures of indirect taxation were to be considered. This was a well-meaning but awkward device which did not allow for the obvious point that no Irish would be present when decisions were taken as to where and in what amounts revenues collected from indirect taxation were to be disbursed within the United Kingdom. Thus under Gladstone's scheme Ireland would have controlled only one-quarter of its revenue of which one-quarter came from the post office and one-half from income tax. Both were difficult to alter. Ireland would therefore have had little financial flexibility.

In setting the Irish contribution at one-fifteenth of the common imperial expenditures, Gladstone did so for a fixed period of thirty years. His thinking was reasonable: since Ireland would not be represented at Westminster, she would not be able to argue against increases in imperial expenditure and therefore should not be vulnerable to any such increases. This was again a problem arising from the hybrid Gladstone solution and it raised other potential problems. The imperial parliament would be able to raise or lower customs and excise duties and Ireland would be affected. If the duties were lowered Irish income would decrease but her imperial obligation would remain constant. Since the remaining revenue would be inadequate, the Irish government would have either to cut back drastically on services and public expenditure or raise income tax to maintain standards and meet her imperial obligation. Nothing could be more certain to exacerbate relations between the United Kingdom and Ireland. If duties were raised, Ireland would experience a windfall which might induce her to lower the income tax. But that would lead to social tensions and possible strife because the lower-income groups would be paying proportionately higher duties while the rich would be relieved of much income tax. Ireland would thus be caught because the use of its direct taxing powers would be directly tied to the way the indirect tax was used by the imperial government. The 1886 solution was therefore inadequate.[47]

In delineating the powers of the "Irish legislative body" and in his financial scheme Gladstone had attempted to tackle, although not always successfully, the three major problems of exclusion or retention, protection of minorities, and Ireland's contribution to the imperial exchequer. Other features of his bill were likewise not altogether free of difficulty. He proposed two orders for the "Irish legislative body." The first was to have 103 members – twenty-eight representative Irish peers and seventy-five elected members. The term of office was to be ten years but half the number had to retire every five years. At the end of thirty years all the seats were to be elective. The second order was to have 204 members made up of all the current Irish members of the Westminster parliament plus an additional member from each of the county and borough constituencies in Ireland. The orders were to deliberate and vote together but if either order desired they could vote separately on a measure which would have to have the support of both orders to pass. A defeated measure could be reintroduced after dissolution or a three-year period – whichever was the longest. The two orders would vote separately but if it passed the first order and was defeated in the second the two orders would be obliged to vote together with a simple majority deciding the issue. This legislative body was to have full taxing powers with the exception of customs and excise. Gladstone's concern to protect the minority while stopping short of a full devolutionary or federal system had resulted in a cumbersome parliamentary arrangement.

As for the police, the Dublin Metropolitan Police were to remain under the control of the lord lieutenant for two years before passing to the control of the Irish legislature. The Royal Irish Constabulary was also to remain under the lord lieutenant's control "while that force subsists." It was clear that the constabulary would eventually be replaced by the new force which was to be established and maintained by the Irish legislature and placed under the control of the Irish counties and boroughs. Trevelyan resigned precisely because he objected to the control of immediate machinery of law and order being withdrawn from direct British authority.[48]

Gladstone was not unaffected by such criticisms. As he prepared his speech for the House, he was obviously still wrestling with some of the basic issues: "Problem before us. How to reconcile Imperial Unity with diversity of Legislatures. Other countries have solved it. Last ½ century rich in lessons. Unity not only preserved but strengthened." He also apparently wondered about the Ulster minority. He considered total exclusion, partial exclusion, separate autonomy, and assigning reserved subjects to provincial councils but he decided none would have sufficient backing for inclusion in the bill.

However, "If any attain general or pre-ponderating approval, may be introduced." On looking once more at the issue of retention or exclusion, he dismissed the inclusion of Irish representatives because it would not be right for them to be present for Scottish and English affairs, and as for participating in the discussion of Imperial affairs: "Inconvenient [and] impossible because of ministerial responsibility. Therefore, Irish members cannot ordinarily sit in the Imperial Parliament." Gladstone then listed five conditions for "a good plan." They were "(1) Imperial unity. (2) Political equality. (3) Equitable distribution of burdens. (4) Reasonable safeguards for minority. (5) It must be a settlement."[49]

In speaking on the introduction of his bill on 8 April 1886, Gladstone argued that home rule was a means of bringing social order to Ireland.[50] Coercion should no longer be the base of Britain's Irish policy. It was necessary to strip the law of its foreign garb and invest it with a domestic character. As he pointed out, the Scots made their own laws but not the Irish. The problem before them was "how to reconcile Imperial unity with diversity of legislation." Gladstone referred to the experience and success of other recent experiments in dividing authority while maintaining unity such as Sweden and Norway and Austria-Hungary. He made it clear that he wished to modify the union, not repeal it or impair the supreme statutory authority of the imperial parliament. It was certainly not his intention to dismember the empire. Gladstone stated flatly that he was not adopting federal arrangements nor did he find it necessary to discuss them. Before detailing his scheme he emphasized that it was not possible to construct an appropriate administrative system for Ireland without legislative change. The fault of the current administrative system in Ireland was that "the motor muscle is English and not Irish." He ended his speech by using the colonial analogy of responsible government to argue that Ireland should have the right to make her own laws. The concession of local self-government would not sap or impair unity but would strengthen and consolidate it. In his estimation, the best and surest foundation to build on was the will of the nation.

Gladstone's home rule bill was subjected to an intensive scrutiny and criticism over the next two months both inside and outside the House of Commons. The majority of speakers and commentators often lost sight of the essential issues and wandered off into personal attacks on the Irish or into a recounting of their own interpretation of Anglo-Irish history. Those who did stick to the point, however, raised questions of fundamental importance about the dispersal of legislative and executive authority within the United Kingdom. A few touched on federalism and examined its implications.

The Ulster Unionists and their English supporters together with a large phalanx of dissident Liberals led by Chamberlain and Hartington were the most punishing critics. They were concerned about Ulster's future in a home rule Ireland and convinced that Gladstone's scheme would lead inexorably to the disintegration of the United Kingdom. Gladstone had paid too little attention to the problem of Ulster, and his "legislative body" with two orders was a weak response to an acute problem. Similarly, the exclusion of the Irish from Westminster predictably led to cries of "taxation without representation" and it also enabled Chamberlain to point out that under such an arrangement the Irish would be effectively excluded from any involvement in the determination of imperial defence and foreign policy. Since the Irish would still be expected to make a hefty contribution to the imperial exchequer and would be vulnerable to changes in customs and excise duties, Chamberlain and others could see no incentive for the Irish to remain faithful to the British connection. It seemed to him that even separation would be more sensible than Gladstone's bill.

These viewpoints surfaced on 9 April, the first day of debate, and were to be reiterated until the vote was taken on 8 June. Colonel Waring of North Down asked how the minority was to be protected. It appeared to him that Ulster would become a dependency and that was intolerable. He advised Gladstone that if Ulster was included in an Irish legislature there would soon be a home rule for Ulster movement.[51] Macnaughton of North Antrim thought Ireland would be made into a colony and would no longer be an integral part of the empire while O'Neill of Mid-Antrim and Walter Long of Wilts, Devizes were convinced an Irish parliament would be a step toward the final repeal of the union.[52]

Joseph Chamberlain spoke for many when he stated that the honour and integrity of the empire were in danger.[53] Chamberlain pointed out that he had always been willing "to give to Ireland the largest possible extension of local government consistent with the integrity of the Empire and the supremacy of Parliament," but Gladstone had gone too far. The removal of the Irish from Westminster and the supremacy of the new "legislative body" in all matters not specifically excluded from its competence were particularly galling to Chamberlain. Unlike Gladstone he did not really believe in extending responsible government to the Irish because that would be tantamount to separation. Chamberlain no longer offered National Councils as a solution for they had always been seen as resolving essentially municipal problems. He now suggested looking for the solution to Anglo-Irish problems "in the direction of federation." He doubted the usefulness of the colonial analogies cited by Gladstone. He thought the tie between Great Britain and "her self-governing and practically independent Colonies" was sentimental only. Canada, for example, might break that tie at any moment if it so desired and "no one would think of employing force in order to tie any reluctant self-governing Colony in continued bonds to this country." Under federation Ireland might "really remain an integral portion of the Empire. The action of such a scheme is centripetal and not centrifugal, and it is in the direction of federation that the Democratic movement has made most advances in the present century." Federation where adopted "has always been in the case of federating States which were previously separate. It has been intended to bring nations together, to lessen the causes of difference, and to unite them more closely in a common union." He referred to Germany and the United States as the best examples of his point, and then he concluded: "... in my view the solution of this question should be sought in some form of federation, which would really maintain the Imperial unity, and which would, at the same time, conciliate the desire for a national local government which is felt so strongly by the constituents of hon. Members. I do not say that we should imitate the great models to which I have referred. Our Constitution and the circumstances of the case are different. I say I believe that it is on this line, and not in the line of our relations with our self-governing Colonies, that it is possible to seek for and find a solution of the difficulty."

Chamberlain was virtually alone in the House in his espousal of federalism. It seemed to pose as many difficulties as Gladstone's proposal. It did not address the pressing needs of the Irish Nationalists and it ignored the lack of interest throughout the United Kingdom in the federal idea. T.M. Healy (Londonderry, S), who was the first to respond to Chamberlain's suggestion, raised the key points. He pointed out that the Irish could not wait. They wanted self-government immediately. "How can you propose to set up a confederate Ireland until you have started some kind of local Legislature? The basis of federation ... is the existence of Parliaments, and you federate Parliaments with the assent of peoples." Could Chamberlain "show us the germ of federation budding anywhere yet?"[54] England clearly did not wish to change its constitution. Englishmen would not surrender their imperial rights in order to get local self-government. He considered Chamberlain's scheme ill-thought out. For example, how did one distinguish between imperial and local questions under a scheme of federation?[55]

Hartington also did not share Chamberlain's seeming interest in federalism.[56] He preferred reform to begin at the local level and not with the imposition of a superstructure. To attempt to establish a federal structure in the United Kingdom would mean "the reconstruction of the whole Constitution" and that was impossible. Nevertheless, he did agree with Chamberlain about Gladstone's constant reference to a model based on the colonial relationship. He pointed out that the distance which separated the colonies from Great Britain made "any analogy which may be drawn between their case and that of Ireland utterly fallacious." He reminded his colleagues that

the connection which exists between our self-governing Colonies and the United Kingdom is purely a voluntary connection. We have granted to these Colonies practical independence. If they are willing still to be bound to, and to form part of, the British Empire; if they are willing to have their foreign policy regulated by the Imperial

Government; if they are willing to submit to the nominal superiority of British law and British authority over their internal affairs, it is by virtue of a voluntary compact by which they accept our direction of their foreign relations that they gain the Imperial protection of our Fleets and Armies. But everyone knows that the real interference of authority exercised by the Imperial Government in the domestic affairs of the Colonies is practically nothing ... We know, also, that if any one of those Colonies were to express a strong, a real, and a determined desire to separate itself from the nominal connection which now binds it to this country, there is no Parliament, there is no statesman, who would attempt at this time of day to prevent that consummation by force. I say that, under these circumstances, there is no similarity between the case of our Colonies and that of Ireland.

Hartington also pointed out that if Scotland and Wales obtained domestic legislatures similar to Ireland's, that would leave an English legislature at Westminster responsible both for English domestic affairs and all colonial, foreign, Indian, and imperial affairs. Such a solution would be considered degrading by the Scots and Welsh, as the current arrangement was by the Irish. It would be unfair to be obliged to contribute financially to the expense of imperial policy but to have no voice in controlling it.

It seemed not to occur to Hartington that the logical solution for such a dilemma would be federalism but it had occurred to John Redmond. He commented favourably on the application of the federal idea to England, Scotland, Wales, and Ireland, since it would solve the problem of exclusion or retention. Under such a scheme all would and should have a say in matters of common concern.[57]

The same range of views found expression outside the House. The *Times* concluded that Gladstone's bill would have perilous consequences for both the interests of the empire and the one and a half million Protestant minority of Ireland. The overall problem "could only be logically solved by a complete federal scheme, embracing the whole of the United Kingdom, with a Central Congress, subordinate local legislatures, and a Supreme Court. This nobody wants and nobody proposes ... The policy of giving Ireland a separate legislature and executive leads either to the complications of federalism or to the colonial position." The *Times* doubted that even Gladstone could persuade the country to take up the cry "Ireland as Canada."[58]

Two writers, Frank Hill and L.G. Power, wrote in favour of a federal solution on American or Canadian lines while another, R.W. Dale, preferred devolution to national parliaments rather than a federation. He wished to preserve imperial sovereignty and he knew federation would not do that. Chamberlain published a letter in the *Times* advocating a federal solution but was subsequently taken to task for not really understanding federalism or being aware of recent Canadian court decisions which had upheld provincial as opposed to federal jurisdiction. The writer doubted that Chamberlain would find that appealing. And, of course, he was right. Chamberlain had never been a pure federalist. At best he favoured home rule all round, which would have been devolutionary in nature and would have preserved the sovereignty of the Westminster parliament. Lord Rosebery, the foreign secretary, seemed to realize that union need not mean centralization, and that local self-government did not necessitate disruption.[59]

The most extensive public comment on both Gladstonian home rule and federalism was made by A.V. Dicey. Dicey found the sudden interest among politicians in constitutional matters rather amusing. He wrote to Bryce on 10 April, two days into the debate on first reading: "It is really too amusing. Now Hartington is apparently trying earnestly to get up the law of the constitn. Suppose we advertise a series of lectures next term on the Constn for statesmen and politicians to be given on Saturday afternoons so as to meet the convenience of MPs. Special reference will be made to H. Grattan's Constn and to foreign systems of federalism or other forms of confederation."[60]

More seriously, he prepared a trenchant criticism of Gladstone's bill. The manuscript of *England's Case against Home Rule* was finished in June but the book did not appear until November 1886 by which time the bill had been defeated and an election had returned the Conservatives and Liberal Unionists to power. The essence of Dicey's position was already well established. He believed home rule, in any form, would destroy parliamentary sovereignty and weaken the unity of Britain and the empire.[61]

In his book he simply elaborated upon those arguments.[62] For Dicey, home rule, of whatever form, had to be consistent with the ultimate supremacy of the imperial parliament. To depart from that premise would involve dangerous if not fatal innovations for the constitution of the United Kingdom. As for federalism, it was an arrangement for the distribution of political power. It usually brought states together and was not a means of disuniting them. If federalism were applied to the United Kingdom, and many saw Gladstone's bill as the first step in that direction, it would mean the break-up of an existing state thereby weakening it. Federalism would necessarily involve a new constitution and implied an elaborate distribution and definition of political powers. For Dicey the disadvantages of federalism were threefold: first, the sovereignty of parliament would be destroyed and all constitutional arrangements would be dislocated; second, the power of Great Britain would be diminished; and third, the chance of further disagreement with Ireland would be increased rather than lessened. As far as Dicey was concerned, parliamentary sovereignty provided the United Kingdom with more flexibility than would an American-style constitution. From the moment the United Kingdom became a federation the omnipotence of parliament would be gone and the authority of central and local parliaments would be limited by articles of the constitution and by the Federal Court. For Dicey, federalism was incompatible with parliamentary government as practised in England.

It would deprive English institutions of their elasticity, their strength, and their life. It did not offer England a constitutional compromise but a fundamental revolution.[63] Dicey was to remain an inveterate foe of both home rule and federalism for the rest of his life. His hostility to Irish nationalism and his a-historical approach to the Anglo-Irish problem weakened his case in the eyes of his critics but Unionists loved to cite him.

None of the comments on federalism either inside or outside parliament provided the sustained, coherent, and searching examination that the topic demanded, but they had arisen naturally from the anomalies in Gladstone's plan and had succeeded in raising the possibility of an alternative approach to the constitutional issue. Only a few individuals had a close familiarity with colonial practice and with the American example. In years to come that lack of knowledge and understanding was to be partially remedied. In 1886 most observers were suspicious of the concept and of the ramifications of its adoption.

The second-reading debate ended early in the morning of 8 June and shortly afterwards Gladstone's bill was defeated 343–313. Ninety-three Liberals voted with the Conservatives to ensure victory for the opposition. A few weeks later Gladstone went to the country in an election bid. He and the Parnellites could muster only 276 seats (191 Liberals and eighty-five Irish Nationalists) while Salisbury's Conservatives and the Liberal dissidents won a clear majority with 394 (316 Conservatives and seventy-eight dissident Liberals). Gladstone resigned and Salisbury formed a new government. For the time being home rule was no longer centre-stage. This did not stop discussion, of course, and over the next decade there were numerous opportunities to explore the phenomena of home rule, devolution, federalism, and home rule all round.

CHAPTER THREE

Home Rule All Round, 1886–1899

Throughout the intense debate over Gladstone's home rule bill of 1886 federalism, home rule all round and devolution had received no sustained consideration. Chamberlain's remarks on federalism had been isolated ones. Gladstone had been well aware of the overall lack of interest in such ideas and on the one occasion when he had been asked to incorporate provisions in his bill for the self-government of England, Wales, and Scotland he had refused, partly on the grounds of the difficulty of including such extensive provisions in one bill but primarily because "the question seems to imply that the wants and wishes of England, Scotland, Wales and Ireland are the same. I have no evidence before me which would lead me to assume that this is the case."[1] Despite this lack of general concern, the discussion of home rule for Ireland did partially reawaken interest in both Scotland and Wales in home rule and increasingly therefore in home rule all round. A number of commentators and politicians raised the possibility of Irish home rule becoming the stepping-stone to imperial federation, and federalism was explored in occasional articles. But this reassertion of Scottish and Welsh interest in home rule and the increased speculation about home rule all round and federalism did not result in specific schemes. Scottish home rulers within the Liberal party did introduce home rule bills and move resolutions for discussion in the House of Commons but no details of any wider proposals were ever forthcoming. Hence there was a general awareness that a major overhaul of the constitution might be appropriate but no considered ideas. Needless to say any discussion that occurred was initiated by Liberals and by Scottish and Welsh home rulers. At this time Conservatives and Liberal Unionists were not interested in the issue of satisfying Scottish and Welsh grievances or in resolving the problem of congestion.

In the weeks and months that followed the parliamentary debate there were various scattered references to federalism as a solution of United Kingdom difficulties. In July 1886 a Canadian observer, L.G. Power of Ottawa, argued that the House of Commons could not long continue to do the variety and volume of work demanded of it. Congestion and the need to recognize "the existence of Ireland as a distinct national whole" suggested that the only solution was "the adoption of the federal system in a form akin to those which we find at work in the United States and Canada." Initially it might apply only to Ireland but Power foresaw the day when the federal system would have to be extended to Scotland and Wales, while England would have to be divided into two provinces with London as a possible third. Until that were achieved, however, Power's provision of thirty-five Irish MPs in the imperial parliament would have caused difficulties.[2]

Julius Vogel of New Zealand pointed out that home rule for Ireland "has special interest to the colonies because of its intimate connection with the larger question of federation of the Empire." He believed that if imperial federation were dealt with first the granting of any degree of self-government to Ireland would be accepted.[3] Lord Monck, the former Canadian governor general, raised the crucial issue of the difference between delegation, devolution, and federalism. He pointed out that delegation of powers and devolution were similar but not devolution and federalism. The latter two were virtually opposite. Delegation of power would retain the supremacy of the central parliament and would mean decentralization rather than disintegration and devolution rather than federalism. It could be done for all regions of the United Kingdom, not just Ireland. The delegation of power to the Irish, Scottish, Welsh, and English members of the imperial parliament to handle the affairs of each region would not be an organic revolution, although he did admit that agreement on what should be delegated would be contentious.[4]

Chamberlain continued to sympathize with the principle of autonomy that lay behind the home rule bill but not with the method of achieving it. He believed the government had proceeded on the lines of separation or colonial independence, "whereas they should have adopted the principle of Federation." For him the "key of the position is the maintenance of the full representation of Ireland in the Imperial Parliament." He expressed a sympathy for home rule all round.[5]

One ingenious scheme called for a form of federation without any elaborate constitution. The members elected to the House of Commons for each of the four "nations," England, Scotland, Ireland, and Wales, would meet separately to form four National Houses of Commons. Each House would pass whatever bills it liked through all stages except final reading. The House of Commons of the whole United Kingdom would then meet to pass or reject but not amend the bills. A bill could be rejected only because it dealt too much with imperial or United Kingdom affairs or involved the "safety, honour, or integrity of the U.K. or Empire." There would be no attempt to determine beforehand what were national and what imperial or United Kingdom questions. The United House of Commons would decide in each case. Parliamentary and administrative functions would quickly develop in each nation. The author, Aneurin Williams, argued that his scheme departed least from tradition; gave the fullest play to nationality consistent with security of the empire; protected minorities while ensuring democracy; and could be easily modified if necessary. He argued that "Constitution-making is abhorrent to English ideas, and we do not love leaps in the dark; but from Select Committees to Grand Committees, from Grand Committees to National Houses are easy steps: we can see where we are treading and draw back if we like." It would enable home rule to be granted to Ireland, and if there was no strong cry for home rule in Scotland or Wales there was considerable demand for local self-government, decentralization, and restored efficiency at Westminster.[6]

Henry D'Esterre Taylor believed that in imperial federation one had the solution to the Irish problem: "Under an Imperial Federation Parliament, the local parliament for managing the affairs of Great Britain would naturally divide itself into three smaller ones for England, Scotland and Ireland, with possibly a fourth for Wales, the very crowning point of local government. Each of the colonies would possess a similar legislative body, and, without doubt, as the population and resources of many of the present ones increased, succeeding years would see further additions to those already in existence."[7]

Edward Freeman had watched the developments of the past few months with more than passing interest. He admitted that federation would be one way of resolving the Irish difficulty, but he believed the words "federal" and "federation" had been used too freely and too vaguely. Federation was after all a definite form of government which could not be applied to Great Britain and Ireland, for "two members are not enough for a federation. But a federal relation between England, Scotland, Ireland, perhaps Wales, perhaps some other members, would be perfectly possible."

Its different members might agree to vest certain powers in purely English, Scotch, Irish, assemblies, and to vest certain other powers in an assembly common to the whole body. The establishment of such a federation would be a very singular event in history. For federations in general have been formed by an exactly opposite process, the union of several smaller members into a greater whole, not by the splitting of a greater whole into several smaller members. Still this relation also is perfectly conceivable.

Nevertheless, Freeman was well aware that such a scheme had inherent difficulties "and they may not have come into the heads of some who have glibly used the words 'federal' and 'federation' without stopping to think what they meant." Undoubtedly, a federation of as few as three or four members

would be awkward to work but that would be a relatively minor problem compared to the one posed by the overwhelming majority of votes in a House of
Representatives commanded by a single member, England.

The only way to establish real federal equality would be to abolish England, Scotland
and Ireland, as separate wholes, to cut up each country into several smaller cantons,
and to make those cantons the constituent members of the federation. In other words,
"Repeal the Union, restore the Heptarchy." A beautifully mapped out federation might
be in this way devised; only are either Englishman, Scotsmen, or Irishmen ready to
wipe out thus the existence of England, Scotland, and Ireland, as distinct and more
substantive wholes?

Clearly Freeman thought not. But despite the strength of his objections to
the application of the federal system to the United Kingdom, he did admit
it would have one distinct advantage: "It would supply, and, as far as I can
see, no other scheme would supply, a ready way out of the Ulster difficulty."
That part of Ulster that was not of the same mind as Leinster, Munster, and
Connaught might have "as fair a claim to Home Rule as against the rest of
Ireland as Ireland has to Home Rule as against the rest of the United Kingdom. And under the federal system that Home Rule might at once be given
to it." In any event, Freeman did not doubt that the recent cries for home rule
emanating from Scotland and Wales would in time necessitate the introduction of another scheme, possibly "on the same general lines as Mr. Gladstone's,
possibly on the federal principles, possibly on some other."[8]
    As he indicated to Bryce in July 1886, Freeman hoped that if Gladstone
won the election he would "either bring in the old bill in its main features.
1. Parliament at Dublin. 2. *No Irish at Westminster* – or else make something
quite different – federation if he likes; there seems to be more tendency to it
in Great Britain than I fancied. I don't want it, because I am sure that
England, Ireland, Scotland, Wales, would not do; you would want smaller
centres, & I do care for the integrity of the Kingdom of Ireland, though not
for any absurd Empire."[9]
    Apart from the shrewd and, indeed, prescient remarks of Freeman, these
various responses were desultory at best. They were either the second thoughts
and reaffirmations of close participants or the idle musings of professional
public men. The home rule debate of 1886 had nevertheless aroused considerable interest in some quarters of Scotland and Wales, and discussion soon
spread to include Scottish home rule, home rule for Wales, and increasingly
home rule all round.

Before 1886 there had been no outburst of political nationalism in Scotland
comparable to that in Ireland. Nevertheless, since mid-century there had been

a stirring of romantic nationalism and a call for the protection of Scottish rights. A "National Association for the Vindication of Scottish Rights" was founded in 1853. Its primary concerns were, first, the proportionate under-representation of Scotland in the House of Commons where it had only 53 seats as against 468 for England, 32 for Wales, and 105 for Ireland, and, second, the lack of a secretary of state for Scotland. Since 1782 Scottish affairs had been handled by the Home Office. Although the association gained little public support in Scotland, its twin concerns were partially remedied over the next thirty years. In 1863 the number of Scottish MPs was raised to 60 and in 1885 to 72 in a House of 670. It took somewhat longer to effect any change in the administration of affairs. Despite the petition of Scottish MPs in 1869 and a royal commission recommendation the same year, neither Gladstone nor Disraeli had taken any action by the late 1870s. This led to mounting irritation among Scottish MPs and in 1877 Sir George Campbell, the member for Kirkcaldy, suggested that if the matter was not satisfactorily resolved fairly soon some system of federation might have to be devised.[10] Not even Campbell took this suggestion seriously but it underlined the level of frustration over the inefficient administration of Scottish affairs. The log-jam was finally broken in 1885 by the earl of Rosebery, who introduced legislation to establish a separate Scottish office headed by a secretary. Such was the general support for the proposal that although the Gladstone government fell before second reading of the bill, the Salisbury administration ensured that it was passed before parliament dissolved.[11] Thus by the end of 1885 there had been some improvement in the handling of Scottish interests.

Throughout the thirty years it had taken to achieve these changes in representation and administration there had been no evidence of a desire among the Scots for separation or for home rule, and the Liberal party continued to have solid support in Scotland. All this changed with Gladstone's decision to extend home rule to Ireland. Scottish nationalism not only became more vibrant but it took on a decidedly political edge. The Scottish Liberal party split and many Scotsmen abandoned the party and its leader. Those who remained identified with the party were staunch supporters of home rule for Scotland, and, generally, of home rule all round. After 1886 there was always an element in Scotland supportive of home rule, while the Scottish Liberals were among the leading advocates of "home-rule-all-round," "devolution," and "federalism" through to the 1920s. But it should be underlined that at no time during those thirty-five years were the Scottish home rulers ever in a majority in Scotland, and separation was never their goal. The union was always to be preserved as was the supremacy of parliament. They were in fact, not, pure federalists but straightforward devolutionists.

There was little public debate or comment in Scottish journals about home rule for Scotland before Gladstone introduced his home rule bill. However, one publicist, Arthur D. Elliott, opposed any drastic constitutional change. He pointed out that home rule for Scotland would probably mean home rule for England. If that were to happen, "the importance of Scotland in the Kingdom as a whole would inevitably be very seriously diminished ... England constitutes such a large portion of the kingdom that its affairs are necessarily of more than local importance."[12] English home rule would mean the exclusion of Scotland from the chief internal politics of Great Britain. It would be difficult, Elliott claimed, "to conceive how any severer blow could be given to the importance of Scotland than by separating its legislature from that of the sister country." Government would be weakened by dividing it. He agreed that much might be done to relieve parliament by transferring private bill legislation to local bodies or officials, but public legislation should continue to be handled by parliament, perhaps with the assistance of standing committees. He scorned a federal solution and urged that all efforts should be concentrated on the removal of inequalities, the remedying of grievances, and the firm administration of the law so that all the inhabitants of the islands could be welded "into *one* contented and united nation."[13] Elliott's point about the implications of English home rule for Scotland was perceptive and in future other commentators would often return to it.

In May 1886, a month after the introduction of Gladstone's home rule bill, a Scottish Home Rule Association was founded with G.B. Clark, MP for Caithness, as its first president. The association was a primarily Liberal body and was to be the foremost champion of home rule for Scotland until its demise at the outbreak of war in 1914.[14] In 1886 its professed aim was to obtain for Scotland a national legislature for the management of purely Scottish affairs, while maintaining the integrity of the empire and retaining an undiminished Scottish voice in the imperial parliament.[15]

Two months later the *Scottish Review* wrote in favour of decentralization in order to take care of the arrears of legislation and the difficulties of congestion faced by parliament. If municipal and county boards, a home rule parliament, and a national parliament were in place then an imperial parliament could be effected: "It points the way to the grandest ideal in modern politics, the union of the mother country with the colonies in one real United Empire, *The United States of Greater Britain.*"[16] To the *Review* there was nothing extraordinary in the demand for home rule. Devolution of local matters had been adopted by most successful large states and empires. In fact,

If we look back into history we find that really free states have been either small, or consisted of a federation under which much provincial self-government or Home Rule is left to the component parts. Accustomed as we are in England to a system of large consolidated states we are apt to look upon a federal system as a system of disunion, and therefore of weakness. In reality, however, federalism is a form of closer union ... Self-government has been reconciled with Imperial unity under the British Crown in the Channel Islands and the Isle of Man. The Imperial Parliament has adopted this as a fixed principle in dealing with all its Colonies of European race ... Federalism is a principle more akin to natural, free and beneficial legislation than this forced centralization.[17]

The article called for a Scottish parliament with exclusive and final authority over Scotland's purely domestic affairs. Imperial, national, and local affairs would need to be divided and assigned and there would continue to be Scottish representation in the imperial parliament. This home rule proposal was modelled deliberately on Canadian and American federal lines but from what was outlined it was clear that sovereignty would remain with Westminster. Therefore it was not a truly federal scheme but a devolutionary one. It was an intriguing idea that received little attention.[18]

The Scottish home rule movement had gathered sufficient momentum by late 1886 to worry some sectors of the Liberal party. James Bryce wrote to Gladstone about his concerns in late November:[19]

If the movement continues, it is likely to divide the Liberal party in Scotland more seriously than the Irish issue has divided it. It can hardly fail to prejudice the Irish question in the minds of Englishmen, because it will point, not to such a solution as that of the Bill of last spring, but to a reconstruction of the British constitution on federal lines, with a supreme legislature for the United Kingdom, and local parliaments for such division. The basic idea of so great a change will, I fear, affright persons who might be willing to let Ireland have such a legislature as you have proposed, and may seriously retard a settlement of our Irish difficulties.

Speaking as a Scotchman, I cannot see that Scotland has any need of a separate legislature – a Scotch Grand Committee with a relegation of private bills to some extra Parliamentary tribunal, would meet all she has at present to complain of – and it would be a loss to both countries for Scotchmen not to have a voice in specially English legislation.

The idea has not yet taken so much hold in Scotland but what it may be successfully discouraged. But it seems to be growing under the influence of a rather thoughtless agitation, conducted by people more active than weighty, and one cannot but fear that it may greatly injure the prospects of Irish self-government.

Henry Campbell-Bannerman, to whom Bryce had written in a similar vein, was not convinced and was, in fact, more perceptive: "I hardly take your view of Home Rule for Scotland. It is difficult to set it aside, as the case for it is logically strong but I do not think the volcano is in so active a state as might be judged from the noise it sometimes makes. From all I could see or hear Scotland is quite staunch on the Irish question – we rather gain than lose; and if the Scotch movement is kept in its proper place it will do us no harm. I do not think there is much sympathy with the men who wish to rush it."[20]

During the late 1880s Scottish home rule continued to be promoted by Scottish Liberals and opposed both by Scottish Liberal Unionists and by those fearful of its impact on Irish home rule and the integrity of the empire. The *Scottish Review* conducted a symposium over two years examining Scotland's place in the union from the legal, the political, the administrative, and the financial standpoints. What was contemplated was essentially a business arrangement – "a mere affair of decentralisation, of devolution, of relieving the Imperial Parliament and Executive of 'local-National' legislation and administration." Scottish home rulers had given little attention, unlike the Irish, to "the sentimental or national aspect of the agitation." One writer, W. Wallace, recognized that such an appeal to nationality would be appropriate but that it might in turn foster English nationalism which would work to Scotland's disadvantage. He wondered if some means other than home rule and the fostering of the sentiment of nationhood could not be found to redress Scotland's legal, administrative, and financial concerns.[21]

W. Mitchell, the honorary treasurer of the Scottish Home Rule Association, writing in the same journal, did not agree. In fact, he went so far as to argue that

The problem now before the United Kingdom is to give to each of its component nationalities such a measure of Home Rule as will enable them to manage their own affairs better than the Imperial Parliament can do for them, and at the same time to preserve to each of these nationalities representation in the Imperial Parliament. This problem once successfully solved, the Imperial Parliament would then have time to give its whole attention to those Imperial interests which of late have been so much neglected, and the way would thus be opened for each of the British Colonies to become a member of the Federation and to send representatives to the Imperial Parliament.

Those who advocate such a policy are the true "Unionists" and those who oppose it are really "separatists."

This scheme did not seem to apply to Wales because there was only reference to "the three Kingdoms" but it was obviously a step toward home rule all round as well as an indication of the essentially conservative imperial interests underlying much of the Scottish home rule agitation. For example, Mitchell wished to preserve the supremacy of the imperial parliament and envisaged his scheme as a step toward some form of imperial federation.[22] In 1888 the same dual attachment to local self-government and imperial unity was reflected in the commitment of the newly founded Scottish Labour party to "Home Rule for each separate nationality or country in the British Empire with an Imperial Parliament for Imperial affairs."[23] One of the founders of the party was Keir Hardie, a vice-president of the Scottish Home Rule Association, who stood on a home rule platform at Mid-Lanark in 1888. The pledge of the Scottish Labour party to home rule within the United Kingdom remained firm over the next forty years.[24]

The commitment to home rule in Wales was never as deeply rooted as in Scotland. While there was a cultural resurgence in Wales in the mid-to-late nineteenth century and considerable political pressure was mounted over the issues of disestablishment and education, political nationalism and thus home rule were never major issues or concerns even in the late 1880s and early 1890s. There was nothing in Wales paralleling the Parnell parliamentary party of Ireland or the Scottish Home Rule Association. Although a general emotional commitment to home rule for Wales did spread in the eighties and nineties and was taken up by Tom Ellis and Lloyd George, it was never a separatist commitment. Self-government for Wales meant devolution and the continued sovereignty of the Westminster parliament. That was to remain the case until the 1920s. Of the kingdoms, Wales was the least committed to home rule or devolutionary ideas. No plethora of bills and motions spilled forth as they did from Scotland and no sustained examination of the constitution took place. There was little sympathy in Protestant Wales for the aspirations of Catholic Ireland, and Irish home rule lacked the support in Wales it could easily garner in parts of England and Scotland. Nevertheless, the introduction of Gladstone's home rule bill meant that certain Welshmen began to ask if what was good for Ireland might not be good for Wales, and a general Welsh commitment to the idea of home rule developed. Wales did after all claim to be a nation and presumably nationhood did imply some means of national self-government.[25] One immediate consequence of this new mood was the formation in 1886 of *Cymru Fydd* ("Young Wales") to preserve and advance the Welsh cultural and linguistic tradition.[26]

Welsh proposals for constitutional change were always modest. In 1888 Tom Ellis, a leading Welsh nationalist and committed home ruler, moved an amendment to the local government bill. He recommended the establishment of a general advisory council for Wales. Although the amendment was withdrawn, section 81 of the new act did permit county councils to consult each other and, if need be, work together on matters of joint interest. This provision was used later by some home rulers, particularly Lloyd George, to press Welsh claims.[27] A year later, W.J. Parry, vice-chairman of Carnarvonshire County Council, drafted the outline of a home rule bill for Wales which he circulated for discussion. A cautious devolutionary proposal, it came to nothing.[28] Home rule for Wales was also the subject of a "Round Table" discussion in the *Westminster Review* in 1890 but the exchange of views revealed a far less extensive attachment to home rule than one might have expected and a commitment to little more than administrative devolution.[29] One leading Welsh politician, Stuart Rendel, a man close to Gladstone and in many respects the father of the Welsh parliamentary party, doubted if many professed Welsh home rulers were really clear about what they wanted: "should be much interested to know from many of those who advocate Home Rule for Wales what in precise terms they mean by Home Rule. It has struck me that they either do not know or do not agree what specific shape Home Rule for Wales should take & therefore what they are demanding." Rendel pointed out that home rule for Ireland meant the restoration of an Irish parliament; but when the term home rule was used for Scotland and Wales very few people meant it "in the same sense as that which they give it in the case of Ireland."[30] For his part, Ellis believed the "tendency of the Home Rule question is towards Federalism."[31]

The aims and aspirations of the Welsh and Scottish home rulers received their first full and formal airing in the spring of 1889. On 9 April Dr G.B. Clark, one of the Highland leaders of the Scottish Home Rule Association, moved in the House of Commons that "it is desirable that arrangements be made for giving to the people of Scotland, by their representatives in a National Parliament, the management and control of Scottish affairs."[32] In introducing the resolution Clark was at pains to make it clear that he did not mean separation: "I have no desire to repeal the Union between England and Scotland."[33] But while the union had been mutually beneficial it had been better for England than Scotland. Clark wanted to keep all the benefits the Scots had under the union without any of the disadvantages. He frankly admitted that his motion was based mainly on practical considerations, but he pointed out that there was a strong sentimental basis, a national one, for the growing home rule movement in Scotland. Nevertheless, the main initial concern was the sad neglect of Scottish affairs such as education, public health, the police, the liquor traffic, and finance. The House was doing its work "very badly and inadequately" and something was required to enable parliament to discharge its duty to the whole country. The remedy in Clark's estimation was "devolution upon lines of nationality, to devolve on each of the national elements of which this great Empire is composed, its own local or national business." The devolution should be twofold. In regard to legislation, "Give to your national Parliaments, or your national Councils ... the powers and functions parallel to those you are going to devolve on County Bodies, and such as you have long devolved on Municipal bodies – powers to act in their own business and with a free hand. If those bodies attempt to go beyond this, the Imperial Parliament can veto the proceedings, but, so far as their powers are conferred, they should have a free hand." The newly created bodies should also have executive responsibilities "or you will have this condition of affairs, that the men carrying out the laws passed by the bodies would be under the control of the Imperial Parliament." Some would see this as a difficulty but Clark saw no reason why it should be. "We do not want an elaborate Executive. I think the Scotch secretary supported by the Scotch people, would be sufficient, and the Lord Advocate might be left to devote more time to his practice at the Bar. There must be a Board of Supervision, a Board of Trade, and heads of these departments of course. I think this would be sufficient for carrying on the national work." He continued:

This seems to me the only solution of our present difficulty – you should do it on the lines of Nationality. The Scotch are a separate nation; we have our separate laws, our separate methods of jurisprudence and administration, and our special technical language, which English lawyers cannot understand. Now, is it not far better that our business should be transacted by a body which has some knowledge of these matters than by others who frankly admit they have no knowledge at all on the subject? You have passed special Bills for Ireland, and the claims of Wales cannot be long neglected. The Welsh people will make their demand before long, and you will be no longer able to settle their affairs on English lines. This question of Home Rule can be settled in one of two ways, on the principle of dualism, or by the method of federalism.

Dualism would never work. The only solution in Clark's estimation was that proposed by Butt in the 1870s. Clark then put his finger on a key point:

The country will never consent to Irish Members being driven out of this House as a consequence of Irish Home Rule, but at the same time I do not think the country would submit to Irish members, while settling their own National affairs, having a finger in the Scotch and English pie. So under the circumstances it seems to me that we are logically bound, and I have long held this view, to have Home Rule all round, and a Federal Parliament representing every section of the Empire ... The Home rule feeling is growing strongly in Scotland as it is in Wales and Ireland, and I hope the time is not far distant when this Parliament will be freed from the discussion of such questions as whether a Scotch Railway Company should have an hotel in Edinburgh, or Belfast have a system of drainage. Other great and Imperial questions will then have a chance of discussion. We have an immediate responsibility. We are responsible for the government of a third of the human race – three hundred millions of people look to the House of Commons for guidance. I trust that in the consideration of Home Rule propositions we shall still preserve intact the great Anglo-Saxon Union that has done so much for civilization, that has so much still to do.[34]

One would be hard-pressed to find another speech that so clearly summed up the various conflicting pressures and emotions or so starkly revealed the essential weaknesses of the home rule position. Clark and his supporters wished to retain the sovereignty of parliament and thus the essential unity of the country. Federation was a misnomer. Divided or coordinate sovereignty was not what the Scottish home rulers wanted. They simply wanted control of local matters. They were not nationalists in the separatist mould but devolutionists. Moreover, they were proud of the empire they had helped create. They wanted it strengthened and, if possible, unified, and they clearly wished to continue to help run it.

Dr W.A. Hunter (Aberdeen North), also a leading member of the Scottish Home Rule Association, supported the motion. He thought the best way to resolve the congestion in parliament, to preserve representative institutions, and to avoid the perils of democratic government would be "to frame a scheme of Home Rule equal for all four divisions of the United Kingdom while maintaining absolute the sovereignty of Parliament ... so a very large devolution of powers could simply be made, while the best division for such devolution will be found in following national lines." Although he referred to his idea as a "Federal form of Union" and looked forward to the day when England should be merged in "a higher unity ... namely, the United States of Europe," he clearly did not have a federal system in mind nor apparently much knowledge of existing federal structures. [35]

During the initial debate on Scottish home rule there were many references to home rule all round and also to federalism but it was clear that many of the speakers were really more concerned with relieving parliamentary congestion than realizing a national dream. Their ideas were vague and lacking in clarity. Their critics were quick to point out not only the lack of detail but also the dearth of any obvious and widespread demand for major constitutional and organizational change. Wedded as they were to a centralized system of government, many of the critics had difficulty envisaging how home rule for Scotland might work. Would Scottish members continue to sit in the House of Commons for all business or only imperial business? Either way there would be difficulties. [36] One speaker also pointed to the great disparity in size between Scotland and England which would make a federal bond most difficult. [37] Gladstone, while appreciative of Scottish concerns and aware of the demands for devolution, did "not think that we have yet reached the situation when the circumstances are ripe for an ultimate and final consideration of this question on its merits." Nevertheless, he did not agree with those critics who said devolution would weaken parliament. On the contrary, "I hold that all judicious devolution which hands over to subordinate bodies duties for which they are better qualified by local knowledge, and which at the same time sets free the hands of Parliament for the pursuit of its proper business, does not weaken it but strengthens it, gives vitality to it, and makes the people more than ever disposed to support the supremacy of Parliament." [38]

In his turn, and on behalf of the government, Arthur Balfour, the Irish secretary, rejected the notion that there was a growing sentiment in favour of Scottish home rule. "Surely," he said, "we should be mad if at the time when every nation in America and in Europe is drawing closer the bonds which unite separate parts, we were to scatter and divide." He maintained that

Scotland had not been overshadowed by England. Its national life had not been crushed. Scotland, on the contrary, had "gained the inestimable privilege of feeling ourselves citizens of one great community, and of our taking full share in the management of this great Empire." Balfour refused to be party to anything which in the smallest degree diminished that bond and that heritage.[39] He was to adhere to this general position over the next thirty years. Neither Clark nor Hunter expected a majority in favour of the motion and in fact it was resoundingly defeated 200–79 with twenty-two of the seventy-two Scottish members voting against and only nineteen in favour.

Despite the ease with which the motion for Scottish home rule had been brushed aside, many Liberals were concerned at the mounting pressure in Scotland and Wales and realized that it would soon be necessary for their party, the only one committed to home rule, to define its aims. Rosebery was particularly anxious that any proposed constitutional change should be thrashed out long before it was publicly expounded. In July and August 1889 he urged Gladstone to appoint a party committee to go over the 1886 bill in detail and raise criticisms and ideas for discussion. While sympathetic and prepared to encourage debate within the party, Gladstone thought the moment inopportune for such a detailed move. Gladstone's stalling only frustrated his senior colleagues, many of whom thought Rosebery's contention "unanswerable."[40]

Gladstone's reluctance to generate a detailed plan in part stemmed from his awareness that the exigencies of the moment would undoubtedly determine many details, but primarily he was conscious of the deep differences of opinion within his party. He reasoned that a broadly defined aim was more likely to keep the party together than would a particular scheme. For example, one of the major difficulties the Liberals faced after 1886 was to resolve the disagreement within their ranks over whether or not Irish MPs should be included in or excluded from the House of Commons. A policy of retention would clearly have undermined the "obstructionist" arguments that had lain at the bottom of many home rule arguments in 1885–6 and would have devalued the position of those who argued that only complete exclusion would ensure any real degree of self-government. Partial retention raised the possibility of serious constitutional problems if it led to two majorities in the House of Commons, one with the Irish MPs present and one with them absent. Total exclusion, of course, still seemed to many a step toward separation and to others it reduced Ireland from a constituent part of the United Kingdom to little more than a tributary province.

Many of the Liberals who continued to think about home rule after 1886 favoured retention, Sir William Harcourt because he thought it was necessary for a Liberal majority, others such as the Scottish and Welsh Liberals and the Liberal imperialists because they thought it would lead to wider imperial reform, possibly imperial federation. Many Liberals suggested retention, because it enabled them to rebut the Unionist argument that home rule would lead to the disintegration of the empire.[41]

Gladstone's 1886 bill had been too "separatist" for many Liberal imperialists because it excluded Irish MPs. H.H. Fowler, for one, was satisfied "that the growing feeling in favour of Home Rule (& it *is* growing) is accompanied by a determination, far stronger than in 1886, to resist to the uttermost not only separation but even the appearance of weakening the supremacy of the Imperial Parliament";[42] while both R.C. Munro-Ferguson and Herbert Asquith linked devolution to wider imperial interests.[43] Morley, on the contrary, thought it should be known that "we do not intend to put parliament on a federal basis ... It is to be delegation, and not federation. We shall have to be careful, as Scotland is rather wide awake, but I, for one, am dead against breaking up the old British parliament as it was before the Irish Union."[44]

By the autumn of 1889 it was clear to a reluctant Gladstone that the issue could not be long avoided and in October the decision was taken to reverse the 1886 arrangement and retain some Irish MPs in the House of Commons in the next Liberal home rule scheme. Predictably, the announcement did more to enliven debate than to dampen it because the implications of the decision were not clear. As Gladstone's close adviser, Hugh Childers, pointed out, the Liberal party's intentions on home rule were the "merest shadow." Their moderate supporters were getting increasingly uneasy about the outline of a future Liberal bill. "The great question as it appears to me, is are we to have an Imperial Parliament for all the imperial affairs of the Empire, with separate Legislatures for England, Scotland, Ireland, & Wales, or is Ireland alone to be dealt with? ... although individuals have used language hostile to or favourable to, the Federal idea, nothing like an authoritative pronouncement on the subject exists. To my mind it must either ... be repudiated or adopted."[45] Gladstone doubted that the Liberal party would be called upon "as a condition of settling Irish HR to say aye or no to Imperial Federation," but Childers assured him that "I do not see how, in the present state of Scottish and Welsh opinion, this can be deferred long ... From the moment when the presence of the Irish MPs at Westminster was conceded, the question ... became vital."[46] As expected, Spencer was distinctly opposed to a separate legislature for each part of the United Kingdom, while Campbell-Bannerman, basically sympathetic to the idea, did not think Englishmen had given thought to having a local English parliament distinct from the imperial one, and since "Scotch Home Rule involves *English* H. Rule ... Scotch Home Rule must wait until the sluggish mind of John Bull is educated up to that point." Nevertheless, he was convinced that Irish home rule would involve Scottish home rule "as sure as eggs is eggs."[47]

One of the young Liberal imperialists who had been pressing for some policy definition was delighted by Gladstone's decision. Herbert Asquith interpreted it as a victory for the "imperialist" position that he and his friends, particularly Rosebery, Haldane, and Grey, favoured:

under the Bill of '86, the Irish Parlt. was (in effect) to be a body with exclusive legislative powers in Irish matters. The supremacy of the Impl Parlt was to be retained by indirect methods – thro' the Lord Lieut's power of veto etc, and by express restrictions upon the legislative competence of the Irish body. With the retention of the Irish members this is no longer necessary. It cannot be said that a Parlt. in wh. Ireland is still directly reptd has no moral authority (even after Home Rule) to legislate for Ireland shd an extreme case arise. Hence it wd seem that in any future scheme the Irish legislature should be treated as a subordinate body with delegated powers; in wh. case no question cd. arise as to the continued supremacy of the Impl Parlt.[48]

Asquith believed the same delegation of powers could be applied to Scotland and Wales; so that "out of Irish Home Rule would emerge a vast new scheme of imperial reconstruction."[49]

Despite the pressures upon him to commit himself to some form of home rule all round or federalism, Gladstone refused to budge. He simply believed the time inappropriate and the prevailing ideas too inchoate. When the question of Scottish home rule was raised in February 1890 during the debate on the Address, Gladstone referred to the various demands for devolution in the United Kingdom: "Between these extremes, between a remedy for private business on the one side, and a remedy in the shape of a Federal Parliament on the other, there are floating ideas perfectly immature and not yet reduced to shape – vaporous forms that are still in the atmosphere and driving about like clouds in the wind, which it is totally impossible to grasp and totally impossible to define ... in these circumstances this is a time of reserve."[50]

While the debate raged within the Liberal party, the Scottish and Welsh home rulers attempted to combine their efforts. On 25 February 1890 a meeting was held in London between representatives of the North and South Wales Liberal Federations, the Cymru Fydd Society, and the Scottish Home Rule Association. Among those present were Dr Clark, J. Hubert Lewis, Henry Lewis, J. Parry, Lloyd George, W.H. Tilston, and Charles Waddie. It was moved "That this Conference is of the opinion that the time has now arrived when the people of Scotland and Wales should be entrusted with the management of their own national affairs still preserving the supremacy of the Imperial Parliament." The resolution carried despite efforts to insert England and Ireland before Scotland. W. Mitchell of Edinburgh and W. Jones of London did attempt to move "That in the opinion of this meeting the true solution of the Home Rule question is to be found in a union upon federal lines and for that purpose the meeting appoints a Committee to make arrangement for the formation of a Federal Union League of the British Empire," but after much discussion the resolution was finally withdrawn. Instead a committee was set up composed of five representatives of the North Wales Liberal Federation, five from the South Wales Liberal Federation, two from the Cymru Fydd Society, and twelve from the Scottish Home Rule Association, and was instructed to report to another joint conference which, if necessary, could include English and Irish representatives.[51]

Two months later a second meeting was held in London with representatives present from Scotland, Wales, and England. The conference adopted a recommendation "that in the final settlement of the Home Rule question a Legislature should be granted to each of the four nationalities, England, Ireland, Scotland, and Wales, for the control and management of all purely local affairs, still maintaining the supremacy of the Imperial Parliament, in which each nationality will be represented."[52] This was clearly devolutionist, at best home rule all round, but certainly not federalism. Nevertheless, Charles Waddie of the Scottish Home Rule Association continued to refer to a "Federal plan of government" and a simultaneous change in all four countries, and was joined in his plea by other Scottish home rulers at the annual meeting of the association in September 1890.[53]

John Leng, who had organized the second London meeting, did write specifically of devolution but his scheme would have had the representatives at Westminster of England, Scotland, Wales, and Ireland meeting alone or with others to deal with each nation's affairs. Although Leng referred to his scheme as home rule all round, it differed markedly from other plans in that it had dual representation. Such a cumbersome solution underlined the essential conservatism of the Welsh and Scottish response.[54] In fact, in 1890 Dr Clark, considered by many to be one of the more radical Scottish home rulers, had declared that he and his fellow home rulers would "repudiate and refuse a scheme of Home Rule" that would prevent them from being members of the imperial parliament and taking part in imperial affairs.[55] Some writers, of course, still did not believe in any form of home rule. They thought the problems were essentially administrative and would be resolved by improvements in House of Commons business, by the use of Grand Committees, and by improvements in local government. If drastic changes were required, however, even the cautious William Wallace agreed there should be a pentarchy, i.e., home rule all round for England, Scotland, Wales, and the two Irelands.[56]

Over the next two years both the Scots and the Welsh attempted to draw attention to their aims. In March 1891 and again in April 1892 Dr Clark introduced a motion in the House of Commons calling for home rule all round. He urged that "in order to increase the efficiency of the Imperial Parliament to deal with Imperial affairs and in order to give a speedier and fuller effect to the special desires and wants of the respective nationalities constituting the United Kingdom, it is desirable to devolve upon the representatives of England, Ireland, Scotland and Wales respectively, the management and control of their domestic affairs." Clark wanted to relieve congestion in parliament, preserve imperial unity, and ensure that the self-governing colonies had a proper say in the determination of imperial policy. "Federal devolution" within the United Kingdom would give the four countries control over their domestic affairs, thereby appeasing local needs, and would enable the imperial parliament to concentrate on foreign and imperial business. For Clark, as for some later federalists, the first step toward imperial federation was the devolution of purely local affairs on to "National Assemblies, Parliaments, or Councils, such as the States of America have, or as different parts of the Canadian Dominion have." In both 1891 and 1892 Clark referred favourably to the American, Canadian, Swiss, and German federal systems. His primary aim was "the stability of the Empire" and he urged his parliamentary colleagues to make "some change." If they adopted federalism, he believed it would be "as successful here as it has been in other countries, and we shall be able to solve local and Imperial problems on lines which will tend to strengthen and develop the Empire rather than to weaken it." Not unexpectedly, Clark's pleas and those of his few supporters fell on deaf ears. In 1891 the House was counted out and in 1892 the motion was lost 74–54. On neither occasion had Clark ventured beyond generalities. He had provided no detailed plans nor had he tackled such key issues as Ulster. Although he always spoke of federalism and used the contradictory phrase "federal devolution" to describe his own ideas, it is doubtful that he really had federalism in mind. His speeches revealed both a basic lack of thought and the essentially imperial and conservative caste of his interests, while the response to his motions underlined the widespread lack of interest not only in the House of Commons but in the country generally in home rule all round.[57]

The Welsh had also been making some efforts to advance their interests and in early 1891 a national institutions (Wales) bill had been introduced into the Commons by Alfred Thomas (Glamorgan East). It had the backing of, among others, Tom Ellis, who had strongly supported Clark's motion, and Lloyd George. The bill proposed the establishment of a National Council for Wales representing the sixteen Welsh counties and boroughs. Two conferences were held to discuss the bill and in early 1892 it was reintroduced into the Commons. The proposal would have given Wales more than Scotland then had, but far less than Gladstone had suggested for Ireland. It was inferior to home rule and was certainly not federal. At best the proposal represented administrative devolution. The idea came to nothing and was dropped as soon as it was introduced.[58]

In addition to the debates in the Commons, a number of interested commentators and political activists turned to the periodicals and magazines to explore the possibilities of home rule all round. In fact, the *Scots Magazine* remained particularly faithful to the cause throughout the 1890s, providing both a platform for advocates and editorial backing. Henry Gow, an ardent Scottish home ruler, often used its pages to promote home rule all round which he considered essential for the relief of congestion and the continued unity of the empire.[59] By 1892 debate was intensifying in the knowledge that the Liberal party had formally adopted a program at Newcastle in October 1891 in which home rule led the way. Gladstone had quickly confirmed his commitment both to the program and to home rule. Nevertheless, in the heightened atmosphere the devolutionists did not have it all their own way. When R.T. Reid advocated home rule all round in the *Contemporary Review* in April 1892, his argument drew criticism from G. Pitt-Lewis, who argued that colonial precedents were unhelpful; that it was impossible to apply a federal solution to the relationship of England and Ireland because of the dominance of England; that it would be difficult to decide between imperial and national issues; and that home rule all round did not address the problem of Ulster.[60]

The Salisbury government was defeated in the House in June and was immediately granted a dissolution. In the ensuing July election the Liberals won a narrow home rule majority of forty. The Liberals had 273 seats; Irish home rulers 81; Conservatives 269; Liberal Unionists 46; and Independent Labour 1. The government finally fell on 11 August and Gladstone, four months short of his eighty-third birthday, formed his fourth administration. It was clear that he would move quickly to introduce a second home rule bill, and the extent of the legislation and its specific details were awaited with keen anticipation[61]

In the event, the devolutionists and federalists were disappointed by Gladstone's bill. It was an exclusively Irish bill and Gladstone initially resisted any temptation to claim it as the first step toward home rule all round. In contrast to the 1886 bill, this one was not prepared by Gladstone alone. The new bill was drafted by a cabinet committee composed of the prime minister, John Morley, James Bryce, Spencer, Campbell-Bannerman, and Lord Herschell. No memoranda on constitutional issues seem to have been generated and the committee contented itself with tinkering with the 1886 bill. Nevertheless, some discreet soundings were made. For example, shortly after the election Bryce approached Sir Edward Blake, the new Irish Nationalist MP for South Longford and the former Liberal premier of Ontario, and arranged for Blake to dine with Gladstone and himself to discuss the Irish situation. Later in the year Bryce asked Blake about the Canadian experience of single and two-chambered legislatures. Blake recommended two chambers but suggested they should meet separately rather than together as under the 1886 bill.[62] Undoubtedly similar soundings were taken both in and outside party ranks, particularly over the size of the Irish representation in the imperial parliament. But since John Morley, one of the strongest advocates of reduced representation, was on the committee it was unlikely that members of the party who favoured retaining the Irish representation intact, such as Sir William Harcourt, would have been given much of a hearing. Certainly men like Munro-Ferguson, Asquith, and Rosebery who favoured some form of devolution or home rule all round were not included in the soundings. Asquith was especially annoyed. Three days before Gladstone introduced his bill in the House of Commons, Asquith wrote to Rosebery: "I understand that on Monday a Bill (to 'amend the provision' for the Government of Ireland), which neither you nor I have seen, is to be introduced into the House of Commons. I send you word of this, as you may possibly like to be present, and hear what Her Majesty's Government have to propose."[63] Clearly Gladstone and his committee kept their ideas pretty much to themselves and took only limited outside advice on constitutional matters. They did need expert advice on finance, however, and arranged for Treasury assistance. In December Hamilton, Welby, and Milner of the Treasury provided an exhaustive analysis of the Anglo-Irish financial relationship and made recommendations for the new legislation.[64]

The home rule bill that Gladstone introduced on 13 February 1893 differed in seven significant ways from the 1886 bill on which it was modelled. First, the new Irish legislature was again to have two component parts, a Legislative Council of forty-eight members and an Assembly of 103, but, as Blake had advised, they were now to sit separately and any disagreement between them was to be resolved by a joint majority vote if the bill in question was reintroduced after dissolution or a lapse of two years. Second, the supremacy of the imperial parliament was emphatically stated in the preamble. Third, the viceroy's term was to be fixed at six years and the office was freed from any religious disability. Fourth, special provision was made for the appointment of an executive committee of the Privy Council in Ireland, in effect, an Irish cabinet. Fifth, in future, appeals would be to the Privy Council alone and not to the Privy Council and the House of Lords. Sixth, there were to be eighty Irish MPs in the imperial parliament who would be entitled to vote only on matters relating to Ireland and imperial affairs. Specifically, they were prevented from voting upon any bill or motion expressly confined to Great Britain or to one of its parts (i.e., England, Scotland, Wales); on any motion or resolution relating to a tax not raised in Ireland; on any vote or appropriation of money otherwise than for imperial services; and on any motion or resolution exclusively affecting Great Britain or person or persons therein. These restrictions were listed in clause 9 which was soon labelled the "in-and-out" clause. Finally, following the advice of the Treasury officials, all Irish customs duties were to be collected by the United Kingdom exchequer and treated as Ireland's contribution to imperial expenditures. Apart from these major changes the 1893 bill resembled that of 1886. The Irish parliament was still prevented from legislating on matters related to the crown, peace and war, defence, the army, the navy, treaties with foreign states, dignities and titles, treason, aliens, external trade, coinage, currency, and various subsidiary subjects. And as in 1886, the Irish legislature was barred from making any law relating to the establishment or the endowment of religion, the imposition of a disability or the conferring of a privilege as a consequence of religious belief, and the abrogation of the right to establish or maintain a denominational school.[65]

In introducing his bill, Gladstone stated the object of it was to establish a legislative body in Dublin for the conduct of Irish legislation and administration distinct from imperial affairs.[66] Even so, he aimed to do nothing inconsistent with imperial unity; rather "we believe that a wise extension of the privileges of local self-government has been shown by experience to be the most effective instrument" for the maintenance of imperial supremacy. Retention of Irish members in the imperial parliament would make Ireland feel she had a full voice in imperial matters, and since British budgets would continue to have an impact on Ireland it was essential for Irish members to be present. He claimed that the controversy over home rule could not be unduly prolonged for then the Irish demand for self-government would become a cry for repeal of the union and dual supremacy, and that, he maintained, would be a dangerous development. Gladstone made no references to home rule all round or federalism in his introductory speech.

Not unexpectedly the bill was subjected to heavy criticism. Balfour was the most pungent. Speaking on 14 February, Balfour referred to the bill as an "abortion of a measure" and a sad comment on seven years of Liberal reflection. He, like so many others who followed him in the debate, was particularly concerned by the in-and-out clause which he thought inoperable. Gladstone could not have been surprised at such criticism for in his own introductory speech he had admitted the difficulty in finding "an absolute and accurate line of cleavage between questions that are Imperial and questions that are Irish." He probably would have preferred to omit Irish representation altogether, as he had in 1886, but he had been obliged to bow to party pressure and maintain one of the key symbols of unity. His refusal to broaden the debate by introducing either home rule all round or a federal proposal condemned his bill on the ground of illogicality, if nothing else. As Balfour acidulously put it: "A Federal Government may be good. Colonial Government may be good. The British Constitution as it stands may be good; but this bastard combination of the three is ludicrous and impossible." Balfour, like all Unionists at this stage, feared that home rule would lead to separation and thus imperial weakness. He argued, much as Dicey did, that "the process of every great community has been towards further integration." Gladstone was asking them "to retrace our steps and make our progress towards disintegration." In doing so he was reversing the necessary evolutionary steps by which great empires were built up and maintained.[67]

Chamberlain, of course, believed that the retention of the Irish members at Westminster was "an essential condition of the maintenance of our existing Parliamentary supremacy, and also of the unity of the Empire." But if retention was accepted there were only two practical and logical ways to do it: first, "that the Irish Government and the Irish Legislative Body should be a wholly subordinate body – something like an enlarged edition of the London County Council," or, second, "that at the same time that you give a Parliament to Ireland you should give a Parliament to England, a Parliament to Scotland, and a Parliament to Wales, and that you should set up over these four Parliaments a fifth for the United Kingdom." He thought that would be a large order. Unfortunately, the government's scheme was neither one thing nor the other.[68]

Again and again throughout the debates on first and second reading the in-and-out clause was the focus of discussion. Many members followed Chamberlain's lead and pointed out that federalism was the only logical solution to the dilemma that Gladstone had posed by attempting to combine colonial self-government and the federal system. But these references to home rule all round or to federalism were only made in passing. There was no sustained analysis or discussion. It was clear that most Unionists were uninterested and most Liberals confused. Balfour put the opposition to home rule all round most succinctly: "I do not believe that this childish imitation of the American Constitution is either fitted to the needs of our people or commends itself to the judgement of our people." The fact that England so exceeded Scotland, Wales, and Ireland in population, wealth, and power would "make the idea of co-ordinating them all as equal elements in one system an absolute impossibility."[69]

Even the Scottish home rulers were divided in their response. Not surprisingly, John Leng (Dundee), who had organized the meeting three years earlier between the Welsh and Scottish home rulers, supported Gladstone's bill as a step towards home rule all round. He believed the in-and-out clause was a recognition of the federal principle. On the other hand, Dr MacGregor (Inverness-shire) thought the only solution to the problem of retaining members in the imperial parliament was "Federal Home Rule or Home Rule all round" and he regretted that Gladstone had not introduced a bill dealing concurrently with Scotland, Wales, and Ireland. Congestion necessitated "a devolution of work to the various Provinces" which would "allow local Bodies to deal with local affairs, with one Parliament supreme over all." He was convinced that the real reason for the opposition to home rule was not a fear of either disintegration of the empire or separation but "the fact that the privileged classes, feeling their monopoly of power slipping from their grasp, were making a last desperate effort to retain it. Would it not be more wise and prudent for the governing and privileged classes to make reasonable concessions to the democracy in time, before the democracy by more violent means swept every obstacle from their path?"[70]

Most of the MPs were less apocalyptic but no less troubled by the bill. Naturally the in-and-out clause and the financial provisions attracted most comment, but the assertion of the supremacy of the imperial parliament in a preamble rather than in a clause was not considered sufficiently concrete by many critics. Similarly, the fact that Gladstone had designated the legislative areas that Ireland could not intrude upon had seemingly left the residual power to the Irish legislature. Many commentators both in and out of the House would have preferred Gladstone to have listed the powers of the Irish legislature thus leaving the residual power to the imperial parliament. Ulster was an additional sore point. Gladstone had made no provision for Ulster in his bill, and had made no reference to her distinctive needs. Chamberlain warned that since Protestant Ulster was not protected by the bill it would undoubtedly fight against inclusion in a home rule Ireland. His warning was echoed throughout the debates by many Ulster sympathizers.

Gladstone was finally obliged to bow to the criticism of the in-and-out arrangement. The clause was changed to permit the Irish representatives to vote on all matters at Westminster. This shift in position resolved the problem falling to the speaker, who would have had to decide what was a fully imperial or British issue, and it averted the possibility of two separate majorities in the House, but it created other equally difficult problems. The Unionists were outraged that the Irish would now be able to vote on all English, Scottish, and Welsh matters but British MPs would still not be able to touch Irish affairs. Many thought that Gladstone had reopened the door to party deals and obstruction which his bill was purportedly designed to resolve. Others believed it was a step much closer to federation than ever before, and were aghast.[71]

Gladstone also had to make changes to the financial provisions. He had initially proposed that the British exchequer should be credited with Irish customs duties, estimated at £2,358,000, which would then be considered Ireland's contribution to imperial expenditure. Such an arrangement would have left the Irish with a surplus of £500,000. The scheme had the advantage of simplicity in that Ireland's contribution would be drawn from one source rather than from across the spectrum of Irish revenues, but it probably would have left Ireland incapable of borrowing or lending with so small a surplus at its disposal. It would also have meant that Ireland would never have reaped the benefit of a rise in customs duties, while the size of its contribution would have varied in accordance with fluctuations in British fiscal policy.[72] Whatever its weaknesses, the scheme was probably the best devised before 1919. Unfortunately, Gladstone had to abandon it because of the discovery of a miscalculation in the yield from Irish customs and excise duties which would have reduced the Irish surplus to £140,000. This was clearly inadequate, so while the bill was in committee a new scheme was proposed requiring Ireland to pay a variable rather than a fixed charge equal to one-third of Irish revenue. The remaining two-thirds were to be used for Irish local needs. Since the plan involved estimating Ireland's true revenue, an exceedingly difficult task, it was obviously not a fully satisfactory alternative. Moreover, the Irish taxes were to be collected by the imperial government for a provisional period of six years, at the end of which the policy and procedure would be reviewed. The provisional nature of the scheme plus the fact it was open to many of the objections raised in 1886 aroused much annoyance and concern.[73]

It was clear from the various criticisms of the 1893 financial proposals that the intricate implications of Gladstone's ideas had not been fully considered or explored by his government and that either scheme, if implemented, would have resulted in more problems. It is true that some of the difficulties Gladstone faced were a result of his own hazy blending of colonial and federal ideas and the inveterate conservatism of most Liberal and Unionist observers, who found it hard to imagine devolution in any form and were inclined to isolate the cost-benefit factors. Nevertheless, it was obvious that serious difficulties would always confront those attempting to divide taxing powers in order to meet the needs and responsibilities of a portion of a country which in some matters was self-governing but which in others, such as defence and foreign policy, was clearly dependent. It might have been a simpler task if home rule all round or a federal system had been under consideration, but neither in 1886 nor in 1893 was any thought given to larger constitutional or financial schemes. Occasional references were tossed off by critics to the overall implications for the British taxpayer if Irish home rule were extended to Scotland and Wales, but no one, not even the advocates of home rule all round, drew up full-fledged analyses or proposals.

The debate in the House of Commons over Gladstone's home rule bill was one of the most protracted in parliamentary history. It dragged through a total of eighty-five sittings and Gladstone had to introduce closure in order to move the bill through the committee stage. The seemingly endless debates were wearisome to sit through and equally paralysing to read as each clause was taken apart word by word and five hundred years of Anglo-Irish grievances were picked over and repackaged according to the political persuasion of the speaker. The bill finally passed through the Commons on 1 September 1893 by a vote of 307 to 267, but as Gladstone had always expected it was resoundingly defeated on second reading in the Lords on 8 September by 419-41. Gladstone wanted to meet the challenge and dissolve but his colleagues resisted. Unhappy with this decision and at odds with his cabinet over other issues, Gladstone resigned on 3 March 1894 and was succeeded as prime minister by Lord Rosebery.

The Scottish and Welsh home rulers had been disappointed that Gladstone had not shaped his bill along devolutionary or federal lines but they could not have been altogether surprised. Their interest in home rule all round was not widely shared by their compatriots and certainly the Irish did not believe home rule for Ireland should wait until Scotland, Wales, and England were ready for a more comprehensive scheme. It was also emphatically clear that even if Gladstone had opted for home rule all round it would have fared no better in the House of Lords than his Irish bill. Dominated by Conservative peers, the upper chamber would always rebuff any attempt, whether it was home rule for Ireland or home rule all round, which in its estimation threatened the sovereignty of parliament and the unity of the United Kingdom and the empire.[74]

Despite the setback, the Scots and Welsh continued to press the case for home rule all round on the assumption that the idea might have some chance of support as long as the Liberals were in office.[75] By the end of 1893 Harry Gow was arguing for the supremacy of the national parliaments within their own sphere with no right of interference by the imperial parliament. Nevertheless, he referred to the powers as delegated powers and thus implied the supremacy of the imperial parliament. Gow and his colleagues thought it might be useful to organize among the home rulers of England, Scotland, Wales, and Ireland, and the colonies, a "Federal Union League for the British Empire," in the belief that such a scheme would bring the unity intended. Thus the Scottish home rulers continued to be a most conservative group not much removed in their basic allegiance from the Liberal Unionists.[76] In December 1893 the *Scots Magazine* established a regular feature entitled "The British Federalist" to provide information and discussion about the resolution of United Kingdom difficulties. Its Scottish home rule originators frankly stated their belief "in the devolution of powers to subordinate legislatures with executive authority" and claimed "for each of our four nationalities the common right to legislate for the Empire that belongs to none, but to all."[77]

Throughout 1894 the "British Federalist" section in the *Scots Magazine* addressed a variety of issues pertinent to a redistribution of governmental powers. One of the first questions to be confronted was whether by "federal" they did not in fact mean "devolution." The response was fudged. Too much importance, it was argued, could be attached to "mere names." This was not a particularly satisfactory or enlightening answer.[78] In February Bernard Harden argued eloquently on behalf of "Home Rule All Round" or "Federal Home Rule" as clearly superior to home rule for Ireland, but John Boyd Kinnear poured cold water on the idea, pointing out that England would never agree. He suggested trying to work the existing constitution. In June and July discussion focused on an actual "Victorian Constitution Bill."[79]

In addition to the efforts of individual commentators and supportive magazines, the issue was kept alive by the persistence of Scottish and Welsh home rulers in the House of Commons. On 3 April 1894 Henry Dalziel (Kirkcaldy) introduced a motion in favour of a Scottish legislature "as a practical solution of the difficulty that had arisen through the neglect of Scottish business in the House of Commons." He went on to assert that, in general, the House was too preoccupied with the discussion of local matters. The ideal solution would be "Home Rule all round." He was supported by Augustine Birrell

(Fife, W) who argued that in addition to the neglect of Scottish affairs, "the interests of the Empire were almost entirely over-looked." Herbert Lewis (Flint) took the opportunity to remind the House that Wales should be included in any scheme of home rule all round, for its affairs had also been neglected by an overburdened parliament. He pointed out that Wales, despite arguments to the contrary, was a nation and its population of sufficient size to warrant a distinct legislature. Although the Scottish and Welsh ideas were quite conservative, Balfour was scathing in his remarks. He pointed out that home rule all round would result in "a revolution in our affairs," and he considered it "absurd" to approve a motion that would sanction a fundamental change in the constitution. Despite Balfour's dismissive comments the motion passed 180–170.[80]

A year later Dalziel reintroduced the home rule all round motion that had been debated in 1891 and 1892.[81] Dalziel admitted there was not the same passionate zeal in favour of home rule in Scotland as existed in Ireland but argued that the congestion in parliament and the neglect of Scottish and Welsh business necessitated that "local – and by local he meant national – opinion should as far as possible govern and determine the settlement of purely domestic affairs." He called for the establishment of four legislatures in the four divisions of the United Kingdom "subordinate to the Imperial Parliament." Lloyd George (Carnarvon) seconded the motion, but first he made it clear that Wales "did not want to set up a separate and independent Republic. They did not want an army and navy." They wanted local assemblies to look after local matters. Congestion of business could be remedied by conferring "upon each nationality in the kingdom a Parliament of its own for the discussion of questions affecting it exclusively." He "supported the principle of Home Rule all round, because he believed that it would foster the spirit of local patriotism."

John Redmond (Waterford) did not think either Dalziel's or Lloyd George's speeches had been equal to the magnitude of the subject: "The proposal amounted to nothing short of the entire revolution of the present constitution of this kingdom." In the abstract, Redmond favoured federalism but he pointed out that in England there was no demand at all for a federal arrangement nor was the demand for home rule in Scotland or Wales very urgent or pressing. In fact, Welsh opinion was more concerned with Welsh disestablishment than anything else. Redmond particularly disliked Ireland being placed on the same footing as England, Scotland, and Wales. Ireland was "an entirely exceptional case." Ireland could not wait until public opinion in England, Scotland, and Wales was ready for home rule all round. Home rule to Ireland meant more than getting private bills through the imperial parliament; it meant "the restoration to Ireland of that national Government of which she was robbed by force and fraud." Although he believed in the principle of federalism, he believed it would be a serious injury to the cause of home rule for Ireland "if it were now complicated by coupling with it the demand for the creation of local assemblies for England, Scotland, and Wales." Nevertheless, in granting home rule to Ireland "care ought to be taken that Home Rule should be conceded to Ireland in such a shape and form that it would be possible to fit in afterwards with a complete system of federalism for all these islands." He did not believe for a moment that federalism in the United Kingdom was in the range of practical politics.[82]

Again the critics, of whom there were many, cited the lack of detail behind the proposal. Balfour, in particular, referred to the "ineffaceable air of unreality" of the debate. Did anyone seriously think five executives and five separate representative assemblies would be approved by the people of the United Kingdom? Balfour firmly believed "this federation ... is not a step, and cannot be made a step, in the direction of drawing together closer the Colonies to Britain itself, but as a step for destroying that centre around which the Colonies must crystallize if the British Empire is to remain united." The idea could "have no practical issue" and was "intrinsically ridiculous." The motion was lost 128–102.

Three months after this debate, in June 1895, the Rosebery government was defeated in the House. A new Unionist administration was formed under Salisbury's leadership and was overwhelmingly endorsed in the July election.[83] The Unionists were in power for ten years and during that time home rule for Ireland and home rule all round were impossibilities. At first the Scottish and Welsh home rulers continued much as before to publicize their ideas. Lloyd George initially took the view that it was idle to expect imaginative legislation for Wales as long as England dominated law-making. Parliament had neither the time nor the inclination to attend to the wants of Wales and Scotland. For that reason he maintained all their energies for reform should be concentrated "in one great agitation for National Self-Government."[84] In October 1895 he argued in the magazine *Young Wales* that the only solution was "Federal Home Rule" by which "each nationality would have a Parliament of its own to deal with its peculiar affairs, and return members to the Supreme Parliament to dispose of Imperial concerns. It strikes me therefore that the surest and speediest method of attaining Irish Home rule is by the advocacy of a simultaneous extension of the same boon of self-government to all the four nationalities constituting the United Kingdom." He also stated his belief that if Irish membership of the House of Commons had been conceded before second reading in 1886 instead of a year later, many Liberals might have been retained in the party, the Liberal rout might have been averted, and "a practicable scheme of devolution might have been formulated and Home Rule might have now been an accomplished fact."[85]

Lloyd George continued to campaign for home rule all round during the next three years but he did so with less fervour after the opening months of 1896. In January 1896 his efforts to create a single Welsh Liberal Federation were rebuffed by powerful interests in South Wales who were opposed to Welsh home rule. Two months later, on 24 March, he called a meeting of the Radical Committee of the Liberal Party to consider the desirability of making home rule all round a plank in the Radical platform. The meeting was attended by fifty-six MPs among whom were Haldane, Henry Dalziel, Dr Clark, Augustine Birrell, John Leng, Henry Labouchere, and Charles Dilke. Although most supported the idea in principle, they believed the moment inopportune given the shattered Liberal fortunes and the overwhelming majority of the Unionists. For the time being, they decided to shelve home rule all round as a primary Radical concern.[86] Increasingly Lloyd George devoted his energies to the wider British political stage.

The Welsh home rulers made one final effort to arouse interest before finally conceding the impossibility of their dream. On 15 March 1898 J. Herbert Roberts (Denbighshire, W) moved that "a large measure of self-government" should be devolved "upon bodies representative of the different parts of the United Kingdom." His main reason for recommending home rule all round was congestion in parliament but he was not as coherent as he might have been in making his point. For example, he argued that "the question of the delegation of legislative powers and the devolution of certain powers of the Public Departments must go hand in hand." Clearly Roberts did not fully appreciate the difference between delegation and devolution. Haldane agreed that "there must be some considerable devolution to local bodies in the country of powers of self-government" and he was "not prepared to put any limit upon this devolution," but he found the motion vague. Moreover, there was little demand. For example, in Scotland the sentiment of nationality "so far remains dormant and quiescent, and has not yet assumed political form. What we have to deal with in Scotland at present is a business problem as to how we are to transact our own affairs more efficiently than at present." The same would seem to be true in Wales. Most MPs agreed there was no "urgent necessity" and that, in fact, the whole issue was in rather a "backwater." Only a few such as Campbell-Bannerman and John Dillon were prepared to support the principle of devolution and self-government.

Balfour, as usual, was the most penetrating in opposition. He thought the debate "of a purely academic interest," "premature in its character," and "entirely misplaced," for it was not one between Unionists and home rulers but between two sections of home rulers. Moreover, to talk of an extension of local self-government was false; the proponents were asking for an "absolutely new departure ... setting up new elective bodies to carry out great legislative operations." To Balfour the whole idea was "absurd." Redmond underlined the point that neither the Scots nor the Welsh had put forward any emphatic demand for home rule whereas the Irish had. He, for one, would never vote for home rule all round in advance of Irish home rule. The latter had to come first. Before the debate could continue the House was counted out. That was the last debate in the House on the subject of home rule all round for over ten years.[87]

This desultory discussion emphasized as perhaps nothing else could the lack of interest in home rule all round in all parts of the United Kingdom. For some months after the election of 1895 the Liberals had persuaded themselves that one of the reasons they had been so badly defeated was their failure to push home rule all round sufficiently strongly in Scotland and Wales.[88] Even Rosebery had continued to urge the Welsh to push the idea of home rule all round,[89] but by 1898 Rosebery had decided that the Liberal party would not benefit at the polls if it retained a full-scale commitment to home rule. He believed that the dissolution of the Liberal-Irish alliance provided the opportunity for the party to reconsider its position. Moreover, the passage of the Irish Local Government Act of 1898 provided an opportunity for Ireland to be governed from the base rather than from the summit. He thought it "obvious that this great experiment must be allowed time for development, and that it cannot soon or hastily be encumbered or overshadowed by an Irish parliament or any analogous body." But "more than that it may be said that British constituencies would not permit such a course." He concluded that the Liberal party "must form a fresh Irish policy" based on "complete independence of the Irish alliance," the acceptance of the Irish Local Government Act, and an awareness that "the condition of the world requires the closest concentration and economy of power in a State." Questions relating to Irish government would, therefore, have to be approached "cautiously and tentatively." All this, argued Rosebery, did not imply "the permanent exclusion of Home Rule in some form or another from the contemplation of Liberals, but it does imply perfect freedom of action, great caution in legislation, and (growing at any rate and naturally out of the Local Government Bill) a dramatically different method of approach."[90] The step-by-step approach favoured by Rosebery became accepted Liberal policy and Irish home rule and its relatives, home rule all round and federalism, were placed on the political back-burner. In October 1899 they receded further from the thoughts of most politicians and publicists when war broke out in the Transvaal between the Boers and the British. For three years attention was riveted on South Africa.

Since 1886 home rule all round had been a continuing, if minor, issue on the political stage and discussion of it had broadened the nature of the constitutional debate in the United Kingdom. Despite the undoubted concern among Welsh and Scottish home rulers, there had been little effort to provide detailed constitutional or financial schemes for discussion and many of the knotty constitutional problems had not been fully aired or solutions suggested. The primary cause of concern had been parliamentary congestion and it was rare to come across a reference to Welsh and Scottish nationalism as a secondary, let alone a principal, motive. Most home rulers would have been satisfied with a devolution of powers to local legislatures. A few would have been content with no more than administrative devolution. None wanted to endanger the unity of the empire. Federalism in its pure form was rarely suggested even though the term was used interchangeably with home rule. Home rule all round was the preoccupation of minor politicians and committed theorists. It was rare for leading politicians to take part in public discussions on the platform or in the House. That Arthur Balfour did so was a reflection of his own deep-rooted antipathy to any scheme that might lead to the disintegration of the United Kingdom and hence the empire, no matter how far-fetched that scheme might be or how thin the support from within and outside the political community. Since there was patently little demand for change in Scotland and Wales, and virtually none in England, it was unnecessary to mount a big political offensive in opposition. The proponents of home rule all round or federalism were mainly conservative and imperialist in their thinking. Their opponents made easy pickings of the arguments. It was not until the development of a serious constitutional crisis in the second decade of the twentieth century that home rule all round and federalism emerged once more as topics for debate. They were then to be taken far more seriously, even by Balfour.

CHAPTER FOUR

Devolution, 1900–1909

Over the next ten years there was a marked diminution of activity on behalf of either home rule all round or federalism. The Unionists won the 1900 election and on Salisbury's retirement in 1902 Arthur Balfour became prime minister. There was little likelihood that Balfour, even under great pressure, would have seriously considered any scheme of devolution, but there was no such pressure. For the moment, the Irish home rule movement was quiescent and the Welsh and Scottish organizations had lost heart. The Liberal party, led since 1899 by Campbell-Bannerman, was understandably cautious. Rebuffed twice by the electorate it was anxious to do nothing to alienate its chances of regaining office. The Liberal imperialists, particularly Asquith, Sir Edward Grey, and R.B. Haldane, ensured that the step-by-step approach to home rule became the party line. As late as the election of 1906, when it had already formed a government in the aftermath of the fall of Balfour's administration, home rule was not specifically identified as a goal of the Liberal party.[1]

Despite this official lack of party interest there remained an undercurrent of discussion and pressure on the sidelines of political life. A few men long committed to the cause continued to publish articles, make speeches, write letters to the editor, and generally lobby hard for both devolution of Irish affairs and home rule all round. One of the Scottish Liberals remained particularly active. J.A. Murray Macdonald was a longtime devolutionist who had sat in the House for Tower Hamlets in the early nineties. Like so many other parliamentarians he had grown increasingly concerned about the congestion of business in the Commons, not only because of the impact it had on the handling of Scottish and Welsh affairs but also because it interfered with any possibility of achieving closer imperial union. Although not himself an advocate of imperial federation, Macdonald appreciated the need to strengthen the British empire at a time of increasingly acute economic, military, and naval competition. He reasoned that the imperial parliament at Westminster should be free to get on with the vital task of dealing with foreign and imperial affairs. In a reflective article in the May 1901 issue of the *Contemporary Review*, Macdonald called for home rule all round "on the ground that the attempt to conduct the strictly local business of the United Kingdom and the business of the Empire by one Parliament is fast breaking down. The injury to the interests of the State caused by the inadequacy of our present governmental machinery to the work it has to perform is every year becoming more obvious, and will, as the years go by, unless the remedy is devised, become more and more serious." It was essential, Macdonald argued, for imperial and local interests to be discussed and dealt with separately. If there was to be any chance of drawing the self-governing colonies into the conduct of imperial affairs, "local legislatures with power to deal with local interests in the three parts of the United Kingdom" would have to be constituted.[2]

Macdonald's linking of domestic and imperial affairs was not unusual. The relationship of home rule all round to a wider imperial federation had often been made by advocates of constitutional change. In the late nineteenth century it had never received much serious attention and Gladstone had peremptorily dismissed any suggestion that he should tie some form of devolution within the United Kingdom to any broader imperial scheme. By the turn of the century, however, the situation was somewhat different. The United Kingdom was under severe pressure from the protectionist policies of its major rivals, while its own policies in South Africa had aroused considerable international criticism. It seemed important to many observers of the imperial and domestic scenes to preserve Britain's status and stature on the world's stage. To do so it would be necessary to streamline the conduct of imperial affairs and, if possible, to associate the self-governing colonies with the mother country in the discussion and formulation of policy. Some imperial unionists favoured closer cooperation on defence and trade matters, while others preferred a more strictly political integration. Increasingly after the turn of the century the relationship of the United Kingdom to its self-governing colonies became a matter of public debate fuelled by the federation of Australia in 1901 and the closer union movement in South Africa. If the Australian and the South African colonies could agree to resolve their major differences and join together in an Australian federation and a South African Union, why could not an equivalent step be taken at the imperial level? Joseph Chamberlain's tariff reform campaign of 1903–6 and the gradual formalization of the colonial conference system after 1902 were but two of the more obvious reflections of this concern over the empire's future. It was only natural, therefore, that after 1900 many of the individuals and organizations interested in home rule all round approached the resolution of United Kingdom difficulties from a decidedly imperial perspective. Even more than their counterparts of the eighties and nineties the advocates of devolution before 1914 had, of necessity, to be sensitive to the imperial dimension. From now on, Irish, Scottish, and Welsh needs and demands would be increasingly confronted by men with experience of empire and aware of its needs.

One such individual was Thomas Allnutt Brassey, the wealthy only son of the first Earl Brassey. He had been born in 1863, educated at Eton and Balliol, and since the mid-eighties had worked actively on behalf of imperial union. He had been editor of the *Naval Annual* since 1890 and in 1900 had been first acting civil commissioner of Pretoria. Most of his efforts had been connected with the work of the Imperial Federation League where he had supported Lord Rosebery. Initially a Liberal, Brassey stood four times for parliament, on each occasion making imperial union a central part of his platform. A man of strongly developed social conscience, he found his views on socio-economic questions readily accepted by Liberals, but many of those same Liberals found his commitment to a strengthened empire and his lifelong work for imperial union difficult to accept, and by the early 1900s the Unionist party seemed his more natural home. His study of imperial problems and his conviction that the empire could maintain its strength only through union led him to an equally passionate conviction that devolution within the United Kingdom had to go hand in hand with imperial federation. Only when the imperial parliament was freed of the myriad local issues it was obliged to consider could proper attention be given to the crucial imperial and colonial issues of the day. Although not a prominent political figure or a widely read publicist, Brassey was well known and respected in imperial circles. He wrote soundly and succinctly and put the case for home rule all round, or federalism as he preferred to call it, as well as anyone.[3]

Brassey had championed the interlinked causes of imperial federation and home rule all round since the early nineties. In 1890, on being asked to stand as a Liberal in Sussex, he had pointed out to his mentor, Lord Rosebery, that he put federation before everything and was not prepared "to work for Home Rule apart from Federation." He preferred to stand as an Independent Liberal rather than as a Gladstonian. He explained that he believed there should be both an imperial parliament and a United Kingdom parliament plus local parliaments for England, Scotland, Wales, and Ireland as in the Dominion of Canada.[4] Brassey repeated these arguments often and publicly throughout the nineties but he did not fully develop his ideas until the turn of the century.[5] By 1901 he was convinced that "the adoption of a Federal form of government is becoming absolutely necessary both for the United Kingdom and the Empire." Home rule did not mean separation either from Great Britain or the empire: "It meant the right of Ireland to manage her own domestic affairs in her own way; but it did not mean, as has been sometimes thought, the grant of the same powers of self-government as those conferred with such beneficial results on the great self-governing colonies." Under home rule the relations of the Irish parliament to the parliament of the United Kingdom would be similar to those of the Canadian provincial parliaments to the Dominion parliament and the Australian state parliaments to the Commonwealth parliament. Ireland's geographical position would preclude placing her in the position of a self-governing colony such as New Zealand. The experiences of 1886 and 1893 had convinced Brassey that it was "impossible to devise a satisfactory measure of Home Rule for Ireland alone." It would have to be approached from a broader standpoint.

Brassey believed that under a scheme of federal government by which England, Scotland, Wales, and Ireland would have local legislatures, the difficulties experienced in devising a satisfactory measure of home rule for Ireland would disappear: "These local legislatures would deal with the special interests of each country, leaving to the existing Parliament (probably with some reduction in the number of members) the management of questions which are of common interest to the whole of the United Kingdom, and all Imperial business, until the time arrives for establishing a true Imperial Parliament, with colonial representation." Brassey wanted the Liberal party to adopt this policy as the main plank in its platform and as a remedy for one of the chief features in the political situation, "the congestion of business in Parliament." He believed the business of both the United Kingdom and the empire would be carried on much better once it was specialized.[6]

In order to promote his cause, Brassey was instrumental in founding the Federal Union Committee to carry on propaganda in favour of home rule all round. A memorandum drafted by Brassey was sent to every Liberal MP, agent, and association in the United Kingdom, and during the two years, 1901–3, of the committee's active life meetings were held up and down the country at which the following resolution was always moved: "That in order to relieve the congestion of business in Parliament, and to give speedier and fuller effect to the domestic requirements of the several nationalities constituting the United Kingdom, and as a necessary step towards Imperial Unity, it is urgently desirable to devolve upon Legislatures in Ireland, Scotland, Wales, and England respectively the management and control of their domestic affairs."

One who joined Brassey in his endeavours to persuade the Liberal party to adopt home rule all round as official policy was Murray Macdonald, but when Rosebery was approached he demurred. He explained his and his party's position to Brassey: "I love your singleminded patriotism, industry and energy. But experience and adversity have made us cruelly practical, and I doubt if the Liberal Party, bled almost to death as it is, can undertake to reconstruct the British constitution. But you may be quite sure that no drop of cold water shall fall on your project from my heedless hand." Although Rosebery appears to have been true to his word, the task that Brassey, Macdonald, and the committee had set themselves was a hopeless one. The memorandum and the resolution attracted a certain amount of attention and comment but home rule all round did not become official Liberal policy.[7]

In November 1902 Brassey carried his campaign into the Royal Colonial Institute where he gave a paper on "Steps to Imperial Federation" in which he argued that the establishment of a federal form of government for the United Kingdom was an essential preliminary to imperial federation.[8] He advised the adoption of a scheme similar to Canada's. "Not the least of the advantages of the establishment of Federal Government in the United Kingdom," argued Brassey, was "that it affords a solution of the institutional difficulties in granting self-government to Ireland alone." As usual, Brassey simply advocated a solution; he did not go into detail about particular schemes. He thus left the impression that he really meant federalism when he used the term, but in fact it became clear later that what he had in mind was an undivided not a coordinate sovereignty within the United Kingdom. He was a devolutionist not a federalist despite his use of the Canadian and Australian analogies.[9]

By early 1904 Brassey had come out in support of Joseph Chamberlain's tariff reform campaign and at one point planned to stand as a tariff reform candidate in the Rye Division with a pledge of allegiance to the Conservatives. His imperial interests had finally taken him completely out of the Liberal party. This shift, however, did not undermine his commitment to devolution in the United Kingdom. Within months he had pledged support to Lord Dunraven's Irish Reform Association and by early 1905 he was speaking often in Ireland in favour of federalism.[10]

Windham Thomas Wyndham Quin, 4th earl of Dunraven, was born at Adare, County Limerick, in 1841 and it was there he made his home in adult life. A passionate sailor, he had competed for the America's Cup in 1893 and 1895. Earlier his sense of adventure had taken him as a war correspondent to Abyssinia in 1866 and to Paris in 1870. He had spent the winter of 1870–1 at Versailles and had been present when the king of Prussia was proclaimed German emperor in the Hall of Mirrors. He travelled extensively in North America in the 1870s and had shot wapiti and buffalo in the Platte River country during the Indian wars with the famous scouts "Buffalo Bill" (William Cody) and "Texas Jack." In 1876 he published *The Great Divide* recounting his experiences. In 1885–6 he served as under-secretary for the colonies in Salisbury's first administration and was reappointed on the formation of the second but he resigned in 1887, convinced that the government had been unfair to Newfoundland over the "French shore" question. Dunraven had been an active opponent of Gladstonian home rule and in 1886 he had been selected by Earl Grey to move the rejection of the home rule bill if it reached the House of Lords. *The Irish Question*, the first of his many pamphlets on Irish affairs, appeared in 1880. His attitude to home rule softened over the years and by the turn of the century he would have been considered a moderate.

Dunraven owned over 16,000 acres of land in Limerick, Kerry, and Clare and, naturally, as a major landholder, he was concerned about British land policies in Ireland. By 1902 a new land agitation had broken out and the Unionist government was under pressure to resolve the problems. A young Galway squire, John Shawe Taylor, suggested in a public letter a conference between representatives of the landlords and the tenants. George Wyndham, the chief secretary for Ireland, and the Nationalist leaders supported the idea but the ultra-conservative Irish Landowners' Convention rejected it. Lord Dudley, the viceroy, made it known that he favoured the suggestion, and a group of landlords led by Lord Dunraven polled the lieutenants and deputy-lieutenants of Ireland on the question and found 103 favoured a conference while only thirty-three were opposed. Eventually four landlords, of whom Dunraven was one, were nominated to meet with the tenants' representatives. When the conference met for the first time, Lord Dunraven was chosen chairman. Under his guidance a unanimous report was adopted recommending a policy of land purchase. The report became the basis of the so-called Wyndham Land Act of 1903 which established that all Irish landlords should be bought out allowing tenants to become the owners. [11]

This was a great success for Dunraven and it prompted him and some of those actively involved in the resolution of the land problem to see whether they might not be able to solve the political problem facing Ireland and Great Britain by similar means of compromise and conciliation. As a result a circular advocating such an approach was distributed in March 1903 by five members of the Landlords' Land Committee. This particular group had no party ties and no Nationalist members but it was viewed with suspicion by the official Unionist body, the Landowners' Convention. It was, in fact, a group of moderate Unionist landowners and its actions were quite unprecedented. In August 1904 the Land Committee was formally dissolved and reconstituted as the Irish Reform Association with Dunraven as president.

At this stage, Dunraven was not altogether clear what he wanted. He admitted to William O'Brien, the Irish Nationalist, with whom he had worked closely during the land negotiations, that the Gladstonian solution of an independent parliament had seemed impracticable to him in 1886 and still did. To Dunraven, Irish representation in the imperial parliament was a necessity. If home rule meant no representation then he was opposed to home rule. But short of that form of home rule Dunraven's mind was "fairly open and unprejudiced. I look for considerable devolution of power in the United Kingdom to relieve the Imperial Parliament ... My mind is open to consider any practical scheme affecting Ireland though I am not prepared to formulate one." [12]

The preliminary report of the association was published on 31 August 1904. It stated the members' belief in "a policy of conciliation and goodwill, and of reform." They wanted to do everything in their power "to promote a union of all moderate and progressive opinion, irrespective of creed or class; to discourage sectarian strife and class animosities, from whatever source arising; to cooperate in recreating and promoting industrial enterprises, and to advocate all practical measures of reform." The statement continued:

> While firmly maintaining that the Parliamentary Union between Great Britain and Ireland is essential to the political stability of the Empire, and to the prosperity of the two islands, we believe that such Union is compatible with the devolution to Ireland of a larger measure of local government than she now possesses.
>
> We consider that this devolution, while avoiding matters of Imperial concern and subjects of common interest to the Kingdom as a whole, would be beneficial to Ireland, and would relieve the Imperial Parliament of a mass of business with which it cannot now deal satisfactorily, and which occupies its time to the detriment of much more important concerns. In particular, we consider the present system of financial administration to be wasteful and inappropriate of the needs of the country.
>
> We think it possible to devise a system of Irish finance whereby expenditure could be conducted in a more efficient and economic manner, and whereby the sources of revenue might be expanded. We believe that a remedy for the present unsatisfactory system can be found in such a decentralization or localization of Irish finance as will secure to its administration the application of local knowledge, interest and ability without in any way sacrificing the ultimate control over the estimates presented, or in respect of the audit of money expended at present possessed by the Imperial Parliament. All moneys derived from administrative reform, together with whatever proportion of the general revenue is allocated to Irish purposes, should be administered subject to the above conditions.
>
> We think that the time has come to extend to Ireland the system of Private Bill Legislation, which has been so successfully worked in Scotland, with such modifications as Scotch experience may suggest, as may be necessary to meet the requirements of this country.[13]

The report met with a mixed response. The *Irish Times*, an arch-defender of the union and a protector of Unionist interests, reserved judgment but not surprisingly other Unionist papers were hostile from the start. They saw the proposals as "home rule by instalments."[14]

In order to develop the preliminary report into a more definite scheme, Dunraven sought the help of Sir Anthony MacDonnell, the under-secretary for Ireland, who was familiar with the aims of the Reform Association. MacDonnell was already under suspicion among Unionists who believed him favourable to home rule because his brother, Dr M.A. MacDonnell, was a member of the Irish Nationalist party. Sir Antony was Irish and a Roman Catholic and had had a distinguished career in the Indian Civil Service before becoming under-secretary on Wyndham's recommendation in 1902. When approached by Dunraven, MacDonnell had no hesitation in lending his assistance. He had often discussed Irish affairs on reform lines with Wyndham and in fact on 10 September he wrote to the chief secretary referring to the assistance he was giving Dunraven.[15]

Sir Anthony and Dunraven spent two days together in Kerry going over the details of a further report. On 26 September 1904 that report was published outlining the program of the Irish Reform Association. The report recommended that control over Irish expenditure, approximately £6,000,000 a year, should be transferred from the Treasury to an Irish Financial Council. Power to raise revenue would remain with parliament as would the duty of collecting it unless parliament chose to delegate that power to the council. The decisions of the council could be reversed only "by the House of Commons on a motion adopted by not less than a one-fourth majority of votes." The exact composition of the council should be carefully considered but it was suggested that the lord lieutenant be president, the chief secretary vice-president and ex-officio member, while twelve members should be elected by amalgamated groupings of county and borough council constituencies and parliamentary constituencies and a further eleven nominated in order to ensure "due representation of the Government, of commercial interests, and of important minorities." One-third of the members should retire at the end of the third year but would be eligible for reelection and reappointment. The report suggested three possible ways the council might obtain the necessary revenue and then turned to the devolution of power to deal with Irish business. The adoption of a Private Bill Procedure Act for Ireland similar to the one in effect for Scotland was considered essential and could not longer be properly denied. But that reform would not be enough in itself. The special needs of Ireland would still not receive adequate attention. "Sufficient relief cannot, in our opinion, be afforded by mere amendment in the standing orders of the House of Commons. Some delegation of authority is necessary. We believe that power to deal with much of the business relating to Irish affairs which Parliament is at present unable to cope with might, with perfect safety, and with advantage both to Ireland and Parliament, be delegated to an Irish body to be constituted for the purpose."

The report suggested delegation of the business with which parliament was unable to deal to a statutory body composed of Irish representative peers and members of the House of Commons, representing Irish constituencies, and permanent members of the Financial Council. This extra statutory body was to have authority to promote bills for purely Irish purposes and to deal with whatever other business was prescribed to it. The report ended with the recommendation for the appointment of a royal commission to investigate the whole subject.[16]

To use Dunraven's words: "The scheme was a modest one. It gave Ireland some control over finance, some incentive to economy and wise and frugal administration: and it gave her some delegated legislative powers. The grants were small and very strictly limited, but held the promise of larger concessions – of development on sound and safe lines." Dunraven hoped moderates in both parties would support it, that the bill would pass, and that once the government saw it working well more and more legislative and administrative functions would be transferred to Ireland "until by degrees Ireland would have full control of her own affairs."[17]

It was the latter goal that Unionists most feared and that made their inordinately hostile reaction to the proposals explicable. The scheme was attacked by both Unionists and Nationalists; on the one hand because it seemed an advance toward home rule which was despised and on the other because it did not go far enough and recommend an Irish parliament. It had fallen victim, as inevitably any similar scheme would have, to the vicissitudes of Irish politics. It pleased neither one side nor the other. The response of the Unionist party was immediate. On 27 September George Wyndham published a letter in the *Times* saying the scheme had come as a complete surprise to him. He repudiated it, disclaiming all knowledge of its genesis. He completely disagreed with the institution of a statutory legislative assembly for Ireland: "Upon that I have to say without reserve or qualification that the Unionist Government is opposed to the multiplication of legislative bodies within the United Kingdom, whether in pursuance of the policy generally known as 'Home Rule for Ireland' or in pursuance of the policy generally known as 'Home Rule all round.'"[18]

That was the end of that particular devolutionist venture. The uproar led eventually to the resignation of Wyndham, his replacement by the more conservative Walter Long, and deepening suspicion in Unionist circles of the English-dominated political parties, which in turn led to the establishment of the Ulster Unionist Alliance. MacDonnell was censured but not compelled to resign, so he did survive to play a part in future schemes of devolution. The whole affair was in many respects based on an unfortunate misunderstanding. If MacDonnell had not misread Wyndham's attitudes and if Wyndham had not mislaid MacDonnell's crucial letter of 10 September, it is arguable that MacDonnell either would not have advised Dunraven in the manner that he did in September 1904 or would have intervened before the report was published. The affair ended Wyndham's political career and blighted the moderate cause in Ireland. It was a severe jolt to the hopes of men such as Dunraven who had been encouraged by developments over the Land Act to further pursue the paths of compromise and conciliation.[19]

Murray Macdonald and Brassey had watched the development of events in Ireland with fascination, and both were quick to take advantage of the heightened interest in devolution. On 15 September Macdonald wrote to the *Times* repeating his earlier call for the adoption of "Federal Home Rule" in the United Kingdom in order to relieve congestion, to extend self-government, and as a stepping-stone to imperial union. On being criticized for his views in a *Times* editorial, Macdonald replied at length in a letter published on 19

September. It undoubtedly struck a responsive chord with both Dunraven and Brassey. His words were a succinct summary of the ideas and attitudes of the majority of those, including Dunraven and Brassey, who wanted to streamline the British constitution.

Macdonald admitted that there would be some difficulty in establishing a demarcation between local and imperial issues, although he thought the worst problems would arise over the division of taxing powers. Nevertheless, he suspected that the critics of "federalism" had misunderstood his position and that of the other advocates of devolution. They were not separatists. They believed in the preservation of the Union. They were also not true federalists, for they believed in the continued supremacy of the imperial parliament. Their intent was simply to make the empire more efficient and thereby stronger. Macdonald pointed out:

though for convenience we loosely use the words "federal" and "federation" in relation to suggested changes in the machinery of our Constitution, no one has ever suggested that we should in these changes follow the lines of a true federal system. The very reverse is the case. The Imperial authority, under any scheme of devolution would be the delegating authority, and would remain, after the delegation had taken effect, as absolutely and as completely supreme as it had been before. And it would exercise its supremacy in two ways ... first ... it would retain the right of refusing assent to measures passed by the Colonial Legislatures ... second ... the Imperial Parliament can never by any act of its own deprive itself of concurrent legislative power on any matter within the legislative jurisdiction of the National Legislatures; and from the very nature of the case no Act of a National Legislature could be filed in any Court against an Act of the Imperial Parliament ... The Imperial authority ... would be absolutely unfettered in its power of determining whether any action of a National Legislature interfered with Imperial interests, and of dealing with that action either by legislation or by administration, or by both as freely and as fully as Imperial interests required. [20]

Dunraven, who had been at pains to point out that his purpose was to secure for Ireland control of its own affairs compatible with both the maintenance of the Union and the supremacy of the imperial parliament, would have been delighted by Macdonald's statement. Brassey certainly was. He had been a firm supporter of Dunraven's land reform activities in the belief that with the "Land Question settled the main objection to the grant of self-government to Ireland is removed; and the way will be there for the establishment of Federal Government in the United Kingdom somewhat on Canadian lines." [21] Despite his use of the term "Federal," it was clear that Brassey did not have coordinate sovereignty in mind. His aim was devolution of power to "subordinate legislatures." He rejected Gladstone's quasi-independent bodies. He could see no difficulty for any imperialist or Unionist in supporting a scheme such as that proposed by Dunraven's Reform Association. To him it was a positive step towards a better understanding of devolution.[22]

Dunraven appreciated the backing he received from Brassey but by early 1905 he was well aware that his venture had failed. As he put it to MacDonnell, "Devolution does not go. It will not move, in my opinion, until after an election. The immediate difficulty is to keep it alive." He recognized that the idea attracted more attention in England than in Ireland and he was anxious to get support across the Irish Sea, "perhaps through the medium of the all round devolutionists" such as Brassey and Bernard Holland.[23]

Dunraven worked hard over the next two years to keep the issue alive. He published both pamphlets and books elaborating the merits of devolution. He made it clear that he was "a landlord, a Protestant; and a Unionist" who still held firm to his "class ... creed, and ... political faith." To his mind, "Ireland should be proud of her distinct nationality, and should cherish and develop it; but that she should also take pride in what in a sense may be called a larger nationality - the honourable share she has in the government of the United Kingdom, and in the conduct of the great Empire of which the United Kingdom is the centre." Dunraven did not believe in an Irish republic, in repeal, or in Gladstonian dualism. He did not even believe in an early adoption of home rule all round. Ireland had to be taken care of first. But it could only be taken care of by the application to Ireland of the two principles which had been applied so wisely in the empire: first, "the reservation to ancient communities of their distinctive characteristics, usages, laws, languages, and governing powers," and, second, "the devolution or delegation of power to new and developing communities." For Dunraven the one failure of the British empire - Ireland - was due to the negation of these two principles. He made it clear that he was not arguing against the union but, quite to the contrary, believed that a close union had to exist between the two islands. Great Britain was Ireland's market and would ever be so. Moreover, Ireland was too small and too poor to stand alone. She required the backing of a great power and a great empire. If she were to stand alone the position would be intolerable: "These narrow seas cannot contain two independent states, and Great Britain is perfectly justified in safeguarding herself." Dunraven refused to accept that there was "no middle course between severing the connection between Great Britain and Ireland and administering Irish affairs by means of a vast number of irresponsible Boards irresponsive to the wishes of the people and ignorant of the needs of the country." There clearly was a middle course and that was the devolution of certain legislative and administrative responsibilities to a subordinate parliament.

Real reform [wrote Dunraven] in the system of Castle Government must proceed on one of two lines - either on the line of federation, as exemplified, for instance in the relation between the Dominion and Provincial Governments in Canada; or by devolution, such as, for example, may be found in the relations between the central and Provincial Governments in India. Federation might be the best line to work upon; but federation, if it ever comes, will come as part of a very much larger measure of an Imperial character, and, in the meantime, Ireland cannot wait. Federation is also open to the objection that, obviously, repeal must precede it, and repeal in my opinion, is quite below the horizon of practical politics.

That left devolution, and it was the method favoured by Dunraven and the Irish Reform Association.[24]

Despite Dunraven's efforts his ideas were given short shrift by most commentators, who went out of their way to underline the difficulties involved in implementing any such scheme. Many critics ignored all his assurances and accused him of recommending a scheme which would inexorably lead to the violation of parliamentary sovereignty and the disintegration of the empire. Dunraven was prepared for debate over his ideas but it must have been galling to be accused of treachery to the union. After all, his scheme was designed to preserve the tie between Ireland and Great Britain and, in fact, was an exceedingly conservative proposal. The degree to which he separated himself from the nationalists was underlined by the ready support he received from men like Brassey and MacDonald, both of whom were interested in strengthening the empire and protecting the supremacy of the imperial parliament. These men wanted above all else to maintain intact both the United Kingdom and the empire. They simply believed that such unity would be more readily assured if the legitimate need for self-government of the Irish, Scots, and Welsh was accommodated, so that the union did not fracture from within. Although Dunraven, Brassey, and MacDonald did not have much support in the Unionist party in 1904–6, the essence of their position came to be more fully appreciated and their ideas more widely espoused once the constitutional problem reached an acute form after 1909.[25]

The activities of Dunraven and the Irish Reform Association may have made a stronger impression on the Liberals than on the Unionists. Although it may not have convinced them of the merits of Dunraven's particular proposal, the devolution campaign of the previous two years had at least sufficiently alerted Liberals to Irish demands that by early 1906 they were formally exploring the possibility of introducing some form of devolution.

The Liberals had formed a government in December 1905 on the fall of the Balfour administration and the ensuing election of January 1906 confirmed them in office under the leadership of Campbell-Bannerman. The election had not been fought over home rule, the Liberals were not dependent on Irish Nationalist votes, and the step-by-step policy still held sway in the party. Nevertheless, there was considerable speculation about the policies the new government would adopt toward Ireland. In November 1905 Campbell-

Bannerman had fuelled that curiosity by offering Ireland "an instalment of representative control" that might "lead up to" home rule. What this meant was unclear but it was well known that Campbell-Bannerman had supported both home rule and home rule all round in the eighties and nineties. John Redmond, the leader of the Irish parliamentary party, immediately warned the Liberals that a rehash of the Dunraven scheme would not be acceptable to the Irish party, but once he was assured that a larger scheme was planned he gave his party's support to Liberal candidates. After the new government assumed office, Sir Anthony MacDonnell, still under-secretary for Ireland, was asked once more to work on a devolution scheme.[26]

MacDonnell sent his first draft to the new chief secretary, James Bryce, on 3 February 1906. Despite Campbell-Bannerman's assurances it was partly based on Dunraven's earlier proposal. There was to be an executive council of thirty members; twenty elected indirectly by delegates from the county councils and ten nominated by the lord lieutenant. The council would simply "advise and assist" the government of Ireland. The supremacy of the imperial parliament would not be jeopardized. Financial administration would be delegated to the council for a five-year period subject to a contract drawn between the Treasury and the Irish government. The police and the high courts would be outside the council's jurisdiction. In forwarding his "outline of Irish Constitutional reform" to Bryce, MacDonnell underlined certain features:

You will perceive that (1) it maintains the unity of Parliament, and its full supremacy over Irish affairs; (2) it is essentially a development of the existing system of Local Government in Ireland; (3) its immediate aims are (a) to co-ordinate and bring under a reasonable measure of popular control, all the Departments of Government now working in Ireland without radically changing the constitution of any (except the Education Department); (b) to confer on the Irish Government such control over Irish expenditure as will enforce efficiency and economy; (4) it subjects the action of the Irish Government to the constant scrutiny and control of the House of Commons if it desires to exercise it; (5) ... it supplies an effective check on hasty or ill-considered action by the Council; and (6) by excluding the higher Judiciary and the Police from control of the Council it furnishes sufficient safeguards for Law and Order.[27]

It was clear that the council was to be little more than an administrative body. It bore a closer resemblance to Joseph Chamberlain's "central board" scheme of the 1880s than it did to Dunraven's subordinate legislature. It was hardly likely to appeal to the Nationalists but, at the same time, was sufficiently different from the *status quo* to attract the jibes of the Unionists who would view it as a step toward home rule.[28]

Although the scheme had been hatched in great secrecy for fear of the reaction of the Nationalists, MacDonnell did mention it to Redmond in February 1906. Redmond had asked if it was Dunraven's and MacDonnell had replied "only in part." Redmond had then reasserted that "of course the Nationalists

could accept no such scheme as a satisfaction of their claims." A half-elected
and half-nominated council would be unacceptable. MacDonnell hoped two-
thirds elected would satisfy them. He pointed out to Bryce that while his own
scheme proceeded on the same lines as Dunraven's, "so far as concerns the
decentralization of finance," the administrative ideas were new. He believed
that "The wisest men among [the Irish parliamentary party] know that this
Devolution scheme will satisfy the wishes of a large mass of Irishmen: and
they hesitate for that reason to touch it." MacDonnell did not think Dunraven
should be associated with the new scheme.[29]

Since he knew Redmond's concerns, it should not have surprised Mac-
Donnell as much as it apparently did to hear Redmond declare in October
that he would fight any "cramped and halting scheme."[30] When Redmond was
finally shown the cabinet proposal two days later, he considered it "beneath
contempt."[31] At further meetings throughout October between Redmond,
Dillon, and Bryce, the Irishmen made it clear that they wanted all the Irish
MPs to sit as the Irish council. Bryce could not accept that.[32]

By mid-November three leading members of the Irish parliamentary party,
Redmond, Dillon, and T.P. O'Connor, had drafted a "Memorandum on the
Constitution of the proposed New Administrative Body to be set up in
Ireland."[33] In forwarding the memorandum to Edward Blake, Redmond
revealed his exasperation: "The Irish administration of Mr. Bryce is lamen-
table in the extreme. He is absolutely under the domination of our friend Sir
Anthony, and ... the latter is every day giving further evidence that he is inclined to utterly disregard popular opinion and the views of the representatives of Ireland."

The Irish leaders disliked the council scheme. It did not include direct
popular election which to them was a fatal omission, and the proposed body
would have no working majority to carry out the wishes of the majority of
the Irish people. Redmond, Dillon, and O'Connor would not support the
proposal unless it could clearly be seen as a step in the direction of a "larger
policy." The scheme also failed to give a working majority to the representatives of the Nationalist movement. The Irish leaders therefore suggested
that the new council be composed of the Irish members of the House of
Commons, together with such a number nominated by the lord lieutenant
so as to give the minority a strong representation while leaving a working
majority to the representatives of the great majority of the Irish people. As
one of their advisers had pointed out, the scheme as it stood did "not bear
upon its features a single sign of trust in the people." It was a scheme not for
representative but for bureaucratic government.[34]

Edward Blake also found the scheme objectionable:

This would be not merely the non-concession of self-government, but the denial
in the directest form of our right to any effective self-government; and our first work
would have to be, not to build on the foundation or enlarge the superstructure, but

to tear down the edifice erected by professedly friendly architects. This would in truth, be an added obstacle to Home Rule set up by professed adherents ... a great part of free government is *administration* ... The more limited for the time being the legislative power to be exercised in Ireland, the more necessary in order for any improvement, however slight, in the constitutional position, become the essential elements of effective *administrative* Home Rule, comprising executive or administrative officers responsible for their acts to a popular elective body. Without this nothing substantial is accomplished.[35]

The memorandum prepared by Redmond, Dillon, and T.P. O'Connor, which was sent to Bryce on 3 December, clearly and firmly stated that "the original proposal for the Constitution of the New Council is Absolutely *Impossible*."[36] A few days later Dillon wrote separately to Morley reiterating the concern and frustration of the Irish leaders:

We are much oppressed by a gentleman of whom you know who moves in an Indian atmosphere quite aloof from the fact of the situation in Ireland and who is incurably convinced that he understands Irish politics better than any of us. This idea appears to me to be to break up the Irish party machine and dominance in Irish politics and get a kind of Indian Council composed of that favourite abstraction of amateur solvers of the Irish problem – non-political business men – and so turn Ireland into a loyal peaceful country very subservient and manageable, purged of politics, and devoted to the breeding of pigs and the making of butter.

I daresay MacDonnell's intentions are excellent but his lights are Indian and therefore so far as Ireland is concerned, they are will o the Wisps.[37]

In the midst of these crucial negotiations in early 1907, Bryce resigned to become the British ambassador to the United States. He was replaced by Augustine Birrell who had the difficult task of picking up the pieces strewn about by MacDonnell and Bryce. A cabinet committee composed of Birrell, Asquith, Grey, Haldane, Lord Crewe, John Burns, Lloyd George, and Morley began meeting in February and initially proposed to reverse the scheme in the light of Redmond's and Dillon's criticisms. MacDonnell was most unhappy with the enlarged powers suggested and objected strongly. The committee then had second thoughts and in March met to consider papers prepared by Birrell and MacDonnell. Gradually MacDonnell's more conservative position won the day and by early May the details of the bill had been settled. The council scheme was much improved over the initial proposal. There were to be eighty-two elected and twenty-four nominated members with the under-secretary an ex-officio member for a total of 107. Over three-quarters of the members were now to be elected but the direct conversion of Irish MPs to membership of the council had been rejected. Moreover, the lord lieutenant remained a political appointee with considerable powers to initiate executive action.[38]

Augustine Birrell introduced the Irish council bill in the House of Commons on 7 May. In doing so he went to some lengths to reassure the Unionists from whom he expected a hostile reception. He pointed out that the bill did not contain "a touch or a trace, a hint or a suggestion, of any new legislative power or authority." The imperial parliament would "remain majestically unaffected by the provision of this Bill." The object was simply to associate directly the Irish people with the administration of Ireland. Nevertheless, he did admit that if after a few years' fair trial the council was a success "it may pave the way to Home Rule."[39] Predictably, Balfour was not mollified by Birrell's assurances. He found the council to be an extraordinary proposal which would satisfy no one whether Nationalist, Ulsterite, or Unionist.[40] Redmond was understandably very cautious. The bill was an improvement on the early draft but the scheme was not home rule and would not be accepted as a substitute for home rule. He reminded the House that good government could never be a substitute for self-government. Although Redmond could in conscience vote for the bill as a step towards home rule, he well knew that many of his colleagues were dissatisfied. He made it clear that he would be bound by the decision of the Nationalist convention in Dublin on 21 May.[41]

There had been surprisingly little comment in the press or in the periodical literature in the run-up to the introduction of the bill, but once it was published the response was immediate and for the most part critical. The Nationalist press was overwhelmingly hostile, while the Unionist response was aptly summarized by the *Edinburgh Review* which referred bitingly to the various Liberal efforts at devolution as "The Separation Bill of 1886; the General Confusion Bill of 1893; the Constitutional Monstrosity of 1907."[42] Even the Irish Reform Association did not think the bill went far enough, for it excluded any powers of a legislative character and the financial proposals were not only inadequate but were likely to cause difficulties. Dunraven himself thought the scheme very modest. It was even less ambitious than Chamberlain's proposals of 1885–6, and he could not see how the passage of such a bill would be deemed injurious to the union.[43] In Ireland the bulk of both the priesthood and Irish lay opinion was opposed as were the majority of Irish MPs, county and district councils, and boards of guardians.[44] Aware of the depth of antipathy in Ireland and realizing the necessity of preserving the credibility of the Irish parliamentary party, Redmond moved the rejection of the council bill at the party convention on 21 May. The motion was unanimously endorsed. Two weeks later Campbell-Bannerman informed the House that the government would proceed no further with the bill in the light of its rejection by the convention.

The Unionists were delighted at the abandonment of MacDonnell's devolution scheme. Even Birrell was not too distressed. The bill had never been enthusiastically supported in the party and Birrell himself had considered it a mistake to touch devolution. The Liberals should have contented themselves with land reform and the university question and left MacDonnell "in the lurch."[45] Needless to say, this episode concluded MacDonnell's influence. He had no more impact on the Liberals and left the under-secretaryship in July 1908. His hope had been to replace the extreme Nationalist and Unionist elements with a moderate group of businessmen independent of various political, agrarian, and clerical pressures. But he had gravely misread his own influence and had ignored the fact that devolution, in any form, was unacceptable to the Nationalists except as a clear step toward home rule and was completely unacceptable to Unionists other than Dunraven's small and uninfluential group.

Over the next two years Dunraven and MacDonnell continued to lobby for devolution. In 1909 MacDonnell prepared a memorandum for both the Irish Reform Association and the Imperial Home Rule Association with a view to promoting their cooperation in the pursuit of Dunraven's policies. MacDonnell argued that home rule was unlikely in the foreseeable future, while if home rule all round was a desirable goal, as many appeared to believe, then Ireland could help its attainment by leading the way. Only devolution offered hope of immediate progress. He called for the creation of an Irish authority with administrative and legislative functions subordinate to the imperial parliament.[46] In the prevailing climate of opinion, MacDonnell's plea fell on deaf ears. Dunraven would have to wait for a more appropriate moment to sound his views.

Since the turn of the century the discussion and promotion of devolution had taken place almost exclusively in the context of Anglo-Irish relations. Scottish and Welsh interests had rarely been mentioned by MacDonnell and Dunraven whose primary concern was always Ireland. Brassey and Mac-Donald had faithfully mentioned home rule all round as a desirable goal but their concern to broaden the discussion to include the imperial dimension had of necessity prevented them from delving too far into the particular needs and interests of Scotland and Wales. After 1900 the Scots and the Welsh had initially done little to draw attention to their constitutional concerns. Even in the heyday of the Scottish and Welsh home rule agitations of the eighties and nineties there had been limited public interest in Wales and no passionate and deep-rooted determination even in Scotland. Now the Welsh were preoccupied with disestablishment and had no interest in the transfer of Irish home rule to Wales. The Scots remained almost equally uninterested, although the *Scottish Patriot* did publish articles in 1904 and 1905 favouring "Federal Home Rule" in the United Kingdom and also helped to found the Scottish National League in 1904 to promote both Scottish home rule and imperial federation.[47]

The Scottish Home Rule Association became more active after the Liberals won the election of 1906. Only two months after the Liberal victory the association sent a letter to all MPs urging the new government to introduce a scheme of home rule all round which would "give to each nation of the United Kingdom perfect control of its own affairs," thus freeing the House of Commons to do "its legitimate work – namely, controlling finance and governing the greatest Empire the world has ever known."[48] This was followed by the introduction of a Government of Scotland bill on 14 June 1906 which attained only a first reading.[49]

Within a few months of the Liberal accession it became startlingly clear to the government and to all interested in home rule and home rule all round that the Unionists were going to use their dominance of the House of Lords to frustrate the Liberal legislative program. Annoyed by the defeat of legislation of great interest to Scotland, the Scottish Home Rule Association intensified its campaign. On 26 May 1908 the Government of Scotland bill was reintroduced by Pirie. Although it met with the same fate as in 1906, it generated far more comment and support in Scotland.[50] By November 1909 the *Thistle*, a strong supporter of Scottish nationalism, called for the establishment of a Scottish National party, for "When there is a Scottish National Party in the House of Commons of say twenty-five members, these joined to the seventy Irish and thirty Welsh members could compel the selfish and reluctant English members to do justice to Scotland, Ireland and Wales. Then, and then only, when we get Home Rule all Round, can we have a happy and a United British People!"[51]

That same month, November 1909, the House of Lords rejected Lloyd George's budget, thereby setting in motion a major constitutional controversy. During the next five years home rule, home rule all round, and federalism were to get a thorough airing as politicians, publicists, and political theorists wrestled with the problem of reforming British constitutional practice. Macdonald, Brassey, Dunraven, and Scottish and Welsh nationalists were all actively involved in the debate.

CHAPTER FIVE

Constitutional Crisis, 1910

The most concentrated and intense discussion of devolution, home rule all round, federalism, and federal home rule took place during the years 1910-14 at a moment of acute constitutional crisis. The elections of January and December 1910 did not give the Liberals a clear-cut victory and in order to ensure the passage of the budget and of legislation restricting the power of the House of Lords they were obliged to rely upon the support of both Labour and Irish Nationalist MPs. The need to obtain support from the latter group raised again the whole issue of home rule which had lain relatively dormant since the 1890s. Home rule was unpalatable to most Unionists and a number began to espouse the cause of federalism in the United Kingdom as a means of keeping the country united. Scottish and Welsh home rulers were annoyed by the government's seeming indifference to the wish of Wales and Scotland for greater local or regional autonomy and they began to push for home rule under the guise of home rule all round. The Liberal government was not unaware of the latter pressure and it did seriously discuss devolution in a United Kingdom setting. Many individuals both inside and outside parliament, some of them long-committed federalists or devolutionists, began writing and speaking on the subject with greater intensity, attempting to put pressure on both the Liberal government and the Unionist opposition.

During the years 1906-9 the Liberals had not had to give serious attention to Irish home rule and certainly not to home rule all round or federalism. The Irish council bill had been severely limited in intent and had never been seen as anything more than an expanded local council scheme. It had been confined to Ireland and the Liberals had given no thought to Scottish and Welsh concerns. With their overwhelming parliamentary majority the Liberals had at last been able to escape the burden of the home rule issue and concentrate primarily on social and economic reforms. Despite this incentive and an imaginative program the Liberal government was stymied in a good deal that it attempted by the unwillingness of the Unionist-dominated House of Lords to pass bills approved overwhelmingly by the Commons. Although this was undoubtedly a legal stance, it was not in the spirit of the constitution. In 1906 the education bill and a plural voting bill were killed by the Lords. In 1907 a small holdings bill for England and an evicted tenants bill for Ireland were passed by the Lords but in mutilated form and a small landholders (Scotland) bill and a land values (Scotland) bill were killed. These actions led to the passage in the Commons in 1907 of a resolution introduced by Campbell-Bannerman, the prime minister, calling for restriction of the powers of the Lords. Ignoring this warning, in 1908 the upper house defeated the licensing bill and on 30 November 1909 it killed the Lloyd George budget which had passed the Commons on 4 November. This was considered by the Liberals and most observers as a breach of the constitution. An election was called for 12 January 1910. The major issue was the House of Lords veto.

It was clear that the Lords was prepared to use its veto to kill any scheme that threatened the entrenched position of its members in British society. There could be no doubt that it would be quickly used to kill any form of home rule bill. As long as the veto power remained home rule was an impossibility. It was therefore understandable that the Irish Nationalists were anxious to see that power reduced, or, if possible, eliminated. Asquith, who had become prime minister in April 1908, knew only too well that there was no guarantee of a Liberal victory in the January election. To ensure the greatest possible success for Liberal candidates and to lay the groundwork for a future alliance, Asquith in his opening speech of the campaign at the Albert Hall on 10 December 1909 deliberately included a pledge that his party was prepared to return once more to the championing of home rule. He declared that the Irish problem could be solved "only in one way, by a policy which while explicitly safeguarding the supremacy and indefectible authority of the imperial parliament, will set up in Ireland a system of full self-government in regard to purely Irish affairs." Although the government had been prevented during the years 1906–9 from seriously considering any such solution, "in the new house of commons the hands of a Liberal government and of a Liberal majority will be entirely free."[1] Since Asquith had never been, and was never to be, an ardent home ruler, this overture was little more than a pragmatic political gesture designed to perpetuate the Liberals in office.

Nevertheless, Redmond, Dillon, and T.P. O'Connor, the principals in the Irish parliamentary party, could not have been more delighted. In the election the Irish stayed scrupulously clear of sure Liberal seats and where possible aided marginal Liberal candidates. When the votes were counted the Liberals had won 275 seats; the Unionists 273; the Irish Nationalists 82; and Labour 40. That left the Liberals seemingly dependent in the House on either the support or the abstention of the Irish members. Since it was certain Labour would not support the Unionists and highly unlikely that Redmond and his colleagues would vote against the Liberals on key issues, the Liberals may have had more discretion than they realized. Nevertheless, most observers and most Liberals assumed the government was now dependent on the Irish in the House of Commons. That would mean securing Irish support for a bill either to curb the Lords' veto power or to reform its constitution. In return, a home rule bill would certainly have to be introduced. The Irish position was firmly stated by T.P. O'Connor in a letter to Dillon at the end of January 1910: "Our policy is quite clear ... go straight ahead and do what we think right, fight through thick and thin with the liberals until we get the veto question tackled and settled, and then ... get them to propose home rule immediately or break with them"[2]

After considerable discussion between the Irish leaders and members of the Liberal cabinet as to the procedures to follow, and in what order, a parliament bill curbing the Lords' veto power was given first reading on 14 April.[3] Four days later Lloyd George's budget was introduced. It was passed in the Commons on 27 April and was approved by the Lords the next day. Although the Lords had accepted the verdict of the election insofar as the budget was concerned, they had not accepted the inevitability of legislation to curb the veto and they had certainly not accepted its corollary, home rule. It became increasingly likely that Asquith would have to ask the king to create additional peers in order to ensure the passage of the parliament bill through the upper house. Thus by the early spring of 1910 a major constitutional crisis had developed. It was in this tense emotional atmosphere that federalism and home rule all round began to be sounded once more as possible alternatives to home rule.

The first group to consider federalism seriously in 1910 was the Round Table movement. The movement had been founded in September 1909 after months of discussion among former members of Milner's "kindergarten," many of whom had played an important role in closer union activities in South Africa. During the years 1906–8 the kindergarten had wrestled with the various merits of a unitary or a federal form of government for South Africa and although much attracted by the federal idea had finally supported a unitary system. One member, Lionel Curtis, had been instrumental in founding the Closer Union societies and had largely drafted the famous "Selborne Memorandum" which had been a crucial catalyst in bringing the four colonies to the conference table. Another, Philip Kerr, had edited *The State*, a quarterly devoted to publicizing the advantages of union. When South African union seemed assured, Curtis and Kerr turned their attention to imperial affairs and were soon convinced that an organization similar to that founded in South Africa should be formed to deal with the union of the empire. Curtis, for as always it was he who took the initiative, had little difficulty in interesting other members of the kindergarten, particularly Milner, Geoffrey Robinson (later

Dawson), Patrick Duncan, Lionel Hichens, Richard Feetham, Fred Perry, George Craik, and Robert Brand, as well as such influential outsiders as Dr Starr Jameson, Lord Robert Cecil, F.S. Oliver, Leo Amery, Arthur Steel-Maitland, Edward Grigg, William Marris, and Lords Selborne, Wolmer, Howick, Anglesey, and Lovat. In meetings in late 1909 and January 1910 the movement defined its aims and mapped out specific objectives. Of paramount importance, of course, was the organic union of the empire and all the movement's activities in its early years in whatever field were related to that primary end. This was the manner in which the problems of home rule for Ireland, home rule all round, and federalism were approached over the next four years.[4]

One of the early associates and longtime supporters of the movement was Earl Grey, the governor general of Canada and an ardent imperial federationist. He had expressed the belief as early as 1907 that "Ireland may still redeem her past by providing the excuse for Imperial Federation ... the Irish question, and the House of Lords, and the discussion which will centre around them will I hope stimulate the processes of evolution, which will one day ... give us some form of organic union."[5] Discussions with Grey in late 1909 convinced Curtis of the interconnection of imperial federation and federation of the United Kingdom. The deadlock produced in the House of Commons by protracted discussion of essentially local or regional matters made it difficult for the imperial parliament to give appropriate attention to imperial affairs. The resolution of that problem would go a long way to making imperial federation a reality. In key meetings in mid-January at Ledbury and in South Africa in early March it was agreed to initiate a study of congestion of business in the Commons and to advocate the establishment of a royal commission to consider the "devolution of powers within the United Kingdom before any measure of Home Rule was accepted." For Curtis, in particular, the surest path to social reform and the proper handling of imperial affairs was the separation of the domestic affairs of the United Kingdom from international and imperial questions. Devolution or the establishment of separate parliaments, i.e., home rule all round, seemed the only logical solution.

Others in the movement were not as easily persuaded and there continued to be no agreed position on the interconnection of imperial federation and federation of the United Kingdom. Kerr concluded by late September that the federation of the United Kingdom was not a necessary stage to be passed before imperial unity could be achieved. The surrender of imperial functions could be made just as easily by a unitary parliament. Moreover, Kerr thought "federation" was a misnomer when applied to devolution in the United Kingdom. In any Round Table scheme the imperial parliament would always remain supreme and there would be no court to interpret the constitution. Nevertheless, for Kerr it was a good fighting word better than either devolution or home rule all round which had unfortunate associations in most Unionist minds. Certainly strong-minded Unionists in the movement such as Amery, Robert Cecil, and Steel-Maitland viewed home rule all round as the first step in the disintegration of the United Kingdom. This was anathema to them, particularly when it was unlikely that such a devolution of powers would lead automatically to imperial union. These arguments and ideas were mulled over in conversation and by means of widely circulated letters and memoranda throughout the spring, summer, and autumn of 1910, while the constitutional conference stumbled wearily closer to a break over Irish home rule.[6]

One man who had no doubts about the linkage between imperial federation and some form of home rule in the United Kingdom was Earl Grey. He was convinced that the empire's strength was directly related to Britain putting its internal house in order. After his conversations with Curtis in December 1909 he reiterated his belief that "Before the road is cleared for the Federation of the Empire we have to put the United Kingdom straight. The time is approaching, if it is not already here, for getting this work done ... Provincial Legislatures of the Canadian rather than the South African type for 1. Ireland 2. Scotland 3. Wales 4. England (4. North? 5. South?) with a Federal Parliament armed with powers of disallowance sitting in London. Each Provincial Unit to be represented in the Federal Parliament in proportion to its population ... When the Irish are thus reduced in the Federal Parliament of the United Kingdom to their proper proportions, we can begin to talk Imperial Federation."[7] During the next few months, and in fact throughout the prewar period, Grey was a zealous advocate of federation for the United Kingdom. After his return to England in 1911 he was often mentioned as a possible leader of a federalist party.

Once the January 1910 election results were clear, Grey was quick off the mark. He wrote to Arthur Balfour from Ottawa on 23 February:

To us over here it looks as if the time had arrived for the moderates of all parties to combine for the purpose of federalizing the U.K. I approach this subject not only as an Englishman, but as a Canadian.

The existence of 72 votes in the House of Commons alway on the watch how to impair the Empire is a danger which alarms every thoughtful and patriotic Canadian. To us out here the importance of cutting out the cancer out-tops the importance of all other questions. The Federalization of the U.K. wd restore the Irish Reptn in the Central Federal Parliament to fair proportions, without giving just ground for offence to Ireland, it wd transfer to England the sympathy largely felt on this side of the Atlantic both in Canada & the U.S. for aggrieved Ireland, & would also settle the question of the H of L. I suppose the Irish wd oppose federalization altho it is difficult to see how they cd do so logically – it is certain they cd not oppose it without forfeiting the sympathy now felt for them in the U.S. & self-governing Dominions ... I am aware that the federalization of the U.K. is a policy which can not be attained by a stroke of the pen.

It appears to me however a policy worth working for, & to be required in the interests not only of the U.K. but of the Empire. The Federalization of the U.K. must precede the federalization of the Empire.[8]

Grey had been keeping in close touch with the Round Table movement and in his letter to Balfour and in another written at the same time to J.L. Garvin, the editor of the *Observer*, he had raised the possibility of a royal commission being appointed to prepare a federal bill. Despite his willingness to intervene as best he could in British domestic politics, Grey's interest was primarily imperial. As he frankly put it to George Wrong, soon to be a leading member of the Canadian Round Table group, "My interest in the federation of the U.K. is based on a belief that the federation of the U.K. must precede the federation of the Empire."[9] Grey strongly believed that the existing impasse at Westminster was "the opportune moment for laying the foundations of a Federalist Party."[10] But as he told Brassey, his fellow federationist, he did not favour a parliament in Dublin which would rank with the dominion parliaments in Canada and South Africa. "My experience out here, and the home situation, have convinced me that the time has come for a serious attempt to federate the United Kingdom, but on the lines which will make Ireland, not into a Canada or Australia, but into an Ontario or Quebec." He envisaged a federation of the British Isles which would give "each portion of the United Kingdom provincial rights like those enjoyed by the Provinces of Canada." Grey was never more specific than this and on the face of it he would seem to be supporting a real federation as opposed to home rule all round, but given his association with the Round Table and the degree to which Dunraven was prepared to support him it is unlikely he desired a division of sovereignty. Grey told Richard Jebb, an expert on the relationship between Britain and the self-governing colonies, that he hoped "to see the Unionist Party take up seriously the question of the Federation of the U.K., which I regard as the foundation of future Imperial evolution."[11]

Jebb, a much respected commentator on imperial affairs, generally agreed that federation would provide a final solution to the home rule trouble and be a step towards imperial federation, but he had some concern about the details. He doubted for example that the dominions would ever wish to enter a United Kingdom federation as additional provinces. Moreover, the discussion over unification and federalism in South Africa had led Jebb "to think that perhaps, after all, the right solution for the UK would be some kind of consolidation of existing local-government divisions, with some enlargement of powers, rather than reconstruction on the federal basis with the three Kingdoms and Wales as the Provincial Units."[12]

While Grey was writing to all and sundry about his federal ideas, two other men, emboldened by success in the January 1910 election, entered the lists. William O'Brien was a prominent Irish Nationalist who had played an instrumental role in the resolution of the land problems in Ireland in the 1890s and early 1900s. He believed deeply in conciliation between Catholic and Protestant in Ireland and he had worked closely with Lord Dunraven in connection with the land problem. He and seven of his supporters had won seats in the House of Commons in the January elections and this had led O'Brien to found the All for Ireland League in March to work for union in Ireland with an inviolable guarantee of the security of Protestant rights and liberties.[13] He became a supporter of federalism because he believed it would aid in the resolution of Irish difficulties and draw the sides closer together. O'Brien did tend to inflate the importance and commitment of his devolutionist, Protestant, landlord friends but he nevertheless made his voice heard.

The second individual was Moreton Frewen, a member of the Anglo-Irish gentry, an uncle to Winston Churchill, and a man with business interests in America. Frewen had also been elected to parliament in January 1910 and generally supported O'Brien's ideas. But Frewen's concerns were less the resolution of Irish problems *per se* than the protection of capitalist and landlord interests threatened by both the Lloyd George budget and the projected parliament act. Frewen was responsible for organizing a League of the Federals in New York in mid-1910 and he actively sought funds in the United States to support a federal solution of United Kingdom difficulties, a solution that he believed would avoid a social revolution. His was essentially an antiradical campaign. He was driven by class and property interests rather than the larger visions impelling Grey and Curtis.

Shortly after arriving in the United States, in March 1910, Frewen wrote to his nephew, Winston Churchill: "Grey's Federal Home Rule will secure a vast endorsement. The Capitalists are saying that the log rolling between Redmond and Keir Hardie threatens the sentiment of property, as indeed it does, here no less than in England. Jump to safety young friend on the Federal Raft, but let me beg of you don't try and bring in your little Welsh "heeler." That won't do! We are determined that a few Welshmen must die for the Nation."[14]

Grey himself wrote to Frewen in early April: "I have heard privately from Arthur Balfour begging me not to make up my mind on the subject of Federation until I have had an opportunity of discussing the whole subject with him. He regards Federation as a means of organising separate communities into one organic whole, and is inclined to regard the proposal to federate the U.K. as tending in the direction of disintegration – as a retrograde step opposed to the teaching of history. He does not appear to appreciate the contention that the Federal government to be is an essential condition precedent to the Federation of the Empire."[15]

Grey was convinced that Balfour and Lord Lansdowne, the Unionist leader in the Lords, should commit themselves and the Unionists to federalism. It would guarantee the self-government that Ireland desired. Moreover, he was convinced there was money available in the United States for the party that favoured federation. Already, he claimed in May, Redmond's financial resources had been stopped primarily because of Frewen's activities. He believed £5,000 had been sent to O'Brien for federalist purposes and that Redmond, lacking funds, would be obliged to accept an offer of federation from a government led by Balfour. Grey feared that "Asquith, realising the altered character of the Irish situation may by some means or another constitute himself the Champion of Federation."[16]

As usual, Grey was much too optimistic. Although Frewen did succeed in attracting some financial support, it did not amount to more than £4,000 in 1910 and the flow was never sustained. Much of that money found its way to O'Brien to support his federal activities through the All for Ireland League. Only a few wealthy friends came forward. There was never widespread support in either the United States or the United Kingdom. By 1912 the American League of Federals had closed its account and the British League of Federals was defunct, while Frewen's attempt to organize a Federal Union League in 1913 and 1914 failed.[17] Committed combatants though they were, Frewen and O'Brien had limited impact on the overall discussion, and even Grey became increasingly marginalized.

In fact, by May 1910 William O'Brien was obliged to write in sober terms to Frewen:

I am quite with you that the Federal solution would be an excellent one, but even that form of Home Rule would, I am afraid, be too strong meat as yet for the Protestant Minority ...

Whenever our movement has reached a certain point of strength, the true way out of the situation would be a Conference for which *I know* men of the utmost importance on both sides are ready to take part. The Federal solution would be more than likely to be their united recommendation. For the moment, it is safer for us to insist upon the general principle of Domestic Self-government, leaving its form to be defined hereafter, as it can without much difficulty be.[18]

Another major advocate of federalism also took the opportunity to reenter the debate and to put pressure on his friends. In the spring and early summer of 1910 Thomas Brassey wrote extensively to leading Unionists trying to persuade them "to put forward Federal government on Canadian lines as the alternative to the Liberal Policy of destruction of the House of Lords and Home Rule for Ireland." Brassey believed that the major obstacle to a measure of self-government for Ireland was "the impossibility of devising a measure for Ireland only which gets over the difficulty as to the position of the Irish members in the Imperial Parliament and the fact that Englishmen have not yet thought of the need of Home Rule as applied to themselves." In particular, he thought O'Brien could help matters by indicating that he would be satisfied "with the power possessed by the Parliaments of Quebec and Ontario." That would, Brassey believed, have an effect on English opinion.[19] Brassey was anxious to persuade Walter Long, the prominent Unionist, to put forward the idea and he wrote and talked to him often on the subject. In addition to pointing out to Long that a scheme of home rule all round or devolution[20] would relieve the congestion of business in parliament, solve the Irish question on the only lines it could be solved, enable tariff reform to be carried at once, and solve the House of Lords issue by removing questions of purely domestic interest from the control of the Lords to subordinate legislatures, Brassey emphasized that it would "remove much of the support which Socialism and Socialistic measures receive in the House of Commons from Irish, Scotch and Welsh members (who in most cases are certainly not Socialists)."[21]

By mid-April even Milner, a most reluctant devolutionist, admitted to Balfour that

I feel we are in for Home Rule in some form, but it makes the whole difference, whether it is provincial Home Rule – ie. Ireland to the United Kingdom like Quebec to the rest of Canada – or National Home Rule, ie. Ireland like Canada, virtually quite independent of the rest of the United Kingdom. I don't suppose the Unionist party can go in for Home Rule in any form, but, if it comes in spite of us, not much harm would be done by Provincial Home Rule. It is Ireland like Canada, which would be so dangerous and so disintegrating. But I don't believe the Irish themselves will want Canadian independence, if they can have a preference in the British market over all comers, including Canadians & Australians.[22]

Thus far much of the discussion and lobbying had taken place against a background of uncertainty and in isolation from the political arena, but by 14 April the parliament bill limiting the power of veto of the Lords and shortening parliamentary terms to five years had been given first reading. It was now clear that home rule would likely follow the passage of a bill limiting the Lords' obstructive power. Then on 6 May King Edward VII died. In order to save the new king, George V, from an embarrassing and difficult constitutional crisis in the first weeks of his reign the Liberal and Unionist parties agreed to a truce and to a conference in order to see if a solution could be found to the problems facing them and the nation. The first meeting of the constitutional conference was held on 17 June.[23] A lengthy interval for the summer recess began on 28 July and meetings did not resume until 11 October. For a few months the efforts of the imperial unionists-cum-United Kingdom federalists took a back seat to Scottish and Welsh arguments which, not surprisingly, surfaced in the late summer and early autumn of 1910 in a form paralleling the aims if not quite the intensity of the 1890s.

After the surge of interest in Welsh and Scottish home rule in the 1880s and 1890s there had been a decided slackening of activity and only sporadic attempts to draw attention to the political aspirations of Wales and Scotland. The new interest in Welsh devolution was stimulated by a middle-aged industrialist, Edward T. John, who was to become Liberal MP for East

Denbighshire in December 1910. Through John's efforts devolution was given a fairly wide play in Wales over the next decade and contacts were established with certain of the Scottish home rulers.[24] As for the Scots nationalists, they had been amazed and frustrated by the declared intention of the Liberals to give home rule only to Ireland and not to Scotland and Wales. One writer thought the Liberals had bowed in the face of violence and political exigency. He argued that Scotland and Wales were every bit as deserving of self-government as Ireland.[25] In early August the Scottish National Committee, composed of Scottish Liberal MPs, issued a manifesto calling for devolution for Scotland as well as Ireland. The Scots wished to establish some form of "representative control over Scottish affairs in Scotland, a principle which, if applied to the different parts of the United Kingdom, would provide for a true expression of the will of each nationality in respect of its own affairs, leaving the Imperial parliament free to transact the business of the Empire." The call was a moderate one but the need was clear and the Scottish Nationalists called for general support.[26]

Three days after the publication of the Scottish manifesto, E.T. John wrote to the *Manchester Guardian* in support. He wanted the adoption of "Federal Home Rule" with four separate bodies dealing with purely local and regional matters with a single supervisory chamber "consisting of peers and Commoners *all* elected, the main charge of which body would be the Imperial interests of the entire British Commonwealth, and whose interference with domestic affairs of the four nations would only arise where the general well-being was likely to be prejudiced." He suggested that the more aggressive Welsh MPs cooperate with the Scottish Nationalist members and jointly come to an understanding with the Irish party. John believed the political salvation of Wales lay in that direction.[27]

During the next two months, E.T. John broadened his campaign. On the initiative and with the advice and assistance of Beriah Gwynfe Evans, a longtime promoter of Welsh home rule, John's letter was translated into Welsh and placed in many Welsh papers while English copies were sent to the English papers.[28] In addition, John was anxious to establish contact with the Scottish Liberal MPs who had recently issued their manifesto. In August he wrote to H.A. Watt, one of the honorary secretaries of the Scottish National Committee, and suggested a joint committee of Welsh and Scottish members: "My personal judgement is that Federal Home Rule could readily be demonstrated to be as beneficial and advantageous to England as to the other parts of the United Kingdom ... Is there any possibility of a joint committee of Welsh and Scottish members meeting to formulate a detailed scheme? In this matter I am convinced that the strength of our proposals will lie in the details thereof."[29]

W.H. Cowan, the second honorary secretary of the Scottish National Committee, replied on 16 August 1910. He was favourably impressed by John's proposal that Wales should cooperate with Scotland "in demanding the control

of her purely local affairs." Cowan also agreed with respect to federal home
rule and England: "We must recognise ... that up to now there has been no
demand for Home Rule for England and it seems to me that the most
promising line of action will be to organise as rapidly and effectively as
possible the strong current of opinion which undoubtedly exists in Scotland
and I imagine also in Wales in favour of Devolution." Cowan agreed with John
about four separate parliaments for England, Scotland, Wales, and Ireland
and with his idea that both peers and commoners should be eligible for election to such bodies, but he disapproved of only a single-chamber imperial
parliament to represent the entire British Commonwealth, including eventually representatives from all the self-governing colonies. Cowan thought
the imperial parliament should have two houses each to be elected by the
people of the empire. He believed that "we should quite unnecessarily estrange
many Federal Imperialists by advocating single Chamber government."[30]

Another Scotsman, H.G. Reid, had also read John's "timely and telling
letter on Devolution for Wales." He believed it was "the only solution; it would
enable each part of the Empire to manage its own affairs with knowledge, and
relieve the Imperial Parliament to discharge efficiently its ever-increasing
obligations."[31] In mid-August he wrote: "Would one could help in this new
departure of *Federated Self Government* – avoid the tainted 'Home Rule' if
possible. What is wanted for Wales is an enthusiastic and eloquent Welsh MP
to make the movement *his one cry* as Thomas did for Disestablishment and
Lloyd George did in his early and devolutionary days ... Scotland is so absolutely self-governed that it is, alas! difficult to awaken general interest in
the movement. The best pamphlet was written long ago by the Marquis of
Bute."[32]

Despite Reid's pessimism Cowan, for one, was determined to do what he
could. He had been in touch with E.W. Davies earlier and had suggested the
establishment of a committee in Wales parallel to the one in Scotland. Cowan
now suggested an informal meeting between the Scottish committee and
Davies's friends sometime between August and mid-October: "The Conference on the Constitutional question has probably been compelled to concern itself with the problem of Irish Home Rule and consequently with the
subject of Devolution generally. This, therefore, would seem to be an unique
opportunity for raising the whole issue of Federal Devolution for the United
Kingdom and the creation of a really 'Imperial' Parliament." He urged the
Welsh to become active as soon as possible.[33] Munro-Ferguson, the chairman of the Scottish National Committee, wrote in a similar vein to John on
1 September. He urged John to undertake the movement for devolution in
Wales. The first task should be to ascertain Welsh public opinion: "We can
then judge better how we can best cooperate."[34]

Three weeks later John invited the attention of all the Welsh Liberal
Associations to the movement in Scotland in favour of federal home rule "and
its bearing upon the interests of Wales."[35] He was successful in carrying a

resolution in favour of the scheme at a meeting of his local Liberal Association in Anglesey on 29 September but he failed with a similar motion at the Welsh National Liberal Council meeting on 20 October 1910.[36] Although John continued to push "Federal Home Rule" during the last months of the year, he had not accomplished all he had hoped by the time an election was called for December 1910.

While the Scottish and Welsh federalists were reorganizing, the constitutional conference reached a crucial stage in its deliberations. Provisional agreement had been achieved on finance bills and on a means of avoiding deadlock on other key issues, but not surprisingly Irish home rule was proving a stumbling block. The Unionists considered it to be of such constitutional and organic significance to the state that they wished it exempt from any special arrangements for the passage of bills.[37] By late July, just before the summer recess, it was clear that an impasse had been reached on this issue. The Liberals were not prepared to treat Irish home rule as a special category of legislation, whereas the Unionists would have it no other way. It was in this context that efforts to bridge the gap between the parties were made. The most suggested and widely debated solution was federalism or home rule all round. Discussion of this idea dominated both public and private efforts until November 1910.

The first initiative came from the new Liberal chief whip, the Master of Elibank. A few days before the conference adjourned for the recess he phone Harold Harmsworth, Lord Northcliffe's brother, and asked for his help in persuading the *Times* to take up the cause of federalizing the constitution by granting legislative powers to Ireland, Scotland, and Wales. Harmsworth willingly approached the editor, Buckle, but came away convinced that he did not understand the issues or appreciate the strength of feeling developing in Scotland. Harmsworth then spoke to J.L. Garvin on 29 July "with a view of inducing him to comment favourably on Federalising the Constitution." Two days later an article by Garvin entitled "The Mystery of the Conference. Mr. Birrell and 'Federalism'" appeared in the *Observer*.[38] The article commented on Birrell's speech of 25 July at the Eighty Club, in which the chief secretary, one of the conferees, made favourable reference to devolution or, as he put it, "federation beginning here at home" which would be a step towards a wider imperial federation. Although Garvin did not at this time come out in support of the federal idea, he did ask if there was not some "middle arrangement" between Gladstonian home rule and Dublin Castle administration that could be devised. He suggested that such moderates as William O'Brien, Tim Healy, Lord Dunraven, or Sir Horace Plunkett might be able to provide ideas. Since Dunraven and O'Brien were well-known devolutionists, Garvin's point could not have been easily missed.[39]

Over the next two months there was increasing public mention of devolution or federalism as a solution to the United Kingdom problem by highly placed figures in the Liberal and the Irish Nationalist parties. Speaking in Wales on 20 September, the Master of Elibank said: "Who knew but that in the evolution of government ... the time was not far distant when, as in the English-speaking Commonwealths across the seas, both Saxon and Celt, both Scots and Welshmen, might be called upon within our shores and under a party system to give free exercise to the genius of self-government with which Providence had so freely endowed them?" From the same platform Lloyd George had spoken of the day when Wales would be "independent and free." And Haldane on October 6 at Tranent had declared that "we might have to make considerable changes in the way of devolution, federal arrangements, and reform of the Councils of the Crown."[40]

Even John Redmond had apparently changed his tune. At Limerick on 11 September he had said: "We demand full executive and legislative control of purely Irish affairs. More than that we are not asking, and less than that we will never accept ... Devolution is as dead as a doornail."[41] But within the month Redmond had stated, to an American audience and to an American reporter, that the Irish Nationalists did not want to break with the British empire nor did they want self-government on the colonial model. "By Home Rule," he said, "we mean something like you have here, where Federal affairs are governed by the Federal government, and state affairs by the State government."[42] Similarly, Redmond's colleague T.P. O'Connor on 5 October had declared to the Ottawa Canadian Club, with Sir Wilfrid Laurier in attendance, that "his mission was to secure Canada's approval of a Federal scheme of Government for the four kingdoms of the British Isles, such as the provinces of Canada enjoy under a central government."[43] By the end of October both Redmond and Dillon had repudiated the reporting and said Redmond had been misquoted. It is more likely that Redmond had been subjected to pressure by wealthy but moderate Irish Americans who were prepared to divert funds to William O'Brien and his federal campaign and away from the parliamentary party unless Redmond toed the line.

Whatever had motivated Redmond and O'Connor, William O'Brien was not deceived and said as much to his backer Moreton Frewen: "Redmond's and T.P.'s declarations for Federalism I presume mean that they have paid that price for Burke Cochran's pecuniary assistance. It complicates the situation considerably. The advocacy of Federalism by the "Mollys" will destroy all chance of its adoption by The Times and by the minority in Ireland. But far the most serious matter of all is that their purse is again well filled ... Redmond after bagging his prize in America will no doubt recant his words when he comes back, under the lash of Dillon. As he recanted his former cable lauding Dunraven's Devolution scheme."[44]

Moreton Frewen continued to keep in touch with both Garvin and Balfour. He was particularly at pains to inform them of O'Brien's struggle in Ireland and the continuing need to support him financially.[45] He also passed on to

Balfour in September an interesting comment on federal precedents by Mackenzie King, then the minister of labour in the Laurier government. In King's words: "What is interesting too in connection with the present discussion, is that speaking of Ontario and Quebec (Upper and Lower Canada, as they were called) they united after Durham had issued his Report, and separated to reunite in a larger Federation in 1867. There is something worthy of consideration in this for England, Scotland and Ireland."[46] King's analysis was accurate and went some way to meet Balfour's long-held contention, no doubt influenced by Dicey, that federation or home rule all round meant disintegration of the United Kingdom. Clearly it did not have to mean that at all.

Earl Grey was of the opinion that Balfour had missed an opportunity: "He might have turned Asquith out at the beginning of last session, and if he had come forward boldly with the Federal plan of Home Rule all round, he would have lifted home politics into a loftier atmosphere, much to the advantage of every part of the United Kingdom and of the Empire." He dismissed the argument that such a policy was "a bid for place at the cost of principle," but he found Balfour's hesitation "a bit too thin-blooded and over-scrupulous. There is as great a difference between Gladstone's Home rule, which would have made Ireland into a Canada, and Federal Home Rule which proposes to give Ireland the status of a Province in a Federal Union; like that enjoyed by the Province of Quebec, in the Dominion of Canada; as between darkness and light." More revealing and perhaps more to the point:

Under our present constitution, the danger of spoliation in my opinion ought to be one of the strongest forces in favour of securing the acceptance of the Federal plan by Unionists. At present we have no security in England against confiscating legislation, but if a Federal Constitution were established, the opportunity would be provided for incorporating into our constitution, certain provisions which would prevent any property or right being taken away from any person except upon due compensation under law. Some provision is necessary if the English liberties given to us by the Magna Charta and the Bill of Rights, are to be secured.

Nevertheless, he admitted that a federal solution was only possible if both sides agreed.[47]

Others also recognized that crucial point and during October a concerted effort was made to persuade Balfour, and then the Unionists generally, to adopt federalism or home rule all round and thereby resolve the constitutional crisis and save the constitutional conference from foundering. The first, and probably the major, overture was made by Frederick Scott Oliver, a longtime friend and adviser of Unionist politicians. F.S. Oliver had published a biography of Alexander Hamilton in 1906 that had really been a brilliant plea for imperial union. The book had influenced Milner's kindergarten in South

Africa and had stimulated them to found the Round Table movement. With the formation of the movement in late 1909, Oliver soon became a close and respected confidant, and he attended all the key Round Table "moots" throughout 1910. He was completely on top of the various arguments in favour of United Kingdom devolution and its connection to the wider union of the empire. He had already played an important role in late May and early June, when under the guise of "Pacificus" he had called for a party truce in three letters to the *Times*. By late September, with the conference in danger of collapsing, Oliver took the initiative once more and drafted a memorandum entitled "The Conference and Its Consequences" which he sent initially to Austen Chamberlain and then to Balfour on 11 October.[48] In forwarding the memorandum to Balfour, Oliver warned him that Austen had found his ideas "*very* wild."

Oliver thought it would be disastrous if the conference failed. "It is of very great importance to give credit to this particular method of settling certain questions – the method of settlement by consent and mutual compromise, after confidential discussion between leading representatives of various parties." If Balfour were going to make an attempt at imperial union, the conference or convention method was the best. Oliver therefore suggested that the Constitutional Conference could advise the assembling of a representative convention "to consider the constitutional question as a whole" rather than simply the matter of the House of Lords. While the Unionist party could not, indeed should not, put forward home rule itself, it certainly could accept it "without dishonour or demoralisation for patriotic reasons ... if a representative Convention, after careful examination, were able to come to an agreement upon a set of proposals." "We could," argued Oliver, "honourably surrender something considerable for the sake of something of even greater imperial importance: as, for instance, for the sake of a constitutional settlement, and for the sake of ending a long and dangerous controversy, and also for the sake of bringing the hope of Imperial Union a stage nearer."

Although the grant of home rule to Ireland did not necessarily mean the grant of home rule to England, Scotland, and Wales, i.e., home rule all round, it did "obviously involve the creation of at least a single domestic Parliament for the United Kingdom to deal with the same set of subjects ... as those which would be allotted to the Irish Domestic Parliament." There would then need to be an imperial parliament to handle imperial affairs, in which Ireland and "the rest of us" would be represented proportionate to population. "This body, under the Federalist plan, would perform two distinct functions (1) It would bear the same relation to the Domestic Parliaments of the United Kingdom and of Ireland as the Dominion Parliament of Canada bears to the domestic legislatures of Ontario, Quebec, etc. and (2) the functions it discharges at present with regard to Imperial affairs." Logically, the second set of duties should be handed over to a "purely Imperial Parliament elected by the Dominions as well as by ourselves." Oliver did not think it necessary to con-

sider such a "visionary problem" at that time, for he doubted if there was yet
a substantial demand in Scotland and Wales for domestic parliaments of their
own.[49] Oliver strongly believed such a solution would best be reached by
means of a representative convention and that "the consequences would be
a gain for sanity." Closure, the destroyer of parliaments, might disappear, the
powers of caucus might be abated thereby restoring principles to the forum,
congestion in the House of Commons might be relieved, and cabinet government might be restored. As long as confusion continued in the United
Kingdom, it would be pointless talking to the other states of the empire about
union; they would "understand nothing clearly out of the babel." In mid-
October Oliver visited Whittingehame to discuss his ideas personally with
Balfour.

The conference resumed the day Oliver forwarded his memorandum to
the Unionist leader. But the knowledge that it might fail unless something
dramatic was done had already prompted Lloyd George to draft a memorandum calling for a coalition government composed of Liberals and
Unionists.[50] Dated the 17 August, it was shown to some of his cabinet colleagues and to Balfour and Garvin in the first two weeks of October at about
the time Oliver's memorandum was circulating.[51] Lloyd George actually gave
little space to Ireland or to devolution in this early draft. Under the heading
"Local Government" he said the whole system was unsatisfactory: "There are
too many Boards and there is no system of intelligent direction, such as is
provided by the Burgomasters on the Continent. Whilst there are too many
small Boards and Councils, there are too few large ones, and a good deal of
work is cast upon the Imperial Parliament which could be much more
efficiently discharged by Local bodies on a large scale." Despite its ambiguity
this statement clearly did not mean home rule all round nor did his suggestion, under the heading "Imperial Problems," that the Irish question would
benefit from nonparty treatment.

This memorandum was the basis for secret discussions between Lloyd
George and Balfour about a Liberal-Unionist coalition which were conducted
parallel to the latter stages of the constitutional conference. During these talks
Lloyd George departed from his own brief and placed increasingly heavy emphasis on the solution of the Irish problem by devolution or federalism. In
a memorandum dated 29 October, he suggested that "a settlement of the Irish
Question and of the difficulties of congestion in the House of Commons
[should] be attempted on some such lines as were sketched by Mr.
Chamberlain in his speech on the First Reading of the Home Rule Bill of 1886.
Ireland to be treated as a unit for the purpose of any measure of self-
government. This settlement should be of a kind which might form a nucleus
for the Federation of the Empire at some future date."[52] It would seem that
this latter memorandum reflected his arguments to Balfour.

Having been shown Lloyd George's memorandum, and aware of the
urgency of finding a solution to the crisis, Garvin wrote a major article,

published on 16 October in the *Observer*, entitled "The Crisis of the Conference. The Case for a Larger Settlement," in which he called for a more broadly representative conference to consider the pressing constitutional and fiscal questions of the day. In doing so he referred favourably a number of times to federalism while not actually advocating it himself.[53]

Garvin's article occasioned an immediate letter to Balfour from Alfred Lyttleton, the former colonial secretary in Balfour's administration. He had found there was "a very great sympathy with Local Federation among our younger intellectuals. I mention F.S. Oliver, Brand, Kerr, and Milner's Kindergarten, Milner himself and Garvin." Lyttleton suggested that a conference such as those held in South Africa in 1908–9 and in America in the 1780s might be the most appropriate setting to discuss such issues: "Whether the devolution proposals are or are not feasible – they are to many minds attractive and plausible and solvent of some great difficulties, and I dread the submission to the Electorate of the House of Lords question – never an advantageous one for us – to which would be added this devolution scheme in bare outline not criticised or fully understood in its weaker parts, with the adherence of all the Dominions and two of our own most important proconsuls, Grey and Milner, besides that of some of our best young men."[54]

Lyttleton's letter must have reached the Unionist leader only shortly before a similar missive from Garvin. The editor of the *Observer* sent Balfour a copy of his article and reiterated his plea for a settlement on possibly federal lines. Garvin was convinced the Unionist party had reached a turning-point and could no longer fight the battle of the Union on the old terms in circumstances that were utterly changed. "To me," he wrote, "the Second Chamber is more important than Dublin Castle." He pointed out to Balfour, as had Oliver and Grey, that a new and quieter Ireland existed now:

How then can we who have worked the economic revolution in Ireland say that we will not recognise the possibility of any Irish administrative change in the direction of limited self-government perhaps no more inimical to the parliamentary union of the United Kingdom – perhaps no less advantageous to it – than is the local autonomy of Quebec to the Parliamentary Union of Canada ... Thinking the present Dublin Castle system now untenable – some form of devolution inevitable – I cannot think it now impossible to frame a safe constructive compromise between the Gladstonian Home Rule which has perished ... and the old Unionist position which has now lost so much of its old basis ... Would not an Ireland under federal Home Rule send a solid majority of Conservatives to help defend in the Imperial Parliament nearly all we care for.[55]

These arguments were very similar to Oliver's and drew heavily, as had the 16 October article, on ideas and arguments contained in the letter of Earl Grey, now widely recognized as one of the leading advocates of a federal solution. The mounting pressure and the nature of the arguments must have given Balfour pause, especially when his faithful adviser and secretary, Jack Sanders, wrote to him on 18 October much in the vein of Garvin: "Is Home Rule exactly where it was? In other words is Home Rule – Parnellite Home Rule – the issue & nothing else? If the larger question of Federation is in any way a matter for consideration & debate, is it possible to get on to this new ground and if so could you consent (or propose) an inquiry into ... this shadowy scheme. After all, Joe ... was apparently ready to go a long way in this direction so that an agreement to a tentative examination of the proposal would not be a shock to some sections of the Unionist party."[56]

Faced with this powerful onslaught from within and outside his party, Balfour had to state his position. He did so in a long letter to Garvin of 22 October. His answer doomed any chance that either the Lloyd George plan or any scheme of federation/home rule all round would be accepted by the Unionists. The final chance to reach a compromise solution to both the Irish question and the larger constitutional issues facing the United Kingdom was rejected in a polite but devastating critique.[57]

Balfour agreed that the present situation was without parallel and that Ireland in 1910 was in many respects wholly different to the Ireland of 1880 to 1890. He was ready to consider the effects of those changes in the most dispassionate manner. Also there were signs that "we have reached a moment ... when the equality of the two great historical parties give undue Parliamentary power to Radical extremists and Irish Nationalists. This is a position full of peril, because it means that while the Unionists cannot hold office at all, the Radicals can only hold office on terms extremely distasteful to the more moderate among them, and very dangerous to the country and the Empire."

Since Garvin believed some form of "Home Rule all round" would help solve both domestic and imperial problems, Balfour explored that solution by means of a number of questions designed to show the difficulties.

(1) Is it not an illusion to suppose (as I gather Albert Grey supposes) that a Federal Constitution in Great Britain would be a step towards ultimately federalising the Empire? Might it not, from many points of view, increase the difficulties of that operation?

(2) Is there not the most serious risk that the public, at home and abroad, will utterly misunderstand the position, if the official and platform arguments are those appropriate to Devolution proper: confined, that is, to purely administrative objects, while the real forces that make for the new policy are Nationalist and Separatist? ...

(3) Is it not further true that such force as lies behind "Home Rule all round" in Scotland and in Wales is also based, not upon administrative advantages, but upon historical sentiment? And is it not in the nature of things that in such cases in-

complete concessions (and provincial powers are necessarily incomplete) only increase the appetites they are intended to satisfy, while they provide new instruments for extorting more?

(4) Is is not a fact that Federalism, as exhibited in the USA, Canada, Australia, and the Cape, is a stage in the progress from separation towards unification; while Federalism in the United Kingdom would be a step from unification towards separation ...

(5) Is not the plain lesson of Irish History on this point somewhat disquieting? Ireland *had* a "subordinate Parliament" till 1782. It took advantage of England's misfortunes to turn it into an "independent Parliament." And why? Because, said Gratton and Flood anything less than this is inconsistent with Irish freedom. This was the argument of loyalists and protestants 140 years ago – is it going to be forgotten by Nationalists and Roman Catholics, merely because Redmond, in order to obtain an instalment of what he considers England's debt to Ireland, promises on behalf of posterity that the instalment shall be for ever accepted as payment in full?

(6) There is in my opinion only one reply to this. It may be said that Irish patriotism in these extreme forms has been and is no more than the romantic disguise in which utilitarian motives flaunt themselves before a sentimental nation. Flood and Grattan when they talked Nationalism really meant that they would stand no more of England's selfish commercial policy: Redmond and his successors, when they talk it, will really mean that their loyalty to the Empire must be paid for in hard cash: and that the pressure of 100 Irish Members in the Imperial Parliament is a sufficient security that the "Subordinate Parliament" in Dublin will have money to play with.

(7) This may be so. But supposing it is not so? You will have established a Parliament and an Executive for one set of reasons, which has been demanded in threatening tones for quite a different set of reasons. These other reasons, which seem to be, and may be, the real reasons undoubtedly require that this Irish Parliament and its Executive shall be (in practice) independent, like the legislature of Canada, not like the legislature of Ontario. You assume that this demand will not be pressed because it will not pay (in a pecuniary sense) to press it. But what if it is pressed? Have you any means, short of two Army Corps, or a Naval Blockade, which can prevent an Irish Parliament and an Irish Executive from defying you? They will have money, police, and organization: In Ireland the Imperial Parliament will have none of these things. Even if it has, would the balance of parties permit them to be used?

(8) re narrower administrative issues. I ask three questions

    (a) Is Ireland to form one province or two? If you prefer the latter, will any Nationalist, of any type, accept this administrative solution? and, if not, why not?

    (b) Is the history of federalism in the USA calculated to reassure us? One civil war, and endless recurrent difficulties show how hard it is to reconcile the claim of Central and Local Authorities, even when there is no "national" sentiment to be reckoned with.

(c) How are you going to deal with England? Is there to be an English as well
as a British Parliament at Westminster? An English as well as a British
Executive at Whitehall? Or are Ireland, Wales and Scotland, to be undivided "nations" while England is cut up into administrative districts?

Balfour felt obliged to raise such objections because they had to be raised
immediately. He assured Garvin that the editor did not stand alone among
strong Unionists, Constitutionalists, and Imperialists. "Many of the best of
our young men are leaning to federalism. The Government are manifestly
moving in the same direction. Redmond will take it, if his supporters allow
him. It seems at first sight to make for peace and goodwill. While the
difficulties and dangers of the time: the balance of parties, ominous revolutionary change make wise men look with friendly eyes upon any scheme which
promises to give increased power to moderate opinion, and offers some hopes
of safeguarding great Imperial interests. And yet – ? ... the risk we run is that
our federalists may indulge in vague aspiration which they have not
sufficiently considered: and will, in their haste, encourage hopes which they
cannot fulfill."

Clearly Balfour was deeply suspicious of the Irish and not at all impressed
by the fuzzy thinking and vague generalities of the federalists. Certainly they
did their cause no good in 1910 by steering clear of any hard-headed analysis
or any tentative constitutional schemes. They did not even draw upon the
plans of the Scottish and Welsh home rulers to fill in the details of their broad
ideas. Perhaps they realized that to do so would only further alarm traditional
Unionists. Balfour's letter firmly indicated that he was not going to deviate
from long-standing Unionist policy. Most Unionists were as alarmed as ever
by any suggestion of home rule all round or federalism which they viewed
as simply home rule under another guise.

Over the next two weeks both Garvin and F.S. Oliver continued to mount
a strong campaign on behalf of federalism. Garvin attempted to draw Austen
Chamberlain onside, and, despite Balfour's criticisms, he continued to argue
strongly on behalf of federalism in the *Observer* on 23 and 30 October. He
singled out William O'Brien and Lord Dunraven as moderates worthy of encouragement and he arranged for both men to write letters to the *Observer* expressing their seemingly spontaneous support for its federal line. Garvin even
tackled the hitherto avoided issue of Ulster in his article of 30 October. If
Ulster was to join in a general Irish settlement, it would have to be brought
in by persuasion and not by force. Federalism could provide the means of protecting Ulster interests while preserving the essential unity of Ireland.[58]

Similarly, F.S. Oliver, having failed to convince Balfour privately, returned
to the public arena as "Pacificus" and in a series of seven articles published
in the *Times* from 20 October to 2 November lucidly and cogently put the case
for a large-scale convention to tackle constitutional difficulties in the United
Kingdom, and outlined what he meant by federalism.[59] Oliver suggested four

subordinate national or provincial parliaments for England, Scotland, Wales, and Ireland and a two-chamber imperial parliament responsible for both overall United Kingdom matters and imperial affairs. Since the sovereignty of the imperial parliament would remain unimpaired, it was evident that once again, like many others, Oliver meant home rule all round or devolution rather than federalism on the American, Canadian, Australian, or even Swiss models. Oliver admitted that financial arrangements would be difficult to work out but considered his idea superior to Gladstone's bills of 1886 and 1893, both of which had left one national parliament, the Irish, subordinate to another national parliament, the British, which in turn was also clothed with imperial sovereignty. His scheme meant that all four regions would have parliaments equal constitutionally but subordinate to an overall United Kingdom parliament. Oliver still did not tackle the continuing confusion of national and imperial issues in the one parliament. He thought it too soon to undertake such a division. Oliver's ideas were well expressed but were by that date not unfamiliar to those who concerned themselves with such issues. He may have succeeded in making the issues clearer to a wider and generally uninformed public but he did not advance the analysis of the problem very far.[60]

Garvin made one more attempt to convince Balfour by exploring his ideas more fully in a letter of eighteen pages sent to the opposition leader on 25 October. He attempted to reassure Balfour on the vexed questions of the union and imperial sovereignty. Union, he argued, would not be touched "if *common affairs remain fully under central control*." By devolving purely local affairs the union would not be impaired "in the slightest." If necessary Ulster should have a separate assembly but he hoped it would only be transitional until the north and south in Ireland could agree on a common assembly.[61] But Balfour was not to be shifted. If he had weakened at all in the face of the concerted efforts of Oliver, Garvin, and Lloyd George it was evident by the end of October that he had thought better of it. On 31 October, the day after Garvin's second major article on federalism, Jack Sanders wrote to the *Observer's* editor: "I am *very anxious*. He has gone back a bit. He shrinks from the Federal issue. He says that *he* is not the man to assist in originating the new policy." Five days later Sanders wrote again to reemphasize the point. He wanted to make it clear "that the *present* issue does not touch Federation. It is whether there shd be *something* or nothing."[62] A day later, on 6 November, Garvin retreated. In an article in the *Observer* he concluded that the chance for a larger settlement with federalism as a component had been lost. All that was now possible was "Something or Nothing."[63]

On 10 November the constitutional conference broke up having failed to reach any decisions. Later that day Asquith saw the king and requested not only a dissolution but a guarantee that peers would be created if the Lords seemed likely to reject a parliament bill. The king finally agreed on 16 November, and Asquith opened the election campaign on 25 November.

Although it had been clear to insiders since the third week in October that the conference would likely fail over Irish home rule, it had not been so clear to those somewhat removed from the discussions. Lord Hugh Cecil, an arch-Conservative, was alarmed by what he read in the press and argued in a letter to the *Times* that no analogy could be drawn between Irish home rule and colonial self-government and that it was foolish to speak of Ireland as if it was a nation. Patently, it was not.[64] Leo Amery, an intimate of the Round Table, did not altogether agree with some of Cecil's arguments. "Most Imperialists," he wrote, would argue "that the question of Home Rule or local federation are entirely different problems." All Unionists would oppose home rule proposals based on the principle of separation but few would object in principle to "some sort of federation or provincial system in the United Kingdom" if the practical details could be worked out. On the other hand, "no internal arrangement of our local affairs can directly help forward the solution of the Imperial problem. The idea that we can federalize the United Kingdom and then ask Canada or Australia to come into that federation on the footing of Ireland or Wales is one that would not occur for an instant to any one at all familiar with public opinion in those Dominions, or with the strictly limited nature of the functions which would be vested in any Imperial Union."[65] Earl Grey was now inclined to agree. "It must," he wrote to Garvin, "be made very clear that the Federation of the United Kingdom has no connection with the Federation of the Empire. They are two separate questions although one leads to the other."[66]

Lord Milner held similar opinions, although he went further than either Amery or Grey. On receiving a copy of Balfour's letter to Garvin, Milner responded in a thoughtful fashion. He appreciated the force of all Balfour's points, particularly the first:

... speaking as an Imperial Unionist of the most advanced type, I certainly do not hold that the grant of any measure of "Home Rule" to Ireland can be made a basis for the wider Federation of the whole Empire. The problems are entirely different. "*Ireland* like *Canada*" might, at first sight, seem a step in that direction. But I believe myself it would be a step in the other – i.e. towards the dissolution of the whole. "*Ireland* like *Ontario*," on the other hand (the whole U.K. standing for Canada) may or may not be a good thing, but it clearly affords no jumping off ground for Imperial Federation.

But as Milner understood it the question before them was one affecting the constitution of the United Kingdom alone. He differed from Balfour in that he was convinced that "we are 'in for' constitutional reorganization in the U.K., whether we like it or not. With an enormous permanent majority in Ireland,

and, as it now appears, a decided majority also in Scotland, not to mention Wales, clamouring for local autonomy, and with half England prepared to move in that direction, what is to be done?" Rather than take up "an attitude of resolute and uncompromising opposition" which would consolidate all sections favourable to change and result in the defeat of the Unionists, would it not be wiser to adopt a less militant course, admitting some change might be necessary and then "try and turn the revolutionary current into safer channels, or at least the safest possible?" He tended to agree with "Pacificus" and to listen, without pronounced hostility, to what the advocates of change proposed. He concluded:

... anything seems better than the Gladstonian plan of dealing with Ireland alone, giving it an exceptional position in the u.k. That it avoids this, is in my humble judgement the great merit of "Federalism" – I hate the word – let me rather say of all-round devolution. I fully realise the colossal difficulties of such a scheme, but they do not seem to me ... insuperable ... On the whole I should be glad if all round devolution – with an unquestionably supreme central authority – were found to be practicable. But, if it is not, I should fight for the status quo with a great deal more heart, and a great deal more hope than I feel today.[67]

By the time Balfour received this letter he had already made his decision not to explore home rule all round. Given his deep-rooted and firmly held convictions, it is doubtful that the receipt of such a letter, even from someone as respected in Unionist circles as Milner, would have had much impact. What the letter did was indicate that if Balfour had been willing to take the lead other well-placed and influential Unionists might have followed and a compromise might have been worked out. How such a compromise would have been received by the hard-liners in the party is hard to assess and so is the degree to which such a decision would have split the party. Nor is it clear how the Irish Nationalists would have reacted. Redmond might have been able to carry the day if a fully rounded scheme of devolution had been offered but probably not. Home rule had become a sacrosanct goal for most Irish politicians. And devolution without special arrangements for Ulster would not have been acceptable even at this relatively early stage in the growth of the Unionist movement.

The emphatic statements of Amery, Grey, and Milner about the lack of direct connection between United Kingdom devolution and imperial federation revealed the extent to which that issue had been clarified within the Round Table movement. By mid-November the London members had formally decided not to devote space to the analysis of federation within the United Kingdom in the larger study of imperial problems being prepared by Curtis or to devote any of the movement's money to promoting the measure. The movement did continue with its investigation of congestion in the United Kingdom and articles in the *Round Table* in 1911 did emphasize the difficulties facing the Commons. Federalism was simply raised in those articles as a possible solution to both the Irish and general United Kingdom difficulties. For the time being, the Round Table movement chose to concentrate on imperial rather than either Irish or general United Kingdom affairs.[68]

Other advocates had mixed reactions. Grey remained hopeful and as committed as ever, and his return to England in 1911 was awaited with anticipation by Frewen. Both Frewen and Dunraven continued to give assistance to O'Brien and ensured that he had sufficient funds to contest the December election in Cork (which he won) and to continue the work of the All for Ireland League.[69] Brassey also supported O'Brien but he was more pessimistic than his friends. In writing to both O'Brien and Garvin his comments were gloomy: "A few days ago it seemed possible that Federal government was to afford a solution which both Parties or at any rate the reasonable men of all Parties might accept. It would have in large part solved the House of Lords question and would have solved the Irish question on the only lines on which it can be solved. But Orange intolerance and Orange prejudices have won the day in the counsels of the Unionist party and the outlook in consequence is bad for the Party, the Constitution and the Empire."[70]

Brassey could not have been pleased by the election results. The electorate had kept the numbers virtually the same as in January with the Liberals winning 272 seats; the Unionists 272; the Irish Nationalists 84; and Labour 42. The result could only be interpreted as a victory for the Liberals, and for the parliament bill. The Unionists prepared themselves for a hard fight in 1911. Both they, in general, and Brassey and his friends, in particular, would have been amazed to learn that shortly after the Liberal victory was assured Haldane had been given Asquith's sanction to prepare "a memorandum on constitutional reform ... Second Chamber Reform (which now that the Conservatives have taken it up we have got to try) Home Rule all round etc. as part of a single scheme."[71] Perhaps the protracted campaign of the Round Table movement, Grey, Dunraven, Brassey, Frewen, O'Brien, and particularly Oliver and Garvin, had had some impact after all.

CHAPTER SIX

Home Rule or "Federalism"?

Since the election results had confirmed the Liberals in office with the support of the Irish Nationalists and Labour, it was now well understood that once a parliament bill was successfully passed a home rule bill would not be far behind. As a result throughout 1911 there was considerable discussion at the higher levels of the Liberal party of devolution or home rule all round as a means of meeting the needs not only of Ireland but also of Scotland and Wales. It was recognized that a number of Liberals, particularly those of Scottish background and/or from Scottish constituencies, were ardent home rulers. It was hoped they would continue to support the party in division if home rule was not made an exclusively Irish program. It was also realized that there was much interest in home rule all round or devolution as a means of resolving the perceived inefficiency at Westminster, particularly the congestion of business. Many Scottish Liberals, in fact, preferred home rule all round to Scottish home rule and it was known they would welcome such a move. It was therefore not altogether surprising that Asquith had encouraged Haldane to look closely at home rule all round in his memorandum on constitutional reform or that a "confidential" paper was circulated among the Liberal cabinet in November 1910 on the subject of the "Division of Powers in Federal Constitutions within the British Empire."[1]

The parliament bill was introduced in the House of Commons on 21 February and for the next six months the debate over the bill in and out of parliament riveted the attention of the country. Although federalism did receive some scattered mention in the House of Commons, the general political atmosphere was not conducive to sustained lobbying by its exponents. For the time being, most of them kept a low profile. As might have been expected, Lord Dunraven and Moreton Frewen were the exceptions.

In January Dunraven had approached Garvin and asked if the editor would recommend someone to him who would be able to "devil up" information on

Irish finance.[2] Clearly he was readying himself for the debate to come over Irish home rule and the federal implications. But Dunraven and Frewen were interested in something more pervasive than their own efforts. They wanted a full-fledged organization. Frewen discussed the possibilities with Earl Grey in Ottawa in February, and Dunraven met with Oliver in London in March. Dunraven hoped that he and Frewen would eventually be able to combine forces with Garvin and Oliver and "rough-hew something for people to stand on;"[3] however, his long meeting with Oliver shattered that hope. Oliver was "satisfied that an organisation is premature – useless until the Federal idea has soaked into men's minds and until a genius arises to take it up." Dunraven's response to that was a sardonic one: "Well! but if we wait for an Alexander Hamilton or a Joe Chamberlain or possibly a Lloyd George we may wait for a long-time." Dunraven wanted, and quickly, a program to which people could adhere and an organization to which they could subscribe:

Of course there is the difficulty of definition; but if we can define a program and objects sufficiently accurately to prevent members of a small committee from quarrelling I think a committee should be formed. I put it brutally to Oliver – "nowadays it is impossible to advance an idea without money. How can people subscribe money without something to subscribe to!" If we could lay our hands on a genius of commanding position in politics to pronounce for Federalism, good! and we would create the organisation after; but as things are we had better create the organisation and trust to its attracting the commanding man of genius.[4]

Despite Dunraven's continued efforts Oliver could not be persuaded. The fact that he was already intimately involved with an organization, the Round Table movement, that had a continuing interest in federalism may have had something to do with Oliver's stance, but he was justifiably cautious. It was not only that the "man of genius" was lacking, but Oliver probably decided it would not be useful for his own purposes to become too closely involved with Frewen and Dunraven, both of whom were supporting William O'Brien, a man not much loved by either Redmondite Nationalists or by Unionists. He was well aware that men like Dunraven and himself were considered "sham Unionists" by the hard-liners in the party because of their "wobbly attitude towards Federalism."[5] The time was inopportune for a prominent organization. Frewen and Dunraven had to be content with Frewen's plea for federalism in his maiden speech in the Commons on 24 April. However, in July Frewen gave up his Commons seat and the federalists lost whatever influence he may have had in the chamber.[6]

Another who continued to promote home rule all round was E.T. John who established a firm contact with the Young Scots Society in his capacity as president of the Welsh National League. In fact, it was Walter Murray of the Young Scots Society who took the initiative. He had seen a speech by John on federal home rule and he wondered if the league and the society could be brought into touch. After emphasizing that the society would favour the introduction of a Scottish home rule bill after the passage of the parliament bill, Murray acknowledged, "Of course, we are federal Home Rulers, and should like to co-operate with Wales in pressing forward the Home Rule all Round policy." Murray believed they should press for "Home Rule All Round" before either a Scottish land bill or Welsh disestablishment. John indicated his willingness to meet with the Young Scots Society regarding joint action: "I should certainly take no part in the Irish Home Rule agitation until similarity and simultaneity of treatment are assured both for Scotland and Wales."[7]

The parliament bill finally received the approval of the House of Lords on 10 August. The act ensured that bills other than money bills would become law if they were passed by the Commons in three successive sessions even though rejected twice by the Lords. Following the passage of the act there was considerable anticipation in the country. A home rule bill was expected soon. Ominously, Ulster opposition to any such scheme began to cohere and become more vocal. Sir Edward Carson, who had become leader of the Ulster Unionists in the House of Commons in February 1910, played an increasingly prominent role in the organization of Ulster opposition. On 23 September he reviewed a march past at Craigavon of the members of the Ulster Unionist clubs and the Orange lodges. The occasion was infused with rhetoric and bombast and general euphoria but those who knew Ulster and Carson were well aware that the situation was highly serious. The federalists now took every opportunity to sound sympathetic politicians and to publicize the merits of their ideas in the newspapers and quarterlies in an effort to prove that only federalism or home rule all round would ensure the continued unity of the United Kingdom and the empire.

Frewen was one of the first to try and persuade the Unionists to take up the federal cause. Shortly after the passage of the Parliament Act, he wrote to Walter Long, a fierce defender of the union, inviting him and Sir Edward Carson to meet with Dunraven, Tim Healy of the Irish Nationalists, and himself. Frewen wanted to substitute a relationship "which will strengthen us" for one "which paralyses us" and he urged Long and Carson to adopt the federal ideal and thus save the United Kingdom and the empire and protect Ulster. Frewen was less patriotic than he sounded. His primary concern was the protection of *"Property"* which, after the passage of a home rule bill, he feared would be "the next article at the Nationalist-Socialist bargain counter." As he cynically put it to Lord Midleton, the leader of the southern Unionists, "You think we Federals are enthusiasts as to the Federal principle; not a bit; we are for the most part Tories, & Tories scared to death!"[8] Whatever his true motive, Frewen had decided that federalism was the solution to the constitutional difficulties facing the country and the only possible protection of the landed interest. Walter Long was not immune to either of these concerns and, in time, he was to adopt the federal solution as the only one which would give Ireland what it wanted while preserving the Union. But in August 1911 he was not ready to change his views so dramatically, especially as he had recently received a lengthy letter from Dicey which would only have confirmed his doubts about federalism.

As we have seen, Dicey had been an inveterate foe of home rule and of federalism since the 1880s and his had been one of the most prolific pens in opposition to either venture. Now, in 1911, he had written a new introduction for another edition of *A Leap in the Dark*. The principal point he wanted to press home was "the unlimited folly of advocating Federal Home Rule."[9] In his anxiety he wrote to Long, an old friend and confidant. Dicey admitted he was a "fanatic" on the Union, and "an unconverted and impenitent Unionist of 1886." He did not believe Unionists should be transformed into federalists. It would be the ruin of English Conservatism and "a total surrender of the fundamental principle of Unionism." Nor would the "federalisation of the United Kingdom" satisfy "the real desires of Irish Nationalists" because it was "absolutely inconsistent with national independence." Could anyone, he asked Long, "suppose that Mazzini would for a moment have accepted a federal government under which Italy should become a province of a federated Austrian Empire?" Moreover, "Federal Home Rule" might be used "as a means of weakening the power and plundering the wealth of England." He also argued, rather weakly and in obvious disregard of the functioning of at least the United States federation, that federalism would make it possible for a provincial authority to beg out of a foreign war or commitment.[10]

Dicey's fears were shared by many leading Unionists, including the influential Lord Salisbury who had become worried by Lord Selborne's apparent readiness to consider a scheme of home rule all round. Selborne had been attending the "moots" of the Round Table movement throughout 1911 and in the aftermath of the passage of the Parliament Act he was less adamant than he had been on the subject of home rule. His experience in South Africa during the debate over closer union had made him realize that it was not beyond the wit of man to devise constitutional forms that would accommodate the interests of all parties. Lord Salisbury was not persuaded:

I look upon Home Rule all round as an evil. Unlike Imperial Federation it is a movement not towards greater consolidation but towards less consolidation – centrifugal not centripetal. But whether you take that view or not consider the effect of this policy at home. England no doubt would gain by it, but it would surrender Scotland and Wales to the very disasters of violent legislation which it is the whole object of your new movement to prevent; in Wales it would disendow the church and destroy the Church Schools and in both Wales and Scotland it would hand over the owners of all kinds of property to their bitter enemies. It is true that even as it is we may not be able to wash off these calamities, but what would our friends think of us – our friends in Scotland and in Wales if we announced it as our policy following on Irish Home Rule to abandon them to their fate? We cannot do it. Moreover there is Ulster. Ulster might resist.

Although not prepared to have separate parliaments, Salisbury accepted that "glorified County Council devolution" was another matter. If the units were made small enough such devolution might work. He reminded Selborne that sweeping change was repugnant to their Conservative supporters: "Whatever your own opinions the Conservative Party can only assimilate change gradually."[11]

F.S. Oliver, like Salisbury, was also beginning to worry about Ulster. He believed that the "shouting and drumbeating and treasonable tomfoolery" would only "weaken the defence of Unionism against Gladstonian and Parnellite Home Rule" because it would convince "the ordinary Englishman or Scotsman (what I fear is an undoubtable fact) that the main reason why *Ulster* is opposed to Home Rule is its blind unreasoning religious jealousy and hatred."[12] Oliver worried that the Unionist party would remain indifferent to alternative solutions but, as yet, he did not think it wise to take up a cudgel on behalf of federalism. Oliver shared his concerns with Milner, a man increasingly identified with the Ulster cause. Milner regretted the turn that events had taken over the previous year: "I dare say you are right and that nothing can now be done to save the Unionists from 'muffing' Home Rule as they 'muffed' the Second Chamber business. They seem to have a genius for putting themselves into positions, in wh. it is always 'too late' to take the right line. No doubt they ought to have taken up Federal Home Rule a year ago, when you started the ball rolling & Garvin came out with his famous screed."[13]

After some reflection, Milner finally agreed that Oliver was probably right to abstain "from immediate direct advocacy of Federal Home Rule." What did concern Milner, however, were the continuing misleading references to colonial self-government when Ireland, and especially Ulster, were under consideration. To Milner, the history of colonial development in the dominions had been "in the direction of *Union* ... coupled with provincial self-government." As long as the supreme authority of the imperial parliament and the same citizenship with the same fundamental rights were preserved in all units of the state, Milner could accept self-government, but not if home rule impaired the sovereign authority of parliament and jeopardized the rights of individual citizens. "The more I think of it," wrote Milner, "the more I feel that, especially as we are going to be doused in references to Colonial experience, it would be invaluable if people could be made to see what the experience really teaches, and where an honest attempt to make use of it would inevitably lead us."

As for Ulster, Milner advised Oliver:

I should be careful to leave the door open to *ultimate support* of a reasonable revolt of Ulster. It may be that an intransigent attitude on the part of Ulster, if it takes a sensible, & not its present intolerable course, is a necessary element in the working out of a settlement on our lines. If the Ulstermen, confronted with proposals which would impair their present British citizenship, as Gladstonian Home Rule did, were to say "No. To this we will not submit. We won't be disinherited," I conceive that we ought to back them. They may or may not make out a case for separate local self-government. I should prefer *not* to have it. I don't like the idea of Two Irelands and a Heptarchic England. But they are undoubtedly entitled to retain their present status, unimpaired, as citizens of a United Kingdom, with the security wh. it alone can give them against oppression.[14]

Clearly some influential Unionists were beginning to have second thoughts about home rule all round and federalism as the inevitability of a home rule bill sank in. Others were still adamantly opposed to any tinkering with the constitutional system and would probably remain so no matter what the cost to the party or the country. For the moment, however, no final decisions would be taken on either a party or an individual basis until the Liberal intention was clear. During the final months before the introduction of the home rule bill, the proponents both of home rule all round and of federalism resorted to the public platform and to the publication of articles, pamphlets, and books in an attempt to emphasize the merits of alternative solutions to United Kingdom difficulties.

One who was particularly active was E.T. John, the Welsh leader. He spoke to students at Oxford, Cardiff, Aberystwyth, and Bangor in late 1911 and wrote on "Wales and Self-Government" and "Federal Home Rule in Relationship to Wales" in the new publication, *Wales*.[15] He abhorred the prevalent congestion in the House of Commons and bemoaned the lack of time for the proper discussion of matters of national importance such as finance and foreign affairs. But for John the primary reason for the Welsh to support federal home rule was the recognition it would give to Welsh nationality. This would not imply separatism, far from it. John believed that "Federal Home Rule facilitates effective Imperial service and cooperation quite as much as it promotes national development and expansion."[16] In fact, the "Federal method happily combines the maximum opportunity for the operation of the deep-seated sentiment of nationality, with the greatest facility for the transaction of the national business."[17] Only by a generous measure of self-government, combined with an adequate share in the running of imperial and international affairs, could Wales serve as fully as it was capable. John believed that efforts to resolve the Irish difficulty alone would founder over the problems resulting from the British retention of customs and the continued representation therefore of the Irish in the House of Commons. The federal solution would meet the problem by creating national legislatures simultaneously in Ireland, Scotland, Wales, and England. The current House of Commons would then concern itself with purely English matters while the existing second chamber, the House of Lords, would be converted into an elective senate, charged with the control of foreign and colonial affairs, the management and maintenance of the army and navy, the responsibility for the national debt, the raising of the necessary revenues for these purposes, the decisions on all questions of import duties, and the superintendence of Indian administration. This novel and radical suggestion was never fully explored by John but it is unlikely that his Welsh and Scottish colleagues found it fully satisfying.

The Scottish, in fact, were fearful that Asquith would decide to resolve the Irish difficulty first rather than introduce a home rule all round bill that would be "the first great step towards the federation and thorough union of the British peoples at home and abroad."[18] Efforts were made in the *Thistle* to keep the Scottish interest in Scottish home rule and home rule all round before the public, especially after Sir Henry Dalziel again introduced a Scottish home rule bill in the Commons on 16 August 1911. Modelled on D.V. Pirie's 1908 bill, it reserved the supreme power of the imperial parliament and specifically enumerated the subjects to be delegated to the Scottish parliament. It was devolutionary rather than federal and was designed to enable a Scottish parliament to consider matters of local importance in Scotland. There was no mention of how Scotland would continue to be represented in the central parliament.[19]

By the end of 1911 a variety of other comments and reflections were available, not so much from active politicians and committed regionalists such as E.T. John as from long-standing advocates and publicists. Basil Williams edited a useful collection of essays entitled *Home Rule Problems* that dealt with some of the constitutional and financial questions surrounding home rule.[20] And Murray Macdonald, who had not contributed much to the discussion in 1910 or 1911, finally broke silence with an article on "The Constitutional Controversy and Federal Home Rule." Although he argued that Britain's constitutional difficulties would never be satisfactorily settled so long as "Federal Home Rule" and imperial federation were dealt with piecemeal and in isolation one from another, the primary issue for Macdonald and the one that justified other action was, as always, the congestion of business in the House of Commons. It was essential to find a scheme to relieve it. The use of closure was one method that had been tried in order to speed up business but it restricted the liberty of debate and increased the power of the executive.

Macdonald claimed the solution lay in federal home rule by which "the control of the strictly separate interests of each of the countries constituting the United Kingdom would be transferred from the Imperial Parliament to secondary and national authorities." He did not agree that federal home rule would lead to disintegration and he cited the British North America Act of 1867 which had dissolved the Union of Upper and Lower Canada and given Ontario and Quebec independent legislative powers within the dominion. The success of that scheme "might at least encourage us to contemplate a modification of the terms of Union between the countries of the United Kingdom without the fear that it would weaken the cohesion of the parts or the strength of the whole." Macdonald went further. He argued that "Federal Home Rule is not inconsistent, in idea, with the terms of the existing Union between England, Scotland and Ireland. Each of the countries has now its own law and its own administrative system regulating and controlling its own domestic interests; and to each of them might be given independent powers of dealing with these interests without any radical departure from the spirit of our present practice." The House of Commons was by its very constitution incompetent to discharge the duty of legislating for local wants of the separate countries of the United Kingdom. Moreover, election issues would be simplified and the federation of the empire might be facilitated by having local, national, and imperial questions separated. He concluded that "Federal Home Rule is at once imperative and inevitable; that it is in itself consistent with the spirit and working of our Parliamentary system; and that it provides the only adequate means of preserving that system from the paralysis and decay which are fast overtaking it."[21]

Dunraven agreed with Macdonald. In two articles in the *Nineteenth Century* and in a book entitled *The Legacy of Past Years: A Study of Irish History*, all published in late 1911, Dunraven asserted that devolution "on federal lines" was essential in the interest of Ireland, Great Britain, and the empire. It would satisfy Ireland, restore efficiency to parliament, strengthen the union, prepare the way for "a federated Empire," and consolidate the empire as a world power.[22] But despite his use of the terms "federal" and "Federal Home Rule" it was clear that Dunraven did not have pure federalism in mind. He referred constantly, as did Macdonald, to the "delegation of authority to subordinate" parliaments and he made it clear that the powers of the central parliament should remain unimpaired. To him, and to many other so-called "federalists," the power of statutory parliaments was "a delegated power." For them the union was all-important. Some delegation of authority might preserve it. Whatever that remodelling of the constitution was called, whether "home rule all round" or "federal home rule" or "federal devolution," the intent was not really federation on the Canadian or American model but rather union on South African lines. Clearly such a solution would not have satisfied even moderate Irish Nationalists by 1911, but the primary frustration for Dunraven, Macdonald, and their associates was that the Unionist party could not or would not understand their basic point.[23] The resignation of Arthur Balfour as leader of the Unionists and his replacement by Bonar Law in November 1911 made it no more likely that they would do so.

The Unionists were particularly active in the early months of 1912. One of their major efforts, a book entitled *Against Home Rule: The Case for the Union*, was published to coincide with the introduction of Asquith's home rule bill. Written by leading Unionists and with an introduction by Sir Edward Carson, it was designed to reveal flaws in home rule thinking. Leo Amery, a Round Table associate, had two articles in it, "Home Rule and the Colonial Analogy" and "The Economics of Separatism," while another by Sir George Cave on "The Constitutional Question" tackled federalism.[24] Rather astutely, Cave did not believe that the "federalists" in fact wanted "pure" federalism, but that they wanted devolution. He doubted if anything like the Irish council scheme would be adequate but he recognized that a moderate and clearly defined "scheme of delegation" might relieve congestion and be acceptable.[25] In his article, "Home Rule and the Colonial Analogy," Amery pointed out that any home rule bill for Ireland would only with great difficulty, if at all, be capable of adaptation to home rule all round or a federation: ... the creation of a federal state, whether by confederation or by devolution of powers, must be in the main, a simultaneous act." Amery was of the opinion that the Liberals were likely to land in a hopeless muddle by trying to appease various interests – Irish and other – by bringing in a bill neither fish nor fowl. "What is needed," argued Amery, "is not the creation of separate parliaments *within* the United Kingdom, but the creation of a separate Parliament *for* the United Kingdom, a Parliament which should deal with the affairs of the United Kingdom considered as one of the Dominions, leaving the general problems of Imperial policy to a common Imperial Parliament or Council equally representative of the citizens of every Dominion. No form of Home Rule can in any sense advance that desirable solution of our Imperial problems."[26]

Amery also wrote a series of seventeen articles for the *Morning Post* on the home rule problem and these were published in 1912 as *The Case against Home Rule*. One of the articles was called simply "The Federal Arguments."[27] Again Amery argued that regardless of the merits of home rule all round the Liberal bill could not be made to fit a federal scheme: "The idea of Nationalist Home Rule and the idea of Federalism are, indeed, essentially incompatible." Uniformity in constitutional and financial arrangements were "the very essence of Federalism." This was unlikely to be included in Asquith's bill. Amery revealed, in both his articles, a sound knowledge of imperial and domestic constitutional developments and particularly of the various forms of federalism. Although not attacking home rule all round in principle, he objected strongly to home rule for Ireland being disguised as a federal step and he refuted the contention that either home rule for Ireland or home rule all round was a step toward imperial federation.[28] Federalists and Unionists alike awaited with considerable anticipation the details of the Liberal home rule bill.

The Liberals had been debating the merits of home rule for Ireland and a general devolutionary scheme for the United Kingdom since early 1911. In late January a small departmental committee "composed of experts" was set up under the chairmanship of Sir Henry Primrose "to consider and report upon the financial relations of Ireland and the United Kingdom."[29] Shortly afterwards, in February, a cabinet committee began to work on home rule. Its responsibilities were strictly constitutional and it never considered fiscal questions nor did it consult with the Primrose committee at any stage. This compartmentalization was not a good omen. It meant that Liberals did not fully appreciate the interlocking nature of fiscal and constitutional matters. To keep consideration of them separate could only lead to confusion.

The cabinet committee, under the chairmanship of Lord Loreburn, was composed of Augustine Birrell, the chief secretary, Lloyd George, Winston Churchill, R.B. Haldane, Herbert Samuel, and Sir Edward Grey. This was a committee much in favour of "federalism" or home rule all round. Lloyd George had floated the federal kite the previous October; Churchill had pursued local devolution with some interest as early as 1901 and again in 1904-5; while Haldane had been interested in reform of both the United Kingdom and imperial constitutions since Gladstonian times and most recently in his involvement with the Pollock Committee. The only strong opponent of home rule all round was Birrell, who knew how deeply opposed the Irish Nationalists were to any deviation from home rule proper. It was he more than any other who worked within the cabinet over the next year and a half to ensure there was no dilution of intent.[30] Loreburn was known to be sympathetic to the idea and even Sir Edward Grey had recently professed enthusiasm for the concept. In a letter to the ardent federalist, Earl Grey, he gave some hint of how he and his colleagues were thinking at this early stage: "We shall, I hope, save the House of Commons by delegating local affairs within the limits of the United Kingdom. The working out of a practical scheme presents many difficulties, but if possible we shall prepare a scheme this year, and proceed to carry it out next year. We shall then have before us a great constitutional Reform: which will include Home Rule for the different parts of the United Kingdom, the reform of the Second Chamber, and a permanent adjustment of the relations between the two houses."[31]

It is a puzzle why Asquith, who was no more than a lukewarm devolutionist, should have appointed a committee potentially so inclined towards home rule all round. It is possible he wanted to oblige the enthusiasts in his cabinet to confront the full complexities of "federalism" and thus dampen their ardour, or he may have thought that a more broadly conceived scheme than one simply dealing with Ireland would eventually be necessary. Whatever his motives, the committee did spend much of its time discussing devolutionary ideas. It may have given the committee pause to read in the *Times* in late January of Redmond's attitudes to home rule all round. The Irish Nationalist leader made it clear that Ireland could not wait until Scotland, Wales, and England were ready to establish a federal government in the United Kingdom. Although he was sympathetic to federalism, he saw home rule for Ireland as the preliminary and necessary first step.[32] Redmond was to adhere to that position throughout the next fifteen months.

In the event only two schemes touching on home rule all round were submitted to the cabinet committee, one by Churchill and the other by Lloyd George. On 24 February 1911 Winston Churchill made his first contribution on the subject of "Devolution." To Churchill it seemed "absolutely impossible that an English Parliament, and still more an English Executive, could exist side by side with an Imperial Parliament and an Imperial Executive, whether based on separate or identical election. Imperial affairs could not in practice be separated from English party politics."[33] For him the "external sphere touches the internal at almost every point." On looking at the inevitable clashes between imperial and English parliaments dominated by different parties, Churchill concluded that it was "impossible for an English Parliament and an Imperial Parliament to exist together at the same time."

Three days later, on 27 February, Lloyd George contributed an idea of his own. He suggested that a complete scheme of Irish home rule with an executive responsible to an Irish parliament should be drafted first but that the government should then undertake "to introduce measures on similar lines dealing with England, Scotland and Wales." "But," he went on, "in order to obviate the inconvenience and injustice which would arise in the interregnum owing to Irish members interfering in purely English, Scottish and Welsh affairs a system of Grand Committees must be set up simultaneously with Irish Home Rule Bill with full and final legislative powers in English, Scotch and Welsh affairs of same character as those delegated to Irish Parliament."[34] The grand committee suggestion was intriguing and for some months the cabinet committee was persuaded in its favour. The committee was led to consider it seriously by the need to respond to further suggestions from Churchill.

Two days after Lloyd George had circulated his proposal, Churchill placed another paper on "Devolution" before the cabinet committee.[35] In it he attempted to meet the concern expressed in his earlier memorandum. He suggested that the imperial parliament should remain unaltered "except by a strict numerical redistribution between countries." The United Kingdom should be divided into ten areas, having regard to geographical, racial, and historical considerations, with a legislative and administrative body, separately elected, for each area. In Scotland, Ireland, and Wales there were to be parliaments "so far as may be desirable in each case." Women were to be given the right to vote and serve on all these bodies except in Ireland where the Irish parliament would decide the practice to be followed. The new bodies would assume all the powers exercised by county councils, certain powers exercised by municipal bodies, and certain powers to be devolved upon them by the imperial parliament including education, licensing, land, housing, police, local judges and magistrates, the poor law, agriculture, fisheries, private bill legislation, roads, boundary questions between counties, towns, and urban and rural areas, and such further powers as parliament from time to time devolved on them. The imperial parliament would retain all powers not specifically devolved. Churchill suggested that his policy be put forward in two separate bills, simultaneously announced but independently justified; one to deal with Ireland and the other with Great Britain. So, even in the Lloyd George and the Churchill plans, Ireland was still to be dealt with separately. Neither full-scale devolution nor federalism was immediately contemplated. Perhaps this was all Asquith had wanted.

Churchill's proposal was shown to Courtenay Ilbert, the clerk of the House of Commons, who almost immediately challenged his ideas and the overall concept of devolution.[36] In reviewing the genesis of the devolution idea, Ilbert concluded that it related to Irish home rule and specifically to whether or not Irish representatives should be excluded from or retained in parliament and if so under what conditions. There had been the "out" plan of 1886 abandoned in 1893; the "in and out" plan proposed in the 1893 bill but dropped in committee; and the "in" plan proposed by the 1893 bill as passed by the House of Commons. The "out" plan was inconsistent with retaining the right to tax Ireland; the "in and out" plan was beset with serious, even insuperable, difficulties; and the "in" plan could not be defended while the powers of parliament remained as they were. Irish representatives could not be allowed a voice in the local affairs of Great Britain while refusing to British representatives a voice in the local affairs of Ireland. Hence the logical move "to some scheme of devolution for Great Britain, some form of 'Home Rule all Round.'" Ilbert agreed with Churchill that the creation of a parliament for England in juxtaposition with an imperial parliament would not work because the English parliament would be too strong. If there was to be any legislative devolution in Great Britain, England would have to be, for purposes of local legislation, divided into provinces.

Nevertheless, he thought the simultaneous announcement of two bills, as proposed by Churchill, would distract the public and confuse issues requiring immediate decision. Nor did he think the kind of devolution suggested was either expedient or practicable. He thought devolution for Ireland and devolution for Great Britain should run on different lines. The Irish demand had always been for an Irish legislature with an Irish executive responsible to it. Scottish and Welsh home rule demands had not, in his estimation, assumed so definite a form. He believed their demands to be essentially administrative rather than legislative. He could find no evidence in England of any demand for provincial councils and there appeared to be no local sentiment or local patriotism which could be appealed to in support of English provinces. There was no homogeneity in any group of English counties corresponding to the homogeneity of Scotland or Wales. He believed that demands for greater local control over legislation of a local character should be met by alterations in parliamentary procedure.

Ilbert was less constrained in private. In a letter to Bryce on 19 March he reacted more critically: "I am rather uneasy about the proceedings of the Cabinet Committee on Irish Home Rule. They seem to be still flirting, probably at Haldane's suggestion, with some wild cat scheme of Home Rule all round. These clever men, when they get together to conclave, are apt to do extraordinarily foolish things, but I hope that when this problem comes before the Cabinet ... saner counsels will prevail."[37]

In fact, the so-called "saner counsels" prevailed at a much earlier stage than full cabinet consideration. Ilbert's salutory remarks had a considerable impact, and during the spring and summer Lloyd George's grand committee scheme was viewed more favourably. It was known that while T.P. O'Connor thought the home rule bill needed to be taken up from the vantage point of "all-round devolution," neither of his Irish Nationalist colleagues, John Redmond and John Dillon, "were willing to complicate the Irish part of the question in that way."[38] Even Loreburn, the chairman of the committee, who believed that "the right principle was *Home Rule all round*," concluded that a beginning should be made with Ireland as the first part of a larger scheme.[39] This was, of course, in line with Lloyd George's thinking. When C.P. Scott, the editor of the *Manchester Guardian* and a friend of many senior Liberals, realized in June that the government still had no plans to deal with "the crucial difficulty of the Irish representation which had baffled Gladstone," he suggested to Lloyd George that the difficulty could only be solved "in principle by a general system of devolution applicable to the same subjects (with the exception perhaps of railways) as were assigned to an Irish legislature e.g. education, land, licensing, and local development." Lloyd George doubted if such a scheme would work in England where "the progressive North would never submit to be placed under the control of the semi-feudal south." While he agreed with Scott that a "big solution" was needed, Lloyd George could not forget that "the people in England were wholly unprepared for such a scheme."[40]

Augustine Birrell, the member of the cabinet committee who had always opposed home rule all round, believed this system would so complicate matters that home rule itself would be wrecked. He much preferred home rule on Gladstonian lines and vowed to do his best to make other solutions, such as some form of devolution, impossible. At a full cabinet meeting in mid-August he protested "against Irish Home Rule being included in a devolution Federal scheme for Wales and Scotland which the country had never discussed."[41] Given the range of concern and the degree of reconsideration, it was not surprising that the second draft bill which circulated among the committee members in August 1911 contained provisions for grand committees based on Lloyd George's idea. Nevertheless, progress overall had been slow and there was still a great deal left to do. Herbert Samuel informed Herbert Gladstone in mid-September that the home rule bill was "in being but with a good many blanks and square brackets. The Cabinet have not discussed it yet, but only our Committee. It is largely Haldane and Loreburn's work, but one ingenious and bold feature is Lloyd George's ... Finance has still to be considered, when the report of the Committee of experts is to hand."[42]

The Liberals had always known that the financial clauses of a home rule bill would be the most difficult to devise and the most contentious. They therefore awaited the report of the Primrose committee with some anxiety but could not have expected recommendations so at variance with their predilections. The Primrose report was handed to the government on 27 October 1911 and printed as a parliamentary paper in April 1912. The committee pointed out that the financial relationship between Great Britain and Ireland had changed a great deal since 1886. Whereas in that year the Irish contributed some £2 million more to the United Kingdom exchequer than they received, in 1910–11 they had a balance of indebtedness of £1 million and the situation could only worsen with the implementation of more social programs. Ireland was rapidly losing the possibility of becoming self-sufficient. The difficulty was that Ireland was largely rural, her natural resources were limited, and she was dependent on customs and excise for the bulk of her revenues. Large expenditures were beyond her capacity under existing financial arrangements. The Primrose committee therefore rejected the various Gladstonian solutions of 1886 and 1893 and recommended that Ireland be given control over all taxation in Ireland, including customs and excise, and that the imperial exchequer should assume the liability for the old age pensions granted up to the date "the transfer of powers" took place. The committee also suggested that Ireland should not be asked to make an imperial contribution until she had reduced her deficit, but that she should assume full responsibility for the whole of Irish local expenditure.[43]

These recommendations would have given Ireland a considerable degree of financial control and were in accordance with the arguments of many of the Irish Nationalist leaders as well as with the views of Erskine Childers, the author of *The Framework of Home Rule*, who favoured dominion status for Ireland. They were not, however, suggestions that a Liberal and traditionally free-trade cabinet found attractive. The possibility of a tariff war between Great Britain and Ireland was anathema to them. Only Birrell favoured the Primrose plan, and it was quickly rejected by the cabinet. Herbert Samuel, the postmaster-general, was asked to examine the financial issue once more and to report directly to the cabinet committee of which he was a member. The consequence was a stream of highly detailed memoranda throughout November. After considerable discussion, Samuel presented his proposals to the cabinet on 4 December 1911 and with some slight modifications they were included in the draft home rule bill of 5 March 1912.

Samuel's scheme was highly complex and it is doubtful that many fully understood it. The frequent and complicated memoranda that he generated underlined the difficulties associated with devising a devolutionary scheme, whether it was to be Irish home rule or home rule all round. The problems associated with establishing Ireland's "real" revenue, dividing taxing powers, and ensuring a "fair" Irish contribution to imperial expenditure were endemic to any devolutionary effort. The difficulties were, of course, compounded by the fact that the examination of the constitutional, legal, and political questions had been largely kept separate from the financial. Even when they were seemingly joined, through Samuel, in the cabinet committee, so few members grasped the full implications that for all intents and purposes they continued to be separate. However, as the months passed, two aspects of Samuel's scheme became increasingly clear. First, it was the antithesis of separation. Its very complexity guaranteed a close connection between Great Britain and Ireland and would have made any future adaptation to home rule all round or federalism for the United Kingdom that much more difficult. And second, Samuel's scheme was based on a 32-county Ireland. Any subsequent plan to grant Ulster, or a portion of Ulster, a special relationship with Great Britain would have disrupted the delicate financial balance of the scheme and perhaps necessitated the withdrawal of the existing home rule bill and the introduction of a new one which might have dragged the issue into an election. It would also have compounded the problem of devising an appropriate financial scheme without being able to draw upon the revenues of industrial Belfast.

In framing his proposals Samuel worked from a number of assumptions. He reasoned that the Irish government should start with sufficient revenue not only to cover its initial expenditure without having to impose fresh taxation but also to ensure a margin of flexibility. He argued that while the Irish parliament should have the power to both raise and reduce taxes, including customs duties, it should not have the power to levy customs duties on articles not included in the customs tariff of Great Britain. With these basic objects in mind, Samuel then proposed that the Irish government should defray the whole of Irish expenditure except the charges for old age pensions, insurance, land purchase, existing constabulary pensions, and the collection of revenue which would be borne by the imperial exchequer. With the exception of the post office, to be controlled by the Irish government which would collect its receipts, all of the existing and future Irish revenues were to be collected by the imperial treasury. The treasury would transfer to the Irish exchequer an annual sum sufficient to its needs. The Irish parliament would have the power to add to any of the customs duties imposed by the imperial parliament as well as to the income tax, excise on beer and spirits, and estate duties but only to a limited extent to be defined by the act, and to add to other excise duties, stamps, land, and miscellaneous taxes without statutory limit. The Irish parliament would also have the power to impose new taxes in areas not included in the above and to reduce any of the taxes paid by Irish people. It would have the right to take over the charge for old age pensions and insurance. In turn, the imperial parliament would have the power to apply to Ireland any increase or decrease of customs, excise on beer and spirits, income tax, and estate duties applied to the rest of the United Kingdom. Essentially, the Irish were to have no primary control over customs and excise. Samuel had clearly rejected the Primrose report and had worked to devise a scheme that would establish a high degree of British control over Irish finance, leaving the Irish with responsibilities but little power, and subject to the whims of British, mainly English, decisions in the imperial parliament. Even so, his proposals were considered too generous by most Unionists and even some Liberals. Needless to say, they did not please the Irish Nationalists who had hoped for much more. The debate over the financial details of the home rule bill was to occupy much energy on all sides and considerable parliamentary time throughout 1912.[44]

Samuel's proposals and those of the long-standing cabinet committee were considered for the first time at a full cabinet meeting on 7 December 1911. Home rule all round, federalism, and Lloyd George's grand committee scheme were all discussed at some length but it was clear at this meeting that there was little support for a wide-ranging shake-up of the British constitution. John Burns found the discussion "very interesting" but concluded that "sweet reasonableness was the only way to win Home Rule for Ireland. Scotland may come. Wales must wait. England does not want it. What was not needed was a welter of parochialisms."[45] Other members of the full cabinet, especially John Morley, McKinnon Wood, and Charles Hobhouse, were equally uninterested in federalism. Asquith, who had admitted earlier in the year the merit of "going on the new line of devolution all round," and who as recently as November had been reminded by William O'Brien of the advantages of the federal system, appears to have remained silent on the question. For Asquith, England was the obstacle. They could not go back to the Heptarchy of Anglo-Saxon Britain. He was certainly not going to divide his cabinet by strongly advocating either home rule all round or federalism.[46] It was decided to send the draft bill incorporating both Samuel's and Lloyd George's proposals to John Redmond and John Dillon for comment.

Although the cabinet committee, which previously had been desultory to the point of negligence in its activity, did meet more frequently in January

1912, its role virtually disappeared in subsequent weeks as the task of preparing a final draft of the bill was increasingly assumed by Birrell, Asquith, and Samuel in close consultation with Redmond and Dillon. The turning-point appears to have been a cabinet meeting on 25 January at which Redmond's and Dillon's response to the draft bill was considered.[47] The Irish leaders had been told that although the financial scheme was "the result of the fullest and gravest consideration," the other provisions "had been thrown hurriedly together, and [were] not to be regarded as expressing the settled view of cabinet." In itself this was a damning comment on the perfunctory treatment given such a vital issue by the Loreburn committee and by the government as a whole, but it did provide Redmond and Dillon with an opportunity to ensure that a revised draft contained no devolutionary references, whether to home rule all round, federalism, or even grand committees.

Redmond and Dillon wanted the 1912 bill to adhere to the Gladstonian models of 1886 and 1893. An Irish legislature should be given power to make laws "with respect to all matters relating to Ireland except those expressly excluded." They believed Irish sentiment would be "profoundly affected" by any change. The chances of litigation would be greatly increased and the Irish parliament degraded in the eyes of the Irish people. They were also upset by Samuel's financial scheme. They believed Ireland "should have distinctly given to her at once the power of imposing all taxes whatsoever," including customs and excise, subject to agreed restrictions. As for keeping the collection of taxes in imperial hands "for all time," it was a "retrograde step" and a severe departure from the 1886 and 1893 bills. They also wanted Part II of the bill, containing Lloyd George's grand committees scheme, eliminated; in part because a proposal to deal with England, Scotland, and Wales as well as Ireland had never been before the electors, but primarily because the "inclusion of such provisions will lead to attempts by at least Scotch and Welsh to enlarge Scotch and Welsh provisions on the proposed Irish lines, and, consequently, to prolonged debates and the possible killing of the Bill, with the inevitable consequence that Home Rule for Ireland will again be postponed indefinitely." Redmond and Dillon approved of the grand committees as temporary expedients for "meeting the crux presented by the continued representation of Ireland in Parliament;" but, they argued, it could "be carried out, in all probability by Standing Orders, and so brought about, would stand as a pledge that the Government intend, at the earliest moment, to complete their scheme of federation for the United Kingdom. Put into the Irish Home Rule Bill, it would, we believe, absolutely shatter the chance of the Bill becoming law in the immediate future."

The cabinet had a mixed reaction to the protests of the Irish leaders. Since there had never been a deep-rooted commitment to federalism or even widespread support for the Lloyd George plan, it was not altogether surprising that the cabinet did not dig in its heels on this issue. Nevertheless, it was only the persistence of Birrell and the continued lobbying of Redmond and Dillon that led to the eventual removal of that section of the bill. When Asquith presented his proposal to the House of Commons in April, it contained no reference to any devolutionary schemes for the United Kingdom. The need to appease the Irish Nationalists and to avoid a cabinet split at a time when government fortunes in the country were low prompted Asquith to relent. However, neither the prime minister nor his cabinet could be shifted on the financial issues. As John Burns put it, "Fiscal Independence was impossible."[48] The Irish would have to be content with the right to raise and reduce, within limits, customs and excise duties. Although not at all satisfied with this arrangement, Redmond and Dillon soon realized they would have to accept it. To remain adamant would endanger the introduction of a home rule bill. Reluctantly, they acquiesced, and the financial clauses in the home rule bill of 1912 were based, with only slight modifications, on Samuel's ideas.

Overall the bill, as it emerged from the intense deliberations of Asquith, Samuel, and Birrell in March and early April, closely resembled that of 1893 as amended in committee. There naturally had had to be some changes in the reserved matters to take account of social reforms since the 1890s, and the financial clauses were markedly different, but in essence Asquith's home rule bill of 1912 was firmly in the Gladstonian tradition. Despite considerable pressure from within and outside his cabinet, Asquith had finally decided to deal only with the immediate and pressing problem of Ireland and not with wider constitutional reform. Home rule all round and federalism were rejected as unnecessary complications for which there seemed no fundamental need.[49]

Asquith introduced the third home rule bill on 11 April 1912.[50] In doing so he suggested that the government considered it "the first step, and only the first step, in a larger and more comprehensive policy" which in the interests of the United Kingdom and the empire would emancipate the imperial parliament from local cares and burdens. If this statement was designed as a sop to the Liberal federalists or the Scottish home rulers – often the same – and as an indirect appeal to the Unionist federalists, it had little chance of success, for the scheme that Asquith outlined was a very modest home rule proposal.

The bill proposed the establishment of an Irish parliament of two Houses, a House of Commons consisting of 164 elected members and a Senate of forty. Disagreements between the two houses were to be settled, as in 1893, by joint majority vote if the bill in question was reintroduced in the next session. Ireland was to continue to have forty-two MPs in the United Kingdom parliament. Supreme power and authority were to remain at Westminster, and there was no question of the Irish parliament being anything other than subordinate. The lord lieutenant was to be the head of the Irish executive representing the crown and his term was now fixed in a nonpolitical fashion at six years. He was to have the right of veto over Irish legislation but would first have to consult the ministry in London. As in 1886 and 1893, a vast range of powers and responsibilities were withheld from the Dublin parliament including defence, foreign affairs, treaties, peace and war, treason, naturalization, trade with any place outside Ireland, merchant shipping, coinage, trade marks, copyright, patents, and lighthouses. The Irish, of course, were also denied control of customs and excise and, under the Samuel scheme, were only given the authority to raise and reduce duties on a narrow range of goods and within prescribed limits. Old age pensions, national insurance, and labour exchanges were reserved to the imperial parliament until the Irish requested their transfer but land purchase and the collection of taxes were reserved in perpetuity. The Royal Irish Constabulary was initially reserved but was to be transferred to Irish control after six years. As in 1886 and 1893 no laws were to be passed by the Irish parliament to establish or endow any religious body. Apart from this clause, designed to protect the interests of the Protestant minority, the bill made no special provision for Ulster despite the obvious antipathy to a 32-county home rule bill in that area of Ireland.

Apart from the financial clauses the most radical break with the 1893 bill – although not with that of 1886 – was the method provided for the revision of the financial arrangements. For the purpose of revising the financial provisions, members of the Irish House of Commons were to be summoned to the Westminster parliament in sufficient numbers to make the representation of Ireland equivalent to the representation of Great Britain on the basis of population. For the purpose of the revision members of the Irish House were to be deemed members of the United Kingdom House of Commons. This was an extraordinary proposal but it did reflect the difficulties associated with devolutionary schemes that were hybrids of the colonial and federal models. By retaining forty-two Irish MPs at Westminster and providing such a contentious means of revising the financial arrangements, Asquith and his colleagues were only creating enormous constitutional problems for the future. These had not been unrecognized or unexplored in the 1880s and 1890s but the Liberals turned a blind eye to those earlier analyses despite Ilbert's reminders. What in effect the 1912 bill did was create three new parliaments: the Irish parliament, a Westminster parliament with a reduced Irish representation, and a parliament especially designed to revise the financial arrangements between Great Britain and Ireland. Not only had Asquith and his colleagues saddled the nation once more with the myriad problems associated with an "in" clause but they had opened up new avenues of constitutional difficulty. And in doing so they had ignored Ulster.[51]

It was not difficult for the federalists and those in support of home rule all round to demonstrate that the bill was not federal in status or a step in the direction of general devolution. There was not a proper demarcation of responsibilities in either the legislative or financial spheres, presumably one of the key features of a federal system, while the right of the Irish parliament to vary customs and excise duties and the continued supremacy of the imperial parliament were markedly antifederal features. Leaving the residual powers in Dublin rather than at Westminster was viewed by many as potentially separatist rather than a step towards a loose federation. In the debates on first and second reading there were a number of critical references to Asquith's claim that the bill was but the initial stage of "a larger and more comprehensive policy." Apart from pointing out that England had never been consulted about such a scheme, most speakers, Unionist and federalist alike, were sharply condemnatory of a piecemeal approach to a general resolution of United Kingdom difficulties. Balfour thought that it was "futile and absurd." A federal system devised on a piecemeal basis would be "unsymmetrical, botched ... utterly unworkable." Other Unionists such as Harry Lawson, George Cave, and Leo Amery were so disgusted by Asquith's suggestions that they took time to remind the Liberal government and the House what the essential features of federalism were. As far as Cave and most observers were concerned, there was no federalism in the bill at all, while Lawson frankly called it antifederal.[52] The Scottish Liberals who favoured home rule all round were bitterly disappointed but were prepared to vote in principle for the bill as a first step toward a more comprehensive scheme.[53]

One of the first criticisms to be levelled at the bill from outside the House was by Oliver, who now reentered the debate over the United Kingdom constitution after a protracted silence. Using his pseudonym "Pacificus," Oliver wrote a lengthy letter to the *Times* criticizing the bill.[54] He suggested that both those Unionists opposed to any change in the existing constitutional system and those who had been willing to consider the alternative of a federal solution would find strong reasons to oppose the bill. Oliver fastened immediately on Asquith's suggestion that the bill might be the first step toward a federal system. He pointed out that "The first essential condition of a federal arrangement is that it should consist of not fewer than two units of an equal *status* entirely independent of one another and entirely without responsibility one to another ... The second condition ... is that there shall be one supreme authority in which all the units are represented fairly and equitably ... This is the essence of a Federation, that the various Federal units should accept the leadership of a supreme Federal authority, and that they should neither make nor meddle in one another's domestic and local affairs." Ireland could be freed to manage its own domestic affairs either by being granted her independence – which was inconceivable to Oliver – or by making the United Kingdom a confederation; there was no middle course. Under the second method England and Scotland would have to have domestic parliaments as well as Ireland. There was no alternative to this because the British constitution could not be turned into a federation piecemeal or by stages. There had to be a supreme parliament but it could not perform its supreme functions and the functions of one or more domestic units as well. The attempt of Asquith and his colleagues "to combine these two sets of functions in one body must inevitably lead to clashing and friction of the most mischievous character." Oliver asserted that if the bill became law and was put into effect it would break down because it was "a botched piece of work."[55]

Other commentators and constitutional experts were equally critical. J.A.R. Marriott preferred devolution to federalism because he was convinced the real problem was parliamentary congestion which could be resolved by an extension of local government. But in assessing Asquith's bill from the federal perspective, Marriott noted that the supremacy of the imperial parliament was left unimpaired and inviolate, which was an emphatic repudiation of one of the cardinal principles of federalism: the distribution of power between a central and a local legislature. The proposed Senate was replete with difficulties, especially as a long-term device for the protection of minorities, and the financial arrangements were "extraordinarily intricate." As for the retention of Irish representatives at Westminster, it had provided "a crumb of comfort for the Federalist," at the expense of constitutional congruity, but there was no genuine federalism in the bill. Marriott's overall assessment of the bill summed up the reaction of most observers. He thought it had been framed

to catch every breath of the wind of popularity. In the distribution of favours nobody had been left out. There is something for the thorough-going separatist, inspired by nationalist fervour; there is something for the timid devolutionist, anxious only to secure 'gas and water' Home Rule; something for the advocate of Colonial self-government; and something for the well-meaning but muddle-headed federalist. But is not the dexterity of the Bill likely to prove its destruction? Is it not, in fact, an ingenious mosaic, cunningly compacted and curiously inlaid ... but grotesquely lacking in consistency of principle, in unity of design, and coherence of construction?

Finally, for Marriott, the failure of the Asquith administration to allow for Ulster's needs was a startling flaw.[56]

J.H. Morgan, a constitutional authority, was no less acerbic. He referred to the bill as "a singular triumph of empiricism. It defies the frontal attacks of the theorist, for the simple reason that there is nothing theoretical about it. It is not 'Federalism,' it is not Dualism, still less is it to be compared with a colonial constitution of the usual type."[57] After the passage of the bill the bond between Ireland and Britain would be tighter than that which united, for example, Massachussetts and the United States: "There is all the difference in the juristic world between the surrender of certain powers by a group of sovereign states like the American 'colonies' to a new Federal Government and the delegation of certain powers by a single sovereign State like the United Kingdom to a provincial legislature." Under the Government of Ireland bill, sovereignty would remain where it was at present – in the imperial parliament. The veto of the crown on Irish legislation undermined the status of the Irish legislature. From whatever aspect the proposed Irish constitution was regarded – executive, legislative, judiciary – it was patently not federal.[58] The bill proposed a delegation of both executive and legislative authority. Unlike a federal constitution, it contemplated no distribution of sovereignty. The imperial government and the imperial parliament would remain supreme. For example, the powers of the Irish legislature were not exclusive of the powers of the imperial parliament, but merely concurrent, and whenever an Irish and an imperial statute conflicted the rule of construction would be in favour of the latter. Nevertheless, Morgan was impressed by the fact that the executive power transferred was co-extensive with legislative authority. He believed it constituted "a grant of a larger measure of self-government" than was to be found in either the 1886 or the 1893 bill. This was not a conclusion that either Unionists or federalists would have found comforting.

The Scottish Liberal federalists were particularly disappointed by Asquith's bill. They had hoped the bill would be more overtly devolutionary in nature. Even if it had to be primarily an Irish bill they had expected some detailed provision for moving toward "federal home rule."[59] They initially supported the principles of the bill in the House but soon put direct pressure on the prime minister in an effort to remind him of Scottish aspirations for some form of self-government.[60] On 6 May 1912 a deputation of Scottish Liberal MPs led by Eugene Wason, Munro-Ferguson, and Murray Macdonald met with Asquith. They urged the prime minister to introduce a Scottish home rule bill next session to satisfy Scotland's desire for control over its own affairs. While admitting that there was no ground-swell of national opinion in favour of home rule, they maintained that there was concern and disgruntlement at the general neglect of Scottish business. That concern would increasingly turn to annoyance in Scottish affairs. Munro-Ferguson was particularly worried that Irish home rule would delay rather than hasten home rule all round. He believed that giving Ireland control of the post office as well as the right to vary customs duties would be particularly difficult to defend "from the Federal point of view." Such arrangements would be impediments to devolution. Both Munro-Ferguson and Macdonald would have preferred "devolution all round" but at least wanted a Scottish parliament which, they assured Asquith, would not endanger the union.

In replying to his visitors, Asquith was sympathetic. He must have realized that the Scottish Liberals were crucial to his majority and that it was imperative not to offend them on the issue of self-government. His problem, of course, was that he was boxed in by the antifederal nature of many of the clauses in the bill, particularly those dealing with finance. He also knew that not all the Scottish Liberals were committed federalists and he must have hoped that some general words of encouragement from him would be sufficient to keep the majority of the Scottish members onside. He expressed sympathy for their desires and their goal. He admitted home rule did need to be viewed in a larger context, and he assured them that while Irish home rule was urgent it was only the first step towards a distant objective. But he reminded them that it was necessary to go "step by step," since it was not possible to take a particular pattern of local autonomy and apply it without modification or qualification to all the different parts of the United Kingdom. The prime minister claimed he would like eventually to apply devolution to all parts of the United Kingdom but "by appropriate methods." He could not promise a Scottish home rule bill next session.[61]

Asquith's blandishments were unconvincing and during the next six months the Scottish Liberals, led for the most part by such federalists as Wason, MacCallum Scott, and Murray Macdonald, proved a major worry to the Liberal government. In July MacCallum Scott introduced his private member's bill for a devolution of "the work peculiar to local administration and legislation" to four local parliaments. The bill was an adaptation of the Government of Ireland bill to home rule all round.[62] Although widely supported in the House, it came to nothing. Increasingly, the Liberal federalists criticized the financial proposals of the bill, fastening on the antifederal nature of the customs provisions. The Unionists were quick to seize on the same issue. While they honestly feared the potential disintegrative impact on the United Kingdom of variable customs duties between Ireland and Great Britain, they were more interested in the nuisance value of the issue. Those who were well informed on the subject probably realized that the bill explicitly ruled out using the right to vary customs duties for protective purposes. The Unionists naturally welcomed any opportunity to embarrass and endanger the government but their real and overriding concern was Ulster.[63] Not so the Liberal federalists who were adamant in their opposition to the financial proposals. When the government appeared to be in danger of losing the support of up to sixty-five MPs on the customs issue, it decided on 21 November 1912 to eliminate the power of the Irish parliament to reduce customs. This naturally infuriated Redmond but again he had to back down for fear of endangering the overall bill. It was the only major victory for the federalists in 1912 and while in itself satisfying it did not particularly advance their cause.[64]

During the latter half of 1912 much of the concern and activity of the Liberals was directed to defending and refashioning its financial proposals. Once the decision had been taken to eliminate from the bill the power of the Irish parliament to reduce customs duties, the major hurdle to the acceptance of the financial proposals had been overcome. On 27 November that amendment was passed by over one hundred votes with the support of seventeen of the Liberal dissidents. Thereafter the remaining clauses were pushed through the House under closure and the report stage was successfully passed on 8 January 1913. By that time Ulster had dominated the thinking of most politicians and publicists for some two months, and once again federalism was being broached as a possible solution of that particular problem.

CHAPTER SEVEN

Ulster and the Federal Solution, 1912–1914

The fact that Ulster would prove an obstacle to the quick and easy passage of a home rule bill should not have surprised the Liberals or Asquith. Gladstone had considered making special provision for Ulster in 1886, and although he had finally abandoned the idea, the serious nature of the problem had certainly been apparent to him and to Bryce. The 1893 bill had also made no provision for Ulster, but the Ulster Defence Union had nevertheless been established that year to ensure Ulster's interests were protected and any home rule bill resisted. Again the devolution crisis of 1904–5 had shocked the Ulster Unionists into loud protests and had led to the formation in 1905 of the Ulster Unionist Council. After it had become clear that the parliament bill would pass the council had chosen as its leader Sir Edward Carson, a southern Unionist and a formidable and successful barrister at the English bar. He joined forces with Captain James Craig to organize a highly efficient opposition to home rule. As he had frankly told Craig, he had not joined for "a mere game of bluff."[1] He was deadly serious about Ulster resistance to home rule, and was prepared to use force if necessary. As we have seen, his personal degree of commitment and the backing that he had among Ulster Protestants had been dramatically underlined on 23 September 1911 by a massive demonstration at Craigavon. On that occasion, Carson clearly stated that if the home rule bill passed a provisional government would be established in Ulster under the leadership of the Ulster Unionist Council.

These developments had not gone unnoticed and throughout 1911 and 1912 a number of individuals had drawn attention to the problem of Ulster and the possible adoption of a federal scheme to resolve the matter. Both Churchill and Lloyd George were intrigued by the idea and had hinted at such a resolution in February 1912. Asquith chose to ignore Ulster in his home rule bill of April 1912, either because he did not appreciate how serious Carson and the Ulster Unionist Council were or because he hoped that once the bill had been passed twice by the Commons the Unionist party would be obliged to bargain and accept a modified and devolutionary scheme in order to protect Ulster. Such a tactic would presumably have removed a major political weapon from the Unionist arsenal and considerably bolstered the chances of the Liberals at the next election. As appealing as this theory is, there is no evidence to support it. There was no long-range planning by the Liberals and no devious manipulation of circumstance. Asquith and his cabinet allowed the situation to drift until virtually the last moment when they scrambled desperately to pull the fat out of the fire by suggesting some modified scheme. The intensity of Unionist opposition to the Liberals, and of support for Carson, was deepened by the choice of Bonar Law, a Canadian of Ulster descent, as leader of the party in place of Balfour on 8 November 1911. Determined and narrow opposition replaced a broader perspective at the head of the Unionists. Increasingly, from the spring of 1912 to the spring of 1914, home rule all round/devolution/federalism were advocated and discussed as the only possible solutions to a situation that was inexorably drawing the United Kingdom to the brink of civil war. The Scottish and Welsh federalists could but watch or cry out weakly and repetitively from the sidelines.

The only men in the Asquith cabinet to give any thought to the Ulster problem and a possible solution were Augustine Birrell, Lloyd George, and Winston Churchill. In August 1911, at about the time the Parliament Act was passed, Birrell had suggested to Churchill that if a referendum on a county basis were held in Ulster probably only Antrim and Down would oppose home rule. Those two counties could then be left out of the settlement for five years when a second referendum would settle the matter one way or the other.[2] Unfortunately, Birrell did not publicly press his ideas, but Lloyd George and Churchill did push them within cabinet. Neither man was a committed home ruler. They recognized, however, that the Liberal party did have a commitment to fulfil. Equally, they were fed up with the amount of time and energy the Irish question demanded. Both men wanted to get the matter settled so that the party could pursue its social and economic reform program. It was clear to them by early 1912 that Ulster would prove a stumbling block, so in February they suggested to cabinet that those Ulster counties with a Protestant majority should be given the option to contract out of home rule. Both Loreburn and Morley strongly opposed any such suggestion, and Asquith finally sided with them. Churchill attempted to raise the issue of exclusion again in March but to no avail. The cabinet decided that the bill should deal with a united Ireland and that no special provision should be made for Ulster. The wish to avoid a major split in cabinet and the uncertainty about the seriousness of the situation in Ulster deterred Asquith and others from employing the twin ideas of a referendum and exclusion.[3] With the decision made, Lloyd George gave the matter of Ulster little attention until November 1913, but Churchill was less easily dissuaded and he soon began seeking counsel on the matter from members of the Round Table movement who were able to place the issue of Ulster in the wider contexts of both United Kingdom and imperial federation.[4]

The issue of partition was raised publicly for the first time in mid-June during the committee stage of the home rule bill. Thomas Agar-Robartes, the Liberal member for St Austell, moved for the exclusion of the counties of Antrim, Armagh, Down, and Londonderry from the provisions of the Home Rule Act.[5] The Liberals and the Nationalists quickly rejected the idea. Redmond viewed it as a wrecking amendment, while Asquith argued that Ireland could no more be split up than could England or Scotland. The Unionists voted for Robartes's motion in order to annoy the Liberals, but made it clear that they were fundamentally opposed to any form of home rule for Ireland. The amendment was easily defeated, but the three-day debate left both the small group of federalist MPs and the larger body of Liberal dissidents unhappy with the cursory attention given by the Liberals to both federalism and home rule all round.[6]

The Unionist party and its leadership were also dissatisfied with the Liberals' attitude to Ulster and took an increasingly provocative stand. On 27 July, at a large Unionist demonstration at Blenheim, Bonar Law stated flatly, and in a menacing fashion, that the government would have to assume full responsibility for refusing to treat Ulster separately: " ... if an attempt were made without the clearly expressed will of the people of this country, and as part of a corrupt Parliamentary bargain, to deprive these men of their birthright, they would be justified in resisting by all means in their power, including force ... if the attempt be made under present conditions I can imagine no length of resistance to which Ulster will go in which I shall not be ready to support them."[7]

This threat overshadowed all discussions of the bill during the next two years. Churchill certainly took Law's words seriously, and was appalled by them, as he indicated to Garvin on 10 August: "I am shocked at these threats of Ulster violence which are made by Conservative leaders. Do they think they will never come back to power? Have they no policy for Ireland except to make it ungovernable? They are the more inexcusable because no one that I know of has ever contemplated the application of force to Ulster. The principle and doctrine lately enunciated would dissolve the framework not only of the British Empire, but of civil society."[8]

A few days later he wrote to Lloyd George about raising once more the question of Ulster exclusion: "The time has come when action about Ulster must be settled. We ought to give any Irish county the option of remaining at Westminster for a period of 5 to 10 years, or some variant of this ... Time has in no way weakened the force of the arguments you used in January [sic], and I am prepared to support you in pressing them."[9] At the end of August he wrote to Redmond in what proved a futile personal attempt to persuade the Nationalist leader to consider giving the Protestant counties of Ulster the option of remaining out of the home rule scheme "for some years,"[10] Churchill also continued to correspond and consult with Curtis and the Round Table. He had talked at length with Curtis during a weekend at Cliveden, and in early September he invited Curtis and Edward Grigg to meet him for a day on board the Admiralty yacht *Enchantress*. The two men proposed "to improve his mind laboriously all day long."[11] Whether or not they had "improved" his mind, they were clearly successful in urging Churchill to take the initiative over federalism.

On 12 September, shortly after his meeting with Curtis and Grigg, Churchill devoted the greater part of a major speech in his Dundee constituency to a consideration of a federal system of government for the United Kingdom. Churchill said the government advocated home rule as a means of solving the Irish question but also because it was intended to be "a forerunner and a preliminary to a genuine system of self-government in all the four countries, which are, and must always remain, united under the Crown and the Imperial Parliament." He thought Scotland and Wales would gain immensely from being able to manage their own national affairs, and there would be no difficulty in extending to them a parliament or a national council. There would, he said, be "no difficulty in applying the federal system to Scotland or Wales as well as to Ireland," but there would be a difficulty with England. England was so great and populous that an English parliament, whatever its functions or limitations might be, could not fail to be almost as powerful as the imperial parliament. If a quarrel developed between the English and imperial parliaments, it might tear the state in two. If it were desired to establish a workable federal system in the United Kingdom, then it would be necessary to face the task of dividing England into several self-governing areas, perhaps as many as ten or twelve, such as Lancashire, Yorkshire, the Midlands, and Greater London. Although he did not mention Ulster directly, it was clear that if England were to be divided it would be natural to establish Ulster, or some portion of it, as a separate parliamentary unit.[12]

Although Churchill had spoken speculatively and not as a representative of the cabinet, his speech raised a furor in both parties and thrust the concept of federalism to the forefront of political debate where it was to remain until early 1914. Churchill had made no mention of Ulster in his speech but understandably the Unionists seized upon his words as evidence that the government might be backing away from a pure home rule bill. To many it seemed the thin edge of the wedge of Ulster exclusion. By that autumn many in the Unionist party were in fact prepared to concede home rule if the Protestant counties of the north east could be protected. Churchill's Liberal colleagues were, of course, shocked by his speech, about which they had been given no preliminary warning. They were appalled that he had resurrected the federal proposals that had been rejected earlier in the year. After all, if it were assumed that the Liberals, or even some of them, were prepared to have ten parliaments within England, why would it be so difficult to have two in Ireland? Courtenay Ilbert, who had penned the devastating critique of Churchill's 1911 proposals, was astounded. The ideas in the Dundee speech were essentially those he had earlier refuted. He was convinced that Churchill's speech owed much to the pressure applied by his "young friends of the Round Table."[13] Ilbert, of course, was absolutely correct.[14]

When it became clear that Asquith had no intention of introducing into the bill any special arrangement for Ulster or of paying any heed to Churchill's ideas, both the Ulster Unionists and the Liberal dissidents attempted to force the issue. D.V. Pirie, the Scottish home ruler and a supporter of federal devolution, tried to have an amendment brought before the House in December by which the nine Ulster counties would be excluded from the bill until a majority of the province's representatives in the House petitioned the king in favour of inclusion. This was similar, although more extensive in scope, to Agar-Robartes's motion of June. Pirie was unsuccessful but that same month, December 1912, the Ulster Unionist Council decided to put down an amendment excluding the whole province from the bill. After a protracted and heated debate in cabinet, during which Lloyd George and Churchill argued vehemently for some concession to Ulster, the Liberals decided not to respond and to stick with the original policy of a united Ireland. Carson moved the amendment on 1 January 1913. It was an historic moment. It was the first time that the Unionists had publicly implied the acceptance of home rule for the three southern and western provinces of Ireland provided Ulster was left out.

Carson and others had already made it clear that to incorporate Ulster would lead to civil war. The debate on the amendment lasted only one day. The government did not budge and Carson's proposal was easily rejected. The rest of the debate on the bill was an anticlimax. Third reading lasted only two days, 15 and 16 January 1913, and the Liberal margin of victory was a commanding 110 votes. While the Liberals were pleased by the successful passage of the bill through the Commons, some of them realized that the problem of Ulster had not been resolved, only avoided. For the rest of the year Ulster held the spotlight. Most observers concluded that in the end some form of exclusion would have to be agreed. Discussion revolved around the possible size of an excluded Ulster. Not unexpectedly, Asquith was slow to respond. In fact, he made no formal offer until March 1914. Much happened before then.

The home rule debate of late 1912 prompted Dunraven, Brassey, and Moreton Frewen to renew their campaign for some form of devolution or "federalism" as a solution to both the Irish problem – more specifically the Ulster question – and the general congestion in the House of Commons. Increasingly too a demand was heard for a conference or convention, i.e., "a settlement by consent," similar to those held in Canada in the 1860s and in South Africa in 1908, in order to thrash out the matter and to find a compromise solution. Many of the federalists were among the leading proponents of such a conference.

As early as September 1912 Dunraven had suggested to Bonar Law that many Unionists were anxious for a compromise in order to preserve the union. He believed Carsonism would "melt away under the approval by the electorate of a moderate scheme on federal lines." He suggested a consultative conference on the whole constitutional question.[15] At the same time, Moreton Frewen wrote candidly to Law referring to himself and Dunraven as "... we pacificators in federal trappings – the worst of wolves in sheep's clothing."[16] Pressure on Bonar Law also came from T.A. Brassey, who urged him to "Settle the Home Rule question on Canadian or Federal lines – give N.E. Ulster a little show of its own if it really desires it – and the Conservative party would receive a large measure of support in Ireland, Scotland & Wales."[17] In late October Dunraven attached his name to a manifesto issued by some twenty-four Irish Unionists, calling for "the adoption of Home Rule by compromise" and suggesting a fully representative nonparty conference to achieve it.[18] He followed up these efforts with an article in the January 1913 issue of the *Nineteenth Century* calling for a settlement of the Irish crisis "by consent," preferably by devolution, "on federal lines," to local legislatures of matters currently cluttering the parliamentary time-table, so that the way to imperial federation could be eased.[19]

For his part, Brassey continued to press the Unionists personally. In fact, in separate letters to Bonar Law and Lord Lansdowne written in early January 1913, Brassey pushed uncharacteristically close to the bone. He suggested the Unionists were carrying their loyalty to the Ulsterites too far. "You are not justified," he admonished Law, "in sacrificing any British Institution ... the interests of the Country and of the Empire on the altar of that loyalty ... you will always have the dead weight of Irish, Scotch and Welsh votes against you until the Home Rule question is settled on Federal lines."[20] He elaborated in his letter to Lansdowne:

The only way out of the *impasse* is to deal with the Home Rule question on Federal or Conservative lines by the establishment of subordinate legislatures in England and Scotland as well as in Ireland. I am as opposed as any Unionist to the present Home Rule Bill, but I do urge upon you and other Unionist leaders that while maintaining your opposition to the present Bill you should seriously consider the alternative policy, and that you should tell the Ulstermen that Home Rule in some shape or other has become a necessity; but that you will resist the inclusion of Ulster with the rest of

Ireland unless the people of Ulster desire to be included ... I believe that if Ulster were offered a separate show of her own she would probably come in from the first, but would anyway not stand out for long.

In any case no durable and satisfactory solution of the Home Rule question can be reached except by consent; and the only way to arrive at agreement is to refer the whole Constitutional question to a Convention on the South African model in which all parties and all the nationalities of the United Kingdom should be represented ... I write strongly because I care.[21]

The Irish Nationalists would not have been impressed by these arguments. John Dillon, for example, was "prepared to go almost any length in the direction of Home Rule within Home Rule for the North-Eastern counties provided always that Ulster remained within the Bill as a part of Ireland, and not as cut out of the Bill and a part of England."[22]

The debate on the bill in the Lords at the end of January provided another opportunity for the federalists to publicize their views and express their concern. Dunraven spoke on the first day, 27 January. He supported the bill because it was "conceived in recognition of the principle of devolution, a principle the adoption of which I believe to be essential for a great many reasons. I believe devolution to be necessary, not by any means only for the welfare of Ireland but for the welfare of the United Kingdom, for the restoring of efficiency to Parliament, and for the permanency of representative institutions, and I do not believe that without the adoption of the principle of devolution any scheme or any device ever will bring closer together the component parts of the Empire." Relief of congestion had to be sought by "delegation, devolution, to subordinate bodies." Dunraven pointed out that Asquith's bill was not founded on federal principles. In fact, it was a bar to federation and if a federal bill were to become law in the future, then the current bill would have to be repealed. He called on the Liberals to "accept the bed-rock principle in this bill – devolution – and then in calm and dispassionate conference see if an agreement by consent cannot be arrived at."[23]

The debate also enabled Earl Grey to outline his views publicly for the first time. He began by informing the House that he planned to vote against the bill because it was a barrier to a federal solution of United Kingdom difficulties. Far from being conducive to harmony and peace, the bill would "promote discord and tend to civil war." He argued that "There are two great opposing principles of local self-government which we have to consider. One is the principle of nationalism, and the other is the principle of federalism. A system of local self-government based on the principle of nationalism leads to separation, but based on the principle of federation leads to unity ... I am opposed to this Bill because I am a convinced Federalist, and because I believe that this Bill being based upon the foundation of nationalism, is one which this House ought not to accept ... it is not suited to the federation of the British Isles."[24]

Having lived in Canada for some years, Grey realized the advantages of the federal system: "It is a system which combines local autonomy on domestic matters with unity of government in matters of common interest." The powers to be granted to Ireland should be those granted to the provinces under the BNA Act. In fact, "Ireland might possibly consist of two Provinces under a federal system – the North-East of Ulster would form one Province, and the rest of Ireland another."[25] Federalism would also relieve congestion in parliament and make of Ireland a friend not a foe. Nevertheless, although Grey believed the federal solution would help the Unionist party, England, and Ireland, his main reason for advocating the federation of the British Isles was "because of the increased strength and security it would bring to the Empire." He called for a conference of men of both parties, selected for their breadth of vision and high patriotism, to work together to create a constitution "most likely to ensure the permanent well-being of the United Kingdom, of the Empire, and of the whole of the English-speaking people."[26]

There were various other reference to devolution and to federalism throughout the debate but most commentators thought such a scheme lay far in the future. Some actually feared a written constitution, the curtailment of the central government's powers, and the need for a Supreme Court. Lord Selborne summed up the thinking of those who favoured imperial federation but balked at federalism for the United Kingdom. He did not think that because a truly imperial parliament might be created it was also necessary to create half-a-dozen subordinate parliaments in the United Kingdom:

We believe that the existing British Parliament relieved of its responsibility for the Navy, the Army, foreign policy, and India would be perfectly capable of dealing with all the requirements of the United Kingdom. We set that deliberately against that other ideal ... of a federal system. Lord Grey thinks that an imitation of the Canadian system would be the only possible solution of the difficulty for the United Kingdom. We do not agree with him. We prefer the South African system to the Canadian system, the unitary system to the federal system.

He was equally critical of Churchill's ideas for England: "I think that England will revolt at that point. I do not think she will exchange willingly her robe of perfect national unity for a patchwork quilt dragged out of the cup-board of the Anglo-Saxons."[27]

It was clear from the debate that the federalists and their sympathizers all too often disagreed with one another. Even Dunraven and Grey differed in their approach. Both agreed that federation was the aim, but Grey wanted to throw out the current bill and devise another while Dunraven was prepared to try and amend it. Nevertheless, Dunraven had liked Grey's speech. As he remarked to Frewen, "Grey has given birth to a baby that will grow into a big strong federal party and that is what we wanted."[28] Dunraven had worked ceaselessly for a compromise solution but he and others like him were on the periphery of political life and had little influence. He glumly admitted to O'Brien: "The trouble is that, at present, we are of no use to anybody. Useless to Unionists because we are Home Rulers though anti-Socialists. Useless to the government because we are anti-Socialist though Home Rulers. Useless to Free Importers and Fair Traders because we take neither side."[29] By mid-February even Brassey, the most optimistic of men, was beginning to have second thoughts about Unionist tactics. He now urged Bonar Law to work for the total defeat of the home rule bill: "There must be no weakening in your loyalty to the Ulster Unionists."[30]

One other familiar voice was heard at this time – that of the constitutional expert A.V. Dicey. In February 1913 Dicey published and widely distributed a book on the home rule bill of 1912 entitled *A Fool's Paradise*. It was not a learned constitutional treatise but a polemic designed to persuade Unionists to do all in their power to defeat the bill. He argued that it would not satisfy the Irish Nationalists or free England or Britain of Irish problems. As for the federal arguments, he quickly dismissed them in a familiar fashion. Federalism would mean a division of powers which would weaken the country; it would mean too heavy a reliance on the courts; it would lead to divided allegiances; it would be a disintegrative step; and it would not at all meet the Irish desire for home rule. As for it being a step toward the wider federation of the empire, Dicey thought that ludicrous. He could not understand how the unity of the British Empire would be enhanced by the disunity of the United Kingdom.[31] Bryce, to whom Dicey wrote, agreed that neither home rule for Ireland nor a federal constitution for the United Kingdom would be a step toward imperial federation. Furthermore, he believed there was no real desire for federalization in Scotland and doubted if there was any in Wales. "It would in my opinion be an injury to the United Kingdom as a whole to give separate legislatures to Scotland, Ireland and Wales. I doubt very much whether this sort of federalisation would even do much to relieve Parliament of its present congestion of business and experience in this country has convinced me that to introduce diversity of legislation where there is now uniformity of legislation would be a step backwards."[32]

Despite the doubts of Dicey and Bryce, E.T. John, the Welsh leader, was more optimistic. Although not "a thorough-going federalist" and thus not in support of separate treatment for Ulster, John was a self-styled "nationalist federalist" who aspired to four parliaments and a single-chamber senate.[33] By April 1913 John believed there were "most interesting movements taking place in Ireland which render the prospect of a settlement by consent highly probable, such settlement will be on federal lines, and will almost certainly invoke the early granting to Scotland of Self Governing powers broadly equivalent and identical with those granted to Ireland. It is pretty obvious that what Scotland gets Wales will also claim and receive."[34] John was, of course, quite out of touch with developments, a reflection of the relative unimportance of Welsh, and even Scottish, home rule aspirations. Nevertheless, he was well aware of how unassertive Welsh nationalism had been and how little prominence Wales had. He thought Welsh interests would best be served in "a compact, well organised, and thoroughly progressive Federal State." By asserting its individuality Wales could "render very material service to the highest interests of the great British Commonwealth."[35]

By the spring of 1913 the advocates of federalism or of home rule all round had had no impact on the fashioning of the home rule bill and had little prospect of success in the near future. The gathering tension in Ulster soon forced a more considered discussion of the constitutional crisis and provided another opportunity for the federalists.

In May Murray Macdonald reopened his personal campaign for a settlement of the crisis generated by the home rule bill with the publication of a pamphlet entitled *The Constitutional Crisis: A Review of the Situation and a Plea for a Settlement*.[36] Macdonald did not believe "ordinary party forces" would be able to avoid grave discontent and unrest nor did he think congestion in the House of Commons could be resolved by changes of procedures. Devolution of functions to subordinate legislatures was therefore essential.[37] A few days after the appearance of Macdonald's pamphlet, Sir W.H. Cowan (Aberdeenshire, E) introduced yet another Scottish home rule bill. It met the same fate as the earlier ones but on this occasion Balfour, while his usual scathing self about "shadowy schemes of federalism," did admit that devolution might be a possible method of relieving parliamentary congestion. Any such scheme would have to be regional rather than national and might well involve cutting up England into "districts" of convenient size.[38] This was quite a shift for Balfour and it was one echoed in the *Nation* which on 7 June supported Macdonald's proposals.

Certainly the king had been impressed.[39] Arthur Ponsonby, like Macdonald a Scottish Liberal member, agreed with Macdonald and pressed the case for a conference on his brother, Fritz, who had recently become the king's second private secretary. He introduced Macdonald to Fritz and the two men talked about Macdonald's federal ideas. Fritz then spoke to the king but by late August not much progress had been made with the conference proposal. The king had indeed written to Asquith about the possibility of an all-party conference "to consider the whole policy of devolution." He was convinced that it would be "better to try to settle measures involving great changes in the Constitution, such as Home Rule all round ... not on Party lines but by agreement." Not surprisingly, the prime minister saw no point in a conference "at that time."[40] The king then appealed to Lansdowne in early September, but Lansdowne argued that devolution would only be possible if the home rule bill was withdrawn, while conferences were only valuable if a certain amount of agreement had been established in advance.[41]

At this time Earl Grey urged F.S. Oliver to prepare a statement outlining "fully the reasons why the Federal solution is a practicable one and ought to be adopted."[42] His reasons for exerting pressure on Oliver were obvious. He hoped that the respect in which Oliver was held in Unionist circles would have some impact. As Grey revealed to Haldane: "I am getting more and more uneasy as we get closer to the Irish calamities impending. I wish the Unionist leaders would do the big thing and adopt the Federal policy and make it possible for you to withdraw your bill and think out a new constitution on the federal basis. This work of course could not be done in a hurry, but a settlement by general consent of the Irish, House of Lords and House of Commons questions, would be worth many sacrifices."[43]

Before Oliver could respond to Grey's urgings, Lord Loreburn decided to take the initiative and in a lengthy letter published in the *Times* on 11 September 1913 he called for a settlement by conference. Loreburn had been chairman of the 1911 cabinet committee on home rule and had always been sympathetic to home rule all round. He had sided with Dunraven and Grey in the Lords debate earlier in the year in calling for a settlement by consent on federal lines. The king had been impressed at the time and so had William O'Brien who had urged him to do all he could for a settlement. Loreburn, however, had had little success with his former cabinet colleagues nor was he able to get through to the Unionist leadership. He therefore made a public appeal in the *Times*, calling for a conference and strongly suggesting that devolution would be the appropriate solution.[44] When asked by Asquith to elaborate, Loreburn prepared a memorandum for the cabinet which argued that Irish home rule should be treated as the first step towards home rule for all parts of the United Kingdom. He also suggested that Ulster could be dealt with as a legislative enclave, so that laws affecting the four northeastern counties could only pass the Irish legislature with the approval of a majority of the representatives from those four counties.[45]

Nationalists were shocked by a proposal which they thought had emanated from the government and the Unionists were fearful of a conference trap. In the light of Loreburn's initiative, Oliver decided not to intervene. He believed a convention would be useful, but it should not "include all sorts of ridiculous people – professors, philanthropists, constitutional lawyers, Morgans, Fred Pollockses, Pacificuses, Erskine Childerses etc. etc. etc. Quite the contrary! It ought to contain nothing but practical politicians."[46] E.T. John was virtually alone in being optimistic that a settlement by conference would be reached and that it would lead to a federal solution. Others were less sanguine. Morley thought Loreburn's suggestions "pure *moonshine*," although he did agree with the diagnosis; and Lansdowne found the proposals too vague.[47]

While the Liberals attempted to sort out their reactions to Loreburn's initiative, the Unionist leadership also found itself under additional pressure.

In the first half of September both Lansdowne and Bonar Law were summoned to Balmoral to see the king, who was more anxious than ever that a settlement by consent be reached, if not by a conference, at least by meetings between party leaders. Lansdowne was predictably cautious about any meetings with Liberals and was opposed completely to any conference on the exclusion of Ulster. Bonar Law was more flexible. He was prepared to take part in a conference to discuss home rule all round but he thought discussions on the exclusion of Ulster would be difficult without the approval of the Unionists in the south and west of Ireland. It was his unwillingness to abandon the southern Unionists that inhibited Bonar Law, because, unlike Lansdowne, he was not unalterably opposed to home rule for the south and west of Ireland. Partition was not unthinkable to Bonar Law if he could be convinced that the southern Unionists would be protected. On the other hand, he was acutely aware of "diehard" feelings and of the need to make no move that would split his party, and he also continued to have his doubts about general devolution. He summarized his position in a letter to Carson: "... I have long thought that if it were possible to leave Ulster as she is, and have some form of Home Rule for the rest of Ireland that is on the whole the only way out because a discussion of the larger question of general devolution even if the Government were ready to consider it would involve the discussion, for instance, of the House of Lords, and probably other questions and would really be impossible I think unless there were something in the nature of a coalition."[48]

When consulted, neither Balfour nor Curzon liked the idea of a conference on devolution, although Balfour was more hopeful about "the limited solution of leaving out Ulster."[49] Lansdowne shared his colleagues' fears about a general conference. As he admitted, "We have none of us any clear ideas on the subject, and should have no proposals to make."[50] He feared being manoeuvred into a position where the party might be made "to *appear* destructive and unreasonable." He thought they might find themselves in such a position "if we were to be offered the exclusion of Ulster, subject to our acceptance of the Bill as it stands. We could not to my mind, go into a conference on such a basis."[51]

By early October Law's views were clear:

There are only two possible bases of settlement; first, a general system of devolution; and second, a form of Home Rule from which Ulster, or part of Ulster, should be excluded. The first of these alternatives is not in my opinion possible, and it is only the second which can be seriously considered.

In my opinion this solution would not be open to the objection, which I have always considered one of the strongest arguments against Home Rule, that our national strength would be fatally weakened. A Parliament for the whole of Ireland would be practically independent, but a Parliament from which Ulster is excluded would in the nature of the case be subordinate, and wd really be in the same relative position to the Imperial Parliament that one of the Provinces of Canada is to the Canadian Parliament.[52]

Despite his reservations Law finally agreed to meet Asquith to discuss the possibility of an interparty agreement on the exclusion of Ulster. Over the next two months the two leaders met three times – 14 October, 6 November, and 9 December.[53] Although the sessions were private, it was generally known in political circles that something of critical importance was afoot. Thus from early October until the end of the year the federalists continued to exert pressure, particularly on the Unionists, and made some efforts to coordinate their own activities.

As usual, Earl Grey was at the centre of things. He wrote to Haldane expressing the wish that "the Unionist leaders would do the big thing and adopt the Federal policy and make it possible for you to withdraw your bill and think out a new constitution on the federal basis."[54] He then urged Oliver to educate the Unionist leadership. What was wanted was "a statement which will show that the present bill is a bad bill because it is based on a vicious principle, namely that of nationality, and that if Ireland is to receive Home Rule the only way in which the principle of Home Rule can be safely applied is by the federal plan."[55] Grey elaborated on his position in a letter published in the *Times* on 11 October. He declared that Asquith's bill should be strongly opposed by all who sympathized with the desire of Ulstermen "to possess those powers of self-government which under the British North America Act are the constitutional right of every Canadian." It was a mistake for the government to try to solve the Irish question on a nationalist rather than a federal basis. Clearly federalism "is the most modern and progressive form of government. It combines the advantages of local autonomy with those of national unity. It provides for self-government in all local matters and for unity in all matters of national concern." Grey personally favoured federalism because "I am a Home Ruler with regard to local affairs but a staunch Unionist with regard to all national affairs." He singled out the United States, Switzerland, Australia, and Canada as examples of successful federal states, and then admitted that he found it hard to understand why Gladstone with his awareness of the Canadian and American examples "never appeared to understand the meaning and possibilities of federalism ... He was always a Nationalist, and the Liberals ... inherited his ideals and his dangerous policy." Grey hoped the Unionist party would accept Churchill's invitation to consider seriously the federal solution.[56]

Oliver finally bowed to Grey's appeals, and initiated a scheme designed to demonstrate to the Unionist leadership that they had not sufficiently thought through the federal alternative. As he pointed out to Milner, the recent moves in a federal direction had been made by "the Liberal men of Peace" such as Munro Ferguson, Macdonald, West-Ridgeway, and Charnwood, whereas in 1910 they had been made by "the Tory Men of Peace." Oliver asked G.L. Craik of "kindergarten" fame, and a Round Table colleague, to help work out "not a bill, but a skeleton of a scheme." It was shown to Milner and passed on to another kindergarten and Round Table man, Geoffrey Robinson, editor of the *Times*, for comment. Oliver and Craik also sent their scheme to Austen Chamberlain. Oliver and Chamberlain had been close friends since the 1880s, so it was not surprising that Oliver should try to persuade his friend of the merits of federalism or devolution. Chamberlain had been attracted by Oliver's and Garvin's proposals of 1910 which he considered bore a favourable resemblence to his father's provincial council schemes. Chamberlain was not dogmatically opposed to home rule in some form provided it did not lead to separation. Therefore a scheme of devolution, or home rule all round, which would preserve the unity of the kingdom and the sovereignty of parliament, had some attractions for him. While awaiting reactions, Craik prepared a digest of the division of powers and functions which had been variously proposed since 1886.[57]

By October 24 Craik was "well satisfied" with the way things were going, particularly after the appearance that day in the *Times* of a proposal by Dunraven, who asserted that "the more closely the Ulster deadlock is examined it becomes more and more clear that, short of absolute surrender on one side or the other, the only working solution is to be found in an application to Ireland of the federal principle." Unlike Grey, Dunraven insisted that Ulster would have to be included. To excise it, in whole or in part, would disrupt traditional, historic, and economic ties. In his estimation, "Ulster is the master log that holds the jam, and to avoid catastrophe it must be loosened gently." That could be done "by federalism and by federalism alone, for federalism involves no loss of citizenship and secures ample protection for all."[58]

At the end of October Oliver met Dunraven and planned a session with Murray Macdonald. By that time he thought more importance was being attached to the issue of Ulster than it deserved. He reminded Craik:

> You will remember that in my notes to your first memorandum I took the view that there would certainly have to be two divisions in Ireland – Ulster in one and the other three provinces in the other. As I see the thing now the above does not seem to be essential.
>
> ... Theoretically it will be possible under a Federal system to realise Sir Edward Grey's notion of Home Rule within Home Rule: but it would be equally possible to retain Ulster as a part of England, Scotland, or the United Kingdom.

But ... it might be practicable ... to have Ireland a single entity and Ulster firmly embedded in it.

The key of the position was "*the strength, composition, and over-riding powers of the Central* or Federal Parliament over the subordinate or National local parliaments and *the coordination of these local or national parliaments* by some means or another is the central pivot upon which everything turns."[59]

During the last weeks of the year, Oliver continued to work behind the scenes. He conferred regularly with Chamberlain and met and corresponded with Carson, Milner, Churchill, Garvin, Brassey, Charnwood, Murray Macdonald, and Horace Plunkett. A major result of his efforts was the publication in November of his pamphlet, *The Alternatives to Civil War*, in which he analysed the constitutional crisis resulting from the home rule bill, and called on the Liberals and the Unionists to cooperate before it was too late. He left his readers in no doubt that he preferred a federal solution.[60] Although Oliver usually met with a sympathetic response from Unionists, few in the leadership were persuaded. Lansdowne spoke for most of his colleagues when he pointed out to Austen Chamberlain that "we are, I suppose, in the abstract, all of us supporters of Devolution, and should like to see Parliament relieved of a good deal of the burden of work which now overwhelms it; but I hesitate to talk glibly about the adoption of the Federal principle until I really know what I mean by the words."[61]

There were, however, occasional, if sometimes reluctant, converts. One, Austen Chamberlain, spent a lot of time in late 1913 talking with Oliver and going over his pamphlets. He became gradually convinced that devolution might be the only way to preserve the union and avoid the dangers of home rule. He acknowledged that such a stance might not be "conservatism in the narrow sense," but it was in keeping with his father's principles of 1886. It was "good Toryism and Unionism." The adoption of provincial councils, or parliaments, might resolve the Ulster question and help avoid anarchy and the breakdown of order that would result if the army and police refused to coerce Ulster into home rule.[62] In informing Lansdowne of the shift in his views, Chamberlain was at pains to explain his position: "I do not for one moment pretend that I am in favour of Home Rule all round, but I think it would be infinitely less dangerous than the present Home Rule bill even with Ulster excluded ... it would be impossible for a Dublin legislature, even though called a Parliament, to establish any kind of rivalry with the Imperial Parliament of Westminster if it were not an isolated excrescence on our system but merely one of several provincial legislatures. In short, though I think that Home Rule all round would be inconvenient and often worrying, I do not believe that it could be dangerous to our unity or would materially lessen our strength."[63] In response, Lansdowne was naturally cautious, and he also underscored a weakness in the federalist/devolution position when he pointed out to Chamberlain that "no one has yet worked out a scheme for the establishment of such local legislatures, and unless we have definite ideas as to how they are to be constituted the proposed reservation as to equal treatment of other parts of the United Kingdom would leave everything quite in the air."[64] Neville Chamberlain, on the other hand, liked his brother's idea. It seemed "the only one that holds any hope of a permanent settlement. I hope if it comes about that the local legislative bodies will not be called Parliaments but that they will simply be Councils with larger powers of local government."[65]

By now Chamberlain had the bit between his teeth and was not to be easily dissuaded. He continued to tackle his colleagues on the issue throughout late 1913, and at least kept the flames of devolution and federalism flickering in the minds if not the hearts of many Unionists. He spoke to Law at the end of October, and urged him to counter the possibility of Asquith suggesting the exclusion of Ulster by raising the possibility of general devolution.[66] He then spoke publicly in November in favour of provincial councils, and during the last weeks of the year he corresponded, and had a number of conversations, with Winston Churchill who showed him his two 1911 memoranda on federalism. Churchill had quickly detected that Chamberlain had not thought through the implications of either federalism or devolution: "It is so easy to talk vaguely about Federalism, but few people try to face the obvious difficulties, or to provide answers to the first questions which arise." He hoped his memoranda would provide Chamberlain with some ideas.[67] Chamberlain read them with great interest. Although he did not share Churchill's opinion about the impossibility of having an English parliament and executive side by side with an imperial parliament and executive, he found "much agreement and no insuperable differences between us" regarding the powers to be devolved, and shared with Churchill the conviction that the "real difficulty in the way of devolution is financial." He did not know how that would be overcome.[68]

Despite his efforts to familiarize himself with federalism, it was clear that Chamberlain's identification with the federalist option was essentially a pragmatic one. As he admitted to his old friend Oliver, "My position is: I don't like federalism for the United Kingdom but I infinitely prefer it to this Bill."[69]

Another convert was Lord Selborne. The former governor general of South Africa had long doubted the merits of applying federalism or devolution to the United Kingdom, but he had gradually changed his mind since the summer of 1913. Like Chamberlain, with whom he had discussed the issue at length, he saw federalism as the most pragmatic solution to United Kingdom difficulties rather than the most meritorious. He had been supportive when Chamberlain had urged Bonar Law to explore with Asquith a scheme of general devolution. Like Chamberlain, he took to the public platform to proclaim his change of heart, and in speeches at Newport on 10 November and Hyde, Cheshire, on 2 December he argued in favour of a federal solution.[70] Even Walter Long, one of the most committed Unionists, was beginning to think there might be something attractive in federalism. In late December he advised Bonar Law, "Every day brings me fresh and reliable evidence of the fact that our Party are getting increasingly anxious. They believe, and I agree with them, that no possible compromise, save perhaps real Federalism, will endure."[71]

Chamberlain, Selborne, and Long had been driven to consider federalism – actually home rule all round – more seriously as it became clear that the Liberals were prepared to try and circumvent the difficulty of Ulster by excluding at least four of the northeastern counties for five or six years, at the end of which time they would be automatically included in the operation of a home rule bill. In November Lloyd George had taken the initiative within the cabinet and had succeeded in persuading his colleagues of the merits of such a temporary exclusion. Only the forceful arguments of Redmond had stayed Asquith's hand. The Nationalist leader was convinced that the crisis in Ulster was exaggerated and that rebellion was unlikely. He believed that the Liberals would be foolish to give up the tactical advantage. Asquith accepted Redmond's analysis, but made it clear to the Irish leader that the cabinet would keep its options open and would not be tied to any particular Nationalist position. Not surprisingly, under such circumstances, the talks between Asquith and Bonar Law proved abortive, leaving the Unionist leader frustrated by Asquith's negotiating style. Bonar Law had, in fact, been ready, albeit reluctantly, to abandon Monaghan, Donegal, and Cavan, the three counties where the Protestants were in a distinct minority. This had alarmed the hard-liners in his party who had declared their intransigence on the issue of exclusion. It was again not surprising that federalism or home rule all round seemed attractive alternatives to many Unionists. The problem was, of course, that the so-called "federalist theorisers" were not in reality federalists. Even if they had been, it is doubtful if at this stage the federal alternatives would have been considered seriously. The fact that nearly all advocates of "federalism" actually meant some form of devolution with "subordinate" parliaments was anathema to the Irish Nationalists. As Churchill had shrewdly pointed out to Chamberlain, the Irish Nationalists wanted some satisfaction in the enjoyment of their parliament.[72] The year ended with both Murray Macdonald and Lord Dunraven, both seemingly immune to political realities, doggedly pleading for a "federal" solution.[73]

The early months of 1914 was a period of gathering tension. As the date neared for the third and last debate on the home rule bill, the Ulster Unionists, under the leadership of Carson and Craig, prepared for the establishment of a provisional government in the province, while Bonar Law, with the support of Balfour, Chamberlain, Lansdowne, and Carson, plotted to use the House of Lords to amend the annual army bill so that the Liberals would be unable to use the army in Ulster. Bonar Law was convinced that if the Liberals could be forced to call a general election, the Unionists would win an overall majority. He was prepared to use the power of the Lords in order to force such an election, thereby forestalling, or so he hoped, a Liberal compromise on the inclusion of Protestant counties. He knew only too well that if the Liberals publicly suggested a compromise it would be difficult for the Unionists to ignore it and have any chance at the polls.

While the Unionist party assessed the wisdom of Law's inclinations, Asquith and the Liberals gradually came to accept that some form of exclusion would probably be essential if anarchy in Ireland were to be avoided. After the failure of his talks with Law, Asquith opened discussions with Carson, but by mid-January those talks collapsed. In February he and Lloyd George concluded there was no alternative but to make an offer that the Unionists would have difficulty turning down. Redmond was shocked and angered by the Liberal change of heart, but in the end he agreed to accept exclusion for a six-year period on a county system basis in order to ensure that the south and west of Ireland would obtain home rule. The alterations were to be embodied in a separate amending bill thus leaving the home rule bill intact. If the amending bill was rejected, the Liberals would still be able to proceed with the home rule bill. Asquith presented his proposal to the House on 9 March.

During these early weeks of 1914, the federalists had not been waiting on events. They took every opportunity to ensure that the federal idea was fixed in the public mind. In February Moreton Frewan and Dunraven joined forces to discuss "federalism" in the pages of the *Nineteenth Century* and to extol the benefits that would accrue to the United Kingdom from its adoption. That same month, Murray Macdonald and Lord Charnwood issued a pamphlet entitled *The Federal Solution* which called for a modification of the home rule bill on federal lines, and Oliver published a typically trenchant pamphlet, *What Federalism Is Not*, which recommended the scrapping of the bill and the introduction of a truly "federal" scheme for the United Kingdom. Oliver, as usual, sent his pamphlet to a variety of politicians on both sides of the House, while Macdonald and Charnwood began working closely with a group made up of experienced civil servants, a financial expert, and men familiar with the South African negotiations of 1908–9 in order to draft a federal plan.[74]

Brassey and Horace Plunkett were equally busy. Brassey continued to write to leading Unionists urging them to consider a convention "on the South African model" at which would be discussed "the amendment of the present

Bill or the drafting of a new measure to meet the Ulster difficulty and to make it the first step in a Federal Solution."[75] For his part, Plunkett had devised a scheme virtually the reverse of most contemporary plans. He outlined it to Asquith in late February and again in early March, a few days before the prime minister was to move second reading of the home rule bill for the third time. Plunkett suggested that Ulster should be included in home rule, but that it should be able "after a stated period, long enough to give the experiment a fair trial and to establish the traditions of good government, to vote itself out if the majority so desire." An independent and impartial tribunal, perhaps the Judicial Committee of the Privy Council, should be established with the power to allow this option of permanent exclusion to be exercised at an earlier period, if it could be satisfactorily proved that Ulster was suffering from misgovernment. Once the principle of temporary inclusion had been accepted, a conference of representative Irishmen should meet to discuss amendments to the home rule bill. If this were all agreed, he recommended the creation of an Irish Territorial Force and the disbandment of both Volunteer Forces. It was an ingenious proposal but since it stood no chance with the Unionists because of its emphasis on inclusion first, exclusion later, and was radically different from the scheme that Asquith, Lloyd George, and the reluctant Redmond had settled upon, it fell by the wayside.[76]

Austen Chamberlain also made another effort to convince his colleagues. As early as mid-February he made it clear to Oliver that he thought a separate council or parliament should be given to Ulster. As he put it, "'Federalism' makes the 'exclusion' of Ulster easy." He asked Oliver to give him a skeleton of the arguments with which he could support his conclusions. But knowing his friend, he added: "Don't write a State paper. Only give me heads of the argument."[77] Chamberlain was looking for two things in an Irish solution:

first, to the prevention of civil war with all the consequences, more terrible than civil war itself ...

second, the defeat of the Nationalist scheme for "Ireland a Nation" in the separatist sense in which they have always employed it. I no more desire to kill or weaken Irish patriotism than I should wish to see Scottish or English patriotism discouraged. The latter two are, and for many years have been, only one ingredient in a wider national spirit which they strengthen and enrich; whereas the claim put forward by the Nationalist Party, from Parnell onwards, has always been destructive of any true spirit of union in the United Kingdom. It does not feed the wider patriotism of which I have spoken but is essentially hostile to it.

I regard the present exclusion of Ulster as essential from both points of view. It may be that a Dublin Parliament might eventually win the affections of Ulster, but it would only be when that Parliament had shown itself as loyal to the flag and the Empire as the local Assemblies of any other part of the United Kingdom would be. Until that time arrives I am opposed not merely as a matter of momentary expediency but on broad general grounds of policy to anything which organises the whole of Ireland as one nation.[78]

There could have been no clearer statement of the primary reason why Unionists such as Long, Selborne, and Chamberlain were interested in federalism.

On 6 March, three days before Asquith addressed the House, Chamberlain had to admit failure. The government appeared to have shut the door on a federal solution. He wrote to Oliver: "As you are aware such a solution would have been to most of us Unionists a *pis aller* at best. If Asquith had acted on the hints thrown out by Lansdowne, Carson and myself, and had confronted us with a definite proposal to cooperate in that solution, I think it might have been carried, but a large section of the Party, from Balfour downwards, abhored it and I should doubt its being possible for Carson or Law to propound it as their own solution."[79] It also seemed clear to Garvin by early March that any hope of federalism had failed. He expressed his dismay to Milner: "I deplore that real federalism – with exclusion as the road to inclusion as a far sounder basis – has failed for the present."[80]

It was made dramatically clear on 9 March that not only federalism had been rejected. In moving second reading of the home rule bill for the third time, Asquith pointed out that there existed a serious possibility of civil war over Ulster. There was clearly need for a compromise. He then outlined the Liberal amendment of exclusion on a county option basis for a six-year period Although he deliberately left the impression that exclusion might become permanent if the Unionists won a general election during the six years, he failed to satisfy Carson. The Ulster leader might have considered the amendment more seriously if there had been no time-limit. He was particularly upset that Ulster would remain a pawn in the political game during the six years. As he tellingly put it in the House, "Ulster wants this question settled now and for ever. We do not want a sentence of death with a stay of execution for six years."[81] Asquith was in no position to respond. The Nationalists had had to be dragged to this point. They would never agree to drop the time-limit. And as far as they were concerned, inclusion should be automatic, not problematic, at the end of six years. Attempts by Asquith to negotiate with Bonar Law were rebuffed by mid-March, and the Unionists became more intransigent.

The Liberals were further undermined in late March by the so-called "Mutiny at the Curragh." Bonar Law had finally bowed to the concern of his party and had abandoned the idea of using the Lords to amend the army bill, but he must have been delighted at the confusion and division engendered in the army and the cabinet by the mishandling of the army's responsibilities in Ulster. The affair effectively removed the possibility that the government would be able to deal easily with any difficulties that arose in the province over the passage of the home rule bill. The brazen and brilliant gun-running by the Ulster Volunteer Force on 24–25 April only emphasized the Liberals' tactical weakness. The UVF was now reasonably well armed and morale was high, while the government floundered. Compromise seemed unlikely. Nevertheless, many of the federalists, particularly the Round Table movement, worked unceasingly over the next few weeks to effect an agreement between the parties on the basis of a federal solution.[82]

Since its success with Churchill in 1912, the Round Table movement had contented itself with periodic discussion of the Irish question and the occasional airing of positions and opinions in the *Round Table Quarterly*. In the main, the London members had adhered to their commitment to some form of home rule all round, but apart from offering support and solace to Oliver, they had not engaged in any sustained campaign. The activities of the London group increased from late 1913 under the pressure of the Ulster problem. Oliver returned to his role of pamphleteer, Selborne gradually lent his weight to Round Table discussion, and in November Robert Brand and Edward Grigg met once more with Churchill on the *Enchantress* to sound him out on Ulster exclusion. Even Leo Amery, linked with Milner in the most intransigent and provocative of Unionist camps, appeared to have second thoughts and to line up on this issue with his Round Table colleagues. He wrote to Bonar Law in December urging him to agree to the summoning of a convention representative of all views "to ascertain the possibility of a federal or devolutionary scheme for the United Kingdom and the reforms required to restore a working constitution."[83] Amery developed his arguments in anonymous articles in the *Quarterly Review* in January, April, and July 1914, in parliamentary speeches, and particularly in correspondence and conversation with Unionist leaders.

The pace picked up in the New Year. Curtis, Oliver, and Brand dined with Horace Plunkett in late January to assess his ideas, and an important "moot" on the Irish problem was held at Oliver's home on 12 February shortly after the publication of his pamphlet, *What Federalism Is Not*. Two days later a full-scale weekend meeting was held at Cliveden, the home of Waldorf Astor, the new proprietor of the *Observer*. According to Plunkett, one of the guests, "All long for a way out."[84] Within the week Oliver and Astor lunched with Lloyd George to discuss ways by which devolution or federalism could be promoted and made acceptable to both the government and the Unionists. Astor was sufficiently angered by the extremists in the Unionist party that he urged Garvin to continue to emphasize the federal solution in the *Observer*. His frustration was acute: "Do try and explain ... what the position is. Some of our people are so thick-headed they cannot see it. They don't realise the talk and drift they advocate ... must mean civil war ... They have not begun to grasp what we mean by Federalism or Devolution – they are such fatheads that they don't see we advocate it as the least bad of the alternatives and not as an ideal policy."[85]

Asquith's failure to persuade Carson of the merits of temporary exclusion and the collapse of subsequent attempts to negotiate with Bonar Law spurred the Round Table group to make extraordinary efforts to effect a compromise. Neither Oliver nor Amery took any significant part. Oliver had lost heart after Austen Chamberlain had failed to persuade Law, Balfour, and Curzon to negotiate with the government on the basis of a federal solution, while Amery had concluded that "to attempt to commit the party [now] to a federal scheme would completely wreck it."[86] Nevertheless, after a "moot" at Blackmoor, Selborne's home, to discuss recent developments, the London group decided to do all they could.[87] In the end, they had two opportunities.

The first resulted from an article in the March issue of the *Round Table* in which Edward Grigg had proposed once more the summoning of a National Convention and the consideration of "Home Rule all round."[88] Lord Roberts, the senior field-marshal of the army, and a firm supporter of Ulster, asked for further details. Grigg drew up a memorandum suggesting that the home rule bill should be abandoned and a federal solution considered. Grigg recommended that the proposal be reviewed by senior representatives of both parties, including Roberts himself. If such men approved the scheme it might be taken seriously. Roberts, while attracted to the idea, did not feel he could act without advice. Therefore on 2 April he forwarded the memorandum to Milner for consideration. Milner by this time had little faith – in keeping with many others – in any scheme of "Home Rule all round" or a federal solution, and he told Roberts as much. Roberts immediately dropped the plan and it went no further. Ironically, the "father-figure" of the Round Table had been primarily responsible for scotching the scheme before it was much advanced.[89]

The second opportunity occurred during April and early May when Lionel Curtis, Bob Brand, Lionel Hichens, Grigg, and Astor attempted to initiate a compromise between the two parties, "who had ceased altogether to be on speaking terms." As Curtis later explained to Richard Feetham, another Round Table member, "A scheme of federalism was only an incident in a vain attempt to get some settlement which would stave off the impending nightmare of civil war."[90] The initiative had apparently resulted from a meeting of Brand, Grigg, and Curtis with Churchill in Oxford on 1 March. When the Round Table members had remonstrated with Churchill about government policy, the minister had challenged them to say what alternative was possible to the bill before the House. They had suggested conferring on England, Scotland, and Wales the same home rule as in Ireland south of Ulster. Ulster should be left as part of the United Kingdom of Great Britain and Ireland. Churchill saw in this idea a possible basis for compromise and asked the Round Table members to prepare a more detailed scheme. This they did and met again with Churchill on 3 and 4 April aboard the *Enchantress*.[91] The Round Table suggestions were as follows:

1. The Government of Ireland Bill to be placed on the Statute Book with the following amendments: (a) the counties of Antrim, Down, Londonderry, Armagh, Tyrone and Fermanagh to be excluded from the operation of the Bill until the Imperial Parliament otherwise provide; (b) the clauses providing for separate Post Offices and a variation between British and Irish Custom duties to be withdrawn; on condition that measures are at once taken to consider a scheme of devolution for the whole United Kingdom.

2. For this purpose two distinct bodies to be constituted to consider separately the British and the Irish question; (a) the British question to be referred to a British Commission or Convention, which should deal with the requirements of Great Britain without reference to the Irish question; re the British Commission – the following suggestions made (1) that it be as small as possible (2) that it include one leader of the Liberal, Unionist and Labour parties (3) that it be an instruction to the Committee to prepare within 6 months a scheme whereby separate provisional representative organs of provincial government should be instituted for England, Scotland, and Wales respectively (4) That these provisional organs be given, to start with, only such powers (e.g. control of municipal govt) and such corresponding revenues as must unquestionably be given under any scheme of provincial devolution (5) that the provincial organs be left to elaborate for themselves proposals for increasing these powers and revenues, or for subdividing their areas, or otherwise modifying their own constitutions (6) that such proposals be submitted to the Imperial Parliament from time to time in the form of private legislation, and that a special committee of the Imperial Parliament be created for the consideration of all such measures and brought up by the provincial organisations. (b) re consideration of Irish questions – an election to be held immediately – the representatives to form an Irish Provisional Assembly which should elect delegates by proportional representation to an Irish Convention – the Convention to consider the terms on which Ireland might be constituted a single self-governing unit in a scheme of devolution embracing the whole U.K.

3. The findings of the British and Irish Conventions to be considered together by the leaders of all parties with a view to their coordination.

4. [and]
    (a) The 6 excluded counties not to be included in the Irish unit of self-government unless by their own consent (b) the 6 excluded counties not to be established as a separate self-governing unit unless with the consent of the rest of Ireland.[92]

The Round Table scheme was forwarded to Churchill before the meeting on 3 and 4 April. He was greatly attracted to it, and thought it could form the basis of a compromise between the parties. On 2 April, therefore, he and F.E. Smith drafted an appeal to the members of the House "as a general basis for H. of C. support to be gathered on." Churchill forwarded it to Lloyd George on 3 April.[93] It read as follows:

We, the Undersigned, are agreed that the outstanding differences on the Irish question can be settled and ought to be settled.

We feel that a solution of a Federal character for the United Kingdom offers the best prospect for a settlement and would in existing circumstances be best for the interests of the country.

We do not at this stage attempt to define in detail how such Federal proposals should be coordinated with or related to the provisions of the Home Rule Bill. The difficulties are obvious, but we believe they can be overcome.

We rely upon the leaders of all parties to make these considerations paramount in order to avoid the National and Imperial misfortunes with which we are now threatened; and we express our earnest desire to support and sustain well conceived proposals to that end when made by the responsible leaders on non-party lines.

Churchill then urged the Round Table members to get in touch with Carson and the Conservative leaders and see if they would consider such a compromise. He and Lloyd George agreed to tackle Asquith. Grigg, Brand, and Curtis saw Austen Chamberlain, Edward Carson, and Bonar Law, in that order, on 7 April and showed them their memorandum. All favoured a compromise, and Carson particularly liked the document. But all had criticisms and all emphasized that the critical factor was not Liberal but Nationalist opinion. They doubted if the Nationalists would accept the scheme unless the government brought considerable pressure to bear on them. As for details, Chamberlain had a good deal to say about the difficulty of establishing a provincial government on federal lines in England. The main difficulty would be finance. Carson welcomed the Irish part of the proposals, thinking them fair and practical, but he did favour the exclusion of all nine counties. Bonar Law accepted the Irish part if Carson did, but had grave doubts about the British government part. He doubted, for example, that Glasgow would defer to Edinburgh and he was sceptical about an English legislature beside the imperial parliament.[94]

Buoyed by these meetings, Grigg got in touch with Maurice Bonham-Carter, Asquith's private secretary and an old school friend of Grigg's, showed him the memorandum, told him of the meetings with Carson and the Unionist leaders, and explained that all had considered them a practical and admissible basis for discussion. Grigg emphasized to Bonham-Carter that no discussion of the Round Table scheme would be profitable unless all parties whose opinion was vital were represented. Bonham-Carter agreed to take the document and Grigg's advice to Asquith.[95] Churchill and Lloyd George also applied pressure, but, as Grigg put it, Asquith initially "behaved like an elephant which puts out first one foot then the other to see if the bridge will hold."[96]

While Asquith was deciding what to do, Selborne wrote to Carson to try and ensure a favourable response from the Ulster Unionist leader:

I believe that you and I think much alike on the question of devolution, or, as some call it, federalism. We should prefer to see the present system of one Parliament for the whole of the United Kingdom remain undisturbed although we think it essential that the Second Chamber should have real power and cease to be a sham as it is now. But we agree in thinking that, whereas all schemes that have been suggested for Home Rule for Ireland would produce a system of government in the United Kingdom impossible permanently to tolerate, by the process of devolution a perfectly workable system could be devised.

Given his South African experience Selborne did not believe there would be great difficulty in settling the proper division of functions between a parliament for the United Kingdom and English, Scottish, and Irish parliaments. The chief difficulty would be finance. He thought differences already existed in law, local government, education, and land and these could be easily accommodated by separate institutions. He also thought the objections to the difficulties arising from the inequality of size of England, Scotland, and Ireland were entirely theoretical and without substance. "There is no reason whatever for cutting England into little bits; indeed I am passionately opposed to any sub-division of England."[97] Carson had, in fact, been much struck by the Round Table scheme, and on dining with Selborne a few days later indicated that "he would certainly, if any scheme of the kind was proposed by the other side, bring it before his own friends."[98] Thus it was not entirely a surprise when, on Churchill's direct approach to him in the Commons on 28 April to consider a federal arrangement, Carson said he was favourably inclined provided the six counties of Ulster were firmly excluded.[99]

Given this impetus the Round Table persisted in their efforts to get the leaders together, and on 5 May they succeeded. A meeting between Asquith, Bonar Law, and Carson took place at Edwin Montagu's house in Queen Anne's Gate, but to the dismay of the federalists the meeting was a disaster. Discussion focused on the terms for Ulster exclusion and did not "touch on the 'Federalist' aspect of the question." It was clear that Asquith, because of his understanding with the Irish Nationalists, would not commit himself to any form of compromise settlement.[100] Despite this setback the movement remained optimistic for a few more days until advised by Milner on 11 May that their scheme would come to nothing.[101]

The failure of the Round Table mission concluded any chance of the adoption of a devolutionary scheme before the passage of the home rule bill.[102]

Matters drifted inexorably on. The home rule bill passed its third reading in the Commons on 25 May. By then Asquith had decided to introduce a separate amending bill in the Lords which would receive the royal assent at the same time as the home rule bill. It was introduced on 23 June and was based on the quite inadequate six-year county option scheme of March 1914. When it reached third reading on 14 July the Lords eliminated the six-year time limit as well as the provision for county option. They substituted instead an amendment by Lansdowne which permanently eliminated all nine counties. This was, of course, quite unacceptable. Under enormous pressure, faced with extraordinary difficulties, and with tension running high in Ireland, Asquith bowed to the king's request, and he and Lloyd George met with Lansdowne, Law, Redmond, Dillon, Carson, and Amery from 21 to 24 July in the Buckingham Palace conference. The discussions broke down over Ulster exclusion. It is unclear how Asquith would have resolved the problem. The gun-running by Childers at Howth on 26 July enabled the prime minister to postpone debate on the amending bill in the Commons to 30 July, but no clear path existed. Asquith and the Liberals were saved by the outbreak of war in Europe and by the immediate offer, in the interests of national unity, of a political truce from the Unionists. The home rule bill was finally placed on the statute book on 18 September, and the amending bill was replaced by a Suspending Act which postponed the operation of the Home Rule Act until after the war. It seems clear that civil war in the United Kingdom was averted by the outbreak of war in Europe.

In those last desperate weeks before war broke out the devolutionists and federalists had had little impact. The Irish Nationalists were not prepared to let home rule for Ireland be diluted by general devolution for the United Kingdom, while the Ulster Unionists were not prepared to sacrifice Ulster interests in a Dublin parliament. Neither group saw devolution or federalism as a satisfactory solution. As Brassey put it in a letter to Murray Macdonald, "I am afraid we are beaten for the moment."[103]

CHAPTER EIGHT

The War Years

With the outbreak of war the Irish question quickly became a secondary consideration for most politicians and certainly for the general public.[1] Similarly, Welsh and Scottish demands for home rule which had received passing attention in the spring of 1914 were dropped not to be revived in a serious form until 1918. Devolution, federal home rule, and home rule all round were not discussed in any context in a sustained way during the first two years of the war. Even F.S. Oliver, perhaps federalism's most ardent champion before August 1914, concentrated on the preparation of his book *Ordeal by Battle*, a critique of Britain's preparedness for war and of the Asquith's government's handling of its early stages.

In March 1915 William O'Brien still believed "the Unionists alone can solve the Irish difficulty with success, and, of course, on Federal United Kingdom lines, leaving the larger question to work itself out later." But first Ireland had "to be favourably disposed, and that could best be done by a Federal Conciliation association, to be modestly started by Irish Unionists of influence." It seemed to O'Brien "clear that, without some Federal proposal, the Unionists could never win a General Election on a mere blind negative anti-Home Rule policy. The mere knowledge that the Unionists were ready for a great Federal experiment would draw the sting of anti-Unionist feeling among the Irish electorate of Great Britain."[2] O'Brien wanted to get Walter Long into a position of power because he was supportive of a moderate federalist approach: "The ideal thing would be if W.L. were made a peer and sent over as Lord Lieutenant (*of course*) with a seat in the Cabinet. On that condition, it is certain that my friends would work with all their hearts to support him, pending the time when he would be in a position publicly to announce the Federal plan, which would quite surely carry all before it."[3] By August, however, he had concluded that the time was not ripe for suggesting the federal solution. Everyone was too preoccupied with the war.[4]

Neither Ireland nor home rule and thus not federalism attracted much attention until the late spring and early summer of 1916. On Easter Monday,

24 April 1916, Padraic Pearse and his colleagues, with contingents of the Irish Volunteers and the Irish Citizen Army, seized control of key buildings in Dublin, and for one week held the British forces at bay. The centre of Dublin was heavily damaged during the Easter Rising and the insurgents had little support from the Dublin populace who spat upon them as they were led away at the end of the bloody affray. The incident might have ended there but the politically insensitive Sir John Maxwell proceeded to execute the leaders at intervals over a period of nine days. Fifteen men died in this way. The people of Ireland were stunned and revolted, and the mood turned against the British. Having only slowly become aware of the implications of Maxwell's actions, Asquith visited Ireland, halted the executions, and after a week of talks concluded that it was essential to try once more to resolve the Irish problem in order to restore confidence in Redmond's Nationalists and to undercut the rise of anti-British feeling in the United States. In late May Lloyd George was given the task of trying to find common ground between Nationalists and Unionists. He talked privately with Redmond, Dillon, Devlin, and T.P. O'Connor of the Nationalists and with Carson and Craig of the Ulster Unionists. He soon appeared to have been successful. Home rule was to be put into effect immediately and the six northeastern counties of Antrim, Armagh, Down, Fermanagh, Londonderry and Tyrone plus the parliamentary boroughs of Belfast, Londonderry, and Newry were to be excluded. The act incorporating the agreement was to remain in effect for one year after the war. If parliament had not managed by then to make a permanent provision for the government of Ireland, the life of the act would be extended by order in council for as long as necessary. The possibility of an imperial conference at the end of the war to consider the Irish question was also raised.

This agreement had a number of intriguing implications, the most important of which concerned the size of the excluded area and whether exclusion was to be permanent or temporary. On the eve of war, the most the Nationalists had been prepared to concede were the four Protestant counties of Antrim, Down, Londonderry, and Armagh. Now Redmond was also prepared to concede Fermanagh and Tyrone and to sacrifice the Nationalist majorities in Belfast, Derry, and Newry for the sake of achieving home rule for the other twenty-six counties; thereby, it was hoped, restoring the waning fortunes of the Nationalists. Lloyd George verbally promised Redmond that the exclusion would be temporary, although the Irish Nationalist leader must surely have wondered how it would be possible to include readily in a united Ireland an area whose right to exist apart from the South had been formally recognized, however temporarily. What he did not know was that Lloyd George had given Carson written assurance that the exclusion would be permanent.

For their part, the southern Unionists were appalled at being sacrificed so readily, and persuaded their cabinet allies, Walter Long and Lord

Lansdowne, to do all they could to thwart the agreement. Lord Selborne was so incensed that he resigned from the cabinet on 16 June. Balfour and Carson and most Ulster Unionists did not share this indignation. The agreement to them was a triumph, for it gave them what they had demanded since 1911: the areas they knew they could control. As Balfour pointed out, the maximum demand of the Unionists at the Buckingham Palace Conference had been the exclusion of six counties; thus their concession to Nationalist demands had already been made in 1914. It was no use arguing, therefore, as Long and Lansdowne were doing, that to concede home rule to the twenty-six counties in 1916 was to bow to rebellion. Balfour simply believed that the Unionists had got what they wanted and without civil war. Nevertheless, Long and Lansdowne were obdurate, and by 19 July had succeeded in persuading their cabinet colleagues to acknowledge publicly that the exclusion of the six counties would be permanent. Their intent was to wreck the arrangement, and they were successful. Redmond had no choice but to reject Lloyd George's new terms. The negotiations collapsed, and matters were left as they had been.

But was the situation quite the same? After all, the Nationalists had accepted the exclusion of six not four counties from the rest of Ireland, and, in time, that was to prove an important precedent for the Ulster Unionists. The episode also meant the virtual end of Redmond's influence and of the relevance of the Irish parliamentary party. Faced with an impossible situation, Redmond had done the best he could, but it had not been sufficient and Sinn Fein reaped the advantages. After 1916 home rule was effectively dead. Separatism and/or dominion status became the rallying cries. Moreover, the incident convinced some southern Unionists of the inevitability of some form of self-government and the need to be more constructive toward the idea.[5]

Throughout the protracted discussions and lobbying of May-July 1916 federalism was rarely mentioned, and then never considered seriously by any individual or group. In writing to Carson just before the start of Lloyd George's negotiations, Oliver suggested that the Home Rule Act would need to be amended before Ulster could consider coming back into a united Ireland. In the first instance, it would have to be stated clearly that Ireland would not become a single federal unit until England and Scotland were each dealt with in the same way; second, each federal unit must be given equality of representation – on the basis of population – in the United Kingdom parliament; third, all unallotted powers must remain with the United Kingdom parliament, fourth, no unit would have the power to touch customs or excise duties; and fifth, the "absolute supremacy" of the United Kingdom parliament must be put beyond doubt.[6]

The first systematic suggestion came from Selborne in August 1916. Selborne had interpreted the developments of the past few months as finally demonstrating the futility of negotiations and suggestions on traditional lines. No such proposals appeared to work. Selborne outlined his thinking in a letter published in the *Morning Post* on 8 August.[7] He argued: "Is it not now manifest

... that on the one hand the great majority of Irishmen and women will accept no solution which divides Ireland and on the other hand that the Unionists of Ulster cannot be forced to accept any solution of which they disapprove?" That being so, neither the 1914 Government of Ireland Act nor autonomy on a Canadian or Australian model would solve the problem. "Does not the solution of 'devolution' alone remain?" He suggested a parliament for the United Kingdom "which should take cognisance only of those matters which are the common concern of all the nations of which the United Kingdom is composed." There would be individual parliaments for Scotland, Ireland, England, and Wales. As for Ireland, it might be possible to set up two legislative bodies and two executives in Ireland, one for the six Ulster counties and one for the rest of Ireland, but he doubted that the Nationalists would accept such a solution.

Selborne admitted that "the cumbersomeness of 'devolution'" compared with the simplicity of the union struck most Unionists very forcibly. Certainly the difficulties in framing such an elaborate constitution, and the objections to it when framed, were manifest. But the objections, grave as they were, did not appear to Selborne to be so grave as those inherent in the Government of Ireland Act which would threaten the union. He recognized that the constitutional process in Canada, Australia, South Africa, and the United States was one of centralization whereas in the United Kingdom it would be decentralization, "but the difficulties which were successfully overcome in those cases and the experience of Canada with its special problem of the Province of Quebec is particularly interesting in this connection." He urged his fellow Unionists to consider seriously the solution of devolution: "If the political unity of the Empire for common imperial purposes (while each part of the Empire retains complete internal autonomy) is to them as it is to me the greatest and dearest political ideal, then they will be careful to carry the public opinion of the Empire with them in their handling of the Irish question."

F.S. Oliver liked Selborne's letter and agreed with his ideas, but he thought there was one other important reason for considering devolution and that was the need to clean up business after the war. As for himself, he thought he should abstain from the controversy that he believed would arise over Selborne's ideas because, as he put it, "crusted Unionists distrust me because I favour Federalism, while crusted Radicals detest me because I have tried to break some of their idols."[8] Encouraged by this support but realizing he would have to take the initiative, Selborne wrote again to the *Morning Post* on 18 August 1916.[9] Having laid the groundwork in his previous letter, Selborne now plunged right in: "Devolution is the only method by which Ireland can be given any form of Home Rule and remain united, the Irish Parliament be manifestly subordinate to the Imperial Parliament, and all Irishmen retain exactly the same share of control as they now possess in the Government of the United Kingdom and of the British Empire." Devolution would mean the imperial parliament would serve as the parliament for the United Kingdom as well as for the empire as a whole. There would also be parliaments for England, Scotland, Ireland, and Wales each of which would concern itself with exclusively English, Scottish, Irish, and Welsh business. Selborne saw no reason to be alarmed at the number of parliaments. There were more in both Australia and Canada, and their systems worked well. Pursuing Oliver's point, Selborne argued that: "Devolution of this sort is the only method by which the legislative machinery can be made adequate to its task. After the war the need for reconstructive legislation will be immense, and there is no possibility of the present Imperial Parliament being able to cope with it. Devolution is also the only method by which we can safeguard the Empire against the disaster which has so often overtaken it, that the men who are elected to govern the Empire are elected on some parish pump issue." He then considered how powers might be divided. He contended that the work of the Foreign, Indian, Colonial, and War Offices and of the Admiralty concerned the United Kingdom as a whole. Similarly, the Home Office responsibility for mines and factories was a United Kingdom matter, but all other Home Office affairs were of a local nature and should be transferred to the subordinate parliaments. Most of the Board of Trade's work was also United Kingdom-wide and only a few issues were local. But the Board of Agriculture, the Local Government Board, the Education Office, the Post Office, ecclesiastical affairs, land, and law, with the exception of the Supreme Court of Appeal, should all be transferred to the local parliaments. Financial matters would be divided according to whatever financial scheme was adopted, but customs and excise would definitely have to remain a United Kingdom matter. In Selborne's scheme nothing that was already local "need for the sake of theory be made United Kingdom." He believed that legislatures could be phased in, thus recognizing the urgency of the Irish problem. He concluded by emphasizing that "it is most important that all powers, which are not expressly delegated to the local Parliaments, should be reserved to the United Kingdom or Imperial Parliament, and not conversely, as in that extraordinarily vicious instrument the present Government of Ireland Act." This clear and frank statement caused concern to many Unionists, but, as Selborne pointed out to Lord Salisbury, it was not possible to "put back the Union or the House of Lords to where it was." He was now convinced that devolution was the only alternative to union and he intended to work for it as actively as he could in conjunction with efflorts to bring about a political union with the dominions for the purpose of defence and foreign policy.[10]

In fact, it was not long before Selborne and Oliver joined forces in a more systematic fashion in order to prepare a full-scale statement on devolution. On 3 November Selborne dined at Oliver's house with Bob Brand, Philip Kerr, and Oliver to discuss a federal bill.[11] They decided to go ahead, but agreed that they would need an assistant to obtain the necessary information and statistics, to write position papers, and generally "to devil" for them. Selborne asked A.L. Smith, the master of Balliol, to furnish a young man to act as secretary. He recommended one of his students, a young Australian named Duncan Hall, who met with Oliver and Selborne on 23 November to confirm the arrangement and to plan the initial stages of the committee's work.[12] Hall had already given some thought to federalism in the empire and had also studied the home rule bills under the supervision of W.G.S. Adams at Oxford. Hall later described his responsibilities, the committee's purpose, and its activities as follows:

We were to study the possibilities of a constitutional settlement of the *Irish issue* within the framework of *devolution* for the United Kingdom. My task was to draft the memoranda on the various aspects of the problem. These were to be discussed at meetings of the Committee which were held several times a month in Selborne's house at 49 Mount St. The members of the Committee all shared a general interest in Federalism: Kerr and Selborne from their S. African experience. Oliver as a student of the origins of the American system ... From the outset I played an active part in the Committee discussions having made it my business to make for this purpose a detailed study of all the Home Rule bills and of each of the federal & union constitutions in the u.s.a. and especially South Africa and Canada. When the general discussions were far enough advanced I put the tentative conclusions into the skeleton framework of a bill. By the late summer of 1917 the draft bill was complete. I went over it with a lawyer in the Temple who gave it greater precision in the matter of legal phraseology at some points. It emerged substantially unchanged and received the approval of the Committee late in the autumn of 1917 and was printed ... it was a very thorough analysis by practical and experienced people. They were fully aware that the bill wd stand or fall as much on its application to Great Britain and the Parliament at Westminster as on the side of Ireland. I remember searching discussions on the effect of devolution on the exercise of powers of taxation of the subordinate legislatures ... By the time the Bill was printed in early 1918 the bottom had fallen out of it as a possible solution of the Irish problem. It was no longer possible to get the Irish leaders to look at a Federal Union.[13]

Throughout the early months of 1917 Oliver, Selborne, and Duncan Hall met regularly to discuss research materials and memoranda gathered and prepared by Hall. In January much of the discussion revolved around financial issues, but by February Oliver was drafting a pamphlet on Ireland which he revised after discussions with Selborne and Hall. It was published on 22 March to coincide with the meetings of the imperial conference and was entitled *Ireland and the Imperial Conference: Is There a Way to a Settlement?*[14] Oliver argued that most parties and individuals were unable to analyse the Irish problem clearly and to suggest a solution agreeable to all. Most were unable to detach themselves sufficiently from their own positions, and all were admittedly stale. Neither their tempers nor their judgments could therefore be relied upon. Perhaps fresh minds would help. Oliver thought that an imperial conference after the war might be the appropriate mechanism for finding an answer. Perhaps "a friendly and sympathetic tutorial, the majority of whose members would be uncommitted beforehand to any particular solution, would have a better chance of arriving at a workable arrangement than any possible convention of pledged partisans." Such an idea should not surprise anyone for "the Irish Question is an Imperial as well as a Local one ... The state of Ireland has been from the beginning, and is now, more than ever, one of the gravest dangers which threatens the unity of the Empire." Oliver concluded by suggesting that in order to prepare for such a postwar conference it might be "desirable to set up at once an independent Commission to consider a single problem, viz., the extent to which it would be necessary to amend the existing Home Rule Act in order to fit it into a Federal system."[15]

The same day that Oliver published his pamphlet, 22 March, Bonar Law announced that the government planned to make another attempt to solve the Irish problem. But it was not until 21 May, almost seven weeks after the United States had entered the war, that Lloyd George finally announced an Irish Convention would be set up under the chairmanship of Sir Horace Plunkett to discuss an Irish settlement using the proposals of May-July 1916 as a starting point. Understandably, Oliver and his colleagues continued their activities, but at a heightened pace. Regular meetings were held between Oliver, Selborne, and Hall. In particular, Hall was most useful preparing memoranda on such subjects as "The Adjustment of United Kingdom Income Taxes," "The Financial Relations between the United Kingdom and Ireland, England and Scotland," and "The Financial Relations between the United Kingdom and the Kingdoms of England, Scotland and Ireland."[16] Much of Hall's work by May-June 1917 was concentrated on the financial side of the committee's work, but he did take pains to remind his employers that "the term 'Federal Union' ... is technically nearer the mark than the term 'Federation' alone. The proposed constitution [i.e., the one recommended by Oliver and Selborne] lies in type between that of Canada and the South African Act. And in theory at least, it is not a Federation but a delegation of power within a Union to subsidiary bodies which according to the Act are liable to extinction or to have their Acts rendered void by an Act of the United Kingdom Parliament."[17] Although Hall was their principal source of information and advice, Oliver and Selborne also conferred in mid-April with Amery and W.G. Adams about Irish finance, and Oliver, at least, had discussions with Murray Macdonald who reiterated his belief in devolution to relieve congestion in parliament.[18] The first stage in the committee's work was completed with the circulation in June of Oliver's and Selborne's privately printed pamphlet entitled *A Method of Constitutional Cooperation: Suggestions for the Better Government of the United Kingdom* in which they recommended the solution of the Irish problem by the adoption of a federal government for the United Kingdom.[19]

In their pamphlet, Oliver and Selborne made it clear that although their proposals were made at that particular moment because of the urgency of the Irish question the settlement of that question was not their primary purpose. Their main object was "the better government of the United Kingdom as a whole." It seemed to them that existing political arrangements were unable to meet immediate legislative and administrative needs and that they would be completely overwhelmed by postwar problems. Obviously the country was endangered by the congestion of business and the overloading of existing machinery. The settlement of the Irish question was therefore only a part, although admittedly an urgent part, of a larger problem which only federalism could resolve. They made it clear that they proposed to deal with England and Scotland upon the same principles they wished to see applied to Ireland, but because public attention was focused on the Irish difficulty they had deliberately dealt more specifically with Ireland in their pamphlet.

Oliver and Selborne pointed out that neither Irish home rulers nor Irish Unionists seemed prepared to accept exclusion either by county option or by any other method as a permanent settlement, and probably not even as a temporary method. The only hope of settlement between such divergent views lay in compromise. It would be foolish to look for a solution which would give either side all it desired. The best compromise would be the application of the federal system to the United Kingdom. This would mean separate legislatures for England, Scotland, and Ireland (Wales was not mentioned in the pamphlet), responsible for the "national" concerns of each of the three kingdoms, and a central parliament to manage the "common" concerns of the United Kingdom. Oliver and Selborne recognized that this solution would not be wholly satisfactory to any political party and probably would be strongly opposed by extremists in all parties. Nevertheless, they believed the proposal gave each party what it most desired, and protected it against what it most feared. If accepted, it would preserve the unity both of Ireland and of the United Kingdom and would give the Irish legislature greater power for developing the resources of Ireland than did the Government of Ireland Act of 1914.

They were emphatic on one point. It was essential that "*from the very outset, the central Parliament, which is to manage the common concerns of the United Kingdom as a whole, must not be encumbered with the management of the purely national concerns of any one or more of the three kingdoms.*" If it was decided to adopt the federal system in order to solve the Irish question, not only an Irish legislature and a United Kingdom legislature would have to be created but also at least one other legislature to manage jointly the "national" concerns of England and Scotland or, preferably, separate legislatures for

England and Scotland. Oliver and Selborne argued that it was essential for the proper working of a federal system that there be a complete separation of "national" from "common" concerns.

On turning to the details of their proposal, the two men immediately emphasized that all powers not specifically allotted to the kingdom legislatures would remain with the United Kingdom parliament. They believed this followed the intent of the preamble to the Government of Ireland Act of 1914; an intent not effectively realized in the clauses. Both Selborne and Oliver wanted a strong federal government on Canadian lines rather than a federation with strong state powers and a weak central government as in the United States and Australia. After all, their purpose was to preserve the union; federalism was only a means to that end. Strong regional or national authority might too easily lead to separation.

The two men recommended that the constitution of the United Kingdom parliament, which was to look after common concerns, should remain the same for the time being except that the membership of the House of Commons should be reduced by about one-half and seats redistributed upon the basis of population. The constitutions of the three kingdom legislatures should be left to separate conventions, but Oliver and Selborne did not think it necessary that there should be uniformity in those constitutions. Each kingdom should be free to adopt the form of constitution most in harmony with its traditions, material interests, and special legislative and administrative needs. They could, for example, envisage, although not necessarily favor, "a constitution for Ireland in which there would be: (a) a single Senate; and (b) two separate lower Houses, one for the six Ulster counties, the other for the rest of Ireland."

As for the distribution of powers, the two men argued that certain powers granted by the Government of Ireland Act of 1914 to the Irish legislature should, in fact, be allocated to the central parliament. Powers for regulating such matters as currency, bills of exchange, bankruptcy, banking, and insurance should be retained in order to secure freedom and equality of commercial and financial intercourse throughout the federal union. It was felt that there was need for uniformity of legislation in these matters in order that friction might be avoided and trade proceed unhampered. For the same reasons the central parliament should assume responsibility for customs and excise. As far as Oliver and Selborne were aware, no successful federation had ever allowed such matters to be regulated by any but the central federal parliament. Postal services and the census should also be retained and judges of the Supreme Court should be appointed by the central parliament. On the other hand, the Land Purchase acts, direct taxation, including income tax and death duties, the Royal Irish Constabulary, old age pensions, and national insurance, all of which had been reserved to the United Kingdom parliament under the Government of Ireland Act, should be granted to the Irish legislature.

In making their suggestions on financial matters Oliver and Selborne tried to keep a balance between two complementary principles which they considered essential to the strength and healthy growth of a federal union. First, to the utmost extent consistent with the safety and solvency of the union as a whole, the individual states or kingdoms should have power over taxation; the power of levying and varying taxation was not only an essential attribute of government but one of the most potent instruments for shaping the development of the people. Second, if certain kinds of taxation were under the control of the local legislatures it would tend to set up barriers between the various parts of the union thus creating friction, ill-feeling, and reprisals all of which were very dangerous to overall unity. With respect to the first principle the authors thought subsidies paid by the federal parliament to the local legislatures should be reduced as far as possible, and with respect to the second that powers over customs and excise should be retained by the central legislature. They reasoned that "To give such powers to the kingdom legislatures is to offer them a temptation to tariff warfare. Human nature being what it is – and, in the case of Ireland, history being what it is – such powers would almost certainly be put in force, would set up friction, and before long would be used by the extremists as a lever for obtaining complete separation."

They recognized, however, the exceptional financial problems of Ireland and realized that unless sources of revenue other than customs and excise could be found an enormous subsidy would be necessary if the Irish government was to cover its expenditure. They therefore recommended that in addition to revenue derived from such miscellaneous sources as licenses the Irish legislature should have wider powers of *direct* taxation, i.e., they proposed that the central parliament should reduce substantially its levy of income tax in order to leave a sufficient portion of this revenue field open to the local legislatures and that all the existing death duties be handed over to the local legislatures. The central parliament, however, would not give up concurrent rights to levy taxation upon Irish incomes and property. Oliver and Selborne also suggested that the following funds, revenue, and property be handed over absolutely to the Irish legislature to deal with as it saw fit: the accumulations of sinking funds under the various Land Purchase acts (about £3,000,000); the annual instalments (i.e., for sinking funds as well as interest) payable by the owners of agricultural land in Ireland which had been already bought under the Land Purchase acts (about £4,250,000); and the whole of the remaining agricultural leaseholds in Ireland (approximate capital value of £60–70,000,000) to be purchased from the present owners – if necessary compulsorily – and handed over to the Irish legislature to deal with as it judged best. For the time being, the proceeds of the super tax would be retained by the United Kingdom parliament. If these suggestions were adopted, Oliver and Selborne believed, the size of the annual subsidy would be reduced to reasonable dimensions. They realized that objections would be raised to the suggestion that £60–70,000,000 should be provided by the United Kingdom to purchase the remaining agricultural leaseholds of Ireland in order to make a present of them to the Irish legislature, but they pointed out that the United Kingdom would have to pay one way or another to start Ireland in a solvent condition. The payments could be made in the form of a capital grant or a flat annual subsidy, and they preferred the former. They reasoned that if the Irish legislature was free to levy direct taxation, and if the whole of the agricultural land of Ireland was under its control, the Irish legislature would have immense powers for promoting national development.[20]

This pamphlet and an accompanying draft bill were circulated privately in June 1917, a month before the first meeting of the Irish Convention. No initial efforts were made to publicize the proposals, and the only ones aware of its existence in the months immediately following were Round Table members and close friends in the Unionist party. At that time there was little interest in federalism. As Monteagle had pointed out in the April issue of the *Quarterly Review*, the federal solution had few charms for Irish Nationalists. It would mean more restricted powers than even the act of 1914.[21] He suggested that "Dominion Home Rule" might be more appealing. Both Smuts, who was in England to attend the Imperial Conference of 1917, and John Redmond were inclined to agree. Smut's "ideal for Ireland was Responsible Government for Ireland as a whole with local autonomy ... for North and South Ireland respectively," while Redmond argued that the "true policy for Ireland was Dominion Government, or something like it, for the whole of Ireland with a subordinate assembly on the Canadian model for Ulster, taking the whole province, and for Munster too if she wanted it."[22]

Although Moreton Frewen had hoped many men of federalist sympathy, including himself, would be appointed to the convention, in the event only Dunraven became a member.[23] Walter Long, by now favourable to the federal idea, had in fact suggested to Lloyd George in February that if an Irish Convention was to be held then someone clearly sympathetic to the federal system, such as Earl Grey, should be appointed chairman. Whether Lloyd George ever considered this suggestion is unclear, but Grey's illness and the need for a well-known Irishman of moderate views led to the appointment of Sir Horace Plunkett.[24] Plunkett was not unsympathetic to the overtures of the federalists, and he ensured that memoranda on such matters as fiscal autonomy, the government of Canada, and the variety of forms of government in the empire, including dominion status and federalism, were prepared and distributed to the members.[25] Despite this Plunkett had difficulty in having the idea discussed.[26] As one of Plunkett's correspondents, Lord Atkinson, pointed out: "When the Sinn Feiners want a Republic, the other

Nationalists independence in the form of the Canadian Government, while the Ulstermen, who are not to be coerced, won't submit to be ruled by either or both the others, how can anything come of it? ... I think the Convention will be abortive."[27]

Shortly after the opening of the proceedings of the convention, Plunkett received from J.X. Merriman, the South African politician, a salutary survey of the financial difficulties to which even a nonfederal devolutionary scheme could be subject. Nevertheless, he thought that "on the whole ... unification was safer than Federation – which always seems to me so dangerously weak in dealing with outside powers."[28] In turn, Plunkett later admitted to Merriman that the rise of Sinn Fein had "enormously added to the difficulties of a constitutional settlement." Sinn Fein was not interested in a federal solution but was now making a strong case for Dominion status.[29]

Despite the obvious difficulties in raising federal proposals in the convention, Lord Dunraven did send Plunkett a federal scheme in mid-August. Unfortunately, Plunkett believed it contained some provisions that unless "expurgated away, would relegate it to the mad list."[30] The scheme followed generally the Government of Ireland Act of 1914, and was capable of being grafted on to that act by the amendment of certain clauses and the exclusion and addition of others. Dunraven's objectives were to give Ireland the fullest possible measure of self-government consistent with imperial unity and safety; to provide a scheme that would fit with minimum amendment into the future complete federalization of the United Kingdom and which might lead to imperial federation; and to conform as closely as possible to the principles which had governed the constitutions of the United States, Switzerland, and the Dominions. Unlike the Government of Ireland Act, Dunraven's scheme gave the Irish more control over taxation and social legislation; offered them more liberty because it prevented the imposition of compulsory military service without the consent of the Irish parliament; and provided for the various sections of the Irish people a greater sense of security not only by a grand committee system but also by the ability of areas ultimately to vote themselves out of the operation of the act. It did not permit partition but it did permit exclusion from the Irish parliament after a fair trial. It also provided for Irish seats in the imperial House of Commons and for consultation on military and naval expenditures.[31]

Whether or not Sir Edward Carson heard of Dunraven's scheme is unclear, but in September he advised Plunkett that a settlement was only possible on federal lines and urged his friends Oliver and Selborne to submit their proposal to the convention. Copies were immediately sent not only to Plunkett but also to St John Brodrick, Lord Londonderry, and "to the Secretariat of the Mandarinate at Downing Street."[32] Selborne subsequently explained to Plunkett that "I have never varied in my opinion that Pitt's solution of the Union was the right solution, but that [sic] when I became convinced that the majority in the United Kingdom had determined to give what is called

Home Rule a trial I set to work to try and frame the scheme which in my judgement would be the least disadvantageous to the Empire and to the United Kingdom, and so of course to Ireland as part of the United Kingdom."[33] In turn, Oliver explained to Plunkett that the danger with the convention was that it might consider "*too much*" the present mood of Ireland and "*too little* the jog-trot businesslike compromise which is most likely to work well in the future." He revealed his true aims when he added, "In particular I think that fiscal autonomy – let alone Dominion status – is incompatible with the firm union, and therefore with the safety, of the United Kingdom."[34]

Plunkett had been delighted to receive the Selborne-Oliver proposal and was quick to congratulate them on "one of the best done things of the kind I have ever seen. Its comprehensiveness in essentials, its lucidity and suggestions and above all its perspective are marvelous."[35] Despite his high hopes the ambience in the convention was not conducive to a discussion of either Dunraven's proposal or the Selborne-Oliver scheme. The majority of members were clearly opposed to federalism. Lord Londonderry did undertake to prepare a federal scheme based on Selborne's and Oliver's ideas for submission to the key Committee of Nine but changed his mind when he realized the hopelessness of gaining Ulster Unionist support. Thus by the end of 1917 neither Dunraven's nor Selborne's and Oliver's proposals had been generally circulated in the convention, and apart from two speeches by Dunraven the matter had not been discussed.[36]

Oliver mistakenly thought that Plunkett had done little to ensure the circulation of the federal scheme and in January brusquely asked for the return of the proposal. He referred scathingly to "the slip-shod, unworkmanlike, less-than-half-thought-out schemes which various highly intelligent men submitted to the Dublin Convention." If the convention failed, "it will do so largely for the reason that nothing of a practical, constitutional character has been laid before it."[37] Oliver now very deliberately turned his attention and efforts elsewhere. Throughout the war he had been dining regularly on Monday evenings with Lord Milner, Sir Edward Carson, Waldorf Astor, and Geoffrey Dawson, editor of the *Times*, and since November 1917 he had been the secretary to a cabinet committee on the economic offensive chaired by Carson. He therefore had unrivalled opportunities to discuss both the general war effort and, more particularly, the Irish question with men who were both well informed and since, December 1916, had had direct access to Lloyd George. In the knowledge that the Irish Convention was having difficulty reaching agreement, and probably would be unable to give the government any clear direction on the Irish question, Oliver pushed the federal case during February and March both in the public arena and privately in an effort to put pressure on the Lloyd George government.

Oliver quickly drafted a pamphlet on *Ulster and a Federal Settlement* in which for the first time since 1914 he publicly stated the case for a federal solution of United Kingdom and Irish difficulties.[38] The arguments for federation were essentially the same as those of his earlier document: supremacy of the imperial parliament, the retention by the central parliament of all powers and functions not expressly delegated and made over to the national parliaments, and the control of customs and excise by the central parliament. There was, however, a significant departure from the earlier document. Oliver now suggested that during the probationary period, and until the fair working of self-government had been proved by experience, it would be necessary that "Ulster should have within its own sphere, a power of veto upon laws, and of control over their enforcement, in such matters as affect her vital interests." He also urged that a federal scheme be quickly prepared and applied. He saw no reason for delay if the statesmen of England and Scotland were in earnest about the evils of congestion and the need for improving the machinery of government. He concluded by asserting that for Ulstermen the union as it stood was the ideal constitution, but since they would retain their security and British citizenship unimpaired under a federation they would be prepared to accept the change. Events were to prove that this was an optimistic interpretation of Ulster's stance on the federal issue, but it was characteristic of Oliver to be blinded by the logic of his arguments. In forwarding the document to Carson, who had recently resigned from the war cabinet in order to have complete freedom of action over the Irish question, Oliver argued that "If your people can bring themselves to put this proposal forward I think (a) they will have England and Scotland and u.s.a. absolutely on their side and (b) they will carry it."[39]

While impressed by Oliver's pamphlet, Carson was despairing about Lloyd George. He had had two conversations with the prime minister "and it is quite clear he does not apply himself to any Federal plan of any kind – owing no doubt to the extent of the problem. What he wants is a patched up truce however unsymmetrical and I feel so much that I am being lured into something I don't really approve that I am thinking of washing my hands of all negotiations and leaving him to frame his proposals."[40]

Alarmed, Oliver hastened to respond. On 11 February he wrote:

It does not seem to me possible to have patched-up temporary arrangement for the duration of the war. That will only entangle people's feet and will increase the bitterness and distrust which are in their hearts.

I suggest that the right plan is to force the hand of the Prime Minister and make Federation a practical way out. That will really be a kindness. It will be done if your people will adopt such a manifesto as I wrote.

Failing that, I might recast it and make it into a manifesto for the Unionist Federalists who number nearly 40 in the House of Commons.

Will you think over these alternatives ... If the case of Ulster were put, and the offer of Ulster were made in the same document, I think the whole issue would at once be changed, and put onto a plane where it could be settled.[41]

Carson doubted the wisdom of pressing the prime minister too hard while the convention was still in session. Nevertheless, he agreed to write to Lloyd George along the lines suggested by Oliver.[42] Carson had clearly been impressed by Oliver's arguments, for his letter of 14 February to Lloyd George depended heavily on his friend's suggestions. Carson indicated to Lloyd George that he had been thinking a great deal recently about a settlement during the war and it was clear that nothing could be devised which would be consistent with the interests of Great Britain and at the same time satisfy the extreme nationalists. Any attempt to bring Ulster into an Irish parliament would result in both Sinn Fein and Ulster being opposed to the new Irish government which would doom it to failure. As far as Carson could see,

The only other possible solution seems to me to lie in a system of Federation for the whole United Kingdom. Averse, as I am, from any change in the present Constitution with its single Parliament for all purposes, I do not deny that the Union, which I regard as the keystone of the British Commonwealth, may nevertheless be preserved upon the principles of a true federation.

In a true federation, it is essential, not only that there should be constitutional equality between the Nations which are to be the federal units, but also that the powers delegated and made over by the United Kingdom Parliament to the National Parliaments, should not be such as to hamper the actual and active supremacy of the former, and to set up impediment against the free intercourse of the federated kingdoms.

If such a policy were adopted, it is easy to see that a settlement of the Ulster difficulty could be found, either by making Ulster a unit or by providing for its particular needs within another unit.

The whole difference is, that in this case the Parliament of the Union would possess a real supremacy and not merely a titular sovereignty, and further, such solution would not be in the direction of separation or secession, which seems to me to be of vital importance. It will be said that the Irish problem is so pressing that it cannot wait for a true federation of the United Kingdom. At any rate let us settle the lines upon which this true federation is ultimately to be made. When this is done, let the South and West of Ireland have their Act, with any necessary safeguards, and let Ulster stand out until such time as England and Scotland can be brought in.[43]

Oliver was delighted with the way Carson had adopted many of his ideas; some of the passages in the letter were virtually verbatim from his pamphlet on *Ulster and a Federal Settlement*. As for Lloyd George, he was by this time prepared to consider "the reorganisation of the affairs of the United Kingdom on a federal basis" in order to preserve the well-being of the empire and the unity of the country and to safeguard the interests of Ulster and the southern unionists. He therefore wrote to Hugh Barrie, the chairman of the Ulster delegation to the convention, suggesting that the settlement reached by the convention should be "compatible with the final realisation of a federal system of the United Kingdom."[44] Oliver did not see Lloyd George's letter to Barrie but heard enough of its contents to believe that the ideas contained both in it and in Carson's letter of the 14th were sufficiently similar to provide the basis for agreement. Oliver suggested to Milner that a leading statesman such as Chamberlain, Smuts, or Selborne should be appointed to devote his whole mind to the problem, and he assured Carson that he was "very hopeful that if we put our backs into it we can bring the thing off."[45]

Throughout these weeks, Oliver, anxious as always to add voices to his chorus, had kept in touch with another close friend, Austen Chamberlain. At the end of February he sent him copies of the pamphlet and draft bill which had been prepared the previous year and attempted to enlist his more active cooperation;

After talking things over with Selborne, I am arranging a dinner for next Wednesday either at Waldor's house or here, to consider whether this is is a suitable moment for making a serious combined effort in Parliament to present the Federal solution as a way out of the present blind alley. If we conclude that it is a suitable opportunity, then we shall have to consider the best means of bringing about the combined action and the right atmosphere. I, personally, am very hopeful indeed, and should feel almost confident of success if you can see your way to take the leading part in the Commons. This I think is Selborne's view also.[46]

On Sunday, 3 March, Oliver had his first opportunity in some weeks to talk with Carson. He wrote of the outcome to Chamberlain:

One thing is pretty clear – *he can accept*, but *he cannot himself stand up and propose* a federal settlement. Ergo: someone else must put it forward and Carson must then reluctantly agree.

Who is the "someone" to be? It should be the government; but the head of that body has neither the time to understand the innards of the problem nor the will to take a bold step of this sort. Can we, therefore, find another "someone"? If we could get even a comparative few from Labour, Liberals and Unionists to act together in a House of Commons motion it would be the next best thing in my opinion.

Almost as an afterthought, Oliver referred musingly to Walter Long: "Now, as Carson says, the worst of W. Long is that he never knows what he wants, but he is always intriguing to get it. I wonder – can't we rope him in?"[47]

Chamberlain met twice with Oliver during the next week, and they were joined by Milner, Carson, Selborne, Astor, Geoffrey Dawson, Leo Amery, and Philip Kerr, Lloyd George's secretary. The main topic of conversation was federalism.[48] By this time Austen Chamberlain was more convinced. He had been impressed by Oliver's pamphlet and the argument that only through federation could one hope to accommodate the wishes of both the Nationalists and Ulster, as well as resolve the problem of congestion in the United Kingdom parliament. Chamberlain outlined his thoughts in a letter to his wife on 9 March:

I have been colloquiescing with Selborne, Fred Oliver and some others about Federalism for the United Kingdom as the only possible solution of the Irish question. Now that half this country has given up the idea of maintaining the Union as it stands we cannot get "resolute government" for the time necessary to let the Home Rule idea die out, even if it would ever die out after all the encouragement it has had. And federalism is the only thing which would make Home Rule safe and the only form of Home Rule which Ulster could be got to accept, whilst for us devolution would seem to have become necessary when you think of the vast mass of work which lies before Parlt in the near future ... It is rather curious to see how far the division of administration has already gone as witnessed by the separate estimates and differing legislation of the three countries. In some ways therefore it would be a smaller revolution than at first sight it appears, but it would still be a prodigious change, and we must test opinion before we go further.[49]

This letter not only reveals the degree of Chamberlain's indebtedness to Oliver for ideas about federalism but also indicates why Chamberlain and Walter Long, both such strong defenders of the union, had become firm supporters of the federal idea. Chamberlain obviously in his heart of hearts did not like the idea of home rule and he would have preferred the maintenance of the union by "resolute government"; but he knew that this was impossible so he adopted federalism as the next best method of preserving the union and the supremacy of the imperial parliament and of fulfilling the requests and protecting the interests of Nationalists and Irish Unionists. It was for him, as it was for Walter Long, the best compromise available.

Oliver continued his behind-the-scenes lobbying. He talked at length with Lloyd George over lunch on 10 March and within the next few days discussed the merits of the federal scheme with Robert Cecil and J.H. Thomas, the railway trade unionist and leading Labour MP. Thomas also read Oliver's pamphlet and was so impressed that during a speech at the Irish Club on 16 March he suggested the application of the federal principle to the United Kingdom and a devolution of responsibilities to Ireland, Scotland, Wales, and England.[50] Interest in a federal solution grew rapidly during March. A number of articles and editorials favourable to the scheme appeared in the newspapers and it was also discussed in political circles, especially among Scottish and Welsh home rulers. Oliver estimated that about fifty Unionists in the House, including some of the most respected leaders, about ninety

Liberals, and an uncertain number of Labour MPs wanted federalism for its own sake. He also felt that there was a much larger number in the House of Commons who only needed to be shown that federalism was the way out of the impasse in order to accept it. By late March Selborne was anxious to know Walter Long's feelings and suggested that Chamberlain might sound him out.[51] If Long were to oppose the federal scheme it would have little chance of success among English Unionists and would lose whatever chance it had of support from the southern Unionists led by Lord Midleton.

At this moment, when matters seemed to be going well for Oliver and his fellow federalists and a ground swell of support appeared to be growing, General Ludendorff's massive offensive broke through the Allied lines on 24 March and threatened the channel ports and Paris. This was a major military disaster which drastically altered the circumstances surrounding the Irish problem. The whole question of conscription for Ireland was raised anew and became inextricably involved with home rule. Oliver was quick to realize the implications of the wedding of conscription and home rule and he promptly arranged for weekly dinner meetings between himself, Selborne, and Chamberlain in order that they might stay abreast of fast-breaking developments and ensure that the federal idea was not lost sight of.[52] Despite opposition from Carson it appeared that Lloyd George was determined to go ahead with both conscription for Ireland and a home rule bill in the belief that conscription would be more palatable if home rule were granted. This reasoning, however, ignored the fierce determination of the southern Irish backed by the Roman Catholic Church to resist conscription at all costs, no matter how it was packaged, and the equally firm opposition of the Ulster Unionists to home rule. It was evident to many observers that such a dual policy would be doomed from the start.

Although dismayed by the sudden turn of events, the federalists remained convinced that the application of federalism would resolve even this dilemma. But the danger was that in order to placate the Nationalists so much would be offered to them that the possibility of devising a federal scheme which would apply to Scotland, Wales, and England, as well as to Ireland, would be highly unlikely. Oliver was particularly concerned that any home rule bill should not contain powers which would imperil the future application of federalism. He urged Philip Kerr to impress this point on Lloyd George and hoped that the prime minister would not delay too long before introducing a federal scheme. There was no time like the present for action; it was "not a time to listen to trembling mediocrities whose nerves are all shaken to bits, and whose lachrymal glands are morbidly overactive."[53] Oliver confessed his anxiety about the proposed Irish settlement to Chamberlain. He feared that under pressure of agitation, and in order to conciliate Irish sentiment over conscription, "they are quite likely to give away vital positions and to make federalism impossible for ever and ever. It will need, therefore, great vigilance, determination and leadership of the Federal Group to bring us safely through this emergency. I wish very much that you and Selborne, who are the real leaders of this Movement, could keep in touch with your people. It is absolutely impossible for me, who am altogether an outsider, to do this for you."[54]

Chamberlain took Oliver's strictures to heart and during April, particularly after his appointment to the war cabinet on 10 April, he discussed at length with his brother Neville their father's – Joseph Chamberlain's – interest in a federal solution of the Irish question. This reaffirmed Austen's conviction that federalism was the only way out of the difficulty. At the same time, Walter Long, while not yet fully convinced of the wisdom of the federal solution, was much dissatisfied with the government's plan to exchange home rule for conscription. He believed it would mean a row with both sides and no satisfaction for anyone. The two issues needed to be dealt with separately.[55]

Oliver was not alone in his concern, and at the end of March Leo Amery entered the fray.[56] He circulated the following question to all Unionist MPs: "If a Home Rule Bill is introduced, would you oppose it or give it support if it was drafted on Federal lines?" One hundred favourable replies were received, a source of much encouragement to Oliver and Amery. The unrest in the Unionist party and the growing strength of the Tory federalists did not escape the attention of Freddie Guest, the government's chief whip. He feared that the Tory party would break up the government rather than split their party over home rule. In order to avoid this he began informal back-stairs negotiations in the first week of April with the Tory federalists. He told them that Lloyd George meant to proceed at all costs with the two bills, that he would lay the order in council – for Irish conscription – on the table simultaneously with the introduction of home rule and that if they decided to split with their party and support Lloyd George they would be welcomed as colleagues. He also advised them to try and get Austen as their leader, "offering him this opening to get ahead of Long." In informing Lloyd George of his actions, he indicated that the Tory federalists "must not be too much relied on. The movement is still academic and many of their numbers will succumb to caucus control. Of course the English, Scottish and Welsh Federalists will rally to you." Guest hoped Lloyd George would not be deflected from his intention to go boldly ahead on his dual course.[57]

It is doubtful that Lloyd George needed this urging or that the knowledge that a split was developing within Unionist ranks between supporters of home rule in a federal guise and the Ulster Unionists had much to do with his decision to go ahead as planned. On 9 April, in a major speech in the House of Commons, Lloyd George announced that the government would extend conscription to Ireland and introduce "a measure for self-government in Ireland." Later that day he asked Austen Chamberlain to join the government with a seat in the war cabinet. He was well aware that if he was to succeed in drafting a home rule bill acceptable to the Unionists Chamberlain would have to be involved. Before agreeing, and at Oliver's urging, Chamberlain sought assurance that the proposed bill would be on federal lines; for it was "the only scheme which would make Irish Home Rule safe and the union of Ireland possible." Furthermore, if it became necessary to treat the Irish case in advance of the rest of the United Kingdom, he wanted to be sure that there would be nothing in the Irish bill inconsistent with the extension of the same system of government to England, Scotland, and Wales. Lloyd George agreed that the government's home rule scheme "must be one which will fit in with a Federal plan." Thus assured, Chamberlain agreed to join the war cabinet and to serve on a committee to frame the Irish bill.[58]

As many observers had predicted, Lloyd George's dual policy had a disastrous effect on Anglo-Irish relations. The home rule party at Westminster voted solidly against the military service bill and then withdrew to Ireland where they lent their support to Sinn Fein. Within the month the Roman Catholic Church had thrown its support behind the Nationalists and a general strike called for 23 April had been carried off with complete success. The report of the Irish Convention published on 12 April only added to the confusion and highlighted the difficulties. As expected, it revealed a serious division of opinion between the Nationalists and the Ulster Unionists and, somewhat surprisingly, between the northern and southern Unionists, the latter, led by Midleton, now being ready to contemplate home rule. It was clear that the Nationalists wanted to have control of customs and excise and that the Ulster Unionists strongly objected. The southern Irish saw in the control of this area of revenue a mark of independence and potential dominion status; the Ulster Unionists considered that control of customs and excise should remain with the United Kingdom parliament in order to ensure the unity and strength of the United Kingdom. It was also clear that the Ulster Unionists were unsympathetic to the federal idea despite favourable references to it in some quarters of the convention. And what gave an air of complete unreality to the whole proceedings was the knowledge that Sinn Fein, by now the most important political organization in Ireland, had dissociated itself from the convention, from home rule, and from federalism, in favour of national independence. The atmosphere in Ireland was tense and ugly, and it was already apparent by mid-April, when the Irish committee began sitting, that both conscription for Ireland and home rule might have to be abandoned by the government.

The Irish committee had been established by the war cabinet on 11 April in order to prepare a home rule bill which could be introduced in the House of Commons before the military service bill had passed its third reading.[59] The committee held its first two meetings on 15 and 16 April in the chief secretary's room at the House of Commons. Walter Long, the colonial secretary, had agreed to serve as chairman and the members were the chief secretary, H.E. Duke; Curzon, George Barnes, Smuts, and Austen Chamberlain, all members of the war cabinet; Dr Christopher Addison, the minister of reconstruction; Herbert Fisher, the president of the board of education; Sir George Hewart, the solicitor-general; and Sir George Cave, the secretary of state for home affairs. Half the members of the committee were Unionist – Long, Curzon, Cave, Chamberlain, and Duke; three were Liberals, Fisher, Hewart, and Addison; there was one Labourite, Barnes; and one respected outsider, General Smuts, who had had to consider federalism during the discussions in South Africa a decade earlier. During these initial meetings it was apparent that the committee would be working constantly within a framework of federalism. All its thinking on political and financial issues during the next three months was determined to some degree by the federal idea. This was natural enough, since federalism was currently "in the air" and much discussed in the press and by politicians, but the idea probably would not have been as predominant if Long and Chamberlain had not from the beginning been committed to the federal solution.

At the first meeting Long pointed out that most members of the House of Commons saw little chance of getting a bill through which did not fit into a federal system. A general discussion followed on the purpose of the committee and Long, supported by Cave, thought they should produce a bill which would pass the House, in other words a federal bill which might persuade the Ulster Unionists to accept one parliament for Ireland. Curzon and Fisher were not convinced that England, Scotland, and Wales were ready for federalism, and they wanted to rule out a federal bill. Because of the urgency of the situation the committee decided to proceed with a draft bill leaving the main debate open.[60] The next day, at their second session, Long informed his colleagues that it had been decided at the war cabinet meeting that morning to have Long draft a bill using the report of the Irish Convention as a framework and submit it to the committee for discussion rather than have the whole group attempt the draft.[61] Long therefore sought advice on three main questions: the position of the Ulster minority; financial proposals; and the form of the representation of the Irish people in the imperial parliament.

Most members of the committee assumed that Ulster would not be given either a separate legislature or remain under the United Kingdom parliament but would come under an Irish parliament in which its interests would be protected by a special Ulster committee with power to reject legislation thought injurious to Ulster. Given the new circumstances in Ireland this attitude begged a number of important questions and seemed particularly inconsistent with the known antagonism within both southern Ireland and Ulster to any such proposal. The members also agreed that customs and excise should remain the responsibility of the central parliament, although they were prepared to transfer revenue powers to an Irish legislature. Long reiterated his opposition to any home rule measure inconsistent with federalism and on this occasion he was given strong support by Chamberlain, Cave, Addison, Duke, and Fisher, while Barnes was willing to apply the federal test provided it did not delay the passage of the urgently needed Irish bill. Chamberlain spoke strongly in favour of a parliament for Ireland "invested with the largest possible powers compatible with the application of federalism to the rest of the United Kingdom." He thought that in introducing the home rule bill the government should express itself in favour of federal reconstruction of the United Kingdom. He wished to keep "each part of the United Kingdom subject to the Imperial Parliament for certain essential purposes, and to give Ireland equality of treatment, with this difference, that Ireland would be dealt with earlier than the other parts of the Kingdom." At Long's suggestion a subcommittee composed of himself, Chamberlain, and Fisher was appointed to deal in more detail with the financial question.[62]

Shortly after these initial meetings Long reported to Lloyd George that the committee's progress was more rapid than expected but there could be no doubt that opinion among the members "had hardened in the direction of a Federal system," and the further they went in the preparation of the bill the more evident it was that once the federal system was adopted the drafting became easier. Long was by now completely convinced that if they could begin to establish a federal system for the United Kingdom all parties to the question could be more easily reassured, especially if the title of the bill was something other than "Home Rule for Ireland." He was not suggesting that parliaments for England, Scotland, and Wales be set up immediately but that a strong commission or committee could be charged with the preparation of schemes for those areas. If his information were reliable, the adoption of the policy by the government would be very popular. Long requested that the question be considered by the cabinet the following week.[63]

While Long and Chamberlain were exerting pressure on Lloyd George, the general campaign for federalism was gaining momentum. The *Times* under the editorship of Geoffrey Dawson favoured the scheme and opened its correspondence columns, its editorial page, and its leading articles to the advocates of federalism. Oliver and Amery were prominent in its pages during late April and considerable care seemed to be taken to publish reports, however brief, of resolutions favourable to federalism adopted by both trade union and party organizations. While Long's committee was holding its first meetings, four Scottish MPs and a Unionist, Arnold Ward, put down separate motions in the Commons calling for the introduction at the earliest possible moment of a measure of federal home rule applicable to each unit of the United Kingdom, and the Provisional Grand Council of the National party argued that any form of home rule for Ireland should be on federal lines and applicable to England, Scotland, and Wales. A more cautious note was struck by Lord Salisbury who while not unsympathetic to the federal idea thought it posed grave problems. He preferred devolution on provincial rather than on national lines. Above all, he believed, time and peace were needed for careful thought.[64]

Neither Amery nor Oliver could agree with Salisbury's plea for delay, and during the next few days both men made efforts to ensure that federalism would be given prompt and adequate consideration by the Irish committee and by Lloyd George. Amery prepared an outline of a draft bill in which he attempted to combine all the essential features of the Oliver-Selborne plan of 1917 within a framework acceptable to the government. He entitled it the "National Governments (Ireland) Bill." It envisaged national parliaments for England, Scotland, Wales, and Ireland and an overall United Kingdom parliament. Provision was made for commissions to examine the nature of the other national parliaments, while the powers to be granted to Ireland were outlined in detail, faithful in all instances to the Oliver-Selborne scheme. Amery made it clear that the supreme power of the United Kingdom parliament would remain unaffected regardless of the degree of devolution. Amery forwarded his scheme to Chamberlain for use in the Irish committee's deliberations and urged Lloyd George to adopt such a plan immediately. He admitted that it was a bold course but he believed it would rally overwhelming support among the British MPs and would be popular in the United States and the dominions and acceptable to both sections of Ireland. He indicated to Lloyd George that "If I were in your place I should have no hesitation in deciding what to do ... I am sure that it is the best way of plucking the flower of safety from the nettle danger."[65]

As for Oliver, he had little faith in the Irish committee's capacity to produce a sound bill. In an effort to guide its deliberations he wrote to Carson asking him if he in turn would write to Long "setting out just two or three points which you regard as *absolutely essential* to have clearly stated, if there is to be the least chance of securing the assent of Ulster." Oliver then went on to suggest four points:

1. A clear reservation of all unallotted powers to the Federal Government.
2. Exclusive authority in the Federal Government in regard to all matters of Navy, Army and Defence (including conscription).
3. Reservation of both Customs and Excise to the Federal Government.
4. Securities for application of federalism all round by some means or other.

Oliver apologized for his "officious" suggestions but he believed it "a duty to warn the Chairman of this rather woolly and perplexed committee of the two or three really fatal reefs on which their ship may be split."[66]

Perhaps the concern revealed in this letter explains the plethora of memoranda and correspondence of the next three weeks. Obviously Oliver and his friends believed that they could not only influence the deliberations and decisions of the committee but that the committee's recommendations would be seriously considered. Oliver continued to funnel information to Austen Chamberlain. Only a day after his plea to Carson, he wrote at length to Highbury reaffirming his earlier argument that no powers, including financial, should be granted to an Irish legislature which could not also be granted to England, Scotland, and Wales. Instead a method of dividing the taxing power between the national units and the federal parliament would have to be devised.[67]

As for Chamberlain, he was pleased with the progress made so far but, as he pointed out to his wife, that was "the least part of the battle. Ireland is full of unreason, North and South alike and what fate awaits us in our Bill I know not. I am sure that Carson would like a settlement and would be reasonable if his people would let him ... If we could federalise the whole U.K. at once, he would accept our proposals and tell the Ulstermen that their case for forcible resistance was gone, but how can we do that *in the time?*"[68] Although Chamberlain was appreciative of the wider difficulties, he was over-sanguine about Carson's attitude. Carson's biographer suggests that by this time the Ulster leader had realized that conditions in Ireland could not be resolved by federalism: "With Ireland on the edge of revolution to try Federalism upon her was like pouring a bottle of rose-water into the crater of a volcano."[69]

On 23 April, in response to Long's request, the war cabinet met to consider the whole problem of Irish home rule and federalism.[70] The discussion indicated that Carson's assessment of the situation was much more realistic than the optimism of Chamberlain, Oliver, and Amery. With the exception of Long and Chamberlain the war cabinet was reluctant to commit itself to a public discussion of federalism during the war or even afterwards when problems of reconstruction would need concentrated attention. Most members were prepared to accept a bill based on the majority report of the convention and Lloyd George's letter of 25 February to the convention, which proposed that jurisdiction over customs and excise should be left to the United Kingdom parliament for a period of years after the war or until a commission had made a full-scale study of Anglo-Irish financial relations. Also, the majority were prepared to make the bill "consistent" with federalism, but no more. Only Long and Chamberlain thought it essential to obtain from the government or from parliament a decision in favour of the federal principle. They were convinced that federalism provided the only chance of appeasing both Ulster and the Nationalists and of obtaining sufficient Unionist support for a home rule bill. Balfour and Curzon were the most reluctant to consider the federal idea. Both men were resigned to a wartime measure intended to relieve the government's difficulties over Ireland and both were ready to agree to a bill "consistent" with federalism, but neither would support a full-scale overhaul of the system. They argued that the British constitution could not be altered so abruptly; such a radical change demanded careful thought. As Balfour pointed out, "It might be the case that there was a growing body of opinion in favour of Federalism, but ... the question had received a very imperfect consideration." The federal solution might be admirable for large countries as an integrating force binding widely scattered regions into a unity, but Balfour doubted its usefulness in a country as small as Great Britain. Although Lloyd George was anxious to secure quick passage of a home rule bill so that he would be in a strong position to enforce the Military Service Act, he was inclined to agree with Balfour and Curzon. A full-scale public discussion of federalism during the war was unfeasible. He was prepared to have the bill "compatible" with a federal scheme, and he was willing to establish a commission to investigate the idea, but "he would not make the passage of the Home Rule Bill dependent on the acceptance of a general scheme of Federalism."

The tenor of this discussion, especially Lloyd George's remarks, indicated that federalism had little chance of success in 1918.[71] Nevertheless, the federalists kept up their barrage, and the idea continually gained adherents in the country if not in the government. Amery, for one, still believed that if federalism were to obtain sufficiently strong support in parliament Lloyd George would be prepared to reconsider his position. He therefore suggested to the prime minister that a bill could be made truly federal, and still remain faithful to the recommendations of the Irish Convention, by inserting a clause stating that the customs and excise question would be reconsidered after seven years "*unless* in the interval a federal scheme shall have been completed which would place Ireland, England, Scotland and Wales on the same equal footing." Amery believed this would satisfy the Nationalists and would convince the Ulster Unionists that whatever the government in power it would have to try and carry a federal scheme unless it was prepared to face a fiscal break-up of the United Kingdom. In fact, Amery thought it would "automatically create a strong federal party in Ulster, and possibly in other parts of Ireland, who would cooperate with the general National-Federal party in Great Britain."[72] Amery believed that the nucleus of such a party was already in existence. At a well-attended meeting of Unionists on 24 April it had been obvious to him that the federal concept was winning many adherents. Amery estimated, perhaps optimistically, that in a vote 150 Unionists could be relied upon to support a federal bill. If their number were coupled with the Liberals, of whom Amery believed the overwhelming majority would prefer a federal to a nonfederal bill, and the bulk of the Labour party, Lloyd George would have "a really solid Parliamentary block which nothing can touch, as well as the germ of a great National-Federal Party in the future."[73]

Amery continued to press Lloyd George hard with memoranda covering all aspects of the federal case,[74] but it was left to Freddie Guest to weigh the strength of the federalists. After a personal survey in early May, he informed Lloyd George that the strongest organized groups looking for a federal solution in one form or another were: 1. Official Liberals who had to support a home rule bill if it was sufficiently democratic and who could not refuse a settlement on federal lines; he estimated their strength at 150, although that number included many Scottish and Welsh home rulers; 2. the Tory federalist group headed by Walter Long and Austen Chamberlain; estimated strength 100; 3. "The little Liberal War Committee" of about twenty-five pledged to Lloyd George; 4. Labour ministers and members, eighteen to twenty in number, who would support a federal home rule bill as long as conscription was postponed; 5. the Scottish home rulers , at least twenty; and 6. the Welsh party of about twenty-five who were unorganized but bound to support federalism. Guest concluded that "Owing to the somewhat chaotic state of public opinion, all of which, however, leans in the direction of Federalism, I believe a clear, statesman-like lead on grounds of urgency and equity, irrespective of Party, will gather to it the majority support. N.B. It is known that Asquith would try and settle on Federal lines."[75]

On 9 May Long's Irish committee held its third meeting to discuss the initial draft of the Irish bill prepared by Long, Cave, Fisher, and Chamberlain. It was clear that they had had difficulty preparing a bill fair to Ulster and yet consistent with the convention report.[76] The bill recommended the establishment of an Ulster committee, and since this had not been suggested by the convention Barnes found it unacceptable. Others were less disturbed, knowing full well that the convention had not considered all contingencies and that Ulster would need to be protected. Long was firm on the matter, and said he would resign if a bill was introduced which did not contain safeguards for Ulster. In fact, Long was sure that any bill devoted simply to Ireland, even if it was compatible with federalism, would be unacceptable to all the various groups in Ireland – nationalists and Ulsterites alike. Only a federal bill stood any chance of success. Many members felt that until the Irish situation had stabilized and the government had asserted its authority by stamping out intrigue and putting down "with a stern hand" the Irish-German conspiracy, neither conscription nor home rule had any chance of success. They all generally agreed that the government should not be too hasty, and should not make any statement in parliament which might imply the introduction of a bill at an early date. Delay was essential if a bill was to have any chance of success. Long, of course, went even further and said only a federal bill had a chance, while Chamberlain, though agreeing with Long, was more cautious because of the difficulties associated with working out the financial powers under a federal scheme.

Sensing that his committee was now more aware of the real problems involved in drafting a bill solely for Ireland and realizing the growing support in the country and in parliament for the federal idea, Long made one last major effort to convince his colleagues of the feasibility of federalism. After his committee meeing he drafted a memorandum for circulation to the war cabinet. It was a strongly argued document which helped to explain why Long had joined the federal camp after having been an inveterate foe before the war.[77] Long pointed out that he had always been opposed to federalism for the United Kingdom mainly on the ground that the country was geographically too small for more than one parliament. He had preferred a scheme of devolution involving the grant of further powers to county councils in certain areas and the setting up of a central representative council of the area, empowered to levy taxation within certain defined limits and to pass legislation dealing with specific subjects. He still believed that if this reform had been adopted twenty years earlier it would have averted the necessity for home rule in any form, but he realized "as I think everybody must do, that events have marched far too rapidly recently to offer the least prospect of such a proposal finding favour anywhere today. And therefore it appears to me that Federalism is the only way in which the pressure on Parliament can be relieved." Long was appalled by the time wasted in the United Kingdom parliament on minor matters. He admitted he had not fully appreciated the enormity of the problem until he had become colonial secretary but his experience in office had soon awakened him to the urgency of the case. He was impressed by the need for a federal solution of the problem of congestion and he was doubly convinced of the need of it if the Irish problem were to be resolved. He believed a federal scheme would have the support of the dominions and the United States and would alter the position of Ulster. Long claimed that support for the idea was growing in the House, especially among Labour members, while opposition was decreasing. He pointed out that if a parliament was set up in Dublin it would raise the problem which had defeated statesman after statesman – what was to be the position of the Irish members in the parliament of the United Kingdom? If the federal plan was adopted this problem would disappear.

What I would like to do would be to make the Irish Bill, not merely as it is now, *consistent* with the Federal plan, but actually in words *a part* of the Federal plan. I would like to set up English, Scottish, and Welsh committees, not to enquire into Federalism, this would be fatal in my judgement, but to prepare the particular constitutional system suited to their various ideas and respective countries; for the *powers* which the subordinate legislatures are to exercise will have been settled by the Government of Ireland Act. They will be the same for England, Scotland and Wales as they are for Ireland.[78]

Long's committee met again on 4 June and it was obvious that the recent threat of a Sinn Fein rebellion and the hostility of the population in southern Ireland had left a deep impression on the members. The drafting of a home rule bill acceptable to either the Nationalists or the Unionists now appeared impossible. The committee was in an awkward position and the government even more so. Long had just returned from a visit to Ireland convinced that it would be impossible for the government to proceed with conscription and that "no measure of Home Rule which the Committee were likely to agree to would be acceptable to any section of Irish opinion." He was supported by Shortt, the new chief secretary. In the ensuing discussion members were anxious that the government avoid the humiliation of having to abandon both its policies. Long, Chamberlain, and Smuts, supported by Addison and Barnes, suggested that the government announce postponement of conscription so that voluntary recruiting might have a chance to work, and asked if the government could "without committing itself to Federalism, announce its intention of appointing a Committee to examine the question?"[79]

In his report summarizing the views of the committee, Long conveyed the opinion that owing to the unrest in Ireland it was *"at the present ... impossible to give effect to the dual policy of the Government."*[80] The committee members thought it would be useless to proceed with the drafting of the bill until the cabinet had considered the general question. Long indicated that a government policy statement on the question of conscription and home rule was essential. Even so, some of the committee – namely, Chamberlain and himself – believed that the question could not be satisfactorily solved, "and indeed that the Draft Bill cannot be effectively proceeded with, except by considering the case of the Irish government as part of the wider problem of a federal constitution for the United Kingdom as a whole." They would be prepared to postpone the Irish bill for the present, but only on the understanding that a commission would be set up to investigate the federal solution and its possible application to every part of the United Kingdom. Long asked for cabinet instruction.

Austen Chamberlain added his voice and weight to Long's with a carefully worded and cogently reasoned memorandum on "The Irish Question and Federalism" which was circulated to the cabinet on 17 June. Chamberlain appreciated the reluctance of his overworked colleagues to consider a novel scheme and realized that the government had agreed at the outbreak of the war to avoid all contentious issues, but new problems of great urgency had arisen demanding solution. He argued that the government could no longer attempt to treat Ireland in isolation from the rest of the United Kingdom, because to do so did not resolve the problem of Irish representation at Westminster; a problem which had not been resolved by Gladstone's two bills, and which had contributed to their defeat. The Irish Committee's work would be to no avail if this course were pursued. It would be equally fruitless if the committee had to prepare a compromise bill, as instructed, somewhere between the convention report, Lloyd George's letter to Sir Horace Plunkett of 25 February, and the Government of Ireland Act of 1914. As it stood the act was incompatible with both the report and the letter. No bill produced under such circumstances would satisfy anyone. The only hope of success in solving the problem was to deal with it in a new form: by federalism or devolution. Chamberlain maintained that only by adopting a federal solution could the government hope to free parliament from its terrible congestion and avoid tensions in British society which could lead to revolution. Devolution, said Chamberlain, was necessary for Great Britain no less than for Ireland, and only when it was agreed to establish a federal system would the problems of Ireland fall into perspective and become more manageable. In the hope of counteracting arguments concerned with the difficulty of the question and the greatness of the change involved, Chamberlain pointed out how far they had in fact gone in both administrative and legislative devolution. Citing Oliver's pamphlet, Chamberlain was able to point out that most of the affairs to be devolved were already the subject of different laws and distinct administrations. He did not think there would be great difficulty in arriving at agreement over the division of powers. He urged that the opportunity should be taken to frame a federal scheme for the United Kingdom. He saw no advantage in the appointment of a commission to investigate the theoretical advantages or disadvantages of a federal system, for at the end no advance would have been made. He favoured a commission with a brief to devise a scheme; in that way they would have practical and definite proposals upon which action could be taken. It was a strong statement but by now Chamberlain had little faith in the persuasive powers of his memoranda and he held out little hope for the success of his appeal.[81]

The war cabinet considered the problem of Ireland and conscription on 19 June and had before them the memoranda from Long and Chamberlain. Lord Curzon pointed out that the government's Irish Policy would be debated in the House of Lords the next day and he should be in a position to state the government's position. The war cabinet was of one mind on the need to delay the implementation of the dual policy and equally aware that they could not and should not abandon it. It was finally decided that Curzon should indicate that the dual policy had not been abandoned, although the government had to be the judge of the time and method of its application. Furthermore, since he was about to receive an all-party deputation led by Brassey on the subject of federalism, Lloyd George thought that before coming to a decision it would be advisable for him to hear what suggestions the deputation had and to see how much support it commanded. It might then be worth considering whether a committee of the House of Commons or a joint committee of both Houses should be struck to consider federalism.[82]

Much of Chamberlain's advice had been ignored, but it was too much to hope that Lloyd George would want to move on such a contentious issue at so difficult a time. In fact, during this period Lloyd George had had very little time to devote to a detailed examination of federalism or even of the Irish problem itself and relied for the most part on his advisers. Chamberlain was disappointed but still capable of some optimism as the following note to his wife reveals: "Last night's Cabinet carried us no farther. The P.M. is waiting to see what support the deputation which waits upon him next week will bring. Meanwhile the outside movement in favour of federalism grows in numbers and strength, and I *think* that the inside opposition shows signs of weakening."[83]

The *Times* held out considerable hope for the success of Brassey's deputation, suggesting that "the future is clearly with the federal solution, and [the] deputation should mark a turning point in the obstinate Home Rule controversy."[84] Walter Long was not as sanguine. He had heard that Lloyd George intended when receiving the deputation to declare himself a lifelong federalist. Knowing Lloyd George, Long was not particularly impressed by this, and he wrote an anxious note to Adams, the secretary of his committee and a confidant of the prime minister: "Now can't you get him to really give a lead on the subject: believe me this is what both Parlt and the country are looking for."[85]

Adams responded willingly to Long's request and quickly drafted two admirable memoranda on "the case for federalism." He argued, much as Long and Chamberlain had done, that a federal solution was essential if the problem of congestion was to be resolved; he considered it of the greatest importance that the machinery of parliament should be overhauled and made as efficient as possible before postwar reconstruction began. He pointed out that much administrative and in practice legislative devolution had already taken place and that the federal idea was growing in popularity in all parties and areas of the United Kingdom. After reviewing the probable division of powers, particularly financial, and the nature of the various constitutions, Adams admitted that a federal scheme did not entirely resolve the special difficulties of the Irish question. There would remain within the federal settlement the problem of Ulster. If if were proposed to treat Ulster as one unit in a federal settlement, Adams thought considerable opposition to a federal scheme would be aroused in both Nationalist Ireland and Great Britain. But a federal scheme which treated Ireland in the same way as other parts of the United Kingdom, reserved to the imperial parliament the control of customs and excise and income tax, and maintained the supremacy of the imperial parliament would give considerable guarantees to Ulster. Adams was aware that the Nationalist press and a large section of Nationalist opinion were opposed to federalism because they felt it would stand in the way of their larger demands for national self-government; nevertheless, he believed that only a federal scheme stood any chance of widespread support. A home rule bill directed solely at Ireland would be doomed before submitted.[86]

By this time, late June, Long had drafted a preliminary version of "a Bill for a federal system for the United Kingdom."[87] It showed a marked resemblance to the Oliver-Selborne scheme. The bill envisaged the simultaneous establishment of national parliaments for England, Scotland, Wales, and Ireland. The supremacy of the United Kingdom parliament was to remain undiminished although the House of Commons was to be reduced to 350 members. Control of peace or war, defence, the treaty-making power, trade agreements, treason, postal services, coinage, trade marks, customs and excise, and income tax were to remain under the control of the United Kingdom parliament. Subsidies were to be paid by the United Kingdom to the local parliaments and in addition Ireland was to receive monies collected under the Land Purchase acts. It was obvious that the bill was still in an early drafting stage; certainly the financial clauses were not fully worked out.

The preliminary draft bill was probably not available when Lloyd George met Brassey's all-party deputation on 26 June but it would not have made any difference, certainly not in its current form, for the prime minister had obviously decided not to rush into federalism. He confessed himself sympathetic to the general ideas of the deputation but he believed there had to be unanimity before a change so drastic could be invoked. While unanimity probably existed in Wales and Scotland, it did not exist in England. Lloyd George argued that such a proposal could not be carried by a bare majority or anything like it. There had to be a call for it from all sections. There should be at least three to one in favour. England had a population of 38 million out of a total of 45 million and unless there was a substantial majority of English representatives in favour of federalism it would be idle to attempt it.[88]

That was obviously the end of federalist hopes in 1918. Efforts continued to be made to bring the subject to the attention of the public and the House in July and August but to little avail. A motion was tabled for debate in the House but it was postponed until October, and then until 1919. Long regretted this and told Lloyd George that he believed the old kind of home rule "as dead as Queen Anne. Federalism is the only substitute."[89] The subject of home rule was discussed once more in the war cabinet on 29 July.[90] Of some concern to Barnes, Fisher, and Addison was the government's policy if the 50,000 recruits asked for under the voluntary scheme had not been obtained by 1 October. Did the government intend to carry out its declared policy, namely, that the Military Service acts could not be enforced without the introduction of home rule? Lloyd George stated that he was determined to consider both conscription and home rule on their merits and not to commit himself in advance. He did not believe anything should be done in the current session. When the House reassembled it could reexamine the problem in the light of the recruitment results. As for federalism, Chamberlain again made a strong plea, but Curzon said he was opposed to a federal solution, certainly to one hastily arrived at. Lloyd George was not anxious to rush the matter, and the true state of his thinking was revealed when he admitted he had not read the home rule bill prepared by Long's committee.[91] He did, however, suggest that another committee might be struck to study the implications of setting up subordinate legislatures in different parts of the United Kingdom. Curzon was strongly opposed; such an action would imply that the government favoured a federal solution. Addison and Fisher were also doubtful. Lloyd George did not press the idea and it was dropped. Interest in federalism nevertheless continued elsewhere. The Labour party, particularly Arthur Henderson and J.H. Thomas, came out strongly in favour of devolution, while Henderson made a special plea to the trade unions to petition the government in favour of a federal scheme.[92] In government circles Adams continued to try and work out the federal idea more fully. This pleased Long who remained "convinced Fedn is the right and only solution."[93] He awaited the results of Adams's activities but of course to no avail. Federalism was formally dead in British government circles by the end of July, and, in practice, had been since late March. Once the government had decided to extend conscription to Ireland federalism was unacceptable; no Irish nationalist would consider it.

Although the federal idea was doomed in 1918, the events of those months are important for what they reveal of English Unionist thinking and F.S. Oliver's influence. In 1918 the English Unionists were struggling with a major dilemma: how to preserve the union and to protect both Ulster and the southern Unionists while at the same time granting Nationalist Ireland what could no longer be avoided – home rule. The solution for many of them was federalism. It alone held the promise of being palatable to both Nationalists and Ulster Unionists. But in opting for federalism the English Unionist leaders were strangely blind to the suspicions and animosities of their compatriots in Ulster. Although they recognized that home rule would always be unacceptable to Ulster, they somehow convinced themselves that federalism would be received differently. But as far as the Ulster Unionists were concerned federalism was just home rule in another guise; they would still be subject to a single Irish parliament and no safeguard such as an Ulster committee would alter that fact. The English Unionists also misread the situation in southern Ireland where interest in home rule declined and commitment to dominion status or independence grew throughout 1918, particularly after Lloyd George announced his "dual policy" in early April. But anxious to preserve the union and to protect the southern Unionists, Chamberlain and Long clung to the federal idea heedless of the opposition and the often sensible criticism of their party colleagues, Balfour and Curzon.

Oliver's role during those months was most influential. It was he more than anyone who supplied the ideas and the arguments during 1918 by dint of remorseless lobbying in all quarters, particularly Unionist. He was in constant touch with Chamberlain and many of his ideas were adopted by Long, Chamberlain, and ultimately the Irish committee. Amery and Astor also played important parts and at one time Amery was even more compulsive than Oliver in his concern to capture Lloyd George for the federal cause. But Lloyd George was a hard man to capture and particularly for a cause that was politically contentious. Lloyd George had to be assured of a general popular clamour in favour of a federal solution. In fact, at the time he made his statement in late July 1918 a considerable amount of support appeared to exist. But it was impossible to assess adequately or to push through parliament in wartime something as drastic as constitutional reform. Balfour and Curzon were right; it was not something that could be rushed. The preliminary draft bill drawn up by Long was incomplete and it would be unfair to assess the nature of the final federal fabric on the basis of it. But the fact that it was incomplete, that the financial sections were woolly, and that certain questions of the relationship between the United Kingdom and the national parliaments had not been worked out despite the many months of labour is an indication of how difficult it would have been to devise an acceptable bill. It might have been different in peacetime but then the issue would probably not have flared up in the same way or with the same intensity, and federalism probably would not have seemed such an urgent option. Ironically, federalism had become topical and possible because of the Irish problem but ultimately it was the Irish problem which made it impossible to either adopt or examine the proposition seriously. The immutable facts of Anglo-Irish affairs, the hazy thinking of the federalists, and the unwillingness of Lloyd George to disturb the party and constitutional balance during the war all served to defeat federalism in 1918.

CHAPTER NINE

Federal Devolution, 1919–1921

Once Brassey's deputation had failed to persuade Lloyd George to consider federalism during the war there was little point in further sustained advocacy. Nevertheless, Ireland remained a problem, and the sudden and unexpected end to the war soon brought new difficulties. Lloyd George decided to call a December election. In that vote the Lloyd George coalition government was returned to office but its support was now predominantly Unionist. The seventy-three MPs elected for southern Irish constituencies refused to take their seats at Westminster and instead met in Dublin on 21 January 1919 and declared themselves the representatives of the first Dáil of the Irish Republic. On that same day Dan Breen, Séan Tracey, and Séamus Robinson killed a policeman at Soloheadbeg in the first act of what was to become a sustained guerrilla action against the British that lasted until the summer of 1921.

The resurgence of Irish nationalism in the last years of the war helped revitalize Scottish and Welsh concern about their future government, and increasingly from the spring of 1918 meetings were held, resolutions passed, and articles written underlining the Scottish and Welsh interest in "federal home rule." These activities were the work of a few and it cannot be argued that there existed a widespread demand in Wales and Scotland for either home rule or United Kingdom devolution. All the same, Scottish and Welsh concerns dovetailed with the traditional interests of long-standing federalists such as Brassey and Macdonald who were increasingly worried that congestion in parliament would hinder postwar reconstruction. The federalists therefore made one more concerted effort to have federal devolution considered seriously. Debates were held in the Lords (March 1919) and the Commons (June 1919) and a parliamentary inquiry into devolution was established under the chairmanship of the speaker in the autumn of 1919. In October 1919 a cabinet committee was created with Walter Long as chairman to consider how self-government might be given to Ireland. Both the cabinet committee and the devolution inquiry wrestled with the federal solution during the winter of 1919–20. A

Government of Ireland bill was introduced on 25 February 1920 and the speaker's conference reported in April 1920.

The debates and the inquiries were what federalists had long wanted, but they came at an inauspicious moment. The Irish troubles dominated domestic political life, and it was clear by the spring of 1920 that the government, while purportedly sympathetic to federal devolution, was determined to resolve the Irish question first. It was equally clear that Ireland would not be satisfied with either a devolutionary or a federal solution. Without Ireland as a factor, and with the ingrained conservatism of the English to overcome, the advocates of federal devolution had little hope of achieving their aim in 1919–20. Nevertheless, the debates in parliament in 1919 on federal devolution were the first held exclusively on that issue, and were the last to be held for over fifty years. Similarly, the discussions surrounding the Irish legislation provided another opportunity for the federal devolutionists to influence government action.

By the late summer of 1918 many leading federalists had begun to withdraw from the frontlines of the battle for federal devolution. Even its most energetic and articulate advocate, F.S. Oliver, decided the time had come for him to relent. As he explained to J.L. Garvin: "I feel that I have already written enough – probably too much – on the Federal matter. I have found also, during the past three months, that the role of one who writes but does not talk in Parliament is necessarily limited. He finds the gate shut in his face at a certain point, and a notice up that only practical statesmen are admitted beyond the barrier ... No man can play another man's game for him ... Federalism has reached a point at which it should be taken out of my hands ... the muse must give way to the governor."[1]

The "governors," however, certainly those interested in federalism, were finding the task equally difficult. In November 1918 A.V. Dicey wrote to Walter Long, one of the "governors," expressing his anxiety about "the prevalent delusion that the difficulty of granting Home Rule to Ireland will be lessened by combining it with an attempt to federalise the Empire." Such an endeavour, argued Dicey, was "far more likely to break up the Empire than to please Irishmen who are preeminently unsuited for taking part in a federal system."[2] Long wished Dicey would reconsider his opinion, and see it from Long's point of view:

Anybody who thinks that the adoption of the federal system or any other plan of devolution would settle our difficulties in Ireland must be wholly ignorant of the true condition of things there. So far from settling things, we are going to have I believe even greater troubles and anxieties hitherto and I do not look at the Federal plan at all from the Irish point of view.

My own belief is that until you federalise the United Kingdom, have local Parliaments for domestic affairs, reserving her central parliament for great Imperial questions, you will not be able to deal with more than a fraction of the problems which present themselves for solution ... As regards Ireland under a Federal plan, if the three Southern provinces declined to adopt it, the only alternative that I can see would be to include Ulster and govern the other three provinces on some different plan and this I believe will be forced upon us so long as Sinn Fein controls the majority of the people as it does at present.[3]

Long had even considered establishing a party to promote "federal home rule" in Ireland to be called the Federal Progressive party, but Midleton, the leader of the southern Unionists, put a damper on the idea. He believed Ulster would be opposed and certainly "No Southern Unionists will listen to a Federal solution if it involves two Parliaments."[4]

Neither Long nor other federalists had made much progress by the time Brassey introduced his motion in the Lords on 5 March 1919 calling attention to the congestion of business in Parliament.[5] The motion read as follows: "That for the purpose of (a) securing prompt and efficient handling of pressing domestic problems and better control over public expenditure, and (b) enabling the Imperial Parliament to devote more attention to the general interests of the United Kingdom and matters of common Imperial concern than is possible under the present system of a single Parliament and Cabinet, the establishment of local legislatures throughout the United Kingdom is an urgent necessity."[6]

Brassey did not submit a detailed scheme for consideration. He simply wished to remind the Lords of the congestion of parliamentary business which would only increase as a consequence of the peace, and to have their assent "to the general principle that devolution is absolutely essential if Parliament is to discharge its duties effectively to the nation." Nevertheless, he reaffirmed his belief that the parliaments established should be subordinate and the supremacy of the imperial parliament indefeasible. The devolution of powers to the subordinate legislatures could be extensive, provided it was consistent with the maintenance of the security and integrity of the United Kingdom, but he did not think the powers to be transferred to the local legislatures or their constitutions needed to be identical in every case. As for Ireland, he held that it was impossible to devise any solution to the Irish question equitable both to Irishmen and to the people of Great Britain if the question of home rule for Ireland was dealt with by itself. Only devolution would permit a reasonable settlement of the Irish question and lead to a better control of the administration and better control of public expenditure. He also believed that having one parliament and one cabinet dealing with both imperial and domestic affairs was "a serious danger to the continued unity of the Empire." It led, particularly at election times, to the confusion of imperial and domestic concerns. Devolution would also help dampen the threat of socialism in that Labour would be given an outlet in the local parliaments. Moreover, reform in procedure alone would not enable the imperial parliament to concentrate more fully on imperial questions, would not lead to increased democracy, and would not result in greater control by the people over administration, legislation, and public expenditure. He ended by suggesting it was "most desirable that there should be set up a Parliamentary Committee to consider the financial and other details of the scheme, and I sincerely hope that His Majesty's Government will accept that suggestion."[7]

The motion was seconded by Lord Selborne.[8] He was strongly of the opinion that "so long as the Irish voters return a majority of members activated by nothing as much as hostility to England and Scotland, Ireland can only be governed in the way she is being governed now. Whatever the form of government in Great Britain may be, Ireland must be governed from the point of view of the safety of the whole of the United Kingdom." He therefore supported devolution not because he saw it as a means of solving the Irish problem, but because he was now convinced "that the interests and the welfare, and indeed the safety, of Great Britain demand some such change in our constitutional procedure." Similarly, he thought that "if we have before us the ideal in the future of some political organisation representative of the whole Empire, Devolution in the United Kingdom is a necessary and an almost essential step towards the realisation of that ideal." Selborne then spoke of the gradual breakdown of parliament and cabinet as a result of the increase in business. No mere procedural changes would resolve the problem. Devolution of business to local legislatures would alone suffice.

The first speaker for the government was the lord chancellor, Lord Birkenhead.[9] He had not been impressed by either Brassey or Selborne, both of whom, he thought, had spent rather a long time delineating the malady but too little time in explaining how devolution would cure it. Birkenhead was not convinced that congestion had been quite the problem Brassey and Selborne made it out to be or that it would remain one. Moreover, he argued, the issue of devolution had not been raised in the 1918 election and no electoral mandate existed for so major a constitutional revolution. He was particularly scathing in reference to Selborne's remark that devolution should not be applied to Ireland. As Birkenhead perceptively commented: "Surely it is obvious that this gives away the whole case. If it be really true that Devolution cannot at this moment be applied to Ireland, but is to be a Devolution which will be limited in its scope to England, Scotland, and Wales, the matter is doomed to failure even before it starts."[10] Like so many of the commentators in the pre-1914 debates, Birkenhead was convinced that if England remained undivided in a devolutionary scheme its parliament would often be in conflict with the imperial parliament. But four subparliaments and an imperial parliament would mean five separate buildings, and five different executives and administrations and that was equally unappealing. Furthermore, the statutory definition of powers that would be necessary would mean the abandonment of a "flexible" constitution and the adoption of a rigid one. There was no demand for such a scheme, certainly not in England, Scotland, or Wales, that was of any significance, and he considered it "altogether inopportune."

Bryce spoke next, and he disagreed with some of Birkenhead's arguments.[11] He thought the subject was on the public mind to a greater extent than the lord chancellor realized, although he admitted that only a minority were truly interested. He agreed completely with Brassey and Selborne about congestion and the defects within the existing parliamentary system due to obstruction. The enlargement of government functions in recent years compounded the problem, and it was not a problem peculiar to the United Kingdom for it was evident in Canada, Australia, and the United States. As for the solution suggested, Bryce doubted it would be found in federalism. He reiterated the point made by Birkenhead about the multiplication of executives and administrative staff, and the difficulty in dividing up the responsibilities of the large government departments. He also thought that England, more than three times as populous and much more than three times as wealthy as Scotland, Ireland, and Wales, would make the federation severely imbalanced and difficult to work. There would be conflict between the English parliament, a powerful body with large responsibilities, and the United Kingdom parliament. He also agreed with Selborne that federalism or devolution would no longer be acceptable in Ireland and thus "any hope of meeting the Irish question by this scheme [i.e., devolution] has, for the present, disappeared."

Lords Crewe and Linlithgow followed but added nothing to what had already been said. The final speaker was Lord Charnwood who expressed surprise that Bryce thought a true federation was under discussion. He reminded his colleagues that what was suggested was not a federation on the American model with a division of sovereignty but rather something analogous to home rule all round with an undivided sovereignty at the centre. Also, since the next best thing to separate executives and administrations already existed as a consequence of the way the business of the separate areas was dealt with in parliament and by the departments, he did not think there would be a major problem in drawing a line between subjects of a local and of a central nature. Nor was Charnwood impressed by Birkenhead's and Bryce's concern about the difference in size between England, Scotland, and Wales. What would it matter? Each would manage its own affairs. Each would also be subordinate to the central parliament which would have its own responsibilities. He thought the potential for friction much exaggerated. Nor was he much impressed by the lack of interest that existed. Public men would draw attention to the problem and the public would grow interested.

Charnwood's speech ended the debate, and Brassey withdrew his motion. The airing of the issue in the Lords was useful but again the federalists had been vague in their advocacy and easily vulnerable to criticism. That the subject had attracted so few speakers was a sound indication of the lack of general interest in federal devolution.[12]

The next major discussion of the issue occurred on 3-4 June 1919 in the House of Commons at which time Edward Wood (later Lord Halifax) attempted to bring Ireland back into the devolution equation.[13] He moved:

That, with a view to enabling the Imperial Parliament to devote more attention to the general interests of the United Kingdom, and, in collaboration with the other Governments of the Empire, to matters of common Imperial concern, this House is of opinion that the time has come for the creation of subordinate legislatures within the United Kingdom, and that to this end the Government, without any prejudice to any proposals it may have to make with regard to Ireland, should forthwith appoint a Parliamentary body to consider and report –

(1) upon a measure of Federal Devolution applicable to England, Scotland, and Ireland, defined in its general outlines by existing differences in law and administration between the three countries;

(2) upon the extent to which these differences are applicable to Welsh conditions and requirements; and

(3) upon the financial aspects and requirements of the measure.

In speaking to his motion, Wood pointed out that the lord chancellor's remarks in the Lords "were at complete variance with what are the known sympathies and indeed beliefs of more than one member of the Government." He believed it necessary to ensure the confidence of the people in the country's institutions by making them more efficient. The current machinery of parliament was overworked at all levels, the executive, administrative, and legislative. If representative institutions were to remain a reality and if MPs were to be more than machines, they must be able to keep in touch with their constituents. Domestic and foreign business had increased dramatically as a result of the war and there needed to be time available to do it. It was essential to free the Westminster parliament from the local concerns of Ireland, Scotland, Wales, and England. Tinkering with procedure was not enough and certainly the grand committee system was unsatisfactory. It was necessary "that we should inquire and inform ourselves as to the extent to which it may be possible to delegate a good deal of the business that we do here to subordinate assemblies, perhaps in different parts of the country." Wood had no fear of the predominance of England. He thought the other areas, particularly Scotland and Wales, would gain by the establishment of subordinate legislatures because the talent would remain at home while English politicians might find the stage too narrow. He thought it essential to restore law and order to Ireland so that it could be given the same self-government as England and Scotland.[14]

The motion was seconded by the veteran campaigner for devolution, Murray Macdonald.[15] As usual, he laid his emphasis on the congestion in parliament which he attributed to the growth of the empire and its responsibilities, the enormous development of industrial life, and the revolutionary changes in men's ideas about government and legislation. Cumulatively and concurrently these developments had added immensely to the mass and volume of the business of parliament. Although changes in procedure had been many over the previous forty years, they had failed in their purpose. Something else was required, and that was devolution. Macdonald made it clear he did not mean a purely federal structure. For him the existing British constitution with its central sovereignty was superior to any federal constitution. Under his devolutionary scheme full and undivided sovereignty would continue to lie at the centre. He did not think the delegation of powers to subordinate legislatures would be either too difficult or too disruptive to the existing system. He did admit financial questions might pose more problems but he believed ways could be found to resolve them. He was opposed to the subdivision of England which he thought would be inconvenient and unnecessary. As for Ireland, he opposed either independence or dominion home rule, and he realized that federalism was unpalatable. He still believed that devolution might work.

Sir Edward Carson was surprised at how much attention Macdonald had given Ireland and he made it clear that while he favoured devolution he did not think it should be based on nationality. He was prepared to see both a divided England and a divided Ireland within a devolutionary scheme. For him it was "really a question of extension of local self-government, and not of splitting up the United Kingdom with emphasis into different nationalities." He admitted that it would be difficult to establish a clear distinction between imperial, national, and local matters; however, not unexpectedly, he rejected the idea that one part of the United Kingdom, Ireland, should be given special treatment as suggested in the motion.

The question of whether or not powers should be devolved to nationally or regionally defined areas surfaced in a number of speeches. Walter Long, for one, supported the basic proposal but he did not like the wording of the motion. He pointed out that he was a federal devolutionist because he wanted to preserve the integrity of the United Kingdom. Like Carson, he did not want Ireland to be treated separately nor the United Kingdom subdivided on national grounds. He recognized that the parliamentary system was congested and needed to be improved and that the only sensible solution was subordinate parliaments, but he insisted the division of the kingdom should be on a regional, not a national, basis. Halford Mackinder, the geographer, was inclined to agree, although he realized it would be difficult to break England up. He suggested that some units might be national and others regional. Opinion in the chamber was also divided over whether or not there should be a separate subordinate parliament for Ulster. Clearly the problem of area and whether or not the determining factor should be national or regional, or some combination of the two, had not been adequately confronted by the federal devolutionists. The disagreements that surfaced in the debate underlined the complexity of the problem and the difficulties that would bedevil any efforts to draft a scheme.

Nevertheless, the bulk of the speeches on 3 and 4 June were in favour of the motion. The Welsh case for home rule was advanced by Sir Robert Thomas and T.A. Lewis, and Scotland's needs were clearly recapitulated by Mackenzie Wood. Most of the speakers simply reiterated the points already made about congestion, reflected on the division of powers, cast glances at Canadian or Australian or American guidelines, and emphasized the devolutionary as opposed to the purely federal nature of their intent. The debate was not well attended, almost being counted out on two occasions on the first day, and less than half the members voted. Ireland was talked about probably more than the movers had expected, although Macdonald himself was partly responsible for that. The majority seemed to realize that the Irish question had moved beyond a federal or devolutionary solution. Most of the speakers were from Northern Ireland, Scotland, and Wales, which again reflected where interest in the scheme predominantly lay. The motion passed 187-34.[16]

While the debate was still in progress, Walter Long wrote to Lloyd George advocating a "parliamentary examination of the question [of devolution] with a view to finding a scheme on the lines of the conference on the franchise."[17] Further discussions were held on the subject in late July,[18] and by early August Brassey was forwarding to Crewe a list of potential members of a conference to examine devolution. Lloyd George finally appointed the speaker, James W. Lowther, to preside over a Conference on Devolution. It was clearly intended to carry out the resolution of the House of Commons. By late August terms of reference had been drafted and letters were being sent out to prospective members asking them to serve.[19]

The composition of the conference was a disappointment. There were sixteen members from the House of Lords of whom nine were English, two Scots, two Northern Irish, one Welsh, and two of dual allegiance. Of the sixteen commoners, five were English, six Scottish, two Welsh, and three Northern Irish; eight were Conservative, three Coalition Liberals, two Liberals, and three Labour.[20] Of the thirty-two members, only Brassey, Charnwood, Herbert Gladstone, and Murray Macdonald had shown any protracted interest in federal devolution. The *Times* commented on the "undistinguished" and "unrepresentative" composition of the conference, and held out little hope for its success.[21] It particularly disliked the fact that Nationalist Ireland was unrepresented, an omission which seemed to suggest that a new constitution for the United Kingdom was not expected to emerge from the conference.[22]

Brassey, whose dream the conference had been for many years, was also dissatisfied with its make-up. He was disappointed that neither Sir Thomas Whittaker nor J.W. Wilson "nor any member of the Unionist Federal Committee in the House of Commons" was included. He could only assume the government wanted to make the proceedings abortive:

There being so few of us in the Conference who are really up in the subject makes our task a difficult one. If there had been, as there ought to have been, ten or fifteen of us who were in favour of the policy and knew what we were driving at, the task of the conference would have been infinitely easier and much more likely to lead to a successful result ...

I look upon Federal Devolution as infinitely more necessary now than ever before. If we are to get back to Parliamentary methods of government and to avoid labour trying to force its wishes by strikes or threats of strikes, Labour must be given the chance of getting its representatives into Parliament. This they would have under Federal Devolution when domestic issues would be submitted to the electorate separately from Imperial issues.[23]

For Brassey, the "weakness of the Conference [was] that none of the Unionist Federal Committee and only one of the Liberal Federal Committee in the House of Commons" were on it.[24]

The announcement was finally made in October, after the recess, and the first organizational meeting was held on 23 October.[25] This occurred only sixteen days after cabinet decided to resurrect its committee on Ireland. Chaired once more by Walter Long, it was instructed to prepare a draft bill for Ireland compatible with federalism. Brassey and Gladstone immediately recognized that this decision relieved the devolution conference of the need to consider the special circumstances of Ireland. Brassey was not displeased with this development. As he put it to Gladstone: "The Cabinet Committee will decide whether Ireland is to have two Parliaments or one or in the latter case what special provisions should be made for Ulster and other similar questions as regards Ireland. This will be a just relief to us in our task – as the discussions on the purely Irish side of the subject would probably have been very animated and strewn with differences of opinion."[26]

At the first meeting of the devolution conference there was a general discussion of the terms of reference after which it was decided to meet three times a week.[27] After the first meeting Brassey felt they had made a reasonably good start and that no one was out to wreck the whole proceedings: "Even my old friend, Ronald McNeill, who has been a vigorous opponent of the policy in days gone by, is prepared to accept Devolution in some form or other." By the second meeting on 28 October, Brassey and Macdonald had drawn up a resolution which immediately forced a discussion of the nature of the devolved areas. Should the deciding principle be national or regional? Should England be included as a full national unit or should it be broken down into regional units?[28] Both Brassey and Macdonald favoured devolution to full national units rather than any subdivision, but some members thought England should be divided because of its overwhelming size and power. The Ulsterites were quick to support a dual parliament for England. If it were accepted it would prove difficult, or so they thought, for Ulster to be denied a similar parliamentary opportunity. Not wishing to see the conference steered so quickly onto the shoals of the Irish problem, Gorell suggested on 4 November that the members should turn their attention to the equally important issue of the division of powers between the central and the subordinate legislatures. Despite the strenuous opposition of the Ulsterites, led in particular by Captain Charles Craig, the speaker finally insisted on that course of action on 11 November. Thus the conference did avoid becoming bogged down on the Irish question. But those early meetings had starkly revealed how impossible it was to discuss the matter of devolution or federation constructively without considering Ireland, and had underlined how difficult it would be to resolve Irish and United Kingdom problems by devolution when Ulster, let alone Nationalist Ireland, found devolution unsatisfactory. The decision to move on to a less contentious topic by no means resolved the basic question of whether the subordinate unit should be national or regional in nature. The next thirty meetings (there were thirty-two in all) did little to clarify matters, and the final report reflected the split in opinion that had surfaced in the initial sessions.[29]

By the time it had been decided to shift to a discussion of the division of powers, Brassey had been seriously injured in a car accident. He died on 13 November. It is difficult to estimate what his loss meant to conference deliberations. He was a persistent advocate, but he was not always as precise and as perceptive as he should have been. In the end his influence might have been marginal, although the Master of Elibank did think Brassey's opponents on the national/regional issue were more effective after his death.[30] Gorell put it well: "As a not very clever specialist on devolution, he was going to be a bore in the conference, but it is frightfully cruel luck that after advocating it for nearly 30 years and getting to this point, he should have been killed."[31]

During five meetings in late November the conference managed to decide upon the division of over one hundred matters between the central and the subordinate legislatures. This was in itself an impressive achievement, but the actual allocation underlined that the frame of reference was decidedly devolutionary and not federal. In addition to reserving all unspecified powers for the central government and preserving the veto of the crown, the members reserved to the central parliament all matters affecting the crown, peace and war, army, naval, and air services, foreign and colonial affairs, all communication services – including the post office, currency, patents and copyrights, the laws of trade, banking and commerce, the regulation of trade, all fisheries, forestry and many agricultural services, industrial legislation, railways and canals, the census, food regulations, marriage law and divorce, major offences under the criminal law and major torts under civil law, university education at Oxford, Cambridge, and London, and finally the metropolitan police. By contrast the powers devolved upon local legislatures seemed miniscule. Among them were the regulation of internal commercial undertakings, professions and societies, such as auctioneers, markets and fairs; order and good government including cruelty to animals and drunkenness; ecclesiastical matters; agriculture and land; the judiciary and minor legal matters; education at the primary and secondary levels and at universities other than Oxford, Cambridge, and London; local government and municipal undertakings; and public health.[32] Murray Macdonald had no objection to this division of powers nor is it likely that Brassey would have objected if he had lived. Both men had always been firm advocates of a unitary constitution as opposed to a federal one on Canadian or American lines, despite their constant use of the term federal.

Unfortunately, the interlude of agreement briefly achieved in late November did not last. The split between all-out-devolutionists of the Brassey-Macdonald camp and the regionalists could not be bridged. At the end of the month Gorell met with Philip Kerr and Lionel Curtis, the latter fresh from advocating and devising schemes for constitutional change in India, to discuss "principally devolution, the Conference and the best way to tackle its ignorance ... Curtis has real knowledge as well as real ability and is a most instructive mentor."[33] That Kerr attended was interesting not only because of his long familiarity with the issue but because he had been named one of the secretaries of the recently revived cabinet committee on Ireland. By early December Gorell was clearly upset with the way the conference was proceeding. On 4 December he commented, "it is not making much headway, too many talkers who know nothing whatever about it," and on 9 December: "A boring morning at Federal Devolution Conference, the Speaker wanting us to agree that members of the subordinate legislatures should be the MPs for the different countries a kind of Grand Committee idea which seems to me a perfectly drivelling suggestion quite at variance with the elementary principles of real devolution."[34]

Distressed, Gorell went to 49 Mount Street and had "a good talk to Lord Selborne and Lionel Curtis about the Devolution conference: both being convinced that only by a good scheme of devolution can government, now hopelessly congested be carried on, are much concerned over the way the Conference is going; Selborne is coming on it in February, in place of Harcourt who is ill, and has resigned, and will be invaluable. He not only does know, but the others will take his knowledge as his prestige after running the Committee on the Government of India Bill is very high. Both surprised at the Speaker's silly proposal and that he should be sticking to it, but Lowther can see things now, I think, only from the House of Commons point of view and also does not want his work on Electoral Reform to need alteration."[35] On 18 December the conference met for the last time until 10 February. Gorell was thankful, for he thought "all the last meetings a waste of time."[36] The next day he sent his notes to Selborne. Since no minutes had been taken of the meetings, Gorell had kept a detailed record himself.[37]

Just before the break two small subcommittees on finance and the judiciary had been struck so that effective work on these matters could be done during the recess. They were headed by Lord Chalmers and Lord Stuart of Wortley respectively. In explaining these developments to Selborne, Lowther was frank about the conference's activities:

We have got a good deal of work done and have agreed on certain matters, but we are just now rather in the Doldrums. We have gone through all the subject matters of legislation and administration which have occurred to us and allotted them provisionally to a central or to local legislative bodies. On that matter we have had very general agreement. The difficulties immediately before us are the nature of these local bodies, whether they could be formed out of the members of the United Kingdom Parlt, or whether they could be formed by indirect election from county councils and then we always have in our minds the over-shadowing difficulty of the division or non division of England. We have discussed this pretty fully but postponed a decision. That is how we stand ...[38]

During the recess the speaker continued to work on his scheme. He did not like the proliferation of parliaments and executives or the expense of new buildings and administrations. He had therefore drafted a paper recommending a system of grand committees or councils composed of the representatives of the existing constituencies of England, Scotland, and Wales which would sit at Westminster, Edinburgh, and Cardiff respectively. These sessions would be held in the autumn and the meetings of the United Kingdom parliament would therefore take place earlier in the year. Lowther's object was to provide a gradual transition to a new constitutional system. His intent was to make as few changes as possible while at the same time meeting as best he could legitimate demands for change. His scheme was not fully regional in nature and it was certainly not close to full-scale devolution. Its primary weakness, as Lowther realized, was its failure to relieve overworked MPs.[39]

After receiving a copy of Lowther's draft proposal, Herbert Gladstone, for one, began to question the scheme and the assumptions that lay behind it. In a detailed critique sent to Lowther on 20 December, Gladstone said that after "many hours" effort he had "arrived at 8 or 10 points of difficulty, of wh

3 or 4 seemed to me very serious obstacles." Apart from his doubts concerning the uncertain role of the House of Lords and the prolonged strain on both members and officials of the House of Commons, Gladstone found himself "absolutely at sea" on the new executive. Did not "the setting up of three additional executive authorities within the existing House of Commons composed of its own members yet removed from its direct authority alter the whole principle and balance of the existing authority?" Also, at least six major departments would have to be reorganized on English, Welsh, and Scottish lines which would involve not only additional expense to the tax-payer but a loss of prestige for the individuals reassigned. Gladstone did not much like separately elected "Parliaments" but "it seems to me the only well defined comprehensible plan *if* administrative powers are to be given. Why not limit the Grand Council plan to *legislation?* It would be strictly 'Devolution' and it gets rid of serious and complicated problems. Legislation and not administration is the chief clog on the House of commons."[40]

In response, Lowther admitted that there would be difficulties if the grand councils were going to work as parliaments. But that was not his intention. No individual responsible for the administration of devolved powers would be a minister of the crown. If the Grand Councils were going to work at all, Lowther was convinced they would "have to work more on County Council lines than on Parliamentary." Those responsible to the grand councils for such matters as education, health, agriculture, or finance would be called "Presidents of the Board of Education, Health, Agriculture, Finance etc. or Directors, or Controllers, or Chiefs, or Chairmen, or any other suitable expression, but they will not be Ministers of the Crown." Lowther also tended to agree with Gladstone about devolving only legislative powers. At least he found the proposal "attractive." Nevertheless, he reminded his colleague that the conference's terms of reference required them to prepare a scheme involving both administrative and legislative devolution.[41] Lowther was clearly an active chairman, and his position as speaker made it difficult for those who disagreed with his ideas and the way he was steering the conference to curb his interventionist tendencies.

Gladstone unconvinced by Lowther's arguments, remained concerned. By the end of January he was at his gloomiest. He found "the personnel of the Conference with few exceptions incompetent," and feared the whole venture would land on the rocks. The more he had pored over the speaker's scheme, "the more impossible it seems to me as a workable, or *initial* solution. For these are the two ways of looking at it. *Can* the "National Grand Councils" work such a scheme? If not what is the position? Apparently, we avoid every single difficulty by shunting the conundrums off our line. For what were we appointed? Probably the main reason was convenience for the Government. We however must assume that we are expected to offer a plan based on examination, such experience as we have, and on evidence." Lowther had not answered his objections. What was really wanted was "a Committee of 12 or 15 of the very best men" to recommend a scheme rather than the "mere sheep" currently involved. Gladstone was particularly worried because the grand councils scheme had been fathered by Lowther whose reputation would give it weight.[42]

Neither Gladstone's nor Gorell's gloom and sense of frustration was lifted by the resumption of meetings. On 11 February Gorell noted in his diary: "A wasted morning of recapitulated talk, during which Lord Selborne, now a member and the one expert, could hardly speak calmly so great was his sense of the stupidity and ignorance round him." Five days later Murray Macdonald organized a meeting of those, some fifteen in number, "who are of opinion that the Speaker's proposals are quite unworkable."[43] He had by then devised an alternative scheme based on the establishment of subordinate national legislatures, separately elected, and wanted to rally support for it among the conference membership. But the clash between the two schemes could not be resolved. A vote taken on 17 February narrowly approved the speaker's proposal and during the remaining sittings much of the time was given over to fleshing out its details. Macdonald, Selborne, and Gladstone attempted to devise a detailed and more fully devolutionary scheme. They worked in the knowledge that to do so was not only difficult without adequate support in the conference but that little parliamentary or countrywide support existed for bold devolutionary or federal proposals. By late February Gladstone realized that the speaker's report would probably reflect the divisions in the conference. The most he could hope for was that it would have some educational value.[44] Gorell was just happy to have the conference done with. On 27 April he made his last notation in his diary: "the final meeting, thank goodness."[45]

The final report of the conference was sent to the prime minister on 27 April 1920 in the form of a letter from Lowther. The only substantial agreement was on the powers to be given to the subordinate legislatures. There had been no consensus on the question of whether or not those legislatures should be established within national or regional areas, and there had been no resolution of the differences between Lowther's transitional grand councils scheme and Murray Macdonald's instant devolution proposal. Each received the support of thirteen members while five others signed both reports, indicating in doing so that although they supported the fundamental principle underlying Macdonald's scheme they believed Lowther's would be a more acceptable initial step. There was little prospect that Lloyd George's government would give so unsatisfactory a report much attention.[46]

And so it proved. The speaker's report was laid on the table of the House of Commons on 10 May but it received no governmental attention, and its publication on 12 May aroused little interest among the public. Some of the supporters of the Macdonald scheme, and others sympathetic to the federalist cause, organized a meeting of interested English, Scottish, and Welsh MPs at the House of Commons on 6 July. The gathering was chaired by Walter

Long, at that time deeply engrossed in the preparation of the Government of Ireland bill. Murray Macdonald also spoke, while Austen Chamberlain sent along his support. After discussing the difficulties posed by congestion and the accumulation of problems from the war, the meeting passed a resolution calling for a measure of legislative and administrative devolution, applicable to England, Scotland, and Wales, to be introduced in the next session of parliament by the government. The conveners of the meeting were appointed to take the resolution to the prime minister.[47] The *Times*, ever supportive of the principle of devolution, opened its columns in early July to Murray Macdonald who in five lengthy articles sketched the background to the current demand, underlined the problems posed by parliamentary congestion, and, in order to assuage fears and clear up misconceptions, emphasized that the goal was devolution not federalism. Sovereignty would remain undivided and the union unimpaired.[48]

The deputation had difficulty gaining an audience with the overburdened Lloyd George, and it was not until 16 December, after a number of postponements, that Lloyd George and Austen Chamberlain met with the deputation led by Murray Macdonald. While expressing his "complete sympathy" with the object of the deputation, Lloyd George pointed out that there were difficulties in the way. He reminded them that common agreement did not exist even among supporters of federalism. He emphasized once more the problem of England with its population of 36 million. How was that to be dealt with? Lloyd George said the government could not possibly move in advance of public opinion.[49]

That was effectively that, although Murray Macdonald did introduce a private member's bill on 28 April 1921 providing for the establishment of subordinate parliaments in England, Scotland, and Wales, much on the lines of his proposals of the previous year. The bill was supported by many longtime federal devolutionists but died on the order paper when the government did not provide facilities.[50]

By the time the Conference on Devolution had reported there had been major developments with respect to Ireland. The government had been under pressure since January 1919 to give some further consideration to Ireland. The 1914 Home Rule Act would come into effect within six months of the signing of a peace treaty with Germany if nothing else was instituted beforehand. Calls for independence from Sinn Fein and for dominion status from moderates such as Horace Plunkett were becoming insistent while the attacks on British troops, the police, and installations in southern Ireland increased rapidly throughout the spring and summer of 1919.[51]

Walter Long went to Ireland in early September to assess the situation for himself. On his return he wrote a memorandum for the war cabinet.[52] He emphasized the necessity of making "an early and definite declaration ... on Irish policy."

What, therefore, is to be done? ... Home Rulers believe with a touching confidence that if only we would grant a full measure of Home Rule, all would be well. They ignore the fact that an Irish Parliament on Dominion lines – and none other would be accepted by the Home Rule Party in Ireland – would be immediately used...to set up a Republic, and would be manned by those who are largely responsible for the present state of lawlessness. Opponents of Home Rule believe with equal confidence that all measures of self-government should be denied, and that all that is required is a firm administration of the law. They in their turn, ignore the fact that in a considerable part of Ireland there is an irrepressible desire for some form of Home Government, and that this demand is strongly supported in our Dominions and in the United States of America.

Was it not possible to find "a middle policy," asked Long. He recommended that the government of Ireland should be given public assurance of the confidence and support of His Majesty's Government and

That on the adoption of the Federal Scheme for the United Kingdom, Ireland shall receive such Parliaments as may be thought necessary. Obviously there must be two – one for Ulster and another for the three Southern Provinces. In some quarters it is thought that it would be better if there were more than this, and the Southern Provinces divided up – but this is a detail.

It will be urged that these proposals will not satisfy Sinn Fein: granted. But nothing short of the setting up of a Republic will satisfy Sinn Fein. Therefore why not recognise the fact and say so frankly? If the Federal System be adopted, England who does not care much about it, will loyally accept and make the best of it. Scotland and Wales, where the feeling in favour is much stronger, will do the same. Ulster will accept and make a success of it. What then is to be done with the three Southern Provinces, assuming that they decline to adopt the Federal plan, or adopt it and proceed to use it as I have indicated above? In either of these circumstances His Majesty's Government should now state frankly and deliberately that if either of these conditions arise, they will be compelled to govern that part of the United Kingdom which refused to accept and make proper use of a measure of self-government which is being granted all round, as if it were a Crown Colony.

On 7 October the situation and policy in Ireland was assessed at a full-scale meeting of the war cabinet. After considering either postponing the Home Rule Act of 1914 or introducing a new home rule bill, it was decided that a cabinet committee, with Long as chairman, "should examine and report on the probable effect on Ireland, on Great Britain, and on opinion abroad of

226 Ireland and the Federal Solution

each of the possible alternative Irish policies, and should advise the Cabinet as to the policy they recommend for adoption." The committee was asked to consider particularly

(1) What would happen in the event of a Home Rule Bill being passed and put into operation (i) If the Irish people refused to touch it; (ii) If a sufficient number of moderate Nationalists were prepared to accept it and form a Parliament; or (iii) If the Sinn Fein Party accepted the Irish Parliament set up under the proposed Act, and used it in every possible way to thwart the British Government. (2) The Financial Position of Ireland in relation to Great Britain, particularly in regard to the collection of Customs duties, Irish indebtedness on account of Land Purchase Act, and the Irish contribution to the cost of the war. (3) The effects of a further postponement of the Home Rule Act, 1914. (4) Whether, in the event of the Home Rule Scheme being decided on, power should be given to His Majesty, by Order in Council, to postpone the operation of the new scheme by resolution of both Houses of Parliament.

The committee was to be free to consider "a general Federal Scheme for the United Kingdom," and in order to facilitate that approach the war cabinet instructed the secretary to circulate the memoranda on the application of a federal scheme to the United Kingdom prepared by Long and Chamberlain in 1918. Once the committee had come to a conclusion its recommendations were to be presented in the form of a draft bill.[53]

At the first meeting of the committee on 15 October it was decided "That there should be two Chambers; one for the north and another for the south of Ireland with a Common Council with certain powers for the whole of Ireland. Such a scheme not to be inconsistent with a Federal system for the United Kingdom."[54] Clearly Long and others still hoped that the recently established Conference on Devolution might recommend a federal solution to United Kingdom difficulties.[55] Over the next two weeks the committee made considerable progress although it did not examine the financial features. Before going into that question and other matters of detail the committee wanted to know if the cabinet approved of the fundamental basis of the scheme it had prepared.

The committee's first report was considered by the war cabinet in early November.[56] The committee was agreed, in view of the situation in Ireland, and of public opinion in Great Britain, the dominions, and the United States, that it could not recommend either the repeal or the postponement of the Home Rule Act of 1914. In its judgment it was essential, now that the war was over, and the peace conference had dealt with so many analogous questions in Europe, that the government "should make a sincere attempt to deal with the Irish question once and for all." On considering home rule in its practical aspects, the committee found itself limited in two ways: on the one hand, "the Government was committed against any solution which would break up the unity of the Empire," while on the other hand, "it was committed that Ulster must not be forced under the rule of an Irish parliament against its will." The first condition excluded any proposal for allowing Ireland or any part of Ireland to establish an independent republic, while the second precluded the establishment of a single parliament for all of Ireland on the lines of the home rule bills of 1886, 1893, and 1912.

There seemed to the committee to be three possible courses. First, "to establish a Home Rule Parliament for all Ireland" and provide for "the exclusion of some part of Ulster either by the clean cut, or by allowing the people of Ulster to vote themselves out by county option or some system of plebiscite"; second, "to create a single Parliament for Ireland, but to secure Ulster against forced Dublin control, either by the constitution of an Ulster Committee within that Parliament possessed of veto powers so far as the application of Irish legislation and administration to Ulster was concerned, or by the artificial over-representation of Ulster in the Irish Parliament on the lines suggested by a considerable section of the Irish Convention of 1918"; and third, "to establish one Parliament for the three Southern Provinces and a second Parliament for Ulster, together with a Council of Ireland composed of members of the two Irish Parliaments, to discharge certain immediate functions, but mainly to promote as rapidly as possible, and without further reference to the Imperial Parliament the union of the whole of Ireland under a single legislature."

The committee rejected the first because the area to be excluded after a plebiscite would be administratively unworkable and a plebiscite fought on the issue of exclusion would inflame religious and political passions and thus promote partition and hinder eventual Irish unity. If the policy of exclusion were applied to either the nine or the six counties it would lead to large nationalist majorities under British rule, "which would clearly infringe the principle of self-determination." Finally, exclusion meant the retention of British rule in some part of Ireland. There was good reason to doubt whether "it would ever be possible to convince Irishmen themselves or Dominion or American opinion that Great Britain was sincere in its policy of Home Rule unless it withdraws its control from the domestic affairs of Ireland altogether."

As for the second alternative, the committee was convinced it would be quite unworkable, even if Ulster were prepared to accept it, for it would "enable the Ulster Committee to block and stultify the work of the Irish Government and Parliament, without enabling it to develop Ulster itself according to the idea of the Ulster people." Nor would overrepresentation work, given the advance in democratic practice since 1914, or the method of allowing a minority to override or block the will of the majority. Both proposals were vitiated by the assumption "that it is within the power of the Imperial Parliament to impose unity on Ireland."

The committee therefore recommended the third alternative, i.e., the establishment of two parliaments, one for Ulster and one for the three southern provinces, and the complete withdrawal of British rule from all

Ireland in all matters not specifically reserved. This scheme would meet the demand for British withdrawal in the sphere of domestic government; it was also consistent with the fact that there was "a majority in Ulster as opposed to Dublin rule as the nationalist majority in Ireland is opposed to British rule." Similarly, Ulster would not be coerced, and would retain both full representation in the imperial parliament according to population and its citizenship in the United Kingdom. The committee also believed the proposal would minimize the partition issue, for no nationalists would be retained under British rule. The committee favoured a nine-county Ulster.

In setting up two parliaments, the committee attached the greatest importance to doing everything possible to promote Irish unity and it therefore made two further proposals. First, that for one year certain services such as agriculture, technical education, transportation, old age pensions, health, unemployment insurance, and labour exchanges should be reserved to the imperial parliament, but that "a Council of Ireland should be established," consisting of twenty representatives from each parliament, which the lord lieutenant or the British minister in charge of the temporarily reserved services would have to consult about policy.

Second, and in the committee's eyes much more important, "the two Irish Parliaments should be given far-reaching constituent powers." It proposed that the two parliaments, by passing identical legislation, should have the power, without further reference to the imperial parliament,

(a) to transfer at any time even within the first year, any of the temporarily reserved services, or any of their own powers, to the control of the Council of Ireland.
(b) to revise the constitution of the Council of Ireland itself in any way they think fit, so that it may, if both Parliaments agree, become a parliament elected by electors for the whole of Ireland, either on a unitary or a federal basis, controlling all or any of the temporarily reserved services, and all or any of the powers originally allotted to the North and South Ireland Parliaments.
(c) to ask the Imperial Parliament to retain control of the temporarily reserved services beyond the first year, if they want further time to deliberate about their common affairs. Failing such a request, however, these services would automatically be divided between the two Parliaments.

The committee believed that, having started from the assumption that "regard must be had to the principle of self-determination," it had done all it could do to bring about Irish unity without infringing Ulster's freedom to decide its own relationship to the rest of Ireland. In particular, the Council of Ireland would compel representatives of the whole of Ireland to meet and do business together. At the same time, the two parliaments "will have complete power by agreement to bring about Irish unity on any basis ranging from federation to what is practically Dominion status."

The committee proposed to reserve to the imperial parliament complete control over the crown, peace and war, army, navy, and airforce, treaties and foreign relations, dignities and honours, treason, naturalization, trade outside Irish jurisdiction, quarantine, navigation, wireless, postal services outside Ireland, and coinage and trademarks, all of which were essentially those powers reserved under the 1914 act. The imperial parliament would also initially reserve customs and excise, income tax, excess profits duty, and internal postal communications. The future of such powers would depend upon the decision reached by the two Irish parliaments as to the future constitution of Ireland. The committee favoured a transfer of such powers if a single legislature for Ireland was established. This would place Ireland on the same basis as a dominion except in the sphere of defence. Otherwise, the powers would remain with the imperial parliament. Similarly, as long as the imperial parliament exercised taxing powers in Ireland, Ireland would have the right to be represented at Westminster on the basis of population with the understanding that Irish members would not be allowed to speak or vote on any question lying within the scope of the Irish legislature.

In summing up its submission to the war cabinet, the committee indicated that it proposed "to follow the Peace Conference by respecting the principle both of responsible government and of self-determination and to give the two parts of Ireland immediately *state rights* together with a link between them, and to give them also the power to achieve Irish unity on any basis ranging from federal unity for the United Kingdom to a qualified Dominion status" which they could agree upon among themselves. The committee thought the proposal a fair one that offered a "road to Irish Home Rule, to Irish unity, and to a reconciliation between Ireland and Great Britain."

These were critically important recommendations that were to have an unforeseen impact on the future not only of Ireland as a whole, but particularly on Northern Ireland and its relationship to Great Britain. Despite the protests of Worthington-Evans and Birkenhead, who did not think Ulster would welcome the proposals and who were sure Sinn Fein would reject them out of hand, and of Balfour, who wanted to retain Ulster as an integral part of Great Britain, the war cabinet decided to direct Long's committee to prepare a formal scheme.[57] Work proceeded quickly and by 21 November an initial draft of the financial implications of the scheme had been prepared. It was circulated to Long's committee on 24 November, and was in turn forwarded to the war cabinet along with an outline of the scheme entitled "Heads of Proposal." By 2 December a draft bill and a memorandum recommending an increase in the number of powers to be transferred to the two Irish parliaments, including local government, public health, housing, transportation, agriculture, old age pensions, unemployment insurance, and employment exchanges were in the hands of the cabinet. The committee considered its proposals to be final. This was a very rapid accomplishment that had taken little more than six weeks. The committee's suggestions of early December were all translated into the bill of 25 February, which was subsequently little altered before receiving the royal assent as the Government of Ireland Act of 23 December 1920.[58]

The memoranda of December 1919 did not touch upon federalism despite Walter Long's continuing support for the idea and the references to it in the November memorandum. By December it was clear to the cabinet that the Conference on Devolution was divided within itself and that the general concept had little support in the country at large. Throughout that month and up to the eve of the introduction of the bill in February the dominating issue in cabinet was the size of the northern Ireland parliamentary area. Debate raged between those who wanted a nine-county area, thinking that the presence of Cavan, Monaghan, and Donegal in the north would facilitate the union of Ireland, and those such as Balfour and the Ulster Unionists who argued for six on the grounds that it was doubtful that a northern parliament, predominantly Protestant and Unionist, would be able to control the three Catholic counties. Finally, on 24 February, the day before the bill was to be introduced in the House, the cabinet decided that the area of Northern Ireland would "consist of the parliamentary counties of Antrim, Armagh, Down, Fermanagh, Londonderry and Tyrone, and the parliamentary boroughs of Belfast and Londonderry."[59] This decision was greeted with delight by many in Ulster and Great Britain because it effectively ensured the unlikelihood of union with the rest of Ireland. Certainly the decision raised the probability of partition.[60]

It is important to emphasize that the British government's primary intention throughout these months had been to devise a scheme that would eventually result in the union of Ireland. The scheme that emerged was predicated on the assumption that Irish unity would eventually be established and that the whole of Ireland would remain in some way associated with the United Kingdom. The British hoped, in the end, that out of two parliaments they could get one. The glee with which the scheme was met in Ulster and many parts of Britain emphatically revealed that all such hopes were ill-placed.

Although federalism, or federal devolution, was clearly a dying issue by February 1920, Walter Long continued to cling to the idea. At a meeting of his committee in Bonar Law's room at 11 Downing Street on 17 February, when the possibility of handing customs and excise over to Ireland was raised, Long said he would fight the bill to the bitter end on that question "because by handing over Customs and Excise the Federal idea was being destroyed."[61] That partition was a likely result of the February bill was clear to at least Philip Kerr, one of the secretaries of the cabinet committee. Kerr admitted to C.P. Scott that the bill had defects, but it was the best that could be obtained from the existing government:

It would at least accomplish two essential things: it wd take Ulster out of Irish gn wh it had blocked for a generation & it would take Ireland out of English party controversies. There wd never be another special Irish Bill. [Kerr] defended the "clean cut" of the six counties on the ground (1) that to have taken the whole province as the area of the Northern Parl wd have reproduced on a small scale the same difficulties which Ireland as a whole had presented to us on a gt scale. It wd have given her a disturbed and irreconcilable minority only to be ruled by force (2) that on the other hand to have arrived at a more exact delineation of the northern or anti-nationalist area by dividing the two mixed counties of Tyrone & Fermanagh wd have involved a religious census wh was highly undesirable. [62]

It was obvious that neither independence nor dominion home rule were much favoured as alternatives by the Lloyd George government in mid-1920, and certainly dominion home rule found little favour among the Irish. Plunkett's Irish Dominion League was active in the early months of 1920 trying to organize moderate Irish opinion in favour of what seemed to them the only settlement possible between Ulster and the rest of Ireland. It culminated on 1 July 1920 in the House of Lords where Lord Monteagle, the chairman of the London committee of the Irish Dominion League, introduced a Dominion of Ireland bill. His aim was to give Ireland the largest measure of self-government compatible with the strategic unity of the islands on the one hand and the safeguarding of minorities on the other. In essence, he recommended dominion home rule with defence reserved. Such a scheme had little chance of support in either Ireland or Great Britain and after a brief debate the matter was given a six months' hoist. [63]

Dunraven, who had spoken in the Lords for the first time since before the war in opposition to Monteagle's bill, wrote three letters to the *Times* in July stating his reasons for opposing dominion home rule for Ireland. They underlined his long-standing desire to preserve the union. He argued that dominion status for Ireland was not compatible with the social, economic, commercial, and political relations that existed between two communities so closely connected geographically, and in every other way, as were Great Britain and Ireland. No analogy could be drawn between Ireland and the dominions. He thought the interpenetration between Great Britain and Ireland so complete that Ireland for her own sake must continue to have representation at Westminster. Dunraven did not favour partition nor did he like the idea of dominion status for the south and west of Ireland while the remainder was administered by Great Britain. Since neither independence nor the forcible coercion of the minority in the north were permissible, the only solution was the establishment of two parliaments in Ireland. That would not prevent the establishment of a federal solution for the whole of the United Kingdom. Dunraven believed a federal union between Great Britain and Ireland an appropriate *via media* because, while akin, the two peoples could not be fused into one. It was necessary, Dunraven argued, to aim at a federal union through devolution: "In my opinion Federalism is the best principle upon which to base a Union that will give Ireland the fullest measure of self-government, that will enable the new Irish constitution to fit into complete federation of the United Kingdom when the appropriate time comes, and to form a consistent link in the chain that may lead to constitutional synthesis within the Empire." As usual, it was clear that by federalism Dunraven did not mean the Canadian or American models. In any "federal" union it would be necessary, argued Dunraven, to recognize the superiority of the central body. It had to be ultimately supreme although devolved powers could be large.[64]

Dunraven need have had no fear that dominion status for Ireland, or for southern Ireland alone, was a possibility. Midleton had expressed similar concerns to Long that same month, but Long quickly reassured him: "You need be under no misapprehension: we have no intention of entering into negotiations with S.F., nor could we even if we wished, which we do not, adopt Dominion Home Rule. It is quite incompatible with our present scheme – even if it were not so, you may rely upon it that we could not bargain with men who have been guilty of those awful murders. The thing is unthinkable."[65] That the government would be anxious to negotiate with Sinn Fein in a year's time and that dominion status would be the exact result of such negotiations seemed impossible in July 1920.

Long distributed a memorandum to his cabinet colleagues on 29 September 1920 urging them not to deviate from the essence of the current bill and to spurn dominion status for Ireland because it might lead to independence.[66] Long continued to support the concept of devolution for the United Kingdom throughout the discussions of the Government of Ireland bill. He was ill when the deputation led by Murray Macdonald finally met with Lloyd George on 16 December, only a week before the Government of Ireland Act received royal assent, but he sent a letter which was read out. He strongly supported federal devolution as a solution to the problems of congestion confronting the United Kingdom. Lloyd George, of course, gave the concept little support, and in truth it now had few supporters in or outside the government, even in Scotland or Wales. For example, E.T. John, the most ardent of Welsh devolutionists before the war, had become by 1920 an advocate of dominion status for Wales and Scotland.

The Government of Ireland Act of December 1920 did not establish a federal system in Ireland nor did it transfer key financial powers. It established two subordinate parliaments in Ireland, one for the south and one for the six northeastern counties. In effect, it was a victory for the Ulster Unionists who had not wished to be submerged in a home rule Ireland. Nevertheless, they had never demanded a separate state, and in December 1920 they did not see the passage of the act as the first step towards that achievement. In addition to the two parliaments, there was to be a Council of Ireland which was designed to be the means of uniting north and south. The division of powers followed the recommendations generated by Long's committee. This gave the two parliaments considerable power over a variety of services, a power which was, in fact, illusory since the Westminster parliament hung on to the major sources of revenue: the income tax, the surtax, and custom and excise. These would be transferred only when a constitution for a united Ireland had been established.

The act came into operation on 3 May 1921, and elections were held three weeks later. Since all the Sinn Fein candidates in the south were unopposed, and only four members attended the first meeting of the southern parliament and only two the second, the attempt to put the act into operation in the south was dropped. Only the north implemented the legislation. James Craig became prime minister, and the northern House of Commons assembled for the first time on 7 June 1921. As a consequence of an appeal made by the king on that occasion, a truce ensued between the British and Sinn Fein. Negotiations between the two groups ended on 6 December 1921 with the signing of a treaty that effectively recognized the southern twenty-six counties as the Irish Free State, a dominion within the British Commonwealth with all the rights and privileges belonging to the senior dominion, Canada.

Plunkett was delighted by the result and thought that the terms of the treaty were "in substance" the policy of the Irish Dominion League.[67] E.T. John was similarly pleased and sent a telegram to Lloyd George expressing his "heartiest congratulations" and the hope "that 1922 may bring both to Scotland and to Wales status, dignity and freedom, fully equal to that now achieved by Ireland."[68] Such was not to happen. There was absolutely no demand or interest. Even the conventional demands for Welsh and Scottish home rule were given short shrift when efforts were made to raise the issues in the House in April and May 1922.[69] The establishment of the Irish Free State in 1922 meant that northeastern Ireland remained within an otherwise undivided United Kingdom with severely restricted powers, particularly financial. The governing apparatus and powers assigned the six counties under the Government of Ireland Act had not been designed for the operation of devolved government. They had been designed to facilitate the union of Ireland at which time additional powers would have been transferred. The six counties were condemned to a restricted political and financial existence. Certainly neither devolutionists nor federalists of the 1870–1920 era had had such a form of government in mind when they advocated either a federal or a devolutionary solution to the United Kingdom's woes.[70]

Conclusion

The federal idea has been a constant if minor strand in British political thought for over two hundred years. Since at least the 1760s, and particularly from the 1830s, until well into the twentieth century, British politicians had been obliged to deal with the issue of the transfer or demission of power from the imperial centre to the colonial periphery. In doing so, they wrestled continuously with the problem of maintaining a union while allowing diversity within it. This, in turn, led many enthusiasts in and out of parliament to consider the adaptation of a federal system to the empire-commonwealth and to many of its component parts. Today the federal idea is most often explored in a European context but frequently surfaces as a possible solution to the problems bedeviling both Ireland and the United Kingdom.[1] That this should be so is not surprising, since the essence of a federal system is the reconciliation of central control and local self-government. Ideally, it enables the regions to protect and explore their own interests without interference by the centre while enabling the centre to act on behalf of the overall nation-state unencumbered by the regions. Within a federation sovereignty is divided but coordinate and can, in the best of circumstances, be wielded cooperatively.

Such a constitutional system had natural attractions for many in the United Kingdom, especially from the 1870s to the 1920s when the country was undergoing major internal social, economic, and political change while facing both external threats to its economic, naval, and military supremacy and increasing pressure from its white self-governing colonies/dominions for more autonomy. The fear that the United Kingdom would inexorably be outstripped by the United States, Germany, and Japan prompted many to argue that the British could maintain their competitive place only by uniting with their most "advanced" colonies and pooling their resources in some form of closer union. Similarly, others argued that the self-governing colonies/dominions would not achieve complete nationhood until they participated fully in imperial foreign policy and defence decisions. It appeared that one way to achieve both objectives would be to adopt a federal system of government for the British empire. It would preserve the unity and strength of the empire while enhancing the status of the white dominions. Imperial federal ideas were widely discussed in the periodical and pamphlet literature, in the newspapers, and in a plethora of books from the 1870s through World War I. It was an important and illustrative debate at the heart of the transition from empire to commonwealth. That federation was not ultimately adopted as the solution to the empire's problems makes it no less important as a key ingredient in British political and constitutional thinking at that time. All politicians, no matter of what party, had at least to address the issue of union, and thus of federation, if they wished to play a useful role in the ongoing debate over the future of the empire.

Inseparable from that debate was the discussion over the relationship of Ireland to Great Britian and, increasingly, of Scotland, Wales, and Ireland to England. From the 1870s, and particularly after Gladstone's conversion to home rule in the mid-eighties, the nationalist demand for a greater degree of autonomy for Ireland was constant and the discussion of its resolution never far from the centre of the political stage. Gradually the Scots and the Welsh began to add their voices to the chorus and increasingly a variety of "federal" ideas were offered as a solution to this acute internal difficulty. As a consequence, "federalism" for the United Kingdom was much discussed during the years from 1870 to 1921 when the relationship of the United Kingdom to the dominions and to the wider empire was gradually being defined. The debate over "federalism" provides an important insight into the ideas and assumptions about the relationship of the state and the individual and the distribution of powers within the state that prevailed at the turn of the century in the United Kingdom. While not always centre-stage, the discussion of constitutional change was a continuous theme during those years and on three occasions – the mid-1880s, 1910–14, 1918–20 – was of fundamental political significance. The analysis of the federal ideas that surfaced during those years is therefore necessary to a general understanding of British political and constitutional thought.

Ireland was, of course, the central concern. The need to find a satisfactory solution to the problems it posed generated most of the schemes and proposals for constitutional change. But there was also considerable anxiety in political circles and among publicists about the inability of parliament to give proper attention to the myriad local, national, and imperial questions before it. It was feared that questions of vital concern to the nation or the empire were suffering from having to make way in the parliamentary timetable for matters of only local interest or ephemeral importance. Attention was drawn to the increased use of closure, to the growth of the committee system, to the limited time available for debate, and to the heavy burden on the ministers. It seemed obvious to many that a redistribution of authority was essential if the government of the United Kingdom was not to grind to a halt or become overly dependent on the civil service. This concern with congestion quickly became inextricably entwined with the Irish question. Many advocates of change believed that Westminster's problems would soon be resolved once some form of self-government was given to Ireland. Increasingly after 1910 congestion in parliament became the rationalization for advocating some form of constitutional change employed by those who did not like to admit that their overriding interest was the preservation of the union and the maintenance of the empire.

Throughout the period the terms "federalism" and to a lesser extent "federation" were loosely used to mean the distribution and sharing of power or authority. They did not necessarily mean the establishment of a federal system in which each government would be supreme in the sphere marked out for it. When the advocates of constitutional change wrote or spoke of federalism, federation, federal devolution, and federal home rule, they usually meant no more than the devolution of certain defined legislative powers to regional or national or provincial parliaments and the retention of sovereignty at Westminster. They were all well versed in their Austin, Dicey, and Freeman and accepted without question the belief in the supremacy of parliament affirmed by those writers. This rather confusing use of terms led to a good deal of unnecessary criticism of the aims and motives of the "federalists," and it led them to devote considerable time and energy to refuting the penetrating arguments of men like Balfour who were rightly scornful of ill-conceived "federal" schemes.

The problem, of course, was that while devolution or home rule all round might have been acceptable to the Scots and the Welsh it fell far short of even the most modest Irish ambition for home rule on the colonial model. That in turn was anathema to the Ulster Unionists and their English supporters. The need to find a means of distributing power satisfactory to all interested parties while retaining the unity of the United Kingdom led many advocates of constitutional change, including Gladstone, to try to combine the colonial and federal systems within the straitjacket of devolution. Not surprisingly, the result was confusion and frustration. The only logical solution to the problems of the distribution of power and the protection of Ulster was a full-fledged federal system modelled on the American or the Canadian example. Those who did propose such schemes ran smack into the deeply ingrained English hostility to a written constitution, the division of sovereignty, and a supreme court.

The hybrid nature of most of the proposals led to considerable difficulty in determining such matters as the allocation of taxing powers and the contribution to the imperial exchequer. At no time throughout the fifty years of debate was an adequate financial scheme proposed, despite the best efforts of Treasury officials and Herbert Samuel. Even the indefatigable F.S. Oliver and his colleagues Lord Selborne and Duncan Hall had no easy solution, while a persistent advocate like Murray Macdonald and a shrewd commentator like Erskine Childers recognized that even if all else could be resolved the financial arrangements would be the stumbling block. They would not have been easy to resolve even if federalism proper had been acceptable but at least models existed which could have provided guidance. The mixture of unitary and quasi-federal features in all schemes from Gladstone's to Walter Long's prevented such explorations.

In fact, one is struck on reading the contemporary press and periodicals, private correspondence, and government documents by the lack of attention given to the ramifications of constitutional change in the United Kingdom whether it be federal or devolutionary in nature. Even at the height of the debate – the 1880s, 1910–14, and 1918–20 – there appears to have been little effort to get in touch with overseas experts or to compile thorough documentation. Gladstone did consult the Canadian and American constitutions but neither he nor his successors made any effort to familiarize themselves with the actual workings of alternative systems. This might have been difficult for the individual publicist to do but not for a government which had serious intentions. One becomes quickly aware of the superficiality of much of the debate in the House and in the press. Many simply urged and affirmed rather than probed and analysed. Their arguments made easy pickings for critics such as Balfour. No one appears to have made an effort to consider the socio-economic or the administrative implications of the adoption of even a limited form of devolution.[2] The approach was a purely political-legal one. There seemed to be little appreciation of national, cultural, social, and economic parameters. This undoubtedly resulted from the nature of the problems to be resolved. Nevertheless, one would have thought that some effort would have been made to come to grips with deeper realities. Instead the problems were usually discussed in an arid theoretical atmosphere.

The majority of the proponents of "federalism" were Unionists who were not interested in federalism *per se* but in finding a way to preserve the union while satisfying local needs and resolving congestion. Certainly later adherents to the "federal" cause from within the Unionist party, such as Lord Selborne, Walter Long, and Austen Chamberlain, saw in it the one possible method of appeasing the Ulster Unionists, satisfying the Nationalists, maintaining the union, and preserving the strength of the empire. Long, in particular, clung to his new faith until the last possible moment. Federalism, of course, meant many things to many people, even to Unionists. Moreton Frewen wanted to find a means of preserving his social class. Others such as Austen Chamberlain and Selborne saw in federalism a means of damping down revolutionary tendencies, while Brassey and Earl Grey were primarily concerned with protecting the integrity of the empire and advancing the cause of imperial federation. Those Liberals who promoted constitutional change either did so because like Murray Macdonald they were distressed about parliamentary congestion or like the Scottish and Welsh nationalists were frustrated by administrative inefficiency and desired parity of treatment with Ireland. None of these various groups and individuals really had the true interests of Ireland uppermost in their thoughts. They either ignored the strength of Irish nationalism or dismissed Irish national demands as pretentious or doubted the capacity of the Irish for self-government. They clung overlong to the assumption that some variant of devolution would be sufficient. As for Ulster, few commentators included it in their schemes until 1912 and even then the English Unionists tended to assume that some form of federalism would meet Ulster's concerns, not realizing that to most Protestants in Ulster federalism was little more than a step towards union with the South.

The crucial point, of course, was that despite the intensity of the debate over constitutional change few really desired it. Most of the Unionists became involved because they wanted to find some means of keeping Ireland within the United Kingdom. If it had not been for the threat of an independent Ireland which they believed implicit in home rule, they would have happily settled for reforms to parliamentary procedure in order to resolve congestion. Similarly, the Liberals had little interest in an immediate and wide-ranging shake-up in the fabric of the British state. They also wished to preserve the union and were convinced that a step-by-step approach to the problem of Ireland would suffice. If there had been powerful Scottish and Welsh nationalist movements coincident with Ireland's, the Liberals would not have been able to avoid at least the consideration of broad-based schemes. No such pressure existed. The Welsh and Scottish national movements were weak in these years and it was not until the 1970s that they had the leverage to force a re-examination of the nature of government in the United Kingdom.

No major constitutional changes in a democracy can be imposed on a reluctant populace. Since England has the largest population in the United Kingdom, it is essential to have its support before venturing in the direction of either home rule all round or federation. The English showed little or no interest in any such form of constitutional change during the years 1870–1921. Not even the threat of civil war in 1914 or the exigencies of world war in 1918 could drive Asquith or Lloyd George in a direction they knew the English and probably most Scotsmen and Welshmen did not wish to go. With the benefit of hindsight, therefore, it appears to have been a hopeless cause. Nevertheless, men concerned with the future of the empire and the stability of the British state used the political arena in a vigorous attempt to force a rethinking of the basic constitutional relationship between Ireland, Scotland, Wales, and England. It was a vibrant and important debate of which we have not heard the last.

Notes

BL   British Library
Cab   Cabinet Office
CUL   Cambridge University Library
FO   Foreign Office
HLRO House of Lords Record Office
HRC   Humanities Research Center, Austin, Texas
ICS   Institute of Commonwealth Studies
LC   Library of Congress
NLI   National Library of Ireland
NLS   National Library of Scotland
NLW   National Library of Wales
NYPL New York Public Library
PAC   Public Archives of Canada
PH   Plunkett House, Oxford
PRO   Public Record Office
TCL   Trinity College Library
UBL   University of Birmingham Library
UD   University of Durham Archives
UTL   University of Toronto Library
WRO   Wiltshire Record Office, Trowbridge

INTRODUCTION

1 See on these matters John M. Ward, "The Third Earl Grey and Federalism,
  1846–1852," *Australian Journal of Politics and History* 3 (1957): 18–32; John M. Ward, *Earl
  Grey and the Australian Colonies 1846–1857: A Study of Self-Government and Self-Interest*

(Melbourne: Melbourne University Press 1958); Bruce A. Knox, "The Rise of Colonial Federation as an Object of British Policy, 1850–1870," *Journal of British Studies* II, no. 1 (November 1971): 92–112; and John M. Ward, *Colonial Self-Government: The British Experience 1759–1856* (London: Macmillan 1976).

2 There is an extensive literature on the background to Canadian federation. See particularly W.L. Morton, *The Critical Years: The Union of British North America 1857–1873* (Toronto: McClelland and Stewart 1964); D.G. Creighton, *The Road to Confederation; The Emergence of Canada 1863–1867* (Toronto: Macmillan 1964); L.F.S. Upton, "The Idea of Confederation, 1754–1858" in W.L. Morton, ed., *The Shield of Achilles* (Toronto: McClelland and Stewart 1968), 184–207; William Ormsby, *The Emergence of the Federal Concept in Canada 1839–1845* (Toronto: University of Toronto Press 1969); and Ged Martin, "An Imperial Idea and Its Friends: Canadian Confederation and the British," in Gordon Martel, ed., *Studies in British Imperial History: Essays in Honour of A.P. Thornton* (London: Macmillan 1986), 49–94.

3 There is an extensive literature on "imperial federation," "empire federalism," and "imperial union." See particularly C.A. Bodelsen, *Studies in Mid-Victorian Imperialism* (London: Heinemann 1960); J.E. Tyler, *The Struggle for Imperial Unity, 1868–1895* (London: Longman 1938); John Kendle, *The Colonial and Imperial Conferences 1887–1911: A Study in Imperial Organization* (London: Longmans 1967); Ged Martin, "Empire Federalism and Imperial Parliamentary Union, 1820–1870," *Historical Journal* 16, no. 1 (1973): 65–92; Ged Martin, "The Idea of 'Imperial Federation'," in Ronald Hyam and Ged Martin, *Reappraisals in British Imperial History* (London: Macmillan 1975), 121–38; John Kendle, *The Round Table Movement and Imperial Union* (Toronto: University of Toronto Press 1975); Michael Burgess, "The Imperial Federation Movement in Great Britain, 1869–1893" (PH.D, University of Leicester, 1976); M.G. Miller, "The Continued Agitation for Imperial Union, 1895–1910: The Individuals and Bodies Concerned, Their Ideas and Their Influence" (D. Phil., University of Oxford, 1980); and Michael Burgess, "Imperial Federation: Continuity and Change in British Imperial Ideas, 1869–1871," *New Zealand Journal of History* 17, no. 1 (April 1983): 60–80.

CHAPTER ONE

1 For a detailed examination of Crawford's ideas and his relationship with O'Connell see B.A. Kennedy, "Sharmon Crawford's Federal Scheme for Ireland," in H.A. Cronne, T.W. Moody, and D.B. Quinn, eds., *Essays in British and Irish History in Honour of James Eadie Todd* (London: Macmillan 1949), 235–54; also Kevin Nowlan, *The Politics of Repeal* (London: Routledge & Kegan Paul 1965), 53, 57–8, 73–8.

2 Crawford to O'Connell, 1 August 1843, *Northern Whig*, 8 August 1843, quoted in Kennedy, "Sharmon Crawford's Federal Scheme," 246.

3 O'Connell's decision followed the publication of a pamphlet on federalism by Grey Porter, the sheriff of Fermanagh, in which the virtues of the American constitution were outlined. Porter wanted sovereign parliaments for each island and an overall

imperial house with responsibility for foreign and colonial affairs. See J.G.V. Porter, *Ireland* (Dublin 1844).

4 This incident and the details of Crawford's scheme are fully treated in Kennedy, "Sharmon Crawford's Federal Scheme," 248–52.

5 Ibid., 249.

6 See Gavan Duffy to Daniel O'Connell, 18 October 1844, *Morning Herald*, 22 October 1844.

7 Russell to Duke of Leinster, [13] September 1844, Russell Papers, PRO 30/22/4C: 242–3.

8 Sir James Graham to Peel, 17 and 20 September 1844, Sir Robert Peel Papers, BL, Add. Mss. 40450: 160–3 and 195–6. O'Connell made it clear to Smith-O'Brien that he believed the fears of Russell and Graham were justified, but he was going to leave the details to the federalists. O'Connell to Smith-O'Brien, 1 October 1844, Ms. 434: 1245, William Smith-O'Brien Papers, NLI, Dublin.

9 See *Morning Herald*, 4 October 1844.

10 Ibid., 26 October 1844.

11 Ibid., 31 October 1844.

12 Ibid., 1 November 1844.

13 For Butt's authorship of the *Herald* articles see Michael Macdonagh, *The Life of Daniel O'Connell* (London: Cassell 1903), 356. There continued to be occasional reminders of the possibilities of federalism. See particularly Michael MacKenna, *Federalism Illustrated; and the Integrity of the British Empire Demonstrated through a Repeal of the Act of Union, with a Federal Constitution, and an Irish Parliament, Addressed to the Right Honorable the Lord Cloncurry* (Dublin 1847).

14 Quoted in David Thornley, *Isaac Butt and Home Rule* (London: Macgibbon and Kee 1964), 97.

15 Isaac Butt, *Home Goverment for Ireland, Irish Federalism: Its Meaning, Its Objectives, and Its Hopes*, 3rd ed. (Dublin 1871).

16 Ibid., ix–XIV.

17 Ibid., xiii.

18 Ibid., 11–12.

19 Ibid., iii–VI.

20 Ibid., 16–18.

21 Ibid., 15–16.

22 For the "Constitution and Powers of the Imperial Parliament" see ibid., 36–48.

23 For the "Constitution and Powers of the Irish Parliament" see ibid., 49–59.

24 Butt never referred to Wales as a separate entity. Like most of his contemporaries he used "England" to mean "England and Wales."

25 For the above see Butt, *Home Government for Ireland*, 60–1.

26 Thornley, *Isaac Butt and Home Rule*, 98–9.

27 Butt, *Home Government for Ireland*, 83.

28 For the fate of Butt's Home Government Association see Thornley, *Isaac Butt and*

Home Rule, passim. The difficulties in demarcating national (Irish) from imperial concerns was raised by many speakers and writers. See for example the *Times*, 27 October 1871. One writer argued federalism would result in purer democracy which would lead to socialism which would fragment the larger nationality. He therefore opposed it. See Cecil R. Roche, *Federalism: The Suppressed Address to the College Historical Society* (Dublin 1873), 5, 8, and 28. Another writer thought a federal system would limit Irish independence and reduce the Irish government to no more than a local board. It would not satisfy Irish demands, and there was no interest in it in England, Scotland, and Wales. See the *Times*, 27 April 1874.

29 See H.V. Brasted, "Irish Nationalism and the British Empire in the Late Nineteenth Century," in O. Macdonagh, W.F. Mandle, P. Travers, eds., *Irish Culture and Nationalism, 1750–1950* (Dublin: Gill and Macmillian 1983), 84–5. See also L. McCaffrey, "Irish federalism in the 1870s: A Study in Conservative Nationalism," *Transactions of the American Philosophical Society*, n.s., 52, pt.6 (1962).

30 The following account is taken from 3 Hansard (H of C), vol. 220, 30 June 1874, cols. 700–92; and 2 July 1874, cols. 874–969.

31 Ibid., cols. 878–84.

32 For the 1876 debate see 3 Hansard (H of C), vol. 230, 30 June 1976, cols. 738–822. Butt again drew on Canadian, Australian, and general colonial analogies in putting his case for a separate Irish parliament.

33 For the above see E.A. Freeman, *History of Federal Government from the Foundation of the Achaian League to the Disruption of the United States* (London 1863), 9, 10, 15, 16, 90–1.

34 E.A. Freeman, "Federalism and Home Rule," *Fortnightly Review*, 22 (1874): 204–15.

35 Frederick William Heygate, "A Suggestion as to Home Rule," *Nineteenth Century* (July 1879): 89–98.

36 G. Campbell, "Home Rule in Several Countries," *Fortnightly Review* 33 (1880): 644–55.

37 See Justin McCarthy, "The Common-Sense of Home Rule," *Nineteenth Century* (March 1880): 406–21.

38 For the above see Edward Wilson, "The Common-Sense of Home Rule: I. A Reply" and Justin McCarthy, "The Common-Sense of Home Rule: II. A Rejoinder," *Nineteenth Century* (April 1880): 567–92. Also Edward Wilson, "Irish Politics and English Parties," *Nineteenth Century* (December 1879): 1068–81, and Justin McCarthy, "Home Rule," *Nineteenth Century* (June 1882): 858–68. Charlotte G. O'Brien, in an article "Eighty Years," *Nineteenth Century* (March 1881): 395–414, argued for the establishment of provincial assemblies for the traditional Irish provinces, making the Irish therefore responsible to themselves and not Westminster. The tie with Great Britain would presumably have been maintained, although O'Brien did say the Irish would never be content with less than freedom and their nationality respected. The *Edinburgh Review* in January 1882 argued that the Irish could not be trusted with a parliament and that Ulster could not be left to its fate.

This was one of the early references to Ulster's needs. "Irish Discontent," *Edinburgh Review* (January 1882): 155–85.

39 Goldwin Smith, "The 'Home Rule' Fallacy," *Nineteenth Century* (July 1882): 1–7. For the Smith-Merriman correspondence see Phyllis Lewson, ed., *Selections from the Correspondence of J.X. Merriman 1870–1890* (Cape Town: Van Riebeeck Society 1960), 49–56, 66–77, and 82–3. See also C.F. Goodfellow, *Great Britain and South African Confederation 1870–1881* (Cape Town: Oxford University Press 1966).

40 A.V. Dicey, "Home Rule from an English Point of View," *Contemporary Review* (July 1882): 66–86.

41 Dicey to Bryce, 1 November 1882, James Bryce Papers, Bodleian, 2: 40–3.

42 Dicey to Bryce, 3 January 1885, ibid., 64–68.

43 A.V. Dicey, *Lectures Introductory to the Study of the Law of the Constitution*, 2nd ed. (London 1886), 127.

44 For the above see ibid., 128–66. Dicey's ideas on federalism also appeared in an article in the first issue of *Law Quarterly Review* (1885); see also Richard A. Cosgrove, *The Rule of Law: Albert Venn Dicey, Victorian Jurist*, (Chapel Hill: University of North Carolina Press 1980) for a clear exposition and analysis of Dicey's ideas.

45 For a full discussion of the Board scheme see C.H.D. Howard, "Joseph Chamberlain, Parnell and the Irish 'central board' scheme, 1884–5," *Irish Historical Studies* 8, no. 32 (September 1953): 324–61.

46 See J. Chamberlain to Duignan, 17 December 1884, in C.H.D. Howard, "Documents Relating to the Irish 'Central Board' Scheme, 1884–5," *Irish Historical Studies*, 8, no. 31 (March 1953): 240–2.

47 Parnell to O'Shea, 5 January 1885, ibid., 242.

48 Parnell to O'Shea, 13 January 1885, ibid., 245–6.

49 Quoted in R. Barry O'Brien, *The Life of Charles Stewart Parnell 1846–1891*, 2 vols. (New York: Harper and Brothers 1898), 38–9.

50 C.H.D. Howard, "Documents," 255–7.

51 Spencer to Chamberlain, 26 April 1885, ibid., 257–9. See also Campbell-Bannerman to Spencer, 30 April 1885, copy, Campbell-Bannerman Papers, BL, Add. Ms. 41228: 259.

52 *Times*, 4 and 15 June 1885.

53 "Local Government and Ireland," *Fortnightly Review* (July 1885): 1–16. This article was reprinted in *The Radical Programme* (preface by Chamberlain) that appeared later in the summer. See D.A. Hamer, ed., *The Radical Programme* (Brighton: Harvester Press 1971), 231–63. Chamberlain acknowledged that his memorandum "Local Government in Ireland" was the basis for the article in the *Fortnightly Review*. See Joseph Chamberlain Papers, UBL, JC 8/5/3/2.

54 *Times*, 9 and 16 September 1885, and Charles W. Boyd, ed., *Mr. Chamberlain's Speeches*, 2 vols. (London: Constable 1914), 1: 241–3.

55 Healy, at Parnell's request, had been investigating a change in the Anglo-Irish constitutional relationship since October. See Healy to Labouchere, 15 October

1885; Labouchere to Chamberlain, 18 October 1885; and Healy to Labouchere, Christmas 1885, printed in A. Thorold, *The Life of Henry Labouchere* (London: Constable 1913), 235-7, 237-9, and 263-4. Also Labouchere to the *Times*, 28 December 1885; and R.J. Hind, *Henry Labouchere and the Empire 1880-1905* (London: The Athlone Press 1972).

56 Chamberlain to Labouchere, 26 December 1885, Thorold, *Labouchere*, 272. Chamberlain also wrote to Sir Charles Dilke, his radical associate, outlining a federal scheme. See Chamberlain to Dilke, 26 December 1885, Sir Charles Dilke Papers, BL, Add. Ms. 43877: 223-6.

57 Chamberlain to Labouchere, 27 December 1885 and 3 January 1886, quoted in Thorold, *Labouchere*, 272-3 and 278-9.

CHAPTER TWO

1 See *Annual Register* (1871), 105-6, for Gladstone's speech at Aberdeen. For a treatment of Gladstone's conversion to home rule see James Loughlin, *Gladstone, Home Rule and the Ulster Question 1882-93* (Atlantic Highlands, NJ: Humanities Press International 1987), 35-52.

2 See the *Times*, 8 November 1877; and Gladstone to Granville, 20 November 1877 in Agatha Ramm, ed., *The Political Correspondence of Mr. Gladstone and Lord Granville 1876-1886*, 2 vols. (Oxford: Clarendon Press 1962), 1: 57-9. See also E.D. Steele, "Gladstone and Ireland," *Irish Historical Studies* 17, no. 65 (March 1970): 58-88.

3 Viscount Hythe, *The Case for Devolution and a Settlement of the Home Rule Question by Consent: Extracts from Speeches* (London 1913), 25.

4 See [W.E.G.], "Devolution and obstruction," 15 November 1880, W.E. Gladstone Papers, BL, Add. Ms. 44642: 78. See also Thomas John Dunne, "Ireland, England and Empire, 1868-1886: The Ideologies of British Political Leadership" (PHD, Cambridge, 1976), 62-3.

5 Gladstone to Granville, 13 September 1881, Ramm, *The Political Correspondence*, 1: 291-2.

6 Gladstone to Granville, 16 September 1881, ibid., 293-4.

7 See Philip Guedella, *The Queen and Mr. Gladstone 1880-1898*, 2 vols. (London: Hodder & Stoughton 1933), 176-8. Granville was uncertain about using Canada as an illustration. He thought Canada was "as nearly independent as possible." Granville to Gladstone, 13 February 1882, Ramm, *Political Correspondence*, 1: 341.

8 Gladstone's "Provincial Councils" scheme was dated 7 April 1882 and is printed in full in J.L. Hammond, *Gladstone and the Irish Nation*, 2nd ed. (Hamden, Conn.: Archon Books 1964), 259-62.

9 Gladstone to Granville, 30 November 1882, Ramm, *Political Correspondence*, 1: 461.

10 Hartington in a speech to his constituents of S.E. Lancs at Bacup on 19 January 1883, *Times*, 20 January 1883.

11 Gladstone to Granville, 22 January 1883, Ramm, *Political Correspondence*, 2: 9-11.

12 See David George Hoskin, "The Genesis and Significance of the 1886 'Home Rule' Split in the Liberal Party" (PHD, Cambridge, 1964), 257.

13 Memorandum by Gladstone, 6 May 1885, in Ramm, *Political Correspondence*, 2: 366–7.

14 On this point see Gladstone to Rosebery, 13 November 1885, in John Morley, *The Life of William Ewart Gladstone*, 2 vols. (London: Edward Lloyd 1908), 2: 358–9.

15 See Gladstone to Hartington, 17 December 1885, in Morley, *Gladstone*, 2: 377, in which Gladstone stated that "the conditions of an admissible plan are: (1) Union of the empire and due supremacy of parliament. (2) Protection for the minority ... (3) Fair allocation of imperial charges."

16 Lord Spencer was Gladstone's principal support during these hectic weeks. See Peter Gordon, ed., *The Red Earl: The Papers of the Fifth Earl of Spencer 1835–1910*, 2 vols. (Northampton: Northamptonshire Record Society 1986), 2: 1–13, 67–130.

17 For the above views and arguments see Castletown, "The Irish Problem: 1. Home Rule and Its Solution," *Fortnightly Review* 44 (1885): 852–64; C. Raleigh Chichester, "The Irish Question: 1. A Policy for Ireland," *Dublin Review* (October 1885): 254–65; Edward William O'Brien, "The Radical Programme for Ireland," *Nineteenth Century* (September 1885): 362–73; J. Leslie Field, "The Burden of Ireland," *Nineteenth Century* (August 1885): 238–48; G.B. Lancaster Woodburne, "Imperial Federation and Home Rule: A Conservative Solution," *National Review* (July 1885): 606–15; and "The Unworkableness of Federalism," *Spectator*, 26 December 1885, 1728–9.

18 "What Home Rule Means, *Times*, 26 December 1885.

19 T.W. Fowle to the editor, ibid., 17 December 1885, and T.P. O'Connor to the editor, ibid., 19 December 1885.

20 T. Brassey to the editor, ibid., 29 December 1885.

21 See Sir James Stephen to the editor, ibid., 4 and 5 January 1886.

22 Merriman to Goschen, 8 February 1886, quoted in Arthur D. Elliott, *The Life of George Joachim Goschen, First Viscount Goschen 1831–1907*, 2 vols. (London 1911), 2: 25–6. H.O. Arnold-Foster adopted a hard position and dismissed the Irish demands as the fruits of "miserable conspiracy." H.O. Arnold-Foster, "'Shall We Desert the Loyalists?'," *Nineteenth Century* (February 1886): 215–25; see also R. Barry O'Brien, "Federal Union with Ireland," *Nineteenth Century* (January 1886): 35–40.

23 James Bryce, "Alternative Politics in Ireland," *Nineteenth Century* (February 1886): 312–28.

24 See A Radical [Joseph Chamberlain], "A Radical View of the Irish Crisis," *Fortnightly Review* (February 1886): 273–84. For proof of Chamberlain's authorship see J. Chamberlain Papers, UBL, JC 8/5/2/2.

25 Edward A. Freeman, "Some Aspects of Home Rule," *Contemporary Review* (February 1886): 153–68.

26 For the above see G. Shaw Lefevre, "Home Rule. 1. Precedents," *Nineteenth Century* (March 1886): 424–42; and Frank H. Hill, "Home Rule: IV. The Impending English Answer," ibid., 476–84. J. Moyes also thought one should see in home rule

"a measure not of disintegration, but of wise devolution by which each country is freed from unnecessary change, control, interference in the domestic affairs of the other; by which all the intelligence, industry, and patriotism in each country is turned full on, with undistracted energy, to the development of its own resources and the working out of its own destinies." J. Moyes, "The Claim for Home Rule, upon General Principles," *Dublin Review* (April 1886): 374–94. For two opposing views see An Irish Catholic Barrister, "The Probable Consequences of Home Rule," *Dublin Review* (April 1886): 394–403; and W.E.H. Lecky, "A 'Nationalist' Parliament," *Nineteenth Century* (April 1886): 636–44.

27 Morley, *Gladstone*, 2: 389. For Gladstone's extensive notes on Burke's writings see "Burke Extracts – Historical," 9 January 1886, W.E. Gladstone Papers, BL, Add. Ms. 44771: 4–19.

28 See Granville to Gladstone, 6 August 1885, in Ramm, *Political Correspondence*, 2: 391.

29 See Gladstone to R. Grosvenor, 9 and 11 October 1885, and Grosvenor to Gladstone, 10 October 1885, W.E. Gladstone Papers, BL, Add. Ms. 44316: 44–9.

30 See K. O'Shea, *Charles Stewart Parnell*, 2 vols. (London 1914), 2: 18–20; also Add. Ms. 44771: 1–2, W.E. Gladstone Papers, BL.

31 Hamilton's untitled memorandum was dated 31 October 1885 and headed "*VERY SECRET.*" See Add. Ms. 44631: 122–9, W.E. Gladstone Papers, BL. James Bryce also supplied Gladstone with a useful memorandum prepared shortly after the "Hawarden Kite." See Add. Ms. 44770: 5–14, ibid. For a valuable treatment of the preparation of the home rule bill see Loughlin, *Gladstone, Home Rule*, 53–80.

32 Gladstone had concluded that home rule would not be possible without a satisfactory solution to the land question, so he decided that a land purchase bill and a home rule bill would have to be introduced virtually together. Two valuable treatments of the preparation of the home rule bill of 1886 are David George Hoskin, "The Genesis and Significance of the 1886 'Home Rule' Split in the Liberal Party" (PHD, Cambridge, 1964); and Thomas John Dunne, "Ireland, England and Empire, 1868–1886: The Ideologies of British Political Leadership" (PHD, Cambridge, 1976), particularly chapter 6, "The Making and Selling of the Home Rule Bill," 235–69. I am indebted to both writers for their insights.

33 See Add. Ms. 44632: 107–39, W.E. Gladstone Papers, BL.

34 Dunne, "Ireland, England and Empire," 240–1.

35 Hugh Childers to Gladstone, 18 March 1886, W.E. Gladstone Papers, BL, Add. Ms. 44132: 226–9. Also Gladstone to Morley, 22 March 1886, ibid., Add. Ms. 44255.

36 [W.E.G.], "Principles of Reconstruction," [March 1886], ibid., Add. Ms. 44772: 51.

37 Ibid., 47–8.

38 See a draft of Gladstone's bill in W.E. Gladstone Papers, BL, Add. Ms. 44772: 37–42, and the comment on the reverse of f. 38; also Add. Ms. 44672 for Gladstone's notes.

39 See Gladstone's notes on March 1886 cabinet meetings in W.E. Gladstone Papers, BL, Add. Ms. 44647, particularly folios 56–7. Also Morley, *Gladstone*, 2: 406–7.

40 W.E. Gladstone Papers, BL, Add. Ms. 44771: 204.

41 Notes of February 1886, W.E. Gladstone Papers, BL, Add. Ms. 44771: 128–83.

42 W.E.G., "Memorandum on Bill for Irish Government. 2nd Reading Division," 5 May 1886, W.E. Gladstone Papers, BL, Add. Ms. 44772: 100–1; also W.E.G., "House of Commons" *Draft. Secret*, 11 May 1886, ibid., Add. Ms. 44772: 108–10.

43 R. Welby and E.W. Hamilton, "Irish Finance. Paper A," 17 February 1886, W.E. Gladstone Papers, BL, Add. Ms. 44771: 77–102; also E.W. Hamilton to Gladstone, 15 January 1886 and enclosure, ibid., 20–7.

44 Gladstone to E.W. Hamilton, 8 February 1886, copy W.E. Gladstone Papers, BL, Add. Ms. 44548: 50.

45 See "Irish Finance. Paper A," W.E. Gladstone Papers, BL, Add. Ms. 44771: 96 and 99.

46 The protracted analysis and debate over the proportion Ireland should contribute to the imperial exchequer can be followed in W.E. Gladstone Papers, BL, Add. Ms. 44771: 77–258; Add. Ms. 44772: 6–31; and Add. Ms. 44632: 192–3, 197–8.

47 See the Government of Ireland bill 1886 plus W.E.G., "Ireland Finance," 31 March 1886, Cab. 37/18/33, PRO; and "The Financial Side of the Home Rule Question," *Economist*, 26 June 1886, 795. See also R. Welby, E.W. Hamilton, A. Milner, "Irish Finance." *Most Confidential*, 14 December 1892, Cab. 37/32/51, PRO, for an exhaustive analysis of the financial relations of Ireland and the United Kingdom under the 1886 bill.

48 Morley, *Gladstone*, 2: 406–7.

49 W.E.G., "Notes for speeches," 8 April 1886, W.E. Gladstone Papers, BL, Add. Ms. 44672: 21, 23, 24, 27.

50 3 Hansard (H of C), vol. 304, 8 April 1886, cols. 1037–85.

51 Ibid., col. 1089.

52 Ibid., cols. 1091, 1093, 1103.

53 For Chamberlain's speech see ibid., cols. 1181–1207.

54 Ibid., col. 1210.

55 Ibid., col. 1218.

56 For Hartington's speech see ibid., cols. 1238–63.

57 For Redmond's remarks see ibid., vol. 305, 13 May 1886, cols. 968–9.

58 Editorial, *Times*, 16 April 1886.

59 For the above see Frank H. Hill, "The Government of Ireland Bill," *Nineteenth Century* (May 1886): 779–92; R.W. Dale, "The Exclusion of the Irish Members from the Imperial Parliament," *Contemporary Review* (June 1886): 761–71; L.G. Power, "Canadian Opinion on the Question of Home Rule," *Dublin Review* (July 1886): 128–44; J. Chamberlain to T.H. Bolton, 7 May 1886, *Times*, 8 May 1886; "R," "After the Battle," *Nation*, 24 June 1886: 524–5; Rosebery to Munro-Ferguson, 4 May 1886, Roseberry Papers, NLS, Edinburgh, Ms. 10017: 23–4. Also Chamberlain to Thomas Gee, 26 April 1886, Thomas Gee Papers, NLW, Aberystwyth, Mss. 8305D: 15a.

60 Dicey to Bryce, 10 April 1886, Ms. Bryce 2: 76–81, Bodleian. Also Dicey to Bryce, 18 May 1886, Ms. Bryce 2: 82–5, for Dicey's regret at his break with the Liberals and his deep-rooted opposition to home rule.

61 For a full discussion of Dicey's views and his use of historical evidence see Richard

A. Cosgrove, "The Relevance of Irish History: The Gladstone-Dicey Debate about Home Rule, 1886-7," *Éire-Ireland* 13, no. 4 (Winter 1978): 6-21; and Richard A. Cosgrove, *The Rule of Law*, particularly chapter six, 114-40.

62 A.V. Dicey, *England's Case against Home Rule*, 2nd ed. (London 1886).

63 For the above see ibid., 54, 161-78, 193, 196-7.

CHAPTER THREE

1 3 Hansard (H. of C), vol. 306, 7 June 1886, cols. 1142-43.

2 See L.G. Power, "Canadian Opinion on the Question of Home Rule," *Dublin Review* (July 1886): 128-44. For a general treatment of the debate over home rule for Ireland during the years 1886-92 see James Loughlin, *Gladstone, Home Rule and the Ulster Question 1882-93* (Atlantic Highlands, NJ: Humanities Press International 1987), 197-219.

3 Julius Vogel to the editor, *Times*, 29 July 1886. See also Raewyn Dalziel, *Julius Vogel: Business Politician* (Auckland: Auckland University Press 1986).

4 Monck to the editor, 18 October and 17 November 1886, *Times*, 20 October and 23 November 1886.

5 The Home Rule Library, No. 6, *Mr. Joseph Chamberlain and Home Rule* (1886), 5. In late June 1886 Sir Alexander Galt of Canada had told the Imperial Federation League that the first and most important step was to secure the confederation of England, Scotland, Ireland and Wales. The *Times* editorial (2 July 1886) was caustic in response: the difficulties in the way of imperial federation were assuredly great enough without rendering them insuperable "by setting forth the confederation of England, Scotland, Ireland and Wales as a condition precedent to the federation of the Empire." For its part the *Nation* did not believe Chamberlain understood either the British North America Act which he had cited in the second reading debate or the radical impact federalization of the United Kingdom would have on the constitution. See the *Nation*, 24 June 1886, 525.

6 A.W. Aneurin Williams, *Home Rule by Development: An Alternative Plan* (Middlesborough 1886).

7 Henry D'Esterre Taylor, *The Advantages of Imperial Federation* (Melbourne 1888), 13. Also Sir George Ferguson Bowen, *The Federation of the British Empire* (London 1889), 9. The link between imperial federation and devolution in the United Kingdom was occasionally made during the eighties and nineties much in the way that Galt and D'Esterre Taylor did but it was not a line of argument supported by the Imperial Federation League. The journal of the league, *Imperial Federation*, rarely mentioned home rule in its nine years of existence but when it did it emphasized that imperial federation did not depend on the granting of home rule to Ireland or to Scotland, England, and Wales.

8 E.A. Freeman, "Prospects of Home Rule," *Fortnightly Review* 46 (1886): 317-33. For a more jaundiced view see Thomas Raleigh, "Mr. Gladstone's Irish Policy," *Westminster Review* 126 (1886): 194-211; also T.B. Scannell, "The English Constitution in Theory and Practice," *Dublin Review* (January 1887): 45-57.

9 Freeman to Bryce, 4 July 1886, Ms. Bryce 7: 236–8, Bodleian. That Freeman had strong opinions about both the Irish and constitutional change had been underlined in May 1886 when he frankly revealed to Bryce: "I do hope Gladstone will stick firm to shutting out the Paddies from Westminster. It is one of the pillars of the whole thing. I am sorry to see so much opposition." Freeman to Bryce, 2 May 1886, Ms. Bryce 7: 216–21; also Freeman to Bryce, 16 January 1887, Ms. Bryce 8: 1–4.

10 3 Hansard (H of C), vol. 232, 23 February 1877, cols. 929–35.

11 For a more comprehensive treatment of these issues see Reginald Coupland, *Welsh and Scottish Nationalism: A Study* (London: Collins 1954), 281–96; and H.J. Hanham, *Scottish Nationalism* (London: Faber and Faber 1969), 50–63.

12 Arthur D. Elliott, "Home Rule for Scotland," *Nineteenth Century* (March 1886): 466–75.

13 Ibid., 475.

14 See Hanham, *Scottish Nationalism*, 92ff; Neil MacCormack, ed., *The Scottish Debate: Essays on Scottish Nationalism* (London: Oxford University Press 1970), 8–9; J.N. Wolfe, ed., *Government and Nationalism in Scotland* (Edinburgh: Edinburgh University Press 1969), 8–10; and Coupland, *Welsh and Scottish Nationalism*, 298.

15 See Charles Waddie to Gladstone, 18 June 1886, enclosed in Waddie to the editor, *Scottish News*, n.d., J. Ramsay MacDonald Papers, PRO 30/69/1186; and Ramsay MacDonald's Scottish Home Rule Association membership card for 1887, ibid., PRO 30/69/1187.

16 "Home Rule for Scotland," *Scottish Review* (July 1886): 1–20.

17 Ibid., 9–10.

18 Some Scotsmen were more circumspect and while prepared to consider very modest changes in Scotland's constitutional relationship with England they were shy of home rule and baulked at the idea of federation. See Boyd Kinnear to the editor, *Scotsman*, 12 October 1886.

19 Bryce to Gladstone, 29 November [1886], Ms. Bryce 11: 155–7, Bodleian. For a more detailed letter about Bryce's concerns regarding Ireland and the Liberal party in Scotland and for his wish to have Gladstone publicly address the issue see Bryce to Gladstone, 22 December 1886, Ms. Bryce 11: 158–61, ibid.

20 H. Campbell-Bannerman to Bryce, 16 December [1886], Campbell-Bannerman Papers, Add. Ms. 41211: 1. For the impact of Gladstone's home rule bill on Scottish Liberals see Coupland, *Welsh and Scottish Nationalism*, 297–8; Wolfe, ed., *Government and Nationalism*, 9; Donald C. Savage, "Scottish Politics, 1885–86," *Scottish Historical Review* 40, no. 2 (October 1961): 118–35; John F. McCaffrey, "The Origins of Liberal Unionism in the West of Scotland," ibid., 50, no. 149 (April 1974): 45–71; James G. Kellas, "The Liberal Party in Scotland 1876–1895," ibid., 44, no. 137 (April 1965): 1–16; James G. Kellas, "The Liberal Party and the Scottish Church Disestablishment Crisis," *English Historical Review* 79, no. 310 (January 1964): 31–46; and Dereck W. Urwin, "The Development of the Conservative Party Organisation in Scotland until 1912," *Scottish Historical Review* 44, no. 138 (October 1965): 89–111. For the impact of land reform and the crofter agitation on party realignment see D. Crowley, "The 'Crofters Party,' 1885–1892," ibid., 35, no. 119 (April 1956): 110–26;

H.J. Hanham, "The Problem of Highland Discontent, 1880–1885," *Transactions of the Royal Historical Society*, 5th ser., 19 (1969): 21–65; and James Hunter, "The Politics of Highland Land Reform, 1873–1895," *Scottish Historical Review* 53, no. 155 (April 1974): 45–68.

21 W. Wallace, "Nationality and Home Rule," *Scottish Review* (July 1888): 177–87.

22 W. Mitchell, "Scotland and Home Rule," *Scottish Review* 11 (1888): 323–46. See also for more general support of Scottish home rule: "The New Round Table," *Westminster Review* 132 (1889): 506–18; and B.D. MacKenzie, "Home Rule for Scotland," ibid.: 553–65.

23 David Lowe, *Souvenirs of Scottish Labour* (Glasgow 1919), 2, quoted in Hanham, *Scottish Nationalism*, 94.

24 For further information see Michael Keating and David Bleiman, *Labour and Scottish Nationalism* (London: Macmillan 1979), 50–8; Jack Brand, *The National Movement in Scotland* (London: Routledge & Kegan Paul 1978), 38–43; and D.N. MacIver, "The Paradox of Nationalism in Scotland" in Colin H. Williams ed., *National Separatism* (Vancouver: University of British Columbia Press 1982), 105–44. Not all Scots were supporters of home rule. On 6 April 1887 at the annual meeting of the Convention of Royal Burghs a motion in favour of establishing a separate parliament and executive for Scotland was defeated 44–17 in order to avoid anything that "might tend to endanger the integrity of the Empire and union with England from which Scotland had derived enormous benefits." *Times*, 7 and 12 April 1887.

25 Coupland, *Welsh and Scottish Nationalism*, 222–3.

26 Although widely supported in the popular press, *Cymru Fydd* did not make much headway until the 1890s and then not extensively in the political arena. See K. Morgan, *Wales in British Politics 1868–1922* (Cardiff: University of Wales Press 1963), 104–6. Gladstone was sensitive to this resurgence of national feeling and in Swansea in June 1887 he made a deliberate appeal to Welsh patriotism and nationalism, and appeared to hint at home rule all round. See the *Times*, 6 June 1887.

27 See Morgan, *Wales in British Politics*, 106–7.

28 *Times*, 26 December 1889.

29 "The New Round Table. Home Rule for Wales," *Westminster Review* (March 1890): 394–416; see also the *Times*, 18 January 1890; and Andrew Reid to Thomas Gee, 8 February 1890, Thomas Gee Papers, NLW, Mss. 8308D: 250, on "The New Round Table."

30 Stuart Rendel to A.C. Humphreys-Owen, 11 December 1888, Glansevern Papers, NLW, Mss. 439.

31 T. Ellis to J. Herbert Lewis, 21 June 1889, Thomas Ellis Papers, NLW, 2882.

32 3 Hansard (H of C), vol. 335, 9 April 1889, col. 74.

33 Ibid., col. 69.

34 Ibid., cols. 69–74.

35 Ibid., cols. 74–81.

36 Ibid., cols. 95–7.

37 Ibid., cols. 96.

38 Ibid., cols. 99–108.

39 Ibid., cols. 108–14.

40 See Edward Hamilton Diary, 7 July 1889, Edward Hamilton Papers, BL, Add. Ms.
48651: 36; Gladstone to Rosebery, 7 August 1889, W.E. Gladstone Papers, BL, Add.
Ms. 44289: 90–1; and Rosebery to Gladstone, 11 August 1889, ibid., Add. Ms. 44647:
92–9. The Scottish Home Rule Association was well aware of the need to put
pressure on Gladstone and the Liberals. It urged its members to attend in full
the annual meeting at Dundee on 25 September 1889 in order to impress upon
the Liberal party the strength of the desire for home rule. It reminded its members
that Scotland was anxious for the restoration of legislative powers and that only
"the Federal principle" could solve the difficulty. See Charles Waddie et al to
members of the Scottish Home Rule Association, 1 September 1889, J. Ramsay
MacDonald Papers, PRO 30/69/1187.

41 Hamer was referred to the two schools of thought that developed in the Liberal
party on this issue as the "imperialist" and the "nationalist." See D.A. Hamer, *Liberal
Politics in the Age of Gladstone and Rosebery: A Study in Leadership and Policy* (Oxford:
Clarendon Press 1972), 156–61.

42 Fowler to Rosebery, 29 December 1888, Rosebery Papers, NLS, Ms. 10087: 310–12.

43 Munro-Ferguson to Rosebery, 30 August 1889, Rosebery Papers, NLS, Ms. 10017:
148–9; and Asquith to Rosebery, n.d., quoted in Hamer, *Liberal Politics*, 157.

44 Morley to Harcourt, 12 October 1889, quoted in Hamer, *Liberal Politics*, 159.

45 Childers to Gladstone, 10 October 1889, W.E. Gladstone Papers, BL, Add. Ms.
44132: 294–7; also Childers to Gladstone, 7 October 1889, ibid.: 292–3.

46 Gladstone to Childers, 11 October 1889, copy, ibid.: 298; and Childers to Gladstone,
18 October 1889, ibid.: 299–300.

47 Spencer to Rosebery, 24 November 1889, Rosebery Papers, NLS, Ms. 10062: 43–4;
and H. Campbell-Bannerman to Donald Crawford, 16 November 1889, copy,
Campbell-Bannerman Papers, BL, Add. Ms. 41233: 46–50.

48 Asquith to Spencer, 12 January 1890, quoted in Hamer, *Liberal Politics*, 161.

49 Ibid., 161.

50 3 Hansard (H of C), vol. 341, 19 February 1890, col. 721.

51 Minute Book, 29 May 1886–2 April 1891, of the North Wales Liberal Federation
founded in 1886, NLW, Ms. 21: 171D.

52 *Times*, 7 May 1890.

53 See Charles Waddie in "The New Round Table: Home Rule for Scotland,"
Westminster Review 133 (1890): 57–69, and *Times*, 25 September 1890.

54 John Leng, "Home Rule All Round," *Westminster Review*, 133 (1890): 573–8.

55 3 Hansard (H of C), vol. 341, 19 February 1890, col. 713.

56 William Wallace, "The Limits of Scottish Home Rule," *Scottish Review* (April 1890):
420–30.

57 See 3 Hansard (H of C), vol. 351, 6 March 1891, cols. 440–56; and 4 Hansard (H
of C), vol. 3, 29 April 1892, cols. 1684–1714. On 26 April 1892, Dr Hunter (Aberdeen
North) moved that Scottish legislative business should be done by the Scottish

members of parliament meeting each autumn in Scotland. The House was counted out immediately after the moving of the motion. See 4 Hansard (H of C), vol. 3, 26 April 1892, cols. 1450-52.

58 Coupland, *Welsh and Scottish Nationalism*, 229-30; and for the text see *South Wales Daily News*, 11 January 1892. The measure is also discussed in Edgar L. Chappell, *Wake up! Wales* (London: Foyle's Welsh Co. 1943), 20-30; and in Morgan, *Wales in British Politics*, 109.

59 See Harry Gow, "Home Rule for Scotland: Political Grievances," *Scots Magazine* (June 1891): 35-46; Harry Gow, "Home Rule for Scotland," *Scots Magazine* (July 1891): 108-15. For a critical view see A.N. Cumming, "Scotland and Her Home Rulers," *National Review* (October 1891): 145-9.

60 See R.T. Reid, "Forms of Home Rule," *Contemporary Review* (April 1892): 472-86; and G. Pitt-Lewis, "Forms of Home Rule: A Reply," *Contemporary Review* (June 1892): 779-90; also Harry Gow, "Imperial Federation," *Scots Magazine* (February 1892): 177-88; Harry Gow, "The Scottish Home Rule Bill," *Scots Magazine* (May 1892): 438-50; Herbert Gladstone, "Ireland Blocks the Way," *Nineteenth Century* (June 1892): 899-904; and J. St. Loe Strachey, "Ulster and Home Rule," *Nineteenth Century* (June 1892): 877-84.

61 In the aftermath of the election the Scottish Home Rule Association attempted to organize a joint parliamentary party of the representatives of Scotland, Ireland, and Wales to lobby for home rule all round. See James Reith (Acting Secretary, Scottish Home Rule Association) to Sir Edward Blake, 9 August 1892, Edward Blake Papers, PAC, Reel M 266.

62 Bryce to Blake, 27 and 28 July and 10 October 1892; and Blake to Bryce, 24 October 1892, Edward Blake Papers, PAC, Reel M 263. For a recent treatment of the preparation of Gladstone's second home rule bill see Loughlin, *Gladstone, Home Rule* 250-72.

63 Asquith to Rosebery, 10 February 1893, Rosebery Papers, NLS, Ms. 10001: 29-30; also Asquith to Rosebery, [c. 1892-3], ibid., 31-2; Munro-Ferguson to H. Gladstone, 18 October 1890, Herbert Gladstone Papers, BL, Add. Ms. 46053: 137-9; and Sir Edward Hamilton Diary, 19 October 1891, Edward Hamilton Papers, BL, Add. Ms. 48656.

64 See R.E. Welby, E.W. Hamilton, A. Milner, "Irish Finance," *Most Confidential*, 14 December 1892, Cab. 37/32/51.

65 See Appendix VII: "The Home Rule Bills," in Earl of Dunraven, *The Outlook in Ireland* (London 1907), 291-5; "Mr. Gladstone's 'Home Rule' Bills Compared" in Sir E. Ashmead Bartlett, *Union or Separation: Mr. Gladstone's Home Rule Plan Analysed* (London 1893), 232-70; and Appendix C: "A Comparison of Irish Home Rule Bills," in Joseph V. O'Brien, *William O'Brien and the Course of Irish Politics 1881-1918* (Berkeley: University of California Press 1976), 254-8.

66 4 Hansard (H of C), vol. 8, 13 February 1893, cols. 1241-75.

67 Ibid., 14 February 1893, cols. 1399-1422.

68 Ibid., 17 February 1893, cols. 1717-44.

69 Ibid., vol. 11, 21 April 1893, cols. 968-91.

70 Ibid., 18 April 1893, cols. 616–8 (MacGregor) and 19 April 1893, cols. 682–8 (Leng). Interestingly, both Michael Davitt and John Redmond, leading Irish Nationalist MPs, spoke in favour of federalism. See ibid., 11 April 1893, cols. 41–62 (Davitt) and 13 April 1893, cols. 235–6 (Redmond). Throughout 1893 the *Scots Magazine* enlightened its readership about the historical background to home rule demands, the social, financial, and political problems currently experienced, and the need for devolution of national affairs upon subordinate parliaments, i.e., home rule all round. See Harry Gow, "Home Rule for Scotland: A Retrospect," *Scots Magazine* (January 1893): 116–25; ibid. (February 1893): 224–35; John Romans, "Home Rule for Scotland," *Scots Magazine* (July and August 1893): 149–55 and 183–90.

71 See particularly "A Fresh Puzzle of Home Rule," *National Review* 21 (1893): 841–4. Other earlier articles worth looking at are Henry Jephson, "Passing the Wit of Man," *Nineteenth Century* (February 1893): 189–202; Robert Stout, "An Experiment in Federation and its Lessons," *Nineteenth Century* (February 1893): 203–18; "The New Irish Home-Rule Bill," *Nation* 56, no. 1440 (2 February 1893): 80–1; Frederic Harrison, "Notes on the Home Rule Bill. I. Clause Nine," and J.E. Redmond, "Notes on the Home Rule Bill. II. Mutual Safeguards," *Contemporary Review* (March 1893): 305–15; J. Chamberlain, "A Bill for the Weakening of Great Britain," *Nineteenth Century* (April 1893): 545–58; "The Creeping-On of Federalism," *Spectator*, 15 April 1893, 476; "Imperial Federation and Home Rule," *Economist*, 15 April 1893, 440; and Hugh Bellot, "The Home Rule Bill and the Canadian Constitution," *Westminster Review* (May 1893): 469–75.

72 For a useful critique of Gladstone's initial financial scheme see J.J. Clancy, "The Financial Clauses of the Home Rule Bill," *Fortnightly Review* 59 (1893): 610–19. For a contrary view see Nemo, "The Financial Scheme of the Home Rule Bill," *Contemporary Review* (May 1893): 609–25. Also J.J. Clancy, "The Financial Aspect of Home Rule," *Contemporary Review* (January 1893): 25–36; "The Financial Aspect of Home Rule," *Economist*, 7 January 1893, 4–6; "Mr. Gladstone's New Scheme of Irish Finance," *Economist*, 18 February 1893, 187–8; "Ireland's Contribution to Imperial Expenditure," and "Some Points in Mr. Gladstone's Scheme of Irish Finance," *Economist*, 25 February 1893, 225–7; "More Light on Mr. Gladstone's Scheme of Irish Finance," *Economist*, 25 March 1893, 349–50.

73 See particularly Redmond to Morley, 20 June 1893, John Redmond Papers, NLI, Ms. 15207.

74 For a cogent summary of the dilemma see T. Bryant to Bryce, 28 July 1893, James Bryce Papers, NLI, Ms. 11011.

75 In September 1893 Rosebery advocated devolution for all countries in the United Kingdom. See the *Times*, 21 September 1893.

76 Harry Gow, "Seven Years of Home Rule Legislation," *Scots Magazine* (October 1893): 393–406.

77 "The British Federalist. A New Departure," *Scots Magazine* (December 1893): 65–9.

78 Publicist, "'Federalist' or 'Devolutionist'? A Canadian Example," *Scots Magazine* (January 1894): 183–92.

79 See Bernard Harden, "The Demand for All-Round Home Rule," *Scots Magazine*

(February 1894): 252–9; John Boyd Kinnear, "Union or Home Rule," *Scots Magazine* (March 1894): 363–7; [Edwin Guthrie], "The Victorian Constitution Bill," *Scots Magazine* (June 1894): 68–76; John Romans, "A British Constitution for the Future," *Scots Magazine* (July 1894): 149–54.

80 For the full debate see 4 Hansard (H of C), vol. 22, 3 April 1894, cols. 1287–1315. In June 1893, in the midst of the debate over Irish home rule, Dr Clark had also moved a resolution in favour of a Scottish legislature. He had made it clear he did not wish to repeal the union but simply to relieve parliamentary congestion by devolving powers upon at least a Scottish legislature but also, he hoped, upon ones in England and Wales. The "Imperial Parliament would then be free to do its Imperial work." He asserted that "Every sensible man had come to the conclusion that the only rational outcome of this business was Home Rule all round." The motion was lost 168–150. See 4 Hansard (H of C), vol. 13, 23 June 1893, cols. 1828–64.

81 4 Hansard (H of C), vol. 32, 29 March 1895, cols. 523–60.

82 John Dillon (Mayo, E), a fellow Irish Nationalist, disagreed with Redmond and thought the Irish MPs should support the national concerns in Scotland and Wales. If one supported home rule for Ireland, one had logically to support it for Scotland and Wales. Ibid., cols. 542–4.

83 The Conservatives won 340; Liberal Unionists 71; Liberals 177; and Irish Nationalists 82.

84 See Lloyd to Thomas Gee, 9 October 1895, Thomas Gee Papers, NLW, Mss. 8310D: 501a.

85 D. Lloyd George, "National Self-Government for Wales," *Young Wales* (October 1895): 231–5; also an interview with Lloyd George in the *Methyr Times*, 28 November 1895, entitled "Home Rule all round," in file A/8/1/50, Lloyd George Papers, HLRO. The magazine *Young Wales* was founded in 1895 and lasted to 1904. It contains only one article of length on home rule all round: Lloyd George's of 1895. It quickly became a literary magazine.

86 For a general treatment of the situation in Wales see Morgan, *Wales in British Politics*, 160–5; for the Radical meeting see the *Times*, 25 March 1896; also D. Lloyd George, "The Place of National Self-Government in the Next Liberal Programme," *Young Wales* (January 1897): 11–15.

87 For the debate see 4 Hansard (H of C), vol. 54, 15 March 1898, cols. 1680–744. In 1899 Pirie introduced a Scottish home rule bill similar to the one of 1892. It did not advance beyond first reading. For the bill see *Parliamentary Papers* (hereafter *Parl. Pap.*) (1899), vol. v, 165–74.

88 See Munro Ferguson to Rosebery, 27 July 1895, Rosebery Papers, NLS, Ms. 10019: 1–2; and Martin Conway to Rosebery, 19 September 1895, ibid., Ms. 10106: 16–19.

89 Rosebery to J. Hugh Edwards, 29 October 1895, ibid., Ms. 10131: 28.

90 See "Rosebery Memorandum," 28 July 1898, ibid., Ms. 10177: 118–21. For the background to the Irish Local Government Act see Andrew Gailey, "Unionist Rhetoric and Irish Local Government Reform, 1895–9," *Irish Historical Studies* 24, no. 93 (May 1984): 52–68.

CHAPTER FOUR

1 As H.H. Fowler succinctly put it: "Home Rule at the present time is ... outside practical politics." Herbert Gladstone and Asquith agreed. See H.H. Fowler to H. Gladstone, 12 January 1900, Herbert Gladstone Papers, BL, Add. Ms. 46047: 257; Also H. Gladstone to Campbell-Bannerman, 8 December 1899, *Secret*, ibid., Add. Ms. 45987: 50-1; and Asquith to H. Gladstone, 8 January 1900, ibid., Add. Ms. 45989: 28-9. On the debate within the Liberal party on this issue and particularly the role of the Liberal imperialists see H.C.G. Matthew, *The Liberal Imperialists: The Ideas and Politics of a Post-Gladstonian Elite* (Oxford: Oxford University Press 1973), especially chapter 8; H.V. Emy, *Liberals, Radicals and Social Politics 1892-1914* (Cambridge: Cambridge University Press 1973); H.W. McCready, "Home Rule and the Liberal Party, 1899-1906," *Irish Historical Studies* 13, no. 52 (September 1963): 316-48; Peter D. Jacobson, "Rosebery and Liberal Imperialism, 1899-1903," *Journal of British Studies* 13, no. 1 (November 1973): 83-107; David W. Gutzke, "Rosebery and Ireland, 1898-1903: A Reappraisal," *Bulletin of the Institute of Historical Research* 54, no. 127 (May 1980): 88-98

2 J.A. Murray Macdonald, "The Liberal Party," *Contemporary Review* (May 1901): 639-48.

3 Another writer who gave serious consideration at the turn of the century to the interconnection of imperial federation and home rule, and who was acutely aware of Canadian precedents and analogies, was Bernard Holland. Holland later became one of the founding members of the Pollock Committee, a small organization established in 1903 for the discussion of imperial problems. See particularly B. Holland, *Imperium et Libertas* (London 1901), especially 220-61 and 281-319. For an appreciation of Brassey see Frank Partridge, *T.A.B.: A Memoir of Thomas Allnutt Second Earl Brassey* (London: John Murray 1921); also Hon. T.A. Brassey, *Problems of Empire: Papers and Addresses of the Hon. T.A. Brassey* (London 1904). New editions of this book were published in 1906 and 1913.

4 T.A. Brassey to Rosebery, 19 January 1890, Rosebery Papers, NLS, Ms. 10088: 130-1.

5 See particularly a speech at Epsom in 1902 entitled "Imperial Government," Brassey, *Problems of Empire* (1906), 1-13; and one at Pokesdown, Bournemouth, on 8 November 1898, Brassey, *Problems of Empire* (1904), 49 - 51.

6 T.A. Brassey, "Federal Government for the United Kingdom and the Empire," *Nineteenth Century* (August 1901): 190-201.

7 For the above see Partridge, *T.A.B.*, 143-5 and 218; *Times*, 20 January 1902; Brassey to the editor, *Times*, 3 March 1902; and Rosebery to Brassey, 18 January 1901, Rosebery Papers, NLS, Ms. 10131: 265.

8 Brassey, *Problems of Empire* (1906), 30-48.

9 Brassey soon afterwards, on 20 January 1903, gave an excellent paper to the Fellows of the Royal Statistical Society on "The Finance of Federal Government for the United Kingdom," one of the first sustained looks at the problem by a publicist. Ibid., 49-72.

10 Few writers addressed the issue of devolution in these years but articles worth looking at are G.R. Benson, "Federal Government for the United Kingdom," *Contemporary Review* (February 1902): 214–20; H. Drummond Wolff, "Home Rule without Separation," *Nineteenth Century* (June 1903) 918–23; Dudley S.A. Cosby, "Home Rule and the King's Visit to Ireland," *Westminster Review* (July 1903): 37–47; and Arnold White, "What Ireland Really Wants," *Fortnightly Review* 82 (1904): 835–45.

11 For a more detailed treatment see Lord Dunraven, *Past Times and Pastimes*, 2 (London 1902); also J.V. O'Brien, *William O'Brien and the Course of Irish Politics 1881–1918* (Berkeley: University of California Press 1976).

12 Dunraven to W. O'Brien, 26 October 1903, William O'Brien Papers, NLI, Ms. 8554/2. For Dunraven's early work with O'Brien see J.V. O'Brien, *William O'Brien*, 143ff.

13 Earl of Dunraven, *The Outlook in Ireland: The Case for Devolution and Conciliation* (Dublin 1907), 271–3.

14 F.S.L. Lyons, "The Irish Unionist party and the Devolution Crisis of 1904–05," *Irish Historical Studies* 6, no. 21 (March 1948): 2–3.

15 Ibid.: 7–9. MacDonnell wrote to Alice Stopford-Green on 1 September 1904 saying he had launched his scheme before the Liberals came back to power because he thought it would have a better chance of being supported by moderate Unionists and Nationalists. See A. MacDonnell to Alice Stopford-Green, 1 September 1904, Alice Stopford-Green Papers, NLI, Ms. 15089/4. Earlier that year MacDonnell had already acknowledged that "the question of greater financial freedom for Ireland ... is the kernel of the question." A. MacDonnell to Alice Stopford-Green, 4 July 1904, ibid.

16 The report is printed in full in Dunraven, *The Outlook in Ireland*, Appendix 1, 273–80; see also 137–76. Dunraven refers to the process of preparation in *Past Times*, 2: 26–8. See also Lyons, "The Irish Unionist Party and the Devolution Crisis," and J.W. Mackail and Guy Wyndham, *Life and Letters of George Wyndham*, 2 vols. (London: Hutchinson 1925), 91–3.

17 Dunraven, *Past Times*, 2: 28.

18 Wyndham's letter is quoted in full in Mackail and Wyndham, *George Wyndham*, 2: 93–5.

19 For the aftermath of the affair see Lyons, "The Irish Unionist Party and the Devolution Crisis"; Mackail and Wyndham, *George Wyndham*; Blanche E.C. Dugdale, "The Wyndham-MacDonnell Imbroglio," *Quarterly Review* 258, no. 511 (January 1932): 15–39; Dunraven, *Past Times*, 30–8, and a memorandum by Sir Anthony MacDonnell dated 8 February 1905, Appendix III, ibid., 186–92.

20 J.A.M. Macdonald to the editor, *Times*, 15, 19, and 21 September 1904; also *Times* editorial, 19 September 1904.

21 T.A. Brassey to A. MacDonnell, 4 January [1903], Anthony MacDonnell Papers, Bodleian, Ms. C350: 19–20.

22 Brassey to the editor, *Times*, 16 September 1904.

23 Dunraven to MacDonnell, 21 January 1905, A. MacDonnell Papers, Bodleian, Ms. C350: 116-21. A few days later he wrote: "Legislative devolution can easily be defended. The difficulty will arise over the Financial Council. People will want to know what amount of control we propose to give it." Dunraven to MacDonnell, 29 January 1905, ibid., 122-5.

24 This synopsis of Dunraven's position as of 1905-7 is based on *Ireland and Scotland under the Unions. Failure and Success: A Comparative Study* (London 1905), 16-20; *The Crisis in Ireland: An Account of the Present Condition of Ireland and Suggestions toward Reform* (London 1905); *Devolution in the British Empire: The Case for Ireland* (London 1906); *The Outlook in Ireland: The Case for Devolution and Conciliation* (Dublin 1907), 168-72, 237. For a comment, not unfavourable, upon Dunraven's and the Irish Reform Association's ideas see James Fitzgerald Kenney, "Devolution and the Future in Irish Politics, *"Fortnightly Review* 83 (1905): 671-80. For a hostile response see Rathmore, "Devolution," *National Review* 46 (1905-6): 814-22. For an anonymous but nevertheless devastating critique of Dunraven's ideas see "The Real Needs of Ireland," *Quarterly Review* 205 (1906): 561-85. Arthur Samuel thought the Irish Reform Association's scheme "a preposterous proposal." See Arthur Samuel to the editor, *Times*, 26 December 1905.

25 Brassey continued to speak on behalf of the Irish Reform Association in late 1905 and early 1906 at meetings in Dublin, Belfast, and Londonderry. He also continued his campaign for "subordinate legislatures" in the *Times*. See Brassey to the editor, *Times*, 16 January and 14 August 1906.

26 See H.W. McCready, "Home Rule and the Liberal Party, 1899-1906," *Irish Historical Studies* 13, no. 52 (September 1963): 316-38; A.C. Hepburn, "The Irish Council Bill and the Fall of Sir Anthony MacDonnell, 1906-07," *Irish Historical Studies* 17, no. 68 (September 1971): 470-98. At this time Michael Davitt informed Redmond that he supported home rule on the Canadian model, implying that a simple devolution scheme would be inadequate for him. See M. Davitt to J. Redmond, 14 January 1906, Redmond Papers, NLI, Ms. 15179.

27 See A. MacDonnell to J. Bryce, 3 February 1906, James Bryce Papers, NLI, Ms. 11012/2.

28 See Hepburn, "The Irish Council Bill," 473. Sir Charles Dilke had recommended "a central board scheme all round" on 7 November 1905. See A.C. Hepburn, "Liberal Policies and Nationalist Politics in Ireland, 1905-10" (PH D, University of Kent at Canterbury, 1968), 47.

29 MacDonnell to Bryce, 11 February 1906, James Bryce Papers, NLI, Ms. 11012/2.

30 Report of Redmond's speech at Athlone, *Weekly Freeman's Journal.* 13 October 1906.

31 Redmond to Dillon, 8 October 1906, cited in Margaret Banks, *Edward Blake: A Canadian Statesman in Irish Politics* (Toronto: University of Toronto Press 1957), 309.

32 Hepburn, "The Irish Council Bill," 477. At the end of September, Lord Loreburn had written to Bryce about the possible reception the scheme would receive from Redmond and Dillon: "To my mind the acceptance of the scheme (with no doubt some emendations) will depend on whether we have the pluck and wisdom to say

that it is intended as a first step leading to a general system of delegating business both administrative and legislative from the House of Commons and London to subordinate legislatures in the three capitals. That is I am more than ever persuaded the true course and the only course." Loreburn to Bryce, 30 September 1906, James Bryce Papers, NLI, Ms. 11014/1.

33 Redmond to Edward Blake, 13 November 1906, enclosing the Memorandum, Edward Blake Papers, PAC, Reel M 266.

34 Undated and unsigned "Private and Confidential Memorandum on the Council Bill," Redmond Papers, NLI, Ms. 15248 (1).

35 Blake to Redmond, 6 December 1906, Edward Blake Papers, PAC, Reel M 266,

36 Redmond to Bryce, 3 December 1906, enclosing "Memorandum on the Constitution of the Proposed New Administrative Body to be set up in Ireland," signed by Redmond, Dillon and O'Connor, James Bryce Papers, NLI, Ms. 11014(4).

37 Dillon to Morley, 18 December 1906, copy, ibid., Ms. 11014(4).

38 The above paragraph is based on Hepburn, "The Irish Council bill," 479–87. For the details of the bill see "Irish Council Bill" (Bill 182) in *Parl. Pap.* (1907), vol. II, 487–506.

39 4 Hansard (H of C), vol. 174, 7 May 1907, cols. 78–103.

40 Ibid., cols. 103–12.

41 Ibid., cols. 112–30.

42 "Ireland – a Nation," *Edinburgh Review* (July 1907): 248–64. See also "Devolution and Home Rule," *Spectator*, 19 January 1907; "Home-Rule and Devolution," *Spectator*, 9 February 1907; L.A. Atherley-Jones, "The Irish Policy of the Government," *Nineteenth Century* (March 1907): 501–8; Walter Long, "A Note on the Irish Question," *Fortnightly Review* (May 1907): 767–72.

43 See the *Times*, 30 May 1907, for the meeting of the Irish Reform Association; also Dunraven, "The Irish Council Bill," *Nineteenth Century* (June 1907): 1033–46.

44 Hepburn, "The Irish Council Bill," 487–91.

45 Birrell to Campbell-Bannerman, 24 May 1907, Campbell-Bannerman Papers, BL, Add. Ms. 41239: 250.

46 For the memorandum see H. Pilkington (Patrick Petterras), "Irish Policy and the Conservatives," *Nineteenth Century* (December 1909): 949–64.

47 See particularly the *Scottish Patriot*, May, June, and October 1904; and February and April 1905.

48 The letter, dated 1 March 1906, was signed by John Romans, the chairman, and C. Waddie, the honorary secretary of the Scottish Home Rule Association. See the *Times*, 5 March 1906.

49 The bill was introduced by Duncan Pirie (Aberdeen, N) and supported by, among other, Murray Macdonald, Keir Hardie, and William O'Brien. See 4 Hansard (H of C), vol, 158, 14 June 1906, col. 1165. For the bill see *Parl. Pap* (1906), vol. II, 591–602.

50 See 4 Hansard (H of C), vol. 189, 26 May 1908, cols. 968–72. For the bill see *Parl. Pap.* . (1908), vol. II, 721–32. It was also printed in the *Thistle* (September 1908):

26–30. For a critique of the House of Lords and of English apathy toward home rule see "The Scottish Home Rule Bill," *Thistle* (August 1908): 11–12; also "Home Rule for Scotland," *Thistle* (October (1908): 45–7. For the sensitivity of Scottish feelings and the antipathy toward certain Englishmen and their arrogant, blinkered assumptions see "Mr. Walter Long's Insult to Scotland," *Thistle* (January 1909): 93–5, and "The Decadence of the Saxon-English," *Thistle* (April 1909): 133–6.

51 "The Young Scots Society and Home Rule," *Thistle* (November 1909): 244–5.

CHAPTER FIVE

1 Quoted in Denis Gwynn, *The Life of John Redmond* (London: George G. Harrap 1932), 169.

2 T.P. O'Connor to J. Dillon, 31 January 1910, John Dillon Papers, Ms. 6740: 164, quoted in Ronan Fanning, "The Irish Policy of Asquith's Government and the Cabinet Crisis of 1910," in Art Cosgrove and Donald McCartney, eds., *Studies in Irish History Presented to R. Dudley Edwards* (Dublin: C. Smythe 1979), 279–303.

3 For a detailed and illuminating analysis of the discussions of February–April 1910, see Fanning, ibid. For a contemporary and representative Unionist view see J. Ellis Barker, "The Parliamentary Position and the Irish Party," *Nineteenth Century* (February 1910): 238–56.

4 For the founding of the Round Table movement and for its various activities see John Kendle, *The Round Table Movement and Imperial Union* (Toronto: University of Toronto Press 1975); also J.E. Kendle, "The Round Table Movement and 'Home Rule All Round'," *Historical Journal* 11, no. 2 (July 1968): 332–53.

5 Grey to Sir Wilfrid Laurier, 12 February 1907, Earl Grey Papers, UD, Box 250.

6 For a full discussion of the points in this paragraph see Kendle, "The Round Table Movement and 'Home Rule All Round'."

7 Grey to L. Curtis, 14 December 1909, copy, Grey Papers, UD, Box 205.

8 Grey to Balfour, 23 February 1910, Arthur Balfour Papers, BL, Add. Ms. 49697. Grey wrote in a similar vein to J.L. Garvin, the editor of the *Observer*. See Grey to Garvin, 20 February 1910, Garvin Papers, HRC. Garvin had already considered the matter and had written in January to J.J. Sandars, Balfour's secretary, asking: "Would Mr. Redmond or Messrs. O'Brien and Healy accept the Quebec or Ontario model. If so the question certainly ought to be discussed in order that we might have some better idea whether the Empire's interests are likely to find a solid footing in this direction." A.M. Gollin, *The Observer and J.L. Garvin 1908–1914: A Study in a Great Editorship* (London: Oxford University Press 1960), 172–3.

9 Grey to G. Wrong, 22 February 1910, George Wrong Papers, UTL.

10 Grey to Brassey, 5 March 1910, copy W. Long Papers, WRO, Ms. 947/129. There is also a copy in the Jebb Papers: see enclosure in Grey to Jebb, 14 March 1910, Richard Jebb Papers, ICS.

11 Grey to Jebb, 14 March 1910, ibid.

12 Jebb to Grey, 24 March 1910, copy, ibid.

13 Joseph V. O'Brien, *William O'Brien and the Course of Irish Politics: 1881–1918* (Berkeley: University of California Press 1976), 197.

14 Frewen to Churchill, 31 March [1910], Moreton Frewen Papers, LC, Box 30; also Frewen to Garvin, 4 April 1910, Garvin Papers, HRC.

15 Grey to Frewen, 2 April 1910, Frewen Papers, LC, Box 30.

16 Grey to a friend in England, May 1910, copy, enclosed in Frewen to Churchill, 31 March [1910], ibid.

17 For a detailed account of the financial and organizational fortunes of Frewen, O'Brien, and Dunraven see Alan J. Ward, "Frewen's Anglo-American Campaign for Federalism, 1910–21," *Irish Historical Studies* 15, no. 59 (March 1967): 256–75.

18 O'Brien to Frewen, 25 May 1910, Frewen Papers, LC, Box 30. See also Tim Healy to Frewen, 12 June 1910, ibid., in which Healy expressed support for a federal resolution of the Irish question.

19 Brassey to O'Brien, 3 and 6 April 1910, copies, Michael Davitt Papers, NLI, Ms. 913.

20 Like so many others Brassey used the terms federal, devolution, and home rule all round interchangeably without recognizing the differences entailed.

21 Brassey to W. Long, 4 April 1910, W. Long Papers, WRO, Ms. 947/460.

22 Milner to Balfour, 17 April 1910, A. Balfour Papers, BL, Add. Ms. 49697: 153–64.

23 The representatives were: Liberals: Asquith, Lloyd George, Augustine Birrell, and Lord Crewe. Unionists: Balfour, Lansdowne, Cawdor, and Austen Chamberlain.

24 See K.O. Morgan, *Rebirth of a Nation: Wales 1880–1980* (Oxford: Clarendon Press 1982), 19.

25 "Denial of Home Rule to Scotland and Wales," *Thistle* (January 1910): 4–7.

26 For the manifesto see the *Manchester Guardian*, 5 August 1910; also "The Scottish Home Rule Manifesto,," *Thistle* (September 1910): 142–5. At about this time, 25 July 1910, Augustine Birrell spoke in favour of federalism in the United Kingdom and the empire at the Eighty Club. See "The Mystery of the Conference: Mr. Birrell and 'Federalism'," *Observer*, 31 July 1910.

27 E.T. John to the editor, *Manchester Guardian*, 8 August 1910. John elaborated upon his devolutionary ideas in a further letter published in the Bangor *Chronicle* in early September. See E.T. John to the editor, 27 August 1910, *Chronicle* (Bangor), 2 September 1910.

28 This letter campaign was organized and administered by Evans. See Beriah Evans to E.T. John, 16, 25 and 31 August, 3 September and 15 October 1910, E.T. John Papers, NLW.

29 E.T. John to H.A. Watt [August 1910], ibid.

30 W.H. Cowan to E.T. John, 16 August 1910, ibid.

31 H.G. Reid to E.T. John, 9 August 1910, ibid.

32 H.G. Reid to E.T. John, 19 August 1910, ibid.

33 W.H. Cowan to E.W. Davies, 27 August 1910, copy, ibid.

34 R. Munro Ferguson to E.T. John, 1 September 1910, ibid; also E.T. John to Munro Ferguson, 2 September 1910, copy, ibid.

35 E.T. John to R.J. James, 20 September 1910, ibid.

36 K.O. Morgan, *Wales in British Politics 1868–1922* (Cardiff: University of Wales Press 1963), 256.

37 For the details see R.C.K. Ensor, *England 1870–1914* (Oxford: Clarendon Press 1936), 422–3; also J.R. Fanning, "The Unionist Party and Ireland, 1906–10," *Irish Historical Studies* 16, no. 58 (September 1966): 147–71.

38 For this episode see Gollin, *The Observer and J.L. Garvin*, 200–1; the quote is from Harold Harmsworth to Elibank, 29 July 1910 cited in ibid., 200.

39 *Observer*, 31 July 1910. Garvin had been in correspondence since April with Moreton Frewen, the advocate of federation and a supporter of William O'Brien's All for Ireland League. He was well aware of federalist plans. See Frewen to Garvin, 4 April and 14 June 1910, Garvin Papers, HRC.

40 Ian Malcolm, "'Home Rule All Round'," *Nineteenth Century* (November 1910): 791–9.

41 Quoted in ibid., 792.

42 See ibid., 795, and "The Irish Nationalists and Home Rule," *Thistle* (November 1910): 180–2.

43 Malcolm, "'Home Rule All Round'," 797.

44 W. O'Brien to Frewen, 4 October 1910, Frewen Papers, LC.

45 See Frewen to Balfour, 21 September 1910, copy, ibid; and Frewen to Garvin, 27 October [1910], Garvin Papers, HRC.

46 Frewen to Balfour, 21 September 1910, Frewen Papers, LC.

47 Earl Grey to G. Prothero, 12 October 1910, copy, Garvin Papers, HRC.

48 The memorandum dated 28 September 1910 was enclosed in F.S. Oliver to Balfour, 11 October 1910, A. Balfour Papers, BL, Add. Ms. 49861: 1–25. For Oliver's association with the Round Table see Kendle, *The Round Table Movement*; and for his background and political leanings see D.G. Boyce and J.O. Stubbs, "F.S. Oliver, Lord Selborne and Federalism," *Journal of Imperial and Commonwealth History* 5, no. 1 (October 1976): 53–81.

49 Somewhat surprisingly, Balfour underlined "*visionary*" and noted "Visionary not in a bad sense. I see this vision and believe in it."

50 See C/3/14/8 in Lloyd George Papers; the memorandum is printed in Sir Charles Petrie, *Life and Letters of the Rt. Hon. Sir Austen Chamberlain*, 2 vols. (London: Cassell 1939), 1: 381–8. For Lloyd George's scheme see G.R. Searle, *The Quest for National Efficiency: A Study in British Politics and Political Thought, 1899–1914* (Oxford: Basil Blackwell 1971), 170–204.

51 Petrie, *Sir Austen Chamberlain*, 1: 286–7; also A. Chamberlain to his wife, 14 October 1910, A. Chamberlain Papers, UBL, AC/6/1/80; and Gollin, *The Observer and J.L. Garvin*, 20.

52 "Lloyd George Memorandum," 29 October 1910, Elibank Papers, NLS, Ms. 8802: 123–7.

53 *Observer*, 16 October 1910.

54 Alfred Lyttleton to Balfour, 16 October 1910, A. Balfour Papers, BL, Add. Ms. 49775: 65–6.

55 Garvin to Balfour, 17 October 1910, copy, Garvin Papers, HRC. Garvin was more specific in a letter to Austen Chamberlain: "I wanted ... to get into such a position that if the Conference broke down *we* could take up federalism at once in our own way, fit it beautifully into the rest of our policy (on fleet, tariff & Imperial Union) & oppose it to the *Gladstonianism* which this government would then be compelled to adopt." Garvin to A. Chamberlain, 25 October 1910, copy, ibid.; also Garvin to A. Chamberlain, 20 October 1910, ibid. Chamberlain himself was less opposed to the federal idea now that he realized its connection with this father's proposals of the 1880s but he was not prepared to advocate federalism publicly. See A. Chamberlain to F.E. [Smith], 21 October 1910, quoted in Petrie, *Sir Austen Chamberlain*, 1: 259–60.

56 J.J. Sanders to Balfour, 18 October 1910, A.Balfour Papers, BL, Add. Ms. 49767: 7–10.

57 Balfour to Garvin, 22 October 1910, Garvin Papers, HRC.

58 "The Conference and the Larger Settlement: Ulster and Empire," *Observer*, 30 October 1910; also "The Conference and the Larger Settlement: The True Basis of Federalism," *Observer*, 23 October 1910.

59 See the *Times*, 20, 22, 24, 26, 28, and 31 October and 2 November 1910. These articles were later published in book form under the title *Federalism and Home Rule* (London 1910) and, with the Round Table members in mind, were dedicated to "Young Men who see Visions."

60 Oliver admired Garvin's article of 30 October: Oliver to Garvin, 31 October 1910, Garvin Papers, HRC.

61 Garvin to Balfour, 25 October 1910, ibid.

62 See Sanders to Garvin, 31 October and 5 November 1910, ibid.

63 "The Last Phase of the Conference. Something or Nothing," *Observer*, 6 November 1910.

64 Lord Hugh Cecil to the editor, *Times*, 28 October 1910.

65 L.S. Amery to the editor, *Times*, 1 November 1910.

66 Earl Grey to Garvin, 1 November 1910, Garvin Papers, HRC.

67 Milner to Balfour, 5 November 1910, A. Balfour Papers, BL, Add. Ms. 49697: 153–64.

68 See Kendle, "The Round Table Movement and 'Home Rule All Round'."

69 Frewen to Redmond, 17 November 1910, Frewen Papers, LC; Frewen to Bourke Cockran, 18 November [1910], W.B. Cockran Papers, NYPL; Grey to Frewen, 14 December 1910, Michael MacDonagh Papers, NLI, Ms. 11447; and Dunraven to Grey, 27 December 1910, copy, Frewen Papers, LC.

70 Brassey to O'Brien, 18 November [1910], M. Davitt Papers, NLI, Ms. 913; also Brassey to Garvin, 18 November [1910], Garvin Papers, HRC; and *Times*, 30 November 1910.

71 Haldane to Grey, 26 December 1910, FO 800/102, ff. 133–6.

CHAPTER SIX

1 The memorandum is dated 2/11/10 and is in Cab. 37/104/56.
2 Dunraven to Garvin, 19 January 1911, Garvin Papers, HRC.
3 Frewen to Grey, 30 March 1911, copy, Frewen Papers, LC.
4 Dunraven to Frewen, [March 1911], enclosed in ibid.
5 St. Loe Strachey to Dicey, 19 May 1911, St. Loe Strachey Papers, HLRO, S/5/5/20. Also Dicey to Strachey, 14 June 1911, ibid., S/5/5/21.
6 Frewen's resignation was ostensibly to give Tim Healy an opportunity to return to the House but, in fact, was a consequence of O'Brien's support of the parliament act and Frewen's own unwillingness to split the O'Brienites over his distaste for an assault on the constitution. See Ward, "Frewen's Anglo-American Campaign for Federalism, 1910-20." For Frewen's speech see 5 Hansard (H of C), vol, 24, 24 April 1911, cols. 1410-17.
7 Walter Murray to E.T. John, 11 April 1911, and E.T. John to J.M. Crossthwaite, 14 June 1911, E.T. John Papers, NLW, 121 and 143.
8 Frewen to Walter Long, 25 August 1911 copy, Frewen Papers, LC; and Frewen to Midleton, 7 January 1912, copy, ibid.
9 Dicey to St. Loe Strachey, 12 July 1911, Strachey Papers, HLRO, S/5/5/21.
10 Dicey to Walter Long, 4 July 1911, Private, W. Long Papers, BL, Add. Ms. 62406.
11 Salisbury to Selborne, 12 September 1911, Selborne Papers, Bodleian, Ms. 6: 116-21.
12 F.S. Oliver to Geoffrey Robinson, 27 September 1911, F.S. Oliver Papers, NLS, Mss. Acc. 7726/84.
13 Milner to Oliver, 3 October 1911, ibid., Mss. Acc. 7726/86.
14 Milner to Oliver, 13 October 1911, ibid.
15 See E.T. John, *Home Rule for Wales: Addresses to "Young Wales"* (Bangor 1912), v, and "Federal Home Rule," 1-15. Also E.T. John, "Wales and Self-Government," *Wales*, 1: 23-5, and E.T. John, "Federal Home Rule in Relationship to Wales," *Wales* 1: 381-5.
16 "Federal Home Rule," 1-2.
17 Ibid., 5.
18 "Automatic Home Rule All Round," *Thistle* (November 1911): 172.
19 A similar bill was introduced the following year on 20 March 1912. See 5 Hansard (H of C), vol. 29, 16 August 1911, cols. 1929-34 and *Parl. Pap.* (1911), vol. 11, "Government of Scotland Bill (Bill 353)," 575-87; also *Parl. Pap.* (1912-13), vol. 11, "Government of Scotland Bill (Bill 96)," 663-75, and 5 Hansard (H of C), vol. 34, 20 March 1912, cols. 1489-90. Also "Scottish Home Rule," *Thistle* (May 1911): 80-1; "Introduction of the Scottish Home Rule Bill," *Thistle* (September 1911): 150-1; and "The Government of Scotland Bill," *Thistle* (October 1911): 164-5. See also R.C. Munro Ferguson, "Why Scotland Wants Home Rule," *Home Rule Notes* (9 December 1911), 29-31.

20 Basil Williams, ed. *Home Rule Problems* (London 1911).

21 J.A. Murray Macdonald, "The Constitutional Controversy and Federal Home Rule," *Nineteenth Century* (July 1911): 33-43.

22 Earl of Dunraven, *The Legacy of Past Years: A Study of Irish History* (London 1911), 268, 271, 272-3.

23 Dunraven wanted the Unionist party to adopt the federal idea. See Dunraven, "The Need for a Re-Creation of Our Constitution," *Nineteenth Century* (September 1911): 401-13; and Dunraven, "The Need for a Constitutional Party," *Nineteenth Century* (November 1911): 981-92. One writer who wondered if the "federalists" really understood federalism was J.A.R. Marriott. See his "The Key of the Empire," *Nineteenth Century* (November 1911): 805-19. Another who confused the terms "home rule all round" and "federalism" was Fabian Ware, "The United Kingdom and the Empire," *Nineteenth Century* (December 1911): 1178-89. Of particular interest in 1911 was the publication of Erskine Childers's *The Framework of Home Rule*. He admitted that home rule all round was in the air but he did not think it a practical issue because Englishmen simply had not thought about it for England. He also thought the term "federal" applied to an Irish home rule bill was meaningless given the disparity in population, resources, and power between Great Britain and Ireland: "In the case of Ireland we have first to dissolve an unnatural union, and then to revive an old right to autonomy, before we can reach a healthy Federal Union." See Erskine Childers, *The Framework of Home Rule* (London 1911), 201. It was in this book that Childers raised the dominion analogy and suggested colonial self-government or dominion status for Ireland.

24 Simon Rosenbaum, ed., *Against Home Rule: The Case for the Union* (Port Washington, NY: Kennikat Press 1970).

25 Ibid., 81-106.

26 Ibid., 130-52; see also 5 Hansard (H of C), vol. 37, 30 April 1912, cols. 1783-4.

27 L.S. Amery, *The Case against Home Rule* (London 1912), 73-81.

28 For a parallel line of argument although with a slightly different aim in mind see Erskine Childers, *The Form and Purpose of Home Rule* (Dublin 1912). The Scots continued to press for home rule for Scotland and to have federal home rule meetings up to the eve of the introduction of the 1912 bill. See the *Thistle*, February and March 1912, and *Home Rule Notes*, 10 February and 9 March 1912.

29 Asquith to the King, 20 January 1911, copy. H.H. Asquith Papers, Bodleian, Ms. 6: 1-2.

30 See P. Jalland, "A Liberal Chief Secretary and the Irish Question: Augustine Birrell, 1907-1914," *Historical Journal* 19, no. 2 (1976): 421-51. The most comprehensive treatments of Liberal deliberations, 1910-14, are P. Jalland, *The Liberals and Ireland: The Ulster Question in British Politics to 1914* (Brighton: Harvester Press 1980) and P. Jalland, "United Kingdom Devolution 1910-14: Political Panacea or Tactical Diversion?," *English Historical Review* 94, no. 373 (October 1979), 757-85.

31 Sir Edward Grey to Earl Grey, 27 January 1911, Sir Edward Grey Papers, FO

800/107/381-2. See also Lady Selborne to Curtis, 14 January [1911], Curtis Papers, Bodleian, in which she describes a lunch with Earl Grey during which he talked enthusiastically about federal ideas.

32 "Home Rule or Federalism," *Times*, 27 January 1911.

33 W.S.C., "Devolution," 24 February 1911, Cab. 37/105.

34 D. Lloyd George, "Home Rule Suggestion," 27 February 1911, Lloyd George Papers, HLRO, C/12/2/8.

35 W.S.C., "Devolution," 1 March 1911, Cab. 37/105.

36 See untitled cabinet paper signed by C.P.I. and dated 9 March 1911, Cab. 37/105.

37 Ilbert to Bryce, 19 March 1911, Bryce Papers, Bodleian, Ms. 14: 15–18.

38 C.P. Scott Diary, 20 July 1911, C.P. Scott Papers, BL, Add. Ms. 50901: 21–2.

39 C.P. Scott Diary, 6–8 September 1911, ibid., Ms. 50901:38.

40 C.P. Scott Diary, 21 June 1911, ibid., Ms. 50901: 17–20.

41 Pease diary, 2: 28, 16 August 1911, Gainford Papers, quoted in Jalland, "United Kingdom Devolution," 767; see also Jalland, "A Liberal Chief Secretary," 421–51.

42 H. Samuel to H. Gladstone, 15 September 1911, H. Gladstone Papers, BL, Add. Ms. 45992: 263. See draft bill 1 August 1911, Lloyd George Papers, HLRO, C/19/2/2.

43 For the Primrose Report see *Parl. Pap.* (1912), Cd. 6153, "Irish Finance. Report by the Committee on Irish Finance" (April 1912).

44 For Samuel's memoranda see Herbert Samuel, "Irish Finance, 6, 13, 14, 22 (two), 23 November and 4 December 1911, Cab. 37/108. The shifting details and various arguments can be followed in P. Jalland, "Irish Home-rule Finance. A Neglected Dimension of the Irish Question, 1910–14," *Irish Historical Studies* 23, no. 91 (May 1983): 233–53. Also useful are R.J. Lawrence, *The Government of Northern Ireland: Public Finance and Public Services 1921–64* (Oxford: Clarendon Press 1965), 7–16; and J.I. Cook, "Financial Relations between the Exchequers of the United Kingdom and Northern Ireland" in D.G. Neill, ed., *Devolution of Government: The Experiment in Northern Ireland* (London: Allen & Unwin 1953), 18–34.

45 John Burns Diary, 7 December 1911, J. Burns Papers, BL, Add. Ms. 46333: 208.

46 See C.P. Scott Diary, 22 July 1911, C.P. Scott Papers, BL, Add. Ms. 50901: 28; and William O'Brien to Asquith, 4 November 1911, Asquith Papers, Bodleian, 36: 7–10.

47 See C.P. Scott Diary, 22 January 1912, C.P. Scott Papers, BL, Add. Ms. 50901: 66–67; Pease diary, 2: 31, 25 January 1912, cited in Jalland, "United Kingdom Devolution,"; and J. Redmond and J. Dillon, "Memorandum on Clauses of the Home Rule Bill," 29 January 1912, Cab. 37/109/8. Lord Loreburn, for one, remained sympathetic to home rule all round. See Loreburn to O'Brien, n.d., M. MacDonagh Papers, NLI, Ms. 11439(1).

48 John Burns Diary, 5 February 1912, J. Burns Papers, BL, Add. Ms. 46334: 46.

49 For the final stages and the preparation of the home rule bill see Jalland, *The Liberals and Ireland*, 37–49, also Jalland, "Irish Home-rule Finance," 233–53. See also Augustine Birrell, "Memorandum," 4 March 1912, Cab. 37/110; Herbert Samuel, "Irish Finance," 5 March 1912, Cab. 37/110/39; Herbert Samuel, "Irish

Finance: Suggested Modifications in the Scheme," 25 March 1912, Cab. 37/105; *Parl. Pap.* (1912), Cd. 6154. Government of Ireland Bill. Outline of Financial Provisions; and *Parl. Pap.* (1912), Cd. 6486. Further Memorandum on Financial Provisions.

50 5 Hansard (H of C), vol. 36, 11 April 1912, cols. 1399–1426.

51 For the bill itself see "Government of Ireland Bill," 16 April 1912, in *Parl. Pap.* (1912–13), vol. 11, 505–82; also Geoffrey J. Hand, "The Parliament Contemplated by the Irish Home Rule Act of 1914," in *Studies Presented to the International Commission for the History of Representative and Parliamentary Institutions* (London 1968), 371–88.

52 See 5 Hansard (H of C), vol. 36, 11 April 1912, cols. 1499–1500 (Lawson); vol. 37, 15 April 1912, cols. 42–4 (Balfour); vol. 37, 30 April 1912, cols. 1772–88 (Amery), cols. 1794–1805 (Cave). See also Amery to Jebb, 21 May 1912, Jebb Papers, ICS, in which he claimed: "I am a very strong federalist, but ... you cannot carry out federalism merely by letting the existing system break down. You must have a practical federal spirit in the air."

53 See particularly 5 Hansard (H of C), vol. 37, 2 May 1912, cols. 2126–30 (Munro Ferguson); and vol. 38, 7 May 1912, cols. 334–41 (Pirie). E.T. John also spoke in favour of the bill despite its defects. See vol. 38, 9 May 1912, cols. 660–5 (John).

54 "Pacificus" to the editor, *Times*, 30 April 1912.

55 See also "Pacificus" to the editor, *Times*, 8 and 9 May 1912, in which he drew attention to the neglect of Ulster in the bill and outlined the consequences that might arise. Horace Plunkett, who preferred "Colonial Home Rule" to either federalism or the *status quo*, thought the bill an improvement over those of 1886 and 1893. Plunkett Diary, 11 April 1912, Plunkett Papers, PH. St. Loe Strachey, in the *Spectator*, agreed that the reason Asquith had not brought in a federal bill was "his Irish masters do not want Federalism they want Nationalism." See "Federalism True and False," *Spectator*, 20 April 1912, 611–12.

56 J.A.R. Marriott, "The Third Edition of Home Rule," *Nineteenth Century* (May 1912): 834–5.

57 J.H. Morgan, "Home Rule and Federalism," *Nineteenth Century* (June 1912): 1230–41.

58 See also J.H. Morgan, "The Constitution: A Commentary," in J.H. Morgan, ed., *The New Irish Constitution: An Exposition and Some Arguments* (London 1912), 3–49.

59 For federal and home rule activity in Scotland in early 1912 see the *Thistle*, February and March 1912, and *Home Rule Notes*, 10 February 1912.

60 One federalist more optimistic than most was Murray Macdonald who believed the bill was "a real instalment of a general system of federation," although he recognized that the financial scheme was inordinately complex and might prove the most difficult problem to resolve. J.A. Murray Macdonald, "The Home Rule Bill," *Contemporary Review* (May 1912): 618–24.

61 See "Deputation from Scottish Liberal Members of Parliament to the Rt. Hon. H.H. Asquith," Asquith Papers, Bodleian, Ms. 89: 3–12; so also "Home Rule All Round: The First Step," *Thistle* (May 1912): 74–6, and *Home Rule Notes*, 11 May 1912, 27.

62 See "Government of the United Kingdom Bill," 3 July 1912 in *Parl. Pap.* (1912–13), vol. 11, 677–708.

63 A.V. Dicey found the financial clauses "very difficult to understand" and suggested to Walter Long, soon after the bill was introduced, that the Unionists have an accountant draw up a statement as to the implications of the provisions. A.V. Dicey to Long, 24 April 1912, Long Papers, BL, Add. Ms. 62406.

64 On this issue see Herbert Samuel, "Variation of Customs Duties in Ireland," Cab. 37/112/116. Redmond's reaction and Birrell's explanation of the cabinet decision are in Redmond to Birrell, 20 November 1912, Redmond Papers, NLI, Ms. 15169(3), and Birrell to Redmond, 21 November 1912, ibid. The episode has been dealt with thoroughly by Jalland, "Irish Home-rule Finance."

CHAPTER SEVEN

1 Quoted in Roy Jenkins, *Asquith* (London: Collins 1964), 274, and H.M. Hyde, *Carson* (London: Heinemann 1953), 287–9.

2 Birrell to Churchill, 26 August 1911, Verney Papers, quoted in P. Jalland, *The Liberals and Ireland: The Ulster Question in British Politics to 1914* (Brighton: Harvester Press 1980), 58–9.

3 The decisions of this important but thinly documented cabinet meeting of 6 February 1912, and the reasoning behind them, are best pieced together by Jalland, *The Liberals and Ireland*, 63–77.

4 See J.E. Kendle, "The Round Table Movement and 'Home Rule All Round'," *Historical Journal* 9, no. 2 (July 1968): 332–53; also L. Curtis to W. Churchill, 17 April 1912, Curtis Papers, Bodleian. Garvin addressed the issue of Ulster in The *Observer* on 28 April. In an article on "Federalism and Home Rule," he made it clear that Ulster was the key to home rule: "... not a single step can be taken on Home Rule lines towards the effective settlement of the Irish question as a whole unless the full will and consent of Ulster can be carried with the purpose."

5 5 Hansard (H of C), vol. 39, 11 June 1912, col. 771.

6 For the debate see ibid., cols. 771–824; 13 June 1912, cols. 1064–1173; and 18 June 1912, cols. 1503–74.

7 *Times*, 29 July and 1 August 1912.

8 Winston Churchill to Garvin, 10 August 1912, Garvin Papers, HRC.

9 Churchill to Lloyd George, 21 August 1912, Randolph S. Churchill, *Winston S. Churchill*, vol. 2, *Companion*, Pt. 3, *1911–1914* (London: Heinemann 1969), 1396.

10 Churchill to Redmond, 31 August 1912, Redmond Papers, NLI, Ms. 15175.

11 Grigg to Willison, 5 September 1912, J.S. Willison Papers, PAC; also Curtis to Churchill, 12 August 1912, copy. Curtis Papers, Bodleian.

12 For Churchill's speech see the *Times*, 13 September 1912.

13 Ilbert to Bryce, 24 October 1912, Bryce Papers, Bodleian, Ms. 14: 63–6.

14 For a comment on Churchill's scheme and a call for proportional representation and a referendum plus a more extensive local government system see "Topics of the Day: Mr. Churchill's Latest Escapade," *Spectator*, 21 September 1912, 396–7. A.G. Gardiner was not as critical as some. While he thought Churchill's proposal for England impossible since England was one and indivisible, he did agree that the

United Kingdom suffered from overcentralization. It was therefore necessary to adjust the relationship between the locality, the nation, and the empire, and apply devolution in the United Kingdom. He did not agree with Churchill that a large local unit such as England would make a federal United Kingdom impossible. The key would be to define clearly the division of powers. See A.G. Gardiner, "Mr. Churchill and Federalism," *Fortnightly Review* (November 1912): 803–12.

15 Dunraven to Bonar Law, 8 September [1912], Bonar Law Papers, HLRO, 27/2/10.

16 Frewen to Bonar Law, 3 September 1912, ibid., 27/2/3.

17 Hythe to Bonar Law, 10 October [1912], ibid, 27/3/27.

18 *Nation*, 26 October 1912.

19 Dunraven, "The Future of Ireland: I. Settlement by Consent," *Nineteenth Century* (January 1913): 199–211. In the December 1912 issue of the *Contemporary Review*, 777–89, Erskine Childers reviewed the situation as of the end of 1912, and reached different conclusions. He argued that one should not entangle the long-held needs of Ireland with the more recent aspirations of Scotland and Wales. In his opinion, there was no uniformity between the parts of the United Kingdom or any concrete scheme of federalism or devolution against which to test the Irish bill or any strong popular move in favour of federalism.

20 Hythe to Bonar Law, 1 January 1913, Bonar Law Papers, HLRO, 28/2/3.

21 T.A. Brassey to Lord Lansdowne, 7 January 1913, quoted in full in Frank Partridge, *T.A.B.: A Memoir of Thomas Allnutt Second Earl Brassey* (London: John Murray 1921), 213–14.

22 C.P. Scott Diary, 15–16 January 1913, C.P. Scott Papers, BL, Add. Ms. 50901: 74–6.

23 5 Hansard (H of L), vol. 23, 27 January 1913, cols. 469–85.

24 Ibid., cols. 496–7.

25 Ibid., cols. 499–501.

26 Grey's full speech is ibid., cols. 496–508.

27 For Selborne's speech see ibid., 29 January 1913, cols. 644–52. Brassey also expressed support for a federal solution of imperial and United Kingdom difficulties in a speech to his constituents on 21 January 1913. See "The Breakdown of Parliamentary Government, and the Remedy," in Viscount Hythe, *The Case for Devolution and Settlement of the Home Rule Question by Consent* (London 1913), 3–22. He also printed excerpts from many of the speeches in the Lords, ibid., 55–101.

28 Dunraven to Frewen, 28 January 1913, Frewen Papers, LC.

29 Dunraven to O'Brien, 1 February 1913, quoted in Joseph V. O'Brien, *William O'Brien and the Course of Irish Politics 1881–1918* (Berkeley: University of California Press 1976), 207.

30 Hythe to Bonar Law, 10 February 1913, Bonar Law Papers, HLRO, 29/1/13. That Brassey was not taken too seriously even by those most in sympathy with him is shown by a correspondence in early May 1913 between Earl Grey and Plunkett. Grey wrote: "I always thought our friend [Brassey] was a bit woolly-headed! Enclosed letter confirms the justice of this impression, for the end of it is a most effective answer to the position he takes up in the beginning." Plunkett replied:

"I return poor T.A.B.'s letter. I wish he had a better head on top of his really good heart." Grey to Plunkett, 1 May 1913, Plunkett Papers, PH, Grey 19, Box 4; and Plunkett to Grey, 5 May 1913, ibid., Grey 20, Box 4.

31 A.V. Dicey, *A Fool's Paradise* (London 1913); also Dicey to Bonar Law, 12 February 1913, Bonar Law Papers, HLRO, 29/1/15.

32 Bryce to Dicey, 28 February 1913, copy, Bryce Papers, Bodleian, Ms. 4: 52–4.

33 See E.T. John to E.A.W. Phillips, 25 and 29 July 1912; also Phillips to John, 21 and 26 July 1912, E.T. John Papers, NLW. Phillips believed locality was of greater importance than race or nationality and favoured seven provinces in England, four in Scotland, four in Ireland, Wales as one, and one each for the Channel Islands and the Isle of Man, making eighteen in all in a federal structure.

34 E.T. John to J.E. Powell, 5 April 1913, E.T. John Papers, NLW. The previous October John had been more explicit. To a close friend, Edward Hughes, he wrote: "There will I am sure be no Ulster in Wales. The irony of the position is that there will [be] infinitely less opposition to give Home Rule to Wales, and its people are undoubtedly far better fitted to exercise the functions of self-government than the very indifferently educated Catholic population of Ireland with their hosts of illiterates." E.T. John to Edward Hughes, 3 October 1912, E.T. John Papers, NLW.

35 See E.T. John, "The Political Aspects of Welsh Nationalism," *Wales* (March 1913): 128–30. On the recent formation of the Scottish Home Rule Council and Scottish willingness to allow Irish matters to take precedence see "Scottish Home Rule," *Thistle* (April 1913): 69–70.

36 A Liberal M.P. [J.A.M. Macdonald], *The Constitutional Crisis: A Review of the Situation and a Plea for Settlement* (London 1913).

37 Two months earlier Charnwood had outlined a possible division of functions under federal home rule. See Charnwood, "Federal Home Rule and the Government of Ireland Bill," *Nineteenth Century* (April 1913): 834–45.

38 5 Hansard (H of C), vol. 53, 30 May 1913, cols. 529–41.

39 Crewe to Asquith, 8 September 1913, Asquith Papers, Bodleian, Ms. 38: 126–7.

40 Fritz to A. Ponsonby, 23 July and 28 August 1913, Ponsonby Papers, Bodleian, Ms. C659: 145–6, 151–4; also Royal memorandum, 11 August 1913, Asquith Papers, Bodleian, Ms. 38: 120–1. For the role of the king in interparty discussions see John D. Fair, "The King, the Constitution, and Ulster: Interparty Negotiations of 1913 and 1914," *Éire-Ireland* 6, no. 1 (Spring 1971): 35–52. In late August William O'Brien, who had been calling for an all-party conference since 1911, presided at the annual meeting of his All-For-Ireland League in Cork, when a resolution was passed asking the government "to advise the King to call a small representative conference." O'Brien was backed at the meeting by Brassey, and Dunraven wrote in support. See Jalland, "United Kingdom Devolution 1910–14: Political Panacea or Tactical Diversion?", *English Historical Review* 94, no. 373 (October 1979), 777; and *Nation*, 23 August 1913.

41 Lansdowne's "Memorandum of Conversation with the King," 6 September 1913, Bonar Law Papers, HLRO, 39/1/7, cited in Jalland, "United Kingdom Devolution,"

778; also Hythe, *The Case for Devolution*, Pt. IV, "Home Rule by Consent: The Proposals of the All-For-Ireland League," 105–18.

42 Grey to Oliver, 10 August 1913, F.S. Oliver Papers, NLS, Mss. Acc. 7726/92.

43 Grey to Haldane, 21 September 1913, Haldane Papers, NLS, Ms. 5910: 114.

44 See Jalland, "United Kingdom Devolution," 778–80; for a favourable comment on Loreburn's intervention see E.T. Cook, "Lord Loreburn's Intervention," *Contemporary Review* (October 1913): 457–66.

45 See H.H.A., "Government of Ireland Bill," 20 September 1913, Asquith Papers, Bodleian, Ms. 38: 188; and Lord Loreburn's Memorandum, 17 September 1913, ibid., Ms. 38: 181–91.

46 See Grey to F.S. Oliver, 26 September 1913; and F.S. Oliver to Grey, 26 September 1913, F.S. Oliver Papers, NLS, Mss. Acc. 7726/92.

47 E.T. John to T.J. Evans, 14 September 1913, E.T. John Papers, NLW; see also Morley to Rosebery, 19 September 1913, Rosebery Papers, NLS, Ms. 10048:41–2; and Lansdowne to Curzon, 11 September 1913, Curzon Mss. Eur. F112/95, cited in Jalland, "United Kingdom Devolution," 781.

48 Bonar Law to Carson, 18 September 1913, Bonar Law Papers, HLRO, 33/5/57.

49 Churchill to Bonar Law, 21 September 1913, Secret, ibid., 30/2/18.

50 Lansdowne to Bonar Law, 23 September 1913, Secret, ibid., 30/2/21.

51 Lansdowne to Walter Long, 3 October 1913, W. Long Papers, BL, Add. Ms. 62403. For the discussions between the king and Lansdowne and Law see Robert Blake, *The Unknown Prime Minister: The Life and Times of Andrew Bonar Law 1858–1923* (London: Eyre & Spottiswoode 1955), 153–59; also A.M. Gollin, *The Observer and J.L. Garvin 1908–1914: A Study in a Great Editorship* (London: Oxford University Press 1960), 409–10. For the differences within the Unionist leadership see Richard Murphy, "Faction in the Conservative Party and the Home Rule Crisis, 1912–14," *History* 71, no. 232 (June 1986): 222–34.

52 Memorandum by Bonar Law, 8 October 1913, Bonar Law Papers, HLRO, 33/5/68. The complexity of the problem was considerable. Even Lansdowne had some sympathy with Asquith's position given the political realities the Liberals faced. He told Law: "I do not think that Asquith is altogether unreasonable in stipulating that, if there is to be Devolution, Ireland should be first served. I have never seen how he could be expected to agree to a compromise under which Home Rule would be side-tracked until such time as Grey, Dunraven and others had elaborated a scheme for the federation of the United Kingdom, or perhaps of the Empire." Lansdowne to Bonar Law, 27 October 1913, ibid., 30/3/56; see also Fred Wrench to Lansdowne, 20 October 1913, copy, ibid., 30/3/47.

53 For the meetings see Blake, *The Unknown Prime Minister*, 160–7.

54 Grey to Haldane, 21 September 1913, Haldane Papers, NLS, Ms. 5910: 114.

55 Grey to Oliver, 3 October 1913, F.S. Oliver Papers, NLS, Mss. Acc. 7726/92.

56 Grey to the editor, *Times*, 11 October 1913. Dunraven had a letter in the same issue calling for "a settlement by consent" by conference.

57 See F.S. Oliver to G. Robinson, 10 October 1913, F.S. Oliver Papers, NLS, Mss. Acc. 7726/84; Oliver to Milner, 23 October 1913, Milner Papers, Bodleian, Ms. 13: 38–41;

and G.L.C. and F.S.O., Untitled Memorandum, [October 1913], A. Chamberlain
Papers, UBL, AC/14/6/72.

58 Dunraven to the editor, *Times*, 24 October 1913; and G.L. Craik to F.S. Oliver,
24 October 1913, F.S. Oliver Papers, NLS, Mss. Acc. 7726/95.

59 Oliver to Craik, 28 October 1913, copy, ibid., Mss. Acc. 7726/95; also Oliver to
Murray Macdonald, 27 October 1913, copy, and Macdonald to Oliver, 28 October
1913, ibid. Oliver also sent a copy of the joint memorandum to Edward Grigg who
was preparing a *Round Table* article on the matter. Oliver was also receiving a good
deal of advice himself. One of the more interesting ideas came from T. Keyes:
"Why not instead of 'Home Rule within Home Rule' have two administrations
similar to those of a Crown Colony and a self-governing colony under a Governor-
General. The Governor-General of India has under him provinces of at least three
degrees of decentralization as well as tracts administered directly by himself and
there is no confusion. I don't think it would be beyond the wit of Macdonnell to
devise a workable scheme." T. Keyes to Oliver, 29 October 1913, ibid.

60 F.S. Oliver, *The Alternatives to Civil War* (London 1913); for similar comments on
this theme read Arthur Ponsonby, "The Future Government of the United
Kingdom," *Contemporary Review* (November 1913): 624–31. See also Earl Grey to
Ponsonby, 19 November 1913, Ponsonby Papers, Bodleian, Ms. C659: 172–5; J.A.M.
Macdonald to Oliver, 24 and 26 November 1913; Oliver to Garvin and Churchill,
24 November 1913; and Brassey to Oliver, 29 November 1913, F.S. Oliver Papers,
NLS, Mss. Acc. 7726/95; Oliver to G. Robinson, 26 November 1913, ibid., Mss. Acc.
7726/84; Carson to Oliver, 3 December 1913, ibid., Mss. Acc. 7726/87; Horace
Plunkett to Oliver, 18 December 1913, ibid., Mss. Acc. 7726/88.

61 Lansdowne to A. Chamberlain, 31 October 1913, A. Chamberlain Papers, UBL,
AC/11/1/47.

62 A. Chamberlain to Willoughby de Broke, 23 November 1913, Willoughby de Broke
Papers, HLRO, WB/6/9.

63 A. Chamberlain to Lansdowne, 29 October 1913, copy, A. Chamberlain Papers,
UBL, AC/11/1/46.

64 Lansdowne to A. Chamberlain, 12 December 1913, ibid., AC/11/1/56.

65 N. Chamberlain to A. Chamberlain, 14 December 1913, ibid., AC/11/1/15.

66 See A. Chamberlain to Lansdowne, 29 October 1913, copy. ibid., AC/11/1/46. In
November Oliver explained to Earl Grey that "Austen is the person on the Unionist
side that I have been in closest touch with ... The great advantage of Austen is
that when once he grips an idea and accepts it he doesn't wobble. I regard him
as the greatest standby at the present juncture." Oliver to Grey, 24 November 1913,
F.S. Oliver Papers, NLS, Mss. Acc. 7726/92.

67 W. Churchill to A. Chamberlain, 1 December 1913, A. Chamberlain Papers, UBL,
AC/11/1/24.

68 A. Chamberlain to W. Churchill, 2 December 1913, *Secret*, copy, ibid., AC/11/1/28.
See also [Austen Chamberlain], "Memo of conversations with Winston Churchill,"
27 November 1913, ibid., AC/11/1/21.

69 A. Chamberlain to Oliver, 6 November 1913, F.S. Oliver Papers, NLS, Mss. Acc.

7726/91. He told Morley on 9 December: "I dislike Home Rule, but I dislike still more the prospect of civil war with its necessary consequences, the destruction of the House of Commons and the demoralization of the Army." See Sir Charles Petrie. *The Life and Letters of the Rt. Hon. Sir Austen Chamberlain*, 2 vols. (London: Cassell 1939), 1: 344-5, 353.

70 For Selborne's earlier views see Selborne to Lady Selborne, 10 September 1912, Selborne Papers, Bodleian, Ms. 102: 60-3, and Selborne to T. Comryn Platt, 19 September 1912, copy, ibid., Ms. 77: 18-22. Another who attempted to influence Bonar Law was Moreton Frewen. See Frewen to Law, 27 October 1913, Bonar Law Papers, HLRO, 30/3/54.

71 Long to Bonar Law, 29 December 1913, ibid., 31/1/62.

72 See [Austen Chamberlain], "Memo of conversations with Winston Churchill," 27 November 1913, A. Chamberlain Papers, UBL, AC/11/1/21.

73 See J.A. Murray Macdonald, "The Constitutional Crisis: A Plea for Settlement," *Contemporary Review* (December 1913): 761-72; Dunraven, "A Last Plea for Federation," *Nineteenth Century* (December 1913): 1125-42. In mid-December, the Liberal, Herbert Samuel, came up with an ingenious scheme to protect Ulster interests through an Ulster House of Parliament. See H.S., "A Suggestion for the Solution of the Ulster Question," 18 December 1913, Cab. 37/117/95. At the same time, looking ahead to a possible federal solution, Samuel argued that the Irish Senate should be chosen by the Irish House of Commons. This indirect method of election would then be transferred to the other constituent second chambers of Scotland, Wales, and England once a federal constitution was adopted. See H.S., "Reconstitution of the Second Chamber," 1 December 1913, Cab 37/117/84.

74 See Moreton Frewen, "Our Unsolved Enigma: On Thinking Federally," *Nineteenth Century* (February 1914): 300-12; Dunraven, "Our Unsolved Enigma: Applied Federalism," ibid.: 312-27; F.S. Oliver, *What Federalism Is Not* (London 1914); and J.A.M. Macdonald and Lord Charnwood, *The Federal Solution* (London 1914). Oliver found Macdonald's and Charnwood's pamphlet "woolly and disjointed," while neither Macdonald nor Charnwood was attracted either by Oliver's detailed ideas or by his philosophic abstractions. See Oliver to A. Chamberlain, 18 February 1914, A. Chamberlain Papers, UBL, AC/60/131; Charnwood to Oliver, n.d., F.S. Oliver Papers, NLS, Mss. Acc. 7726/96; and J.A.M. Macdonald to Oliver, 18 February 1914, ibid. A rambling attack against federalism was levelled by Ian Colvin, "The Dead Hand of Federalism," *National Review* 63 (1914): 52-70, but J.A. Marriott now commented more sympathetically in "The Constitution in Suspense," *Nineteenth Century* (January 1914): 1-18. See also H.B. Lees Smith, "The Future of the Home Rule Bill," *Contemporary Review* (March 1914): 305-10, which contains an assessment of both the Macdonald-Charnwood and the Oliver pamphlets. Selborne did not like the Macdonald-Charnwood scheme. Although not a federal enthusiast, he believed the Ulster problem, and that of Ireland generally, could only be solved by "a federal recasting of the Constitution to be brought into operation simultaneously in all parts of the United Kingdom." See Selborne to

Charnwood, 7 February 1914, Selborne Papers, Bodleian, Ms. 77: 80–2, and Charnwood to Selborne, 7 March 1914, ibid., 85–6.

75 Brassey to Curzon, 22 January 1914, quoted in Partridge, *T.A.B.*, 215–16. Brassey did admit to Curzon that 'I don't think Home Rule with Ireland split into two Provinces would work, but I admit it may be necessary as a temporary solution.' See also Brassey to Selborne, 31 January 1914, ibid., 216–18.

76 For the full Plunkett scheme see Sir Horace Plunkett, *A Better Way: An Appeal to Ulster Not to Desert Ireland* (London and Dublin 1914). Also Plunkett to Asquith, 4 March 1914, Plunkett Papers, PH, Asq. 1, Box 1; Plunkett to Oliver, 18 December 1913 and 30 January 1914, F.S.Oliver Papers, NLS, Mss. Acc. 7726/88; and Plunkett to Erskine Childers, 24 December 1913 and 13 January 1914, Erskine Childers Papers, TCL, Ms. 7850/991 and 993.

77 A. Chamberlain to Oliver, 18 February 1914, F.S. Oliver Papers, NLS, Mss. Acc. 7726/91. Oliver, however, doubted that Protestant Ulster could be made a separate unit on a permanent basis. Oliver to Chamberlain, 18 February 1914, A. Chamberlain Papers, UBL, AC/60/131.

78 A. Chamberlain to F.S. Oliver, 23 February 1914, F.S. Oliver Papers, NLS, Mss. Acc. 7726/91.

79 A. Chamberlain to Oliver, 6 March 1914, ibid., Mss. Acc. 7726/91. In February a memorial urging the establishment of a commission or the exploration of a common agreement to see if a federal scheme could be devised so as to avert civil war was signed by twenty-two Unionists and given to Bonar Law. For the "Memorial" see Bonar Law Papers, HLRO. 39/4/32.

80 Garvin to Milner, 3 March 1914, Milner Papers, Bodleian, Box 100.

81 5 Hansard (H of C), vol. 59, 9 March 1914, cols. 933–6.

82 The most detailed exposition/analysis of Liberal government policy-making and of the negotiations between Liberal, Unionist, and Nationalist leaders is in chapters 5 and 6 of Jalland, *The Liberals and Ireland*, 142–206. Jalland's treatment of the Curragh incident in chapter 7 of her book is the best of many available. In the midst of this political crisis the Scots and the Welsh made a forlorn attempt to wrest attention away from Ulster and Ireland. Scottish and Welsh home rule bills, patterned on previous efforts but also modelled after the current Irish bill, were introduced in February and March, but were essentially ignored. E.T. John introduced the Welsh bill on 11 March 1914 under the ten-minute arrangement, while the Scottish bill had been introduced on 13 February 1914 by I. Macpherson supported by, among others, Murray Macdonald, Pirie, and Cowan. See *Parl. Pap.*. 1914, vol. III, Government of Scotland Bill, 13 February 1914, 69–96; and *Parl. Pap.* 1914, vol. III, Government of Wales Bill, 11 March 1914, 101–24. Also *Welsh Outlook* (March 1919), *Supplement*; E.T. John, "The National Needs of Wales: 11 Self-Government," *Wales*, 6: 71–74; and 5 Hansard (H of C), 13 February and 11 March 1914.

83 L.S. Amery to Bonar Law, 27 December 1913, quoted in L.S. Amery, *My Political Life*, 3 vols. (London: Hutchinson 1953), 1: 437–9. Amery elaborated in a letter

to the Welsh leader E.T. John: "I am not an advocate of federalism myself, though my objections to it, like those of most Unionists, are on an entirely different plane to my objections to any dualist or separatist measure ... If you want to get through a federal scheme there is only one way to do it, and that is to decide first of all quite clearly for the whole United Kingdom what powers can practically and usefully be delegated to the local bodies – thus far you must have uniformity – then let the people of the areas concerned settle for themselves what manner of constitution they prefer to adopt for the exercise of those limited powers," Amery to E.T. John, 10 January 1914, E.T. John Papers, NLW.

84 See Plunkett Diary, 26 and 27 January and 14 February 1914, Plunkett Papers, PH.

85 Astor to Garvin, n.d., quoted in Gollin, *Garvin*, 417–18.

86 Amery to A. Chamberlain, 1 May 1914, A. Chamberlain Papers, UBL, AC/11/1/1; A. Chamberlain to M. Chamberlain, 5 May 1914, ibid., AC/4/1/1131; and A. Chamberlain to N. Chamberlain, 21 March 1914, cited in D. Dutton, *Austen Chamberlain: Gentleman in Politics* (Bolton: Ross Anderson Publications 1985), 105. Chamberlain had calculated that there were about eighty members in the House from both parties prepared to support the idea if given the opportunity by the party leaderships. See A. Chamberlain, *Politics from Inside: An Epistolary Chronicle* (London: Cassell 1936), 636–7. For Oliver's position see "Pacificus" to the editor, *Times*, 27 March 1914. J.A. Spender regretted the loss of an opportunity to advance the federal idea. See J.A. Spender to F.S. Oliver, 9 March 1914, F.S.Oliver Papers, NLS, Mss. Acc. 7726/96.

87 See Lady Selborne to Curtis, 6 March [1914], Curtis Papers, Bodleian.

88 [Edward Grigg], "The Irish Crisis," *Round Table* (March 1914): 201–39.

89 For this episode see Kendle, "The Round Table Movement and 'Home Rule all Round'," 351.

90 L. Curtis to R. Feetham, 4 and 24 June 1914, Curtis Papers, Bodleian.

91 For the provenance of the scheme see C.P. Scott Diary, 1 May 1914, C.P. Scott Papers, BL, Add. Ms. 50901: 117–18; and Curtis to H. Montgomery Hyde, 24 July 1950, copy, Curtis Papers, Bodleian.

92 "Suggestions for a Settlement of the Irish Question," Selborne Papers, Bodleian, Ms. 77: 137–45.

93 Churchill to Lloyd George, 3 April 1914, Lloyd George Papers, HLRO, C/3/16/11.

94 For the above see Curtis to Hyde, 24 July 1950, Curtis Papers, Bodleian; Selborne's notes, n.d., Selborne Papers, Bodleian, Ms. 77: 137–40; A. Chamberlain to Carson, 7 April 1914, enclosed in Carson to Bonar Law, 7 April 1914, Bonar Law Papers, HLRO, 32/2/26; Grigg to Bonar Law, 9 April 1914, ibid., 32/2/27; and Grigg to A. Chamberlain, 9 April 1914, A. Chamberlain Papers, UBL, AC/11/1/35.

95 Grigg to Bonar Law, 9 April 1914, Bonar Law Papers, HLRO, 32/2/27; and Grigg to A. Chamberlain, 9 April 1914, A. Chamberlain Papers, UBL, AC/11/1/35.

96 Curtis to Hyde, 24 July 1950, Curtis Papers, Bodleian.

97 Selborne to Carson, 9 April 1914, copy, Selborne Papers, Bodleian,Ms. 77: 101–3.

98 Lady Selborne to Curtis, 21 April [1914], Curtis Papers, Bodleian.

99 5 Hansard (H of C), vol. 61, 28 April 1914, col. 1591; and 29 April 1914, cols. 1747-53.
100 H.H.A., "Note of Prime Minister's meeting with B. Law and Sir E. Carson, 5 May
1914. Sent to the King," Asquith Papers, Bodleian, Ms. 7: 123-4; Curtis to Hyde,
24 July 1950, Curtis Papers, Bodleian; and Hyde, *Carson*, 367. For Dillon's attitude
see C.P. Scott Diary, 4 May 1914, C.P. Scott Papers, BL, Add. Ms. 50901: 119-22;
and for Redmond's harsh criticism of the Curtis scheme see Redmond to Asquith,
5 May 1914, Asquith Papers, Bodleian, Ms. 39: 167-71. Amery also had grave doubts
about the implications of federalism for the Unionists. See Amery to A. Chamberlain, 1 May 1914, A. Chamberlain Papers, UBL, AC/11/1/1, and Amery to A.
Chamberlain, 4 May 1914, ibid., AC/11/1/2.
101 C.P. Scott had told Geoffrey Robinson and Brand much the same in mid-April:
"I did not see much hope in federal idea which is far too much in the air and too
large and doubtfully practicable for present use." C.P. Scott Diary, 13 April 1914,
C.P. Scott Papers, BL, Add. Ms. 50901: 110. Also entry for 1 May 1914, 117-18. In
May a petition was handed to Asquith signed by seventy-eight Liberal Federalists.
It called on the party leaders "to consider forthwith whether a common agreement might be arrived at to appoint a body, without delay, to devise a federal
scheme with a view to terminating the crisis." See "Petition of Liberal Federalists
of May 1914," Asquith Papers, Bodleian, Ms. 39: 159-60.
102 By late May even Dunraven was pessimistic. He wrote to O'Brien: "It is too late.
We are sitting on the very edge of a volcano and unless something occurs pretty
soon to avoid an immediate catastrophe I do not see what chance a conference
has." Dunraven to O'Brien, 22 May 1914, quoted in J.V. O'Brien, *William O'Brien*,
211.
103 Hythe to J.A.M. Macdonald, 20 July 1914, quoted in Partridge, *T.A.B.*, 222.
Brassey had been attempting since late March to push the idea of setting up "a
Commission for the purpose of devising a federal scheme for the United Kingdom." By now Brassey thought the term "devolution" more accurately described
what he had in mind than did "federal." In June he organized meetings in Oxford
and Hastings attended by leading members of both parties, and on 30 June he
arranged a meeting between Liberal and Unionist "federalists" at his own home.
Although recognizing short-term defeat, he remained convinced of the necessity
to "keep our flag flying." Ibid. See Hythe to Sir John Douglas Hagen, 3 July 1914,
ibid., 221-2; Hythe to Ponsonby, 26 March 1914, Ponsonby Papers, Bodleian, Ms.
C660; Hythe to Lansdowne, 4 April and 22 June 1914; and Hythe to Salisbury,
13 June 1918, *T.A.B.*, 218-21.

CHAPTER EIGHT

1 For a detailed analysis of interparty discussions over Ireland during the first six
weeks of the war see Patricia Jalland and John Stubbs, "The Irish Question after
the Outbreak of War in 1914: Some Unfinished Party Business," *English Historical
Review* 96, no. 381 (October 1981): 778-807.

2 William O'Brien to M. Frewen, 10 March 1915, W. O'Brien Papers, NLI, Ms. 8557/5.

3 O'Brien to Frewen, 21 May 1915, copy, M. MacDonagh Papers, NLI, Ms. 11440/3.

4 O'Brien to Frewen. 4 August 1915, ibid., Ms. 11440/3. In 1915 only one article attempted to grapple with the issue of federalism. H. Douglas Gregory, a Unionist, pointed out that the Government of Ireland Act was antifederal and therefore separatist in scope and neither it nor any conceivable amending bill offered any prospect for final settlement of the question. He suggested legislation that would specifically enumerate the powers of a Dublin, and, if necessary, a Belfast parliament, leaving all powers not actually conferred by name to the central authority. Whatever Irish authorities were established would be merely units in a new constitution for the United Kingdom. He favoured the simultaneous establishment in England, Scotland, and Wales of local parliaments with similar powers. Only by doing so would the sense of union be preserved, allowing representatives to sit proportionally at Westminster, but it would eliminate the interference by one element or more in the purely local affairs of other territories. See H. Douglas Gregory, "The Future of Irish Government," *Empire Review* (May 1915): 172–83.

5 For detailed discussion and analysis of this episode see Patrick Buckland, *Irish Unionism: One. The Anglo-Irish and the New Ireland 1885–1922* (Dublin: Gill and Macmillan 1972), 51–82; David W. Savage, "The Attempted Home Rule Settlement of 1916," *Éire-Ireland* 2, no. 3 (Autumn 1967): 132–45; D.G. Boyce, "How to Settle the Irish Question: Lloyd George and Ireland 1916–21," in A.J.P. Taylor, ed., *Lloyd George: Twelve Essays* (New York: Atheneum 1971), 137–64; David G. Boyce, "British Opinion, Ireland and the War, 1916–1918," *Historical Journal* 17 no. 3 (1974): 575–93; John Grigg, *Lloyd George: From Peace to War 1912–1916* (London: Eyre Methuen 1985), 342–55; and Michael Laffan, *The Partition of Ireland 1911–25* (Dundalk: Dundalgan Press 1983), 51–5. The Lloyd George, Asquith, and Walter Long papers contain extensive correspondence and memoranda which makes possible an almost day-to-day reconstitution of this episode.

6 F.S. Oliver to Carson, 21 May 1916, F.S. Oliver Papers, NLS, Mss. Acc. 7726/87.

7 See Selborne to *Morning Post*, 5 August 1916, copy, Selborne Papers, Bodleian, Ms. 84: 4–6; and *Morning Post*, 8 August 1916.

8 F.S. Oliver to Selborne, 8 August 1916, Selborne Papers, Bodleian, Ms. 84: 12–14. Selborne's and Oliver's activities regarding federalism have been outlined in D.G. Boyce and J.O. Stubbs, "F.S. Oliver, Lord Selborne and Federalism," *Journal of Imperial and Commonwealth History* 5, no. 1 (October 1976): 53–81.

9 Selborne to *Morning Post*, 18 August 1916, copy, Selborne Papers, Bodleian, Ms. 84: 7–9.

10 Selborne to Salisbury, 12 September 1916, ibid., Ms. 6: 185–91.

11 F.S. Oliver Diary, 3 November 1916, F.S. Oliver Papers, NLS, Mss. Acc, 7726/216.

12 See F.S.Oliver Diary, 3 and 23 November 1916, ibid., and H. Duncan Hall to J. Kendle, 28 April 1971, in which Hall outlined his involvement with Oliver and Selborne.

13 Hall to Kendle, 28 April 1971. Brassey (i.e., Hythe) was supposed to be a member of Selborne's committee but was inactive. The draft bill was also sent to Amery.

14 See Oliver Diary, January-March 1917, F.S. Oliver Papers, NLS, Mss. Acc. 7726/217; and F.S. Oliver, *Ireland and the Imperial Conference: Is There a Way to a Settlement?* (London 1917).

15 See Oliver to W. Astor, 3 March 1917, enclosed in Astor to Lloyd George, Lloyd George Papers, HLRO, F/85/1/1.

16 See F.S. Oliver Papers, NLS, Mss. Acc. 7726/148.

17 See H. Duncan Hall to Oliver, 14 June 1917, ibid., Mss. Acc. 7726/89; also Hall to Oliver, 6 and 26 May and 13 and 15 June 1917, ibid.

18 On two occasions, 30 March and 22 June, Oliver, Selborne and Hall met with Snowden, the Labour MP. The subject of their meetings is not clear. See Oliver Diary, March-June 1917, ibid., Mss. Acc. 7726/217; also J.A.M. Macdonald to Oliver, 18 March 1917, and J.A.M. Macdonald to Amery, 8 April 1917, copy, ibid., Mss. Acc. 7726/97; Oliver to Milner, 20 March 1917 and 1 June 1917, Milner Papers, Bodleian, Box 144; and Oliver to Selborne, 26 April 1917, Selborne Papers, Bodleian, Ms. 84: 49–51.

19 Selborne and F.S. Oliver, *A Method of Constitutional Cooperation: Suggestions for the Better Government of the United Kingdom* (London 1917). The pamphlet was reprinted, still for private circulation, in April 1918.

20 Appendix 1 of the pamphlet listed both the powers proposed for the local legislatures and the powers already administered in Scotland.

21 Monteagle, "The Irish Problem," *Quarterly Review* (April 1917): 558–69. At about this time Alfred Perceval Graves of the Irish Literary Society of London called for a separate government for Ulster outside that of the rest of Ireland. While retaining eleven representatives in the British parliament, Ulster would have its own House of Commons and a Senate. See Alfred Perceval Graves, "Ulster Home Rule," *Contemporary Review* (May 1917): 588–96.

22 C.P. Scott Diary, April 30 – May 4, 1917, C.P. Scott Papers, Bodleian, Add. Ms. 50903: 13 and 35. Murray Macdonald, on the other hand, called for an organic union of the empire. Not surprisingly, he viewed United Kingdom federation as a necessary preliminary step to imperial federation. See J.A. Murray Macdonald, *Notes on the Constitutional Reconstruction of the Empire* (London 1917).

23 Frewen to Long, 23 May 1917, and Long to Frewen, 25 May 1917, W. Long Papers, WRO, 947/409.

24 Long to Lloyd George, 26 February 1917, copy, ibid. Earl Grey, in fact, died on 29 August 1917.

25 See "Forms of Government within the Empire," Confidential, I.C. 9 [1917] in Redmond Papers, NLI, Ms. 15265(1); "Memorandum on Fiscal Autonomy" [1917], ibid., Ms. 15265(8); "The Government of Canada: Memorandum on Its History and Working" [1917], ibid., Ms. 15265(2); and "An Analysis of the Fiscal Question," I.C. 24 [1917], ibid., Ms. 15265(2).

26 For an excellent analysis of the convention see R.B. McDowell, *The Irish Convention 1917–18* (London: Routledge & Kegan Paul 1970).

27 Lord Atkinson to Plunkett, 10 July 1917, Plunkett Papers, PH, Atk 1, Box 1.

28 J.X. Merriman to H. Plunkett, 28 July 1917, ibid., Mer 1, Box 6.

29 Plunkett to Merriman, 22 October 1917, copy, ibid.

30 H. Plunkett to Redmond, 18 August 1917, Redmond Papers, NLI, Ms. 15221. Also "An Outline of Irish Self-Government" with preface by Lord Dunraven, ibid., Ms. 15265 (2).

31 At the same time, the minister of labour asked H.J. Hetherington to prepare a memorandum on the advantages and objections to a federal system from the point of view of the Ministry of Labour. Hetherington thought the work of Oliver, Murray Macdonald, and Charnwood to be "unscientific." H.J. Hetherington to W.G.S. Adams, 31 July 1917, Lloyd George Papers, HLRO, F/74/25/1.

32 See Selborne to Lady Selborne, 9 October 1917, Selborne Papers, Bodleian, Ms. 103: 33; and Oliver to Milner, 25 October 1917, Milner Papers, Bodleian, Box 144.

33 Selborne to Plunkett, 22 October 1917, copy, Selborne Papers, Bodleian, Ms. 84:64.

34 Oliver to Plunkett, 28 October 1917, Plunkett Papers, PH, Oli 27, Box 6.

35 Plunkett to Selborne, 11 October 1917, Selborne Papers, Bodleian, Ms. 84: 60.

36 See Plunkett to Oliver, 30 November 1917, F.S. Oliver Papers, NLS, Mss. Acc. 7726/88; and Plunkett to Dunraven, 10 December 1917, Plunkett Papers, PH, Dunr 3, Box 3. Also Plunkett to Bryce, 1 November 1917, Bryce Papers, NLI Ms. 11016(9). In addition to McDowell's book there is valuable material on the convention in Patrick Buckland *Irish Unionism: One*, 83–128; P. Buckland, *Irish Unionism: Two. Ulster Unionism and the Origins of Northern Ireland 1886–1922* (Dublin: Gill and Macmillan 1973), 107–13; and D.G. Boyce, "British Opinion, Ireland and the War, 1916–1918."

37 Oliver to Plunkett, 22 January 1918, Plunkett Papers, PH Oli 35, Box 6.

38 F.S. Oliver, *Ulster and a Federal Settlement* (London 1918).

39 Oliver to Carson, February 1918, quoted in Ian Colvin, *The Life of Lord Carson* (New York: Macmillan 1937), 316.

40 Carson to Oliver, 9 February 1918, F.S. Oliver Papers, NLS, Mss. Acc. 7726/87. By this stage William O'Brien was of the opinion that "The Federalism of five years ago will no longer satisfy Ireland – little less than Dominion Home Rule can now do it." O'Brien to M. Frewen, 10 January 1918, W. O'Brien Papers, NLI, Ms. 8557/5.

41 Oliver to Carson, 11 February 1918, quoted in Colvin, *Lord Carson*, 317.

42 Carson to Oliver, 12 February 1918, Oliver Papers, NLS, Mss. Acc. 7726/87.

43 Carson to Lloyd George, 14 February 1918, Lloyd George Papers, HLRO, F/6/3/6; also enclosed in Carson to Oliver, 16 February 1918, F.S. Oliver Papers, NLS, Mss. Acc. 7726/87; and quoted in Colvin, *Lord Carson*, 326–7.

44 Lloyd George's letter to Hugh Barrie, n.d., is quoted in Colvin, *Lord Carson*, 328–9.

45 Oliver to Milner, 25 February 1918, Milner Papers, Bodleian; and Oliver to Carson, February 1918, quoted in Colvin, *Lord Carson*, 331.

46 Oliver to A. Chamberlain, 28 February 1918, A. Chamberlain Papers, UBL, AC/14/6/75. By this time Waldorf Astor was parliamentary secretary to Lloyd George.

47 Oliver to A. Chamberlain, 3 March 1918, ibid., AC/14/6/77. A few days later Oliver had second thoughts about Long: "He is a very dangerous creature to deal with;

partly because of his limited intelligence ... and jealousy." Oliver to A. Chamberlain, 7 March 1918, ibid.

48 Milner diary, 4 March 1918, Milner Papers, Bodleian.

49 A. Chamberlain to Ida Chamberlain, 9 March 1918, A. Chamberlain Papers, UBL, AC/5/1/64.

50 Oliver to A. Chamberlain, 10, 18, and 31 March 1918, ibid., AC/14/6/79, 81, 84. For Thomas's speech see Times, 18 March 1918. Oliver was delighted by this development and persuaded Chamberlain to write a congratulatory note to Thomas. Oliver to A. Chamberlain, 18 March 1918; A. Chamberlain to J.H. Thomas, 20 March 1918, ibid., AC/14/6/86; and J.H. Thomas to A. Chamberlain, 21 March 1918, ibid., AC/18/2/4.

51 Selborne to A. Chamberlain, 21 March 1918, ibid., AC/18/2/5.

52 Oliver to Selborne, 27 March 1918, copy, ibid., AC/14/6/88, and Oliver to A. Chamberlain, 2 April 1918, ibid., AC/14/6/89.

53 Oliver to Kerr, Good Friday, 1918, copy. Lloyd George Papers, HLRO, F/91/7/3.

54 Oliver to A. Chamberlain, 2 April 1918, A. Chamberlain Papers, UBL, AC/14/6/89.

55 Long to Bonar Law, 4 April 1918, Bonar Law Papers, HLRO, 83/2/2.

56 At this time Amery was working in the Cabinet Office.

57 F. Guest to Lloyd George, 5 April 1918, Lloyd George Papers, HLRO, F/21/2/16; and Colvin, Lord Carson, 348.

58 For the correspondence between Chamberlain and Lloyd George see Sir Charles Petrie, The Life and Letters of the Rt. Hon. Sir Austen Chamberlain, 2 vols. (London: Cassell 1939), 2: 114–17. See Oliver to A. Chamberlain, 10 April 1918, A. Chamberlain Papers, UBL, AC/14/6/97; also A. Chamberlain to Lord Hugh Cecil, 10 April 1918, in which he outlined his reasons for adopting a federal solution, ibid., AC/18/2/9. For other Unionist support see the Times, 10 and 18 April 1918.

59 "Minutes of Meeting. Committee on Government of Ireland Amendment Bill," 11 April 1918, Cab. 23/6/389.

60 See T. Jones, Whitehall Diary, vol. 1, 1916–1925 (London: Oxford University Press 1969), 61; and "Minutes of First Meeting. Committee on Government of Ireland Amendment Bill," 15 April 1918, Cab. 27/46.

61 For the war cabinet decision see "Minutes of a Meeting," 16 April 1918, Cab. 23/6/392.

62 See "Minutes of Second Meeting. Committee on Government of Ireland Amendment Bill," 16 April 1918, Cab. 27/46.

63 Long to Lloyd George, 18 April 1918, Lloyd George Papers, HLRO, F/32/5/83. Brassey urged Long to do his best to ensure the government introduced a United Kingdom bill on federal lines: "The only possibility of bringing Ulstermen in and keeping Ireland united is under a scheme applicable to the whole of the United Kingdom." Long agreed "entirely" with Brassey. See Brassey to Long, 18 and 21 April; and Long to Brassey, 19 April 1918, W. Long Papers, WRO, 947/162.

64 Times, 17 and 18 April 1918; also Salisbury to Selborne, 11 and 29 April 1918, Selborne Papers, Bodleian, Ms. 7: 11–14, 15–18.

65 Amery to Lloyd George, 17 April 1918, Lloyd George Papers, HLRO, F/2/1/18; and
   Amery to A. Chamberlain, 21 April 1918 and enclosure: "Draft Scheme of Bill on
   Federal Lines" by L.S. Amery, 21 April 1918, A. Chamberlain Papers, UBL, AC/31/1/4
   and 5.
66 Oliver to Carson, 18 April 1918, copy ibid., AC/14/6/101. Plunkett met with the committee on 19 April 1918 and found it "a very stupid body." Plunkett Diary, 19 April
   1918, Plunkett Papers, PH.
67 Oliver to A. Chamberlain, 19 April 1918, A. Chamberlain Papers, UBL, AC/14/6/102.
68 A. Chamberlain to Ida Chamberlain, 20 April 1918, ibid., AC/5/1/71.
69 Colvin, *Lord Carson*, 344.
70 "Minutes of a Meeting of the War Cabinet," 23 April 1918, Cab. 23/6/397.
71 Dunraven also now believed that "it will take some years before a scheme of
   federalism all round can be put into operation." He thought that Ireland would
   have to be given first place in a federal scheme and wider powers than the other
   parts of the United Kingdom. Dunraven to Long, 23 April 1918, Long Papers, WRO,
   947/210.
72 Amery to Lloyd George, 24 April 1918, Lloyd George Papers, HLRO, F/2/1/20; also
   L.S. Amery, "The Irish Convention and the Federal Solution," 18 April 1918, enclosed in Amery to Lloyd George, 25 April 1918, ibid., F/2/1/21. Amery carried his
   argument about the need for the United Kingdom parliament to retain control
   of customs and excise into public print: "Irish Grievances: The Demand for Fiscal
   Autonomy," *Nineteenth Century* (June 1918): 1157–67. The article was dated 18 May
   1918. See also F.S.Oliver, "Note on Federal Decentralisation," 26 April 1918, A.
   Chamberlain Papers, UBL, AC/14/6/103.
73 Amery to Lloyd George, 29 April 1918, Lloyd George Papers, HLRO, F/2/1/22. Astor
   was less enthusiastic in his estimate of Unionist support; after a postcard canvass
   he put the figure at sixty but indicated that many would not commit themselves
   in writing. In early May he was prepared to resign in order to help federal home
   rule. See Astor to Lloyd George, [?] May and 6 and 9 May 1918, ibid., F/83/1/17–19.
74 Amery to Lloyd George, 1 May 1918, ibid., F/2/1/23.
75 Guest to Lloyd George, 3 May 1918, ibid., F/21/2/20. At the end of April Liberal
   and Unionist members sought parliamentary time for the debate of a bill granting self-government to Scotland. Ten days later the South Wales Labour party
   decided to formulate a Labour policy for federal home rule for Wales, and the Scottish National Committee, composed of Liberal and Labour members, which had
   been responsible for the preparation of the Scottish home rule bill of 1913, held
   its first meeting since the outbreak of war and decided to ask the government to
   frame the Irish bill "with a view to the immediate extension of a similar measure
   of self-government to Scotland and consequent establishment of a complete federal
   system for the United Kingdom." *Times*, 26 April and 7 and 8 May 1918. See also
   F.S. Oliver, "Ulster and a Federal Settlement," *Times*, 3, 4, and 6 May 1918.
76 "Notes of a Meeting. Committee on Irish Bill," 9 May 1918, Cab. 27/46; also T.
   Jones, *Whitehall Diary*, 62–4.

77 W. Long, "Federalism," 9 May 1918, Lloyd George Papers, HLRO, F/32/5/35. Long had consulted Oliver who liked the document and made some suggestions for change. See Oliver to Long, 7 May 1918, Long Papers, WRO, 947/322.

78 Throughout May interest in federalism continued to run high. Early in the month the Scottish Unofficial Liberal MPs requested the appointment of a commission to examine a home rule scheme for Scotland. On 15 May Welsh members of all parties declared that in any measure of devolution Wales should have both legislative and administrative powers. On 21 May at a Welsh conference at Llandrindod Wells a resolution favouring self-government on federal lines for Wales was passed. On 22 May the Scottish National Association passed a resolution in favour of a federal scheme and the establishment of a Scottish parliament. On 30 May about sixty Liberal MPs met to discuss federalism. And on 1 June the South Wales Labour party called a conference for 13 July to discuss a program of "Federal Home Rule." See "Federation," *Secret*, G.T. 4529, Cab. 24/51; also the *Times*, 9, 16, 17, 22, 23, and 31 May and 3 June 1918. Also F.S. Oliver, "Federalism," *Times*, 21 and 23 May 1918.

79 "Notes of a Meeting. Committee on Irish Bill," 4 June 1918, *Secret*, Cab. 27/46. Unlike his colleague, Addison was prepared to finish drafting a purely Irish bill while embarking on the preparation of a federal bill. Also, George Barnes did not want to be committed to shelving home rule until the government had dealt with federalism. His opinion was shared by others not on the committee. See G. Barnes to Lloyd George, 5 June 1918, Lloyd George Papers, HLRO, F/4/2/30; and "Notes of a Meeting. Committee on Irish Bill," 10 June 1918, *Secret*, Cab. 27/46.

80 W. Long, "Committee on Government of Ireland Bill. Interim Report," 14 June 1918, *Secret*, G.T. 4839, Cab. 27/46; also T. Jones, *Whitehall Diary*, 65–6.

81 A. Chamberlain, "The Irish Question and Federalism," 17 June 1918, *Secret*, G-212, Cab. 24/5. Also A. Chamberlain to Hilda Chamberlain, 14 June 1918, A. Chamberlain Papers, UBL, AC/5/1/87. Also Chamberlain to Long, 3 June 1918, and Long to Chamberlain, 11 May 1918, Long Papers, WRO, 947/180. Selborne also believed federalism would avert the danger of revolution in Great Britain. Selborne to Salisbury, 17 June 1918, Selborne Papers, Bodleian, Ms. 7: 33–40.

82 See "Minutes of a Meeting of the War Cabinet," 19 June 1918, *Secret*, Cab. 23/6/433.

83 A. Chamberlain to Lady Chamberlain, 19 June 1918, A. Chamberlain Papers, UBL, AC/6/1/301.

84 "Ireland and a Federal Solution," *Times*, 19 June 1918.

85 W. Long to Professor Adams, 20 June 1918, Lloyd George Papers, HLRO, F/67/1/24.

86 [W.G.S. Adams], "The Case for Federalism," June 1918, ibid., F/68/32; also [W.G.S. Adams], "Federal Settlement. The situation with regard to the Irish Bill," June 1918, ibid., F/68/33.

87 "Draft of a Bill for a federal system for the United Kingdom, prepared by Mr. Walter Long's Committee, June 1918," *Secret*, G.T. 8239, Cab. 24/89.

88 Lloyd George was accompanied by Smuts, Barnes, Shortt, and Long, while Brassey, Selborne, J.M. Robertson, Adamson (chairman of the Labour party), Laurence Hardy, Murray Macdonald, and Sir Herbert Robert (chairman of the

Welsh party) spoke for the deputation. See the *Times*, 25 and 26 June and 1 July 1918. Two days later the Labour party conference adopted a resolution calling for separate legislatures for Scotland, Wales, and England and home rule for Ireland. *Times*, 29 June 1918.

89 Long to Lloyd George, 20 July 1918, Lloyd George Papers, HLRO, F/33/1/11. Long's commitment was not shared by George Barnes who was now convinced that federalism was not a viable policy at the moment. See G.N. Barnes, "The Future of Home Rule," 23 July 1918, *Secret*, G.T. 5199, Cab. 24/58. For Long's rebuttal see W. Long, "Ireland," 24 July 1918, G.T. 5209, Cab. 24/59.

90 "Minutes of a Meeting of the War Cabinet," 29 July 1918, *Secret*, Cab. 23/7/453.

91 In addition to the federal bill, Long's committee had also prepared a bill dealing only with Ireland. See "Mr. Long's Committee August 1918: Draft Bill for the Government of Ireland," G.T. 8240, Cab. 24/89/271.

92 *Times*, 29 July and 17 August 1918.

93 Adams to Long, 26 August 1918; and Long to Adams, 27 August 1918, Lloyd George Papers, HLRO, F/67/1/38.

CHAPTER NINE

1 Oliver to Garvin, 21 August 1918, Garvin Papers, HRC.

2 Dicey to Long, 22 November 1918, Long Papers, WRO, 947/207.

3 Long to Dicey, 29 November 1918, copy, ibid.

4 Long to Midleton, 4 October 1918, and Midleton to Long, 6 October 1918, ibid., 947/308.

5 Although Welsh and Scottish federalists, particularly, E.T. John, had continued to give publicity to the needs of their areas, and to the necessity of home rule all round in order to meet national and functional needs, there was little prefatory comment from the Welsh and the Scots before the debate in the Lords. See *Welsh Outlook*, vol. 5 *seriatim*, and *Welsh Outlook* (February 1919); also Kenneth O. Morgan, *Wales in British Politics 1868-1922* (Cardiff: University of Wales Press 1963), 285. See also Maud Selborne, "The Federal Solution from a Conservative Point of View," *National Review* 73 (1919): 414-15. This article reflected her husband's commitment to federalism, and was an interesting contrast to the attitudes of her Cecil brothers, Robert, Hugh, and Edward.

6 For the debate see 5 Hansard (H of L), vol. 33, 5 March 1919, cols. 501-50.

7 For Brassey's speech see ibid., cols. 501-12. Reginald Coupland later claimed that Brassey made two new points: "(1) the desirability of dividing England, Scotland, and Ireland, but not Wales, into two provinces each; and (2) the possibility that Ulster might accept this version of Home Rule." Brassey made no such suggestions. See R. Coupland, *Welsh and Scottish Nationalism: A Study* (London: Collins 1954), 316.

8 For Selborne's speech see 5 Hansard (H of L), vol. 33, 5 March 1919, cols. 512-21.

9 For Birkenhead's speech see ibid., cols. 521-31.

10 Ibid., col. 526.

11 See ibid., cols. 531–40.

12 The debate has been dealt with in John Fair, *British Interparty Conferences: A Study of the Procedure of Conciliation in British Politics 1867–1921* (Oxford: Clarendon Press 1980), 230; and Coupland, *Welsh and Scottish Nationalism*, 315–17; and Wan-Hsuan Chiao, *Devolution in Great Britain* (New York: Columbia University Press 1926), 153–60.

13 For the debate see 5 Hansard (H of C), vol. 116, 3 June 1919, cols. 1873–974; and 4 June 1919, cols. 2063–129.

14 For Wood's speech see ibid., cols. 1873–82.

15 Ibid., cols. 1882–94.

16 The debate has been dealt with in Fair, *British Interparty Conferences*, 430–1; Coupland, *Welsh and Scottish Nationalism*, 317–20; and Chiao, *Devolution in Great Britain*, 160–9. In speaking against the motion, Ronald McNeill (cols 2068–80) argued that an extended and more fully developed county council system was preferable to devolution.

17 Long to Lloyd George, 3 June 1919, Lloyd George Papers, HLRO, F/33/2/49.

18 "Summary of discussion at Conference held at 36 Belgrave Square, 22 July 1919," ibid., F/21/4/7.

19 See [unclear] to H. Gladstone, 24 August 1919, H. Gladstone Papers, BL, Add. Ms. 46084: 131; Brassey to Garvin, 21 August 1919, Garvin Papers, HRC; Brassey to Crewe, 6 August 1919, Crewe Papers, CUL, Mss. 1919; and Lowther to H. Gladstone, 12 September 1919, H. Gladstone Papers, BL, Add. Ms. 46084: 131–2.

20 Coupland, *Welsh and Scottish Nationalism*, 321.

21 *Times*, 17 October 1919.

22 The issue of membership had been treated less seriously than it might have been. For example, Curzon who did not like the conference because it had not been discussed in cabinet, had been given the responsibility by Bonar Law of recommending Unionist delegates. The result had been a list containing a number of Ulsterites who had no interest in the basic idea. See Curzon to Bonar Law, 7 August 1919, Bonar Law Papers, HLRO, 98/1/5, and Fair, *British Interparty Conferences*, 232. Certainly the Ulsterites had no faith in federalism as a solution of the Irish problem, and some of them thought the conference nothing more than "an academical affair or a convenient apparatus for shelving the Home Rule question." See Hugh de Fellenberg Montgomery to Carson, 11 August 1919, quoted in Fair, *British Interparty Conferences*, 231.

23 Brassey to Sir Thomas Whittaker, 25 October 1919, quoted in Frank Partridge, *T.A.B.: A Memoir of Thomas Allnutt Second Earl Brassey* (London: John Murray 1921), 232.

24 Brassey to Selborne, 29 October 1919, quoted in ibid., 233.

25 Viscount Ullswater (J.W. Lowther), *A Speaker's Commentaries*, 2 vols. (London: Edward Arnold 1925), 2: 267; and Gorell Diary, 23 October 1919, Gorell Papers, Bodleian.

26 Brassey to H. Gladstone, 25 October [1919], H. Gladstone Papers, BL, Add. Ms. 46084: 268-9.

27 After the first meeting, Brassey felt they had made a reasonably good start and that no one was out to wreck the whole proceedings: "Even my old friend, Ronald McNeill, who has been a vigorous opponent of the policy in days gone by, is prepared to accept Devolution in some form or other." See Brassey to Selborne, 29 October 1919, quoted in Partridge, *T.A.B.*, 233.

28 Gorell Diary, 28 October 1919, Gorell Papers, Bodleian.

29 For a lucid analysis of the conference proceedings see J. Fair, *British Interparty Conferences*, 233-9.

30 Gideon Murray, *Viscount Elibank: A Man's Life* (London: Hutchinson 1934), 242.

31 Gorell Diary, 13 November 1919, Gorell Papers, Bodleian. Apart from the loss of Brassey, the conference also lost Lords Inchcape, Hambledon, Harcourt, and Dufferin through resignation. The first four were replaced by Lords Strafford, Chalmers, Elgin, and Selborne. Dufferin was not replaced.

32 "Conference on Devolution. Letter from Mr Speaker to the Prime Minister," 27 April 1920, *Parl. Pap.*, 1920, Cmd. 692, Appendix III.

33 Gorell Diary, 26 November 1919, Gorell Papers, Bodleian.

34 Gorell Diary, 4 and 9 December 1919, ibid.

35 Gorell Diary, 15 December 1919, ibid.

36 Gorell Diary, 18 December 1919, ibid.

37 Gorell Diary, 19 December 1919, ibid.

38 Lowther to Selborne, 10 December 1919, Selborne Papers, Bodleian, Ms. 87: 60-1.

39 For the speaker's actions and attitudes see Ullswater, *Commentaries*, 269-70; and "Memo circulated by the Speaker at the Request of the Conference, Xmas 1919 ," H. Gladstone Papers, BL, Add. Ms. 46104: 18-23. Also Lowther to Gladstone, 14 December 1919, ibid., Add. Ms. 46084: 169-72.

40 H. Gladstone to Mr Speaker, 20 December 1919, copy, ibid., Add. Ms. 46084: 180-2.

41 Lowther to Gladstone, 23 December 1919, ibid., Add. Ms. 46084: 183-7.

42 H. Gladstone to Chalmers, n.d. and marked "cancelled," in reply to Chalmers to H. Gladstone, 31 January 1920, ibid., Add. Ms. 46084: 201 and 207-8. Also Chalmers to Gladstone, 9 February 1920, ibid., Add. Ms. 46084: 210.

43 Gorell Diary, 11 and 16 February 1920, Gorell Papers, Bodleian.

44 H. Gladstone to Mr. Speaker, 22 February 1920, Private, H. Gladstone Papers, BL, Add. Ms. 46084: 219-20; Emmott to Gladstone, 16 and 29 March 1920, ibid., Add. Ms. 46084: 223 and 227; J.A.M. Macdonald to Gladstone, 20 February, 22 March, 15, 16 and 19 April, 5 and 11 May 1920, ibid., Add. Ms. 46084: 225, 231, 233-5, 247-9.

45 Gorell Diary, 27 April 1920, Gorell Papers, Bodleian.

46 For the full report, including both schemes plus appendices, see "Conference on Devolution: Letter from Mr Speaker to the Prime Minister," 27 April 1920, *Parl. Pap.*, Cmd. 692. The *Welsh Outlook* thought the conference had ended in a "fiasco,"

and it found Lowther's scheme "hopeless" while Macdonald's was not much better. See "The Outlook: The Speaker's Conference," *Welsh Outlook* (June 1920): 134–5. For a more favourable view see A Welsh Nationalist, "Welsh Self-Government and Speaker's Conference," *Welsh Outlook* (July 1920): 158–9.

47 *Times*, 2, 7 and 9 July 1920.

48 Ibid., 5–9 July 1920. The articles were subsequently published as a book, *The Case for Federal Devolution* (1920), and dedicated to the memory of Earl Brassey.

49 *The Times*, 17 and 20 December 1920.

50 Ibid., 29 April 1921.

51 For Plunkett's proposal see the *Times*, 15 April 1919, and Plunkett to Bryce, 9 May 1919, Bryce Papers, NLI, Ms. 11016 (9). Plunkett started a newspaper, the *Irish Statesman*, and helped found the Irish Dominion League in order to advocate dominion status for all of Ireland. Plunkett favoured a Canada-like status for Ireland and a Quebec-like status for Ulster but with control of defence and foreign policy remaining with Great Britain. See Plunkett to Bryce, 11 June and 27 September 1920, ibid.

52 W. Long, "Situation in Ireland," 24 September 1919, *Secret*, G.T. 8215, Cab. 24/89, 33–7. For a recent treatment of Long's role in the making of the Government of Ireland Act see Richard Murphy, "Walter Long and the making of the Government of Ireland Act, 1919–20," *Irish Historical Studies* 25, no. 97 (May 1986): 82–96.

53 "Conclusions of the War Cabinet," 7 October 1919, War Cabinet 628, Cab. 23/12. In addition to Long, the committee was composed of French and Macpherson, *ex officio*, Fisher, Birkenhead, Shortt, Geddes, Horne, Roberts, Worthington-Evans, Hewart, and Kellaway, with Philip Kerr and L.F. Burgis as joint secretaries. Among the other documents circulated to the war cabinet was the draft bill of a federal system for the United Kingdom prepared by Long's committee in June 1918.

54 "Conclusions of a meeting of the Committee on Ireland," 15 October 1919, Cab. 27/68.

55 Two days later, on 17 October, Plunkett spoke with Kerr, and raised his plan for the grant of dominion status to Ireland with Ulster being given provincial status "on the Canadian plan." According to Plunkett, "P.K.'s own postulate was that England should get out of Ireland first and let Ireland and Ulster fight it out!" Plunkett Diary, 17 October 1919, Plunkett Papers, PH.

56 "First Report of Cabinet Committee on the Irish Question," 4 November 1919, C.P. 56, Cab. 27/68.

57 For Balfour's protest see "The Irish Question. Memorandum by Mr. Balfour," 25 November 1919, C.P. 193, Cab. 24/93; also "Note by Birkenhead and Worthington-Evans, 11 November, ibid.

58 See "Report of Sub-Committee on Irish Finance," 21 November 1919, C.I. 35, Cab. 27/68; "Committee on Ireland. Third Report. Heads of Proposal," 24 November 1919, C.P. 90, Cab. 27/68; "Committee on Ireland. Fourth Report," C.P. 247, Cab. 27/68; also C.P. Scott Diary, 30 November 1919, C.P. Scott Papers, BL, Add. Ms.

50905: 212. It was at this time that Erskine Childers spoke with both Kerr and Curtis in Paris, and was frustrated by their attitudes to Ireland. See Childers to his wife, November-December 1919, Childers Papers, TCL.

59 "Conclusions of a meeting of the Cabinet," 24 February 1920, Cab. 23/20.

60 For a full discussion of the negotiations and discussions in the period December 1919–February 1920 see T.G. Fraser, *Partition in Ireland, India and Palestine: Theory and Practice* (London: Macmillan 1984), *27–44*; Sheila Lawlor, *Britain and Ireland 1914–23* (Dublin: Gill and Macmillan 1983), *44–58*; Michael Laffan, *The Partition of Ireland 1911–1925* (Dundalk: Dundalgan Press 1983), 61–71; R.B. McDowell, *The Irish Convention 1917–18* (London: Routledge & Kegan Paul 1970), 196–209; John McColgan, *British Policy and the Irish Administration 1920–22* (London: George Allen & Unwin 1983), 35–52; Charles Townshend, *The British Campaign in Ireland 1919–1921: The Development of Political and Military Policies* (Oxford: Oxford University Press 1975), 33–9; Patrick Buckland, *Irish Unionism: Two. Ulster Unionism and the Origins of Northern Ireland 1886–1922* (Dublin: Gill and Macmillan 1973), 113–26; D.G. Boyce, "How to Settle the Irish Question: Lloyd George and Ireland 1916–21," in A.J.P. Taylor, ed., *Lloyd George: Twelve Essays* (New York: Atheneum 1971), 137–64; and D.G. Boyce, "British Conservative Opinion, the Ulster Question, and the Partition of Ireland, 1919–21," *Irish Historical Studies* 17, no. 65 (1968), 89–112.

61 Committee on Ireland. "Notes of a Meeting," 17 February 1920, C.I. 15, Cab. 27/68. On 24 March Long circulated a memorandum entitled "Government of Ireland Bill. Differences between the Bill and the Act of 1914 with respect to the powers transferred," C.P. 943, Cab. 24/101.

62 C.P. Scott Diary, 15–17 March 1920, C.P. Scott Papers, BL, Add. Ms. 50906: 1–2.

63 For the debate see 5 Hansard (H of L), vol. 40, cols. 1113–62; and for the Irish Dominion League see G.F. Berkeley Papers, NLI, Mss. 10924 and 10925. The lack of interest in any form of home rule at that time was reflected in the sparse attendance and desultory debate of a Government of Scotland bill on 16 April 1920. See 5 Hansard (H of C), vol. 127, cols. 2005–83.

64 The three letters plus Dunraven's speech in the Lords of 1 July 1920 were published in a small book: The Earl of Dunraven, *The Crisis in Ireland: Federal Union, through Devolution* (London 1920).

65 Long to Midleton, 26 July 1920, and Midleton to Long, 24 July 1920, Midleton Papers, PRO 30/67/43: 2473 and 2474. Also Long to Dunraven, 17 August 1920, copy, Long Papers, WRO, 947/214.

66 "Cabinet Committee on Ireland. Memorandum by Mr Long," 29 September 1920, C.I. 87, Cab. 27/70.

67 Plunkett Diary, 7 December 1921, Plunkett Papers, PH.

68 E.T. John to David Lloyd George, [8 December 1921], E.T. John Papers, NLW, 3023.

69 See 5 Hansard (H of C), vol. 153, 28 April 1922, cols. 929–42, for desultory debate on a Government of Wales bill; and ibid., vol. 154, 26 May 1922, cols 1609–48, for much the same treatment of a Government of Scotland bill. A Government of Scotland and Wales bill received only first reading on 8 May 1922, ibid., vol. 153, col. 1808.

70 Carson was bitter at the result. See Carson to F.S. Oliver, 17 December 1921, F.S. Oliver Papers, NLS, Mss. Acc. 7726/87. See also Fair, *British Interparty Conferences*, 244–61.

CONCLUSION

1 See particularly Michael Burgess, ed., *Federalism and Federation in Western Europe* (London: Croom Helm 1986); J.C. Banks, *Federal Britain?* (London: George G. Harrap 1971); Bernard Burrows and Geoffrey Denton, *Devolution or Federalism? Options for a United Kingdom* (London: Macmillan 1980); and Keith Robbins, "Core and Periphery in Modern British History," *Proceedings of the British Academy* 70 (1984): 275–97.

2 I have found only one instance where some effort might have been made to examine an aspect of the problem. See above, chapter 8, note 31.

A Note on Sources

The basic primary sources for this study of federalist thought in the United Kingdom were the manuscript collections of some seventy politicians and lobbyists, the contemporary periodical and pamphlet literature, the newspapers, the parliamentary debates, sundry memoirs, and Cabinet Office material. In addition, there is a considerable secondary literature for this period and I gained innumerable insights from reading widely in a variety of books, articles, and theses. Since all printed materials used in this study receive a full citation in the notes this comment is confined to indicating the location of the most useful manuscript collections and to isolating the most valuable secondary sources.

The manuscript material is mainly located in repositories in Great Britain and Ireland but some key collections have to be consulted in the United States and Canada. In London, the British Library has the Arthur Balfour, Campbell-Bannerman, Herbert Gladstone, W.E. Gladstone, Walter Long, and C.P. Scott papers, while the House of Lords Record Office contains the Willoughby de Broke, Lloyd George, Courtney Ilbert, Bonar Law, Herbert Samuel, and St Loe Strachey papers, all essential to an appreciation of both Liberal and Unionist assumptions and policies. The Bodleian Library, Oxford, houses the papers of H.H. Asquith, Augustine Birrell, James Bryce, Lionel Curtis, Anthony MacDonnell, Milner, and Selborne, all of whom were deeply involved in the debate. A rounded picture of the degree of concern generated by the issue of constitutional change and the extent of lobbying engaged in to achieve personal goals would not have been possible without consulting a number of important collections in Wales, Scotland, and Ireland. The National Library of Wales at Aberystwyth has the papers of Tom Ellis, Thomas Gee, Glansevern, E.T. John, and Thomas Jones. One of the most important collections, that of F.S. Oliver, is held at the National Library of Scotland in Edinburgh along with the papers of the Liberals Elibank, Haldane, and Rosebery. In Dublin, the National Library of Ireland houses a second James Bryce collection and the papers of G.F. Berkeley, Michael Davitt, Michael MacDonagh, John Redmond, William O'Brien, W. Smith O'Brien, and Alice Stopford-Green. The remaining manuscript collections are scattered among a number of repositories. One of the most valuable is the Austen Chamberlain material at the University of Birmingham Library, while the papers of Walter Long, Chamberlain's ally in the fight for a federal structure, are divided between the Wiltshire Record Office and the British Library. Horace Plunkett's papers are in Plunkett House, Oxford; the Earl Grey papers at the University of Durham; Erskine Childer's and John Dillon's in Trinity College Library, Dublin; Richard Jebb's at the Institute of Commonwealth Studies, London, while the Public Record Office, London, holds those of Sir Edward Grey, J. Ramsay MacDonald, Midleton, and Russell plus the essential Cabinet Office files. In North America, the Humanities Research Center in Austin, Texas, houses the J.L. Garvin collection, one rich in information and insight. The Library of Congress has Moreton Frewen's papers, and the New York Public Library has the William Bourke Cockran collection. In Canada, the Public Archives in Ottawa has the Edward Blake and J.S. Willison material and the George Wrong papers are in the University of Toronto Archives.

This subject has received a certain amount of scholarly treatment, particularly since the late sixties when both the "Irish question" and the issue of devolution resurfaced as major concerns. Books such as J.P. Mackintosh's *The Devolution of Power: Local Democracy, Regionalism and Nationalism* (London: Penguin 1968), J.C. Bank's *Federal Britain? The Case for Regionalism* (London: George G. Harrap 1971), Vernon Bogdanor's *Devolution* (Oxford: Oxford University Press 1979), Bernard Burrow's and Geoffrey Denton's *Devolution or Federalism? Options for the United Kingdom* (London: Macmillan 1980), and H.M. Drucker's and Gordon Brown's *The Politics of Nationalism and Devolution* (London: Longman 1980) are concerned primarily with recent problems. Nevertheless, all the books, especially Bogdanor's,. reflect upon the efforts and ideas of the period 1870–1921 and help place them in a wider context. Two particularly valuable books for that purpose are the classic study of *Federal Government* (London: Oxford University Press 1946) by K.C. Wheare and a recent examination of *Federalism and Federation in Western Europe* (London: Croom Helm 1986) edited by Michael Burgess. An older exposition that can be profitably reread is Wan-Hsuan Chiao's *Devolution in Great Britain* (New York: Columbia University Press 1926).

The standard studies of Welsh and Scottish nationalism such as Reginald Coupland's *Welsh and Scottish Nationalism: A Study* (London: Collins 1954), Kenneth Morgan's *Wales in British Politics 1868–1922* (Cardiff: University of Wales Press 1963), and H.J. Hanham's *Scottish Nationalism* (London: Faber and Faber 1969) each look at the issue of federalism/devolution/home rule all round at varying lengths and with differing levels of intensity within the framework of Scottish or Welsh interests but naturally make no effort to provide a synoptic treatment and analysis. Similarly, the standard monographs on the imperial theme such as Seymour Ching-Yuan Cheng's *Schemes for the Federation of the British Empire* (New York: Columbia University Press 1931), J.E. Tyler's *The Struggle for Imperial Unity, 1868–1895* (London: Longmans 1938), and my own books on *The Colonial and Imperial Conferences 1887–1911* (London Longmans 1967) and *The Round Table Movement and Imperial Union* (Toronto: University of Toronto Press 1975) all recognize the degree of overlap in interest and personnel between imperial and domestic advocates of federalism but do not fully explore the phenomenon.

The most suggestive work on the federal theme can be found in monographs and articles concerned with Anglo-Irish affairs. The list is extensive and only a few items can be mentioned here. Of particular importance are D.G. Boyce and J.O. Stubbs, "F.S. Oliver, Lord Selborne and Federalism," *Journal of Imperial and Commonwealth History* 5, no. 1 (October 1976): 53–81, and P. Jalland, "United Kingdom Devolution 1910–14: Political Panacea or Tactical Diversion?," *English Historical Review* 94, no. 373 (October 1979): 757–85. See also my "The Round Table Movement and 'Home Rule All Round'," *Historical Journal* 11, no. 2 (July 1968): 332–53, and "Federalism and the Irish Problem in 1918," *History* 56, no. 187, (June 1971): 207–30. Monographs that should be noted are: Nicholas Mansergh, *The Irish Question 1840–1921* (Toronto: University of Toronto Press 1965); R.B. McDowell, *The Irish Convention 1917–18* (London: Routledge & Kegan Paul 1970), Patrick Buckland, *Irish Unionism*, 2 vols. (Dublin: Gill and Macmillan 1972 and 1973); D.G. Boyce, *Englishmen and Irish Troubles: British Public Opinion and the Making of Irish Policy 1918–22* (London: Jonathan Cape 1972); Patricia Jalland, *The Liberals and Ireland: The Ulster Question in British Politics to 1914* (Brighton: The Harvester Press 1980); Sheila Lawlor, *Britain and Ireland 1914–23* (Dublin: Gill and Macmillan 1983); and James Loughlin, *Gladstone, Home Rule and the Ulster Question 1882–93* (Atlantic Highlands, NJ: Humanities Press International 1987). Each of these books has something valuable to say on home rule and, at least by implication, on federalism.

A good deal of useful work still rests in thesis form. The following are of particular interest: Michael Burgess, "The Imperial Federation Movement in Great Britain, 1868–1893" (PH.D, University of Leicester, 1976); Thomas John Dunne, "Ireland, England and Empire, 1868–1886: The Ideologies of British Political Leadership" (PH.D, University of Cambridge, 1976); A.C. Hepburn, "Liberal Policies and Nationalist Politics in Ireland, 1905–1910" (PH.D, University of Kent at Canterbury, 1968); David George Hoskin, "The Genesis and Significance of the 1886 'Home Rule' Split in the Liberal Party" (PH.D, University of Cambridge, 1964); and M.G. Miller, "The Continued Agitation for Imperial Union, 1895–1910: The Individuals and Bodies Concerned, Their Ideas and Their Influence" (D.Phil., Oxford University, 1980).

Index